Editorial project:
2019 © booq publishing, S.L.
c/ Domènech, 7-9, 2º 1ª
08012 Barcelona, Spain
T: +34 93 268 80 88
www.booqpublishing.com

ISBN 978-84-9936-056-0

© Editions du Layeur
Dépôt Légal : Septembre 2019
ISBN : 978-2-915126-57-0
Imprimé chez Shenzhen Hua Xin Colour
Printing & Platemaking Co., Ltd. en avril 2019

Editorial coordinator:
Claudia Martínez Alonso

Art director:
Mireia Casanovas Soley

Editor:
Cayetano Cardelús

Layout:
Cristina Simó Perales

Printing in China

Multi-family buildings currently constitute the most common residential typology in our cities and, therefore, a fundamental element in the configuration of the urban landscape. However, this building typology, one of the driving forces in the evolution of modern cities, has frequently shown a closer link to the term "construction" than to the term "architecture."

The creation of pleasant living environments that avoid the simple container of human beings and build spaces of coexistence receptive to the needs of users has been one of the objectives of architectural practice for decades. Works such as Le Corbusier's Unité d'Habitation in Marseille (1952) laid the foundations for a new relationship between the building and its inhabitants.

The projects presented in this book are magnificent recent examples of how architecture can create attractive residential buildings aware of their social function, promoting interaction between users and the harmonious relationship of the community with its natural and urban environment. Likewise, all of them transmit a great sensitivity towards issues such as sustainability, eco-efficiency or the integration and conservation of historical and industrial heritage, using construction methods ranging from traditional techniques to the most modern parametric design systems.

Mehrfamilienhäuser stellen derzeit die häufigste Wohntypologie in unseren Städten dar und sind daher ein wesentliches Element in der Gestaltung der Stadtlandschaft. Diese Gebäudetypologie, eine der treibenden Kräfte in der Entwicklung moderner Städte, hat jedoch häufig eine engere Verbindung zum Begriff „Bauen" als zum Begriff „Architektur" gezeigt.

Seit Jahrzehnten ist eines der Ziele des Architekturbüros die Schaffung angenehme Lebensumgebungen, dass bedeutet etwas anderes als ein bloßer Behälter des Menschen, damit sie für die Bedürfnisse der Nutzer empfänglich sind. Einige Werke wie Unité d'Habitation in Marseille (1952) von Le Corbusier die Grundlagen für eine neue Beziehung zwischen dem Gebäude und seinen Bewohnern beschaffen.

Die in diesem Buch vorgestellten Projekte sind großartige Beispiele dafür, wie Architektur attraktive Wohngebäude schaffen kann, die sich ihrer sozialen Funktion bewusst sind und die Interaktion zwischen den Nutzern und das harmonische Verhältnis der Gemeinschaft mit ihrer natürlichen und städtischen Umwelt fördern. Ebenso vermitteln sie alle eine große Sensibilität für Themen wie Nachhaltigkeit, Ökoeffizienz oder die Integration und Erhaltung des historischen und industriellen Erbes mit Bauweisen, die von traditionellen Techniken bis hin zu modernsten parametrischen Designsystemen reichen.

Les immeubles multifamiliaux constituent actuellement la typologie résidentielle la plus courante dans nos villes et, par conséquent, un élément fondamental dans la configuration du paysage urbain. Cependant, cette typologie de construction, considérée comme l'un des moteurs de l'évolution des villes modernes, a souvent montré un lien plus étroit avec le terme « construction » qu'avec le terme « architecture ».

Depuis des décennies, l'un des objectifs de la pratique architecturale est de créer des milieux de vie agréables qui s'éloignent du simple contenant d'êtres humains et construire des espaces de coexistence réceptifs aux besoins des usagers. Des œuvres comme l'Unité d'Habitation de Le Corbusier à Marseille (1952) ont jeté les bases d'une nouvelle relation entre le bâtiment et ses habitants.

Les projets présentés dans cet ouvrage sont des magnifiques exemples récents de la façon dont l'architecture peut créer des bâtiments résidentiels attrayants et remplissant leur fonction sociale, favorisant l'interaction entre les utilisateurs et la relation harmonieuse de la communauté avec son environnement naturel et urbain. De même, tous les projets montrent une grande sensibilité à des questions telles que la durabilité, l'éco-efficacité ou l'intégration et la conservation du patrimoine historique et industriel, en utilisant des méthodes de construction allant des techniques traditionnelles aux systèmes de conception paramétrique les plus modernes.

Los edificios plurifamiliares constituyen en la actualidad la tipología residencial más común en nuestras ciudades y, por tanto, un elemento fundamental en la configuración del paisaje urbano. Sin embargo, esta tipología edificatoria, uno de los motores en la evolución de las ciudades modernas, ha mostrado frecuentemente una vinculación más estrecha al término «construcción» que al término «arquitectura».

La creación de entornos habitables agradables que huyan del simple contenedor de seres humanos y construyan espacios de convivencia receptivos a las necesidades de los usuarios ha constituido desde hace décadas uno de los objetivos de la práctica arquitectónica. Obras como la Unité d'Habitation de Le Corbusier en Marsella (1952) sentaron en su momento las bases de un nueva relación entre el edificio y sus habitantes.

Los proyectos presentados en este libro son magníficos ejemplos recientes de cómo la arquitectura puede crear atractivos edificios de viviendas conscientes de su función social, promoviendo la interacción entre los usuarios y la relación armoniosa de la comunidad con su entorno natural y urbano. Así mismo, todos ellos transmiten una gran sensibilidad hacia temas como la sostenibilidad, la ecoeficiencia o la integración y conservación del patrimonio histórico e industrial, utilizando para ello métodos constructivos que van desde las técnicas tradicionales hasta los más modernos sistemas de diseño paramétrico.

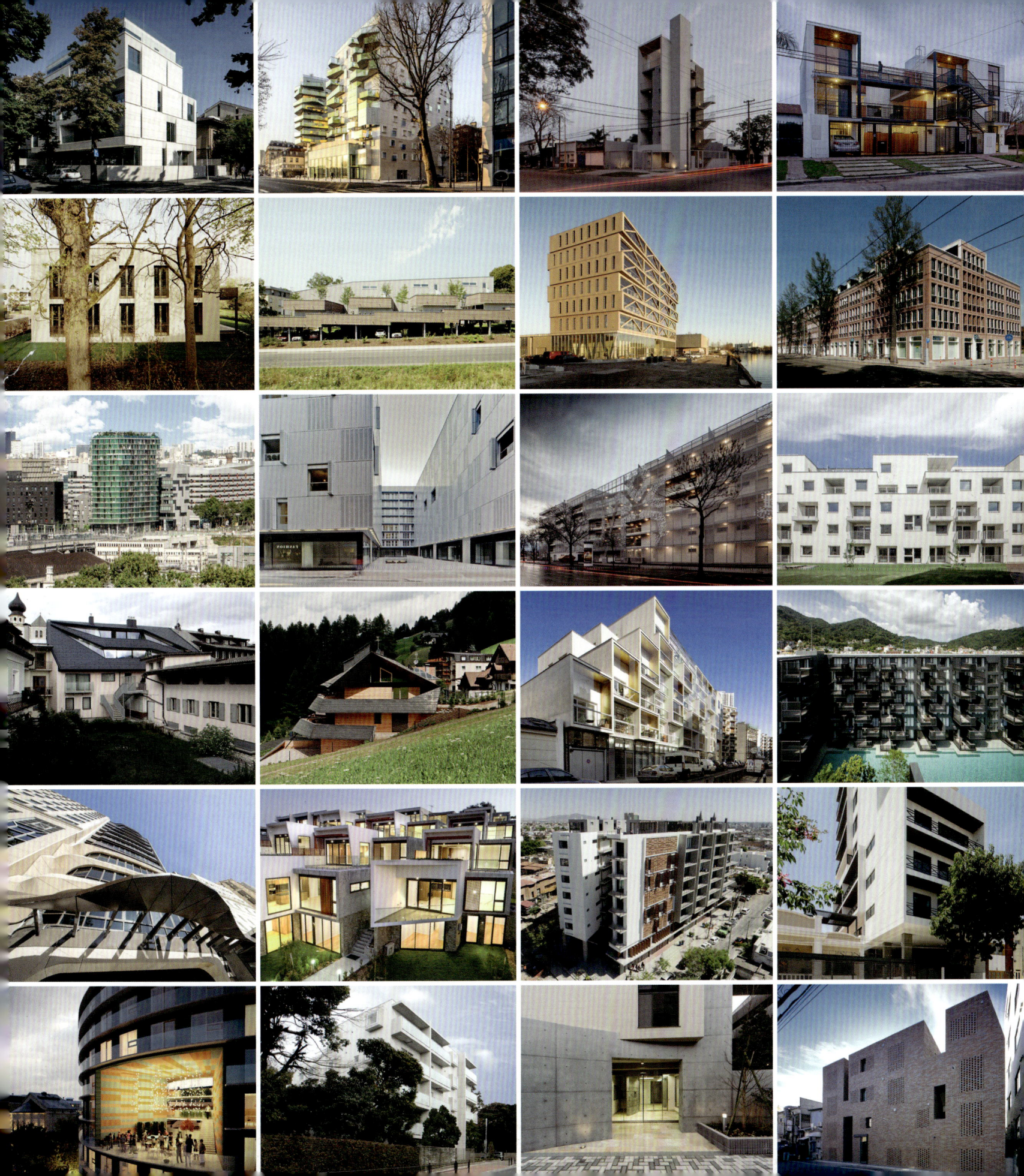

AKIO NAKASA /
NAF ARCHITECT & DESIGN
www.naf-aad.com

naf architect & design was established in 2000 by Akio Nakasa and Tetsuya Nakazono, who both studied architecture at Hiroshima University. Prior to its establishment, Nakasa earned his master's degree at Waseda University in Tokyo and worked at Riken Yamamoto. Since 2001, Nakasa has been Tokyo Office representative mainly working with clients in eastern Japan, while Nakazono continued in Hiroshima to work on projects in western Japan.

They have designed a wide range of projects from private home, clinics, nursery schools and apartment buildings, all of which are concept oriented reflecting the philosophy of the clients. Their goal in design is how best architectural expression and solution are materialized in the project.

Among many awards received, "small village", nursery school, received GOOD DESIGN, JIA award, Kids Design and exhibited during Milano triennale, and "A House Made of Two", private home, and, "Machida Shizen Kindergarten" received JIA award.

naf architect & design wurde im Jahr 2000 von Akio Nakasa und Tetsuya Nakazono gegründet, die beide Architektur an der Hiroshima University studierten. Vor seiner Gründung erwarb Nakasa seinen Master an der Waseda University in Tokio und arbeitete bei Riken Yamamoto. Seit 2001 ist Nakasa Repräsentant des Tokioer Büros, das hauptsächlich mit Kunden in Ostjapan arbeitet, während Nakazono in Hiroshima weiterhin an Projekten in West-Japan arbeitet.

Sie haben eine Vielzahl von Projekten aus dem Privatbereich, Kliniken, Kindergärten und Wohnhäusern entworfen, die alle konzeptorientiert sind und die Philosophie der Kunden widerspiegeln. Ihr Ziel beim Design ist es, wie sich der beste architektonische Ausdruck und die beste Lösung im Projekt verwirklichen lassen.

Neben vielen anderen Auszeichnungen erhielten „small village", Kindergarten, GOOD DESIGN, JIA-Award, Kids Design und wurden während der Triennale in Mailand ausgestellt, und „A House Made of Two", Privathaushalt, und „Machida Shizen Kindergarten" erhielt JIA-Award.

naf architect & design a été fondé en 2000 par Akio Nakasa et Tetsuya Nakazono, qui ont tous deux étudié l'architecture à l'Université d'Hiroshima. Avant sa création, Nakasa a obtenu sa maîtrise à l'Université de Waseda à Tokyo et a travaillé chez Riken Yamamamoto. Depuis 2001, Nakasa est le représentant du bureau de Tokyo et travaille principalement avec des clients de l'est du Japon, tandis que Nakazono a continué à Hiroshima pour travailler sur des projets dans l'ouest du Japon.

Ils ont conçu un large éventail de projets de maisons privées, de cliniques, d'écoles maternelles et d'immeubles d'appartements, tous orientés vers le concept et reflétant la philosophie des clients. Leur but dans la conception est de savoir comment la meilleure expression architecturale et la meilleure solution sont matérialisées dans le projet.

Parmi les nombreuses récompenses reçues, « petit village », école maternelle, a reçu GOOD DESIGN, JIA award, Kids Design et exposé lors de la triennale de Milan, et « A House Made of Two », maison privée, et, « Machida Shizen Kindergarten » a reçu JIA award.

naf architect & design fue fundada en 2000 por Akio Nakasa y Tetsuya Nakazono, que estudiaron arquitectura en la Universidad de Hiroshima. Antes de su fundación, Nakasa obtuvo su Máster en la Universidad de Waseda en Tokio y trabajó en Riken Yamamoto. Desde 2001, Nakasa ha sido representante de la Oficina de Tokio, trabajando principalmente con clientes en el este de Japón, mientras que Nakazono continuó en Hiroshima para trabajar en proyectos en el oeste del pais.

Han diseñado una amplia gama de proyectos que van desde casas particulares, clínicas, guarderías y edificios de apartamentos, todos ellos orientados al concepto que refleja la filosofía de los clientes. Su objetivo en el diseño es la mejor manera de materializar la expresión y las soluciones arquitectónicas.

Entre los muchos premios recibidos por la guardería infantil «El Pequeño Pueblo», se encuentra el GOOD DESIGN, el premio JIA de diseño de espacios infantiles y exhibido durante la trienal de Milán. El proyecto titulado «Una casa hecha de dos», y el «Jardín de infancia Machida Shizen» recibieron tambien el premio JIA.

A-1

Category: Houses in a row

Structure: Wood construction

Number of stories:
3 floors above ground

Maximum height: 9.826 m

Maximum eave height: 8.904 m

Frontal road:
6.360 m on the South

Site area: 180.83 m²

Building area: 111.18 m²

Total floor area: 295.68 m²

Design time:
July 4, 2015 – May 8, 2016

Construction time:
May 9, 2016 – November 20, 2016

Architect:
Akio Nakasa (Principal Architect),
Masaya Kato

Photo credits: © Toshiyuki Yano

Category: Houses in a row

Structure: Wood construction

Number of stories:
3 floors above ground

Maximum height: 9.543 m

Maximum eave height: 9.000 m

Frontal road: 4.000 m on the East

Site area: 167.49 m²

Building area: 88.20 m²

Total floor area: 251.96 m²

Design time:
August 24, 2014 – January 11, 2016

Construction time:
January 12, 2016 – July 12, 2016

Architect:
Akio Nakasa (Principal Architect),
Masaya Kato

Photo credits: © Toshiyuki Yano

E-1

Situated in a dense residential neighbourhood of 2 and 3-storey houses, the building occupies an elongated strip of land that curves to the bottom of the plot and presents a narrow façade to the street. The building is structured into four two-storey volumes that support the owner's home, which occupies the entire upper floor. These volumes contain apartments for rent and other uses linked to the upper floor. The areas between the apartments or "grey areas" house transit spaces and balconies. The shed roof creates an undivided space, flanked by a succession of windows offering views over a sea of outdoor roofs. The project seeks to promote a livable environment by making positive use of the interspace between the houses in the neighbourhood or "passive space."

Das Gebäude liegt in einem dichten Wohnviertel mit 2- und 3-geschossigen Häusern und nimmt einen langgestreckten Landstreifen ein, der sich bis zum Ende des Grundstücks erstreckt und eine schmale Fassade zur Straße hin aufweist. Das Gebäude ist in vier zweigeschossige Volumen gegliedert, die das Eigenheim des Bauherrn tragen, das sich über das gesamte Obergeschoss erstreckt. In diesen Volumina sind Mietwohnungen und andere mit dem Obergeschoss verbundene Nutzungen enthalten. Die Zwischenräume zwischen ihnen oder „Grauzonen" beherbergen Transitzonen und Balkone, die für die Wohnungen gesammelt wurden. Das Sheddach schafft einen ungeteilten Raum, flankiert von einer Reihe von Fenstern, die einen Blick auf das Meer der Außenterrassen bieten. Das Projekt zielt darauf ab, eine lebenswerte Umwelt zu fördern, indem der Zwischenraum zwischen den Häusern in der Nachbarschaft oder der „passive Raum" positiv genutzt wird.

A-1
SETAGAYA WARD, TOKYO

Situé dans un quartier résidentiel dense de maisons de 2 et 3 étages, le bâtiment occupe une bande de terrain allongée qui s'incurve vers le bas du terrain et présente une façade étroite sur la rue. Le bâtiment est structuré en quatre volumes de deux étages qui soutiennent la maison du propriétaire, qui occupe tout l'étage supérieur. Ces volumes contiennent des appartements à louer et d'autres usages liés à l'étage supérieur. Les zones interstitielles entre elles ou « zones grises » abritent les zones de transit et les balcons collectés pour les appartements. Le toit de la remise crée un espace indivis, flanqué d'une succession de fenêtres offrant des vues sur la mer des terrasses extérieures. Le projet vise à promouvoir un environnement habitable en utilisant positivement l'espace intermédiaire entre les maisons du quartier ou « espace passif ».

Situado en un denso barrio residencial de casas de 2 y 3 pisos, el edificio ocupa una alargada franja de terreno que se curva al fondo de la parcela y presenta una estrecha fachada a la calle. El edificio se estructura en cuatro volúmenes de dos plantas que sirven de apoyo a la vivienda del propietario, que ocupa toda la planta superior. Estos volúmenes contienen apartamentos en alquiler y otros usos vinculados a la planta superior. Las zonas intersticiales entre ellos o «zonas grises» albergan zonas de tránsito y balcones recogidos para los apartamentos. La cubierta en forma de cobertizo crea un espacio sin divisorias, flanqueado por una sucesión de ventanas que ofrecen vistas sobre el mar de cubiertas exterior. El proyecto intenta promover un entorno habitable mediante la utilización positiva del interspacio situado entre las casas del barrio o «espacio pasivo».

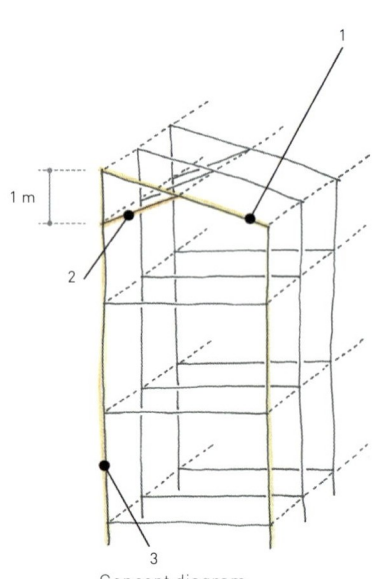

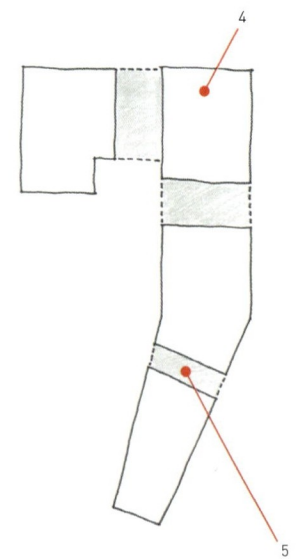

Concept diagram

1. Beam
2. Angle brace
3. Irregular portal structure
4. Four volumes
5. Positive interspace (gray zone)

1 m

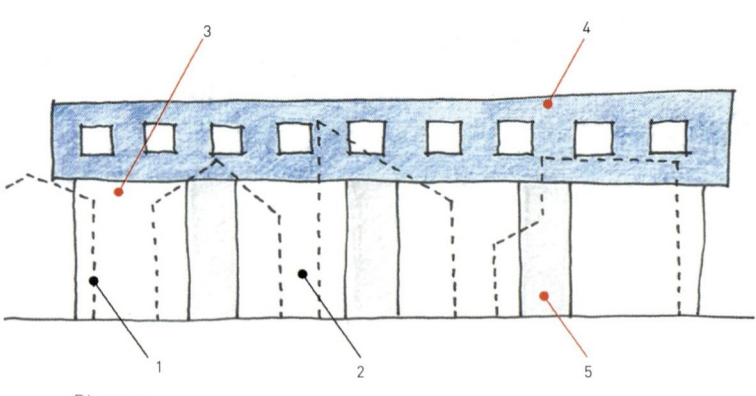

Diagram

1. Surrounding houses
2. Passive interspace
3. Four volumes
4. Owner house
5. Positive interspace
   (gray zone)

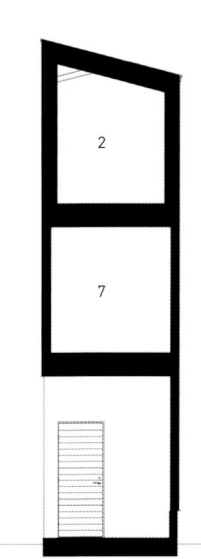

Section

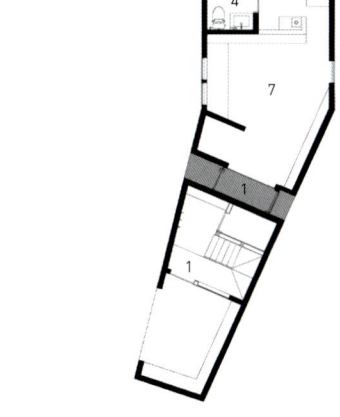

First floor plan

Second floor plan

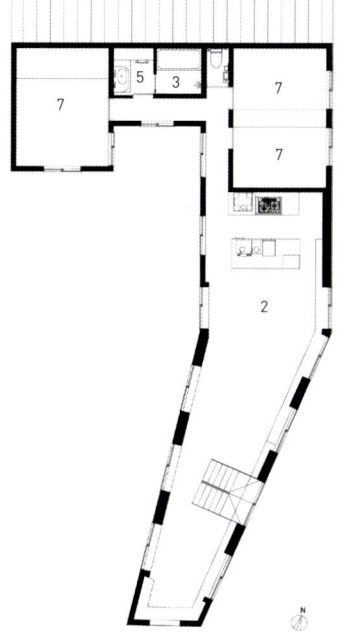

Third floor plan

1. Entrance
2. Living / Dining / Kitchen
3. Bathroom
4. Toilet
5. Washroom
6. Washroom / Toilet
7. Room
8. Balcony
9. Walk-in closet

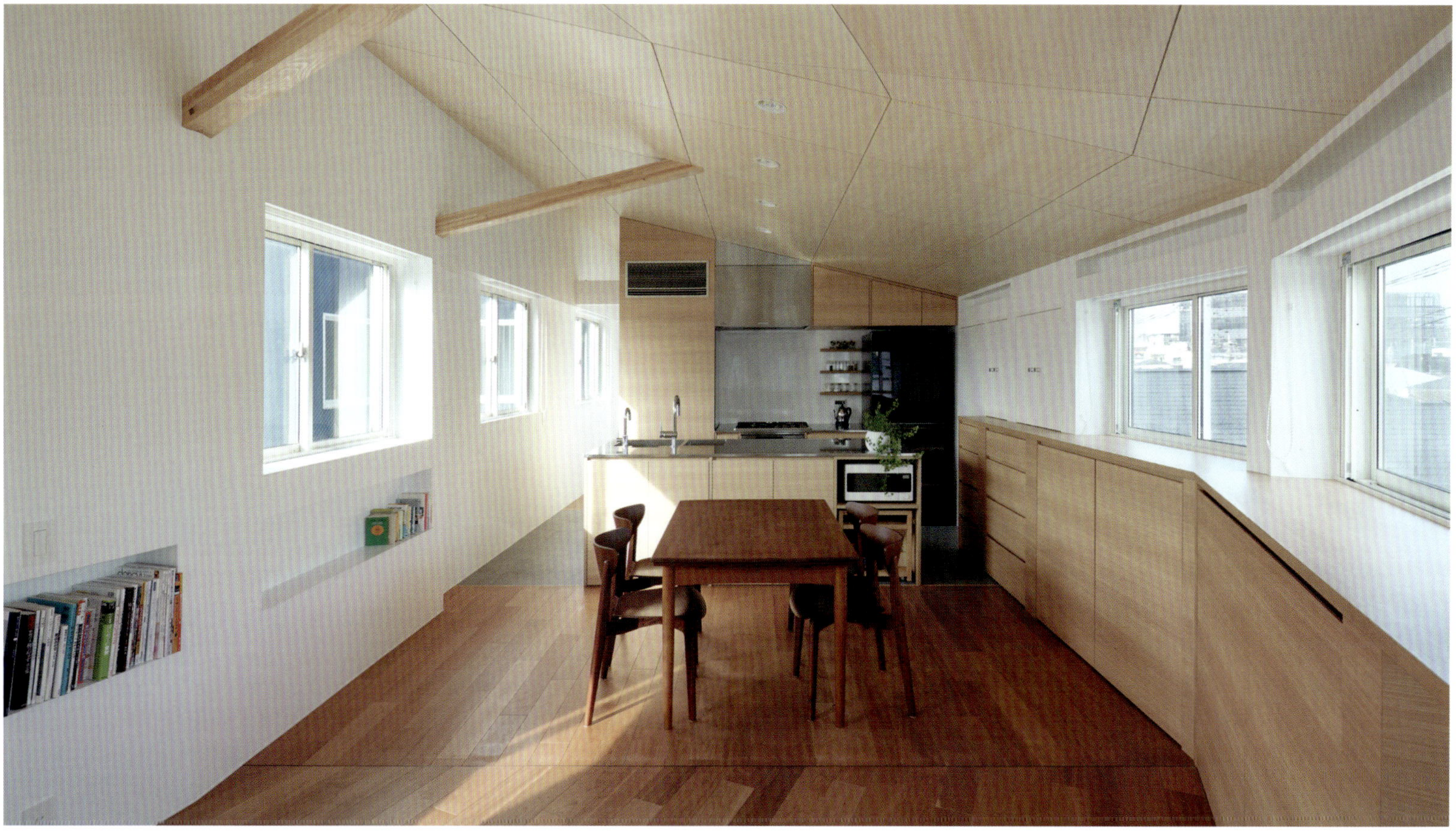

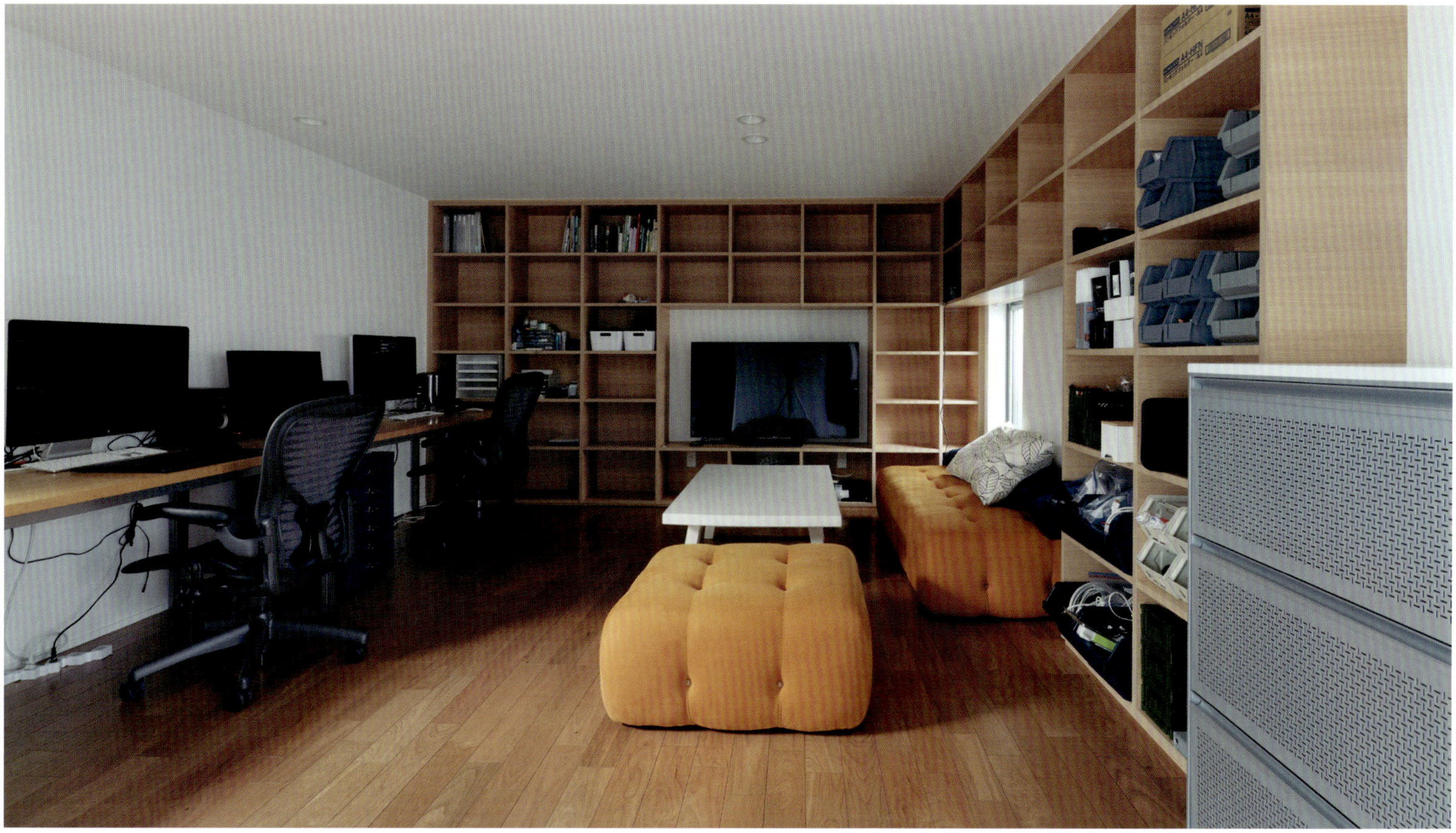

Located in a private passageway in a central area of Tokyo, this elongated building is composed of three floors that house 3 studio-type dwellings and 3 duplexes. The soft curve of the building and the simple design of its façade offer a unitary image from the outside. Behind the south-facing façade, a narrow strip painted entirely white, known as the "white layer", acts as a buffer zone between the exterior and the interior living space. This strip contains the stairs and the access areas to the dwellings and constitutes the internal traffic line, which is also used as a work space or place to sunbathe. The 6 dwellings have different distributions, but maintain the same structure of white layer - habitable space as a common link.

Dieses langgestreckte Gebäude befindet sich in einer privaten Passage in einem zentralen Teil Tokios und besteht aus drei Stockwerken, in denen 3 Atelierwohnungen und 3 Duplexwohnungen untergebracht sind. Die glatte Rundung des Gebäudes und die einfache Gestaltung der Fassade bieten von außen ein einheitliches Bild. Hinter der nach Süden ausgerichteten Fassade zum Durchgang fungiert ein schmaler, vollständig weiß gestrichener Streifen, die so genannte „weiße Schicht", als Pufferzone zwischen dem äußeren und dem inneren Wohnraum. Dieser Streifen enthält die Treppen und Zugangsbereiche zu den Wohnungen und bildet, wenn man sich in ihnen befindet, die interne Verkehrslinie, die auch als Arbeitsplatz oder Sonnenplatz genutzt wird. Die 6 Wohnungen haben unterschiedliche Verteilungen, behalten aber die gleiche Struktur der weißen Schicht / des bewohnbaren Raumes als eine gemeinsame Verbindung bei.

E-1
SHINAGAWA WARD, TOKYO

Situé dans un passage privé dans une zone centrale de Tokyo, ce bâtiment allongé est composé de trois étages qui abritent 3 logements de type studio et 3 duplex. La courbe lisse du bâtiment et le design simple de sa façade offrent une image unitaire de l'extérieur. Derrière la façade sud du passage, une bande étroite, entièrement peinte en blanc, appelée « couche blanche », sert de zone tampon entre l'extérieur et l'espace de vie intérieur. Cette bande contient les escaliers et les zones d'accès aux logements et, une fois à l'intérieur, constitue la ligne de circulation interne, qui sert également d'espace de travail ou de lieu pour prendre un bain de soleil. Les 6 logements ont des distributions différentes, mais maintiennent la même structure de couche blanche / espace habitable comme un lien commun.

Situado en un pasaje privado de una céntrica zona de Tokio, este edificio de forma alargada se compone de tres plantas que albergan 3 viviendas tipo estudio y 3 dúplex. La suave curva que dibuja el edificio y el sencillo diseño de su fachada ofrecen una imagen unitaria desde el exterior. Detrás de la fachada al pasaje, que goza de orientación sur, una franja estrecha y pintada completamente de blanco denominada «capa blanca» funciona como zona de amortiguación entre el exterior y el espacio habitable interior. Esta franja contiene las escaleras y las zonas de acceso a las viviendas y, una vez dentro de ellas, constituye la línea de tráfico interno, que es utilizada también como espacio de trabajo o lugar donde tomar el sol. Las 6 viviendas tienen distribuciones diferentes, pero mantienen la misma estructura de capa blanca/espacio habitable como vínculo común.

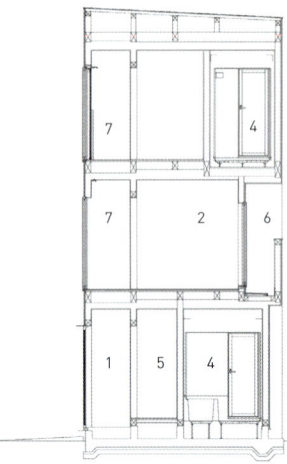

Section

1. Entrance / doma
2. Living / dining room
3. Washroom / toilet
4. Bathroom
5. Kitchen
6. Balcony
7. Sunroom
8. Work space
9. Walk-in closed
10. Room
11. Washroom
12. Toilet

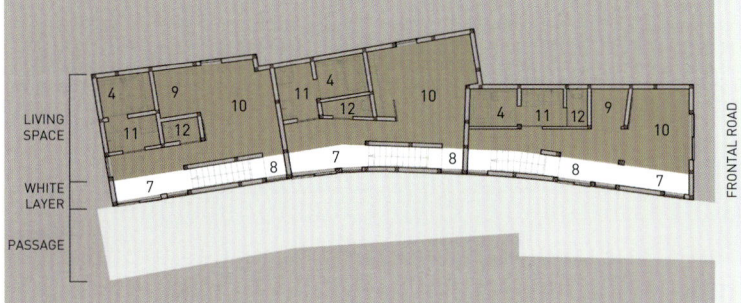

Third floor plan

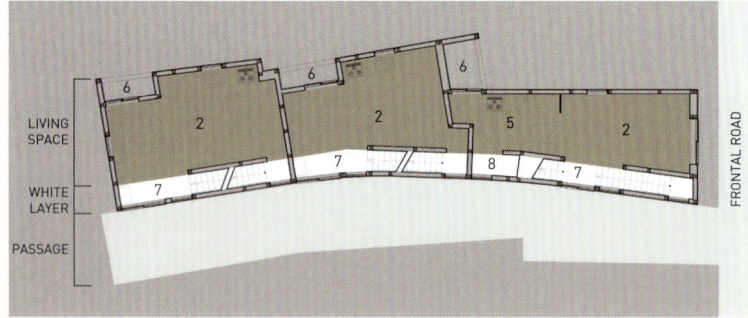

Second floor plan

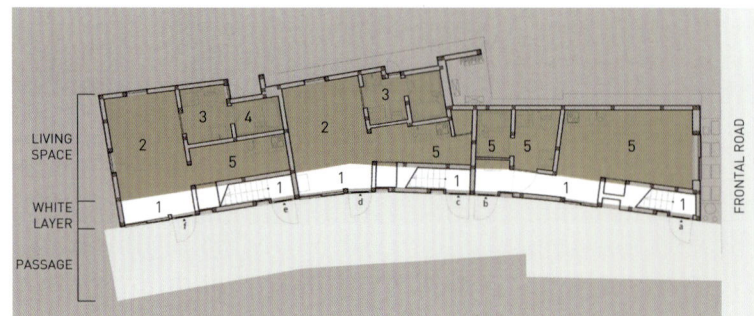

First floor plan

ARCHITEKTI ŠEBO LICHÝ

http://sebolichy.sk/

When designing projects, we encourage a discussion with partners who share our values and views. We do not pretend to know everything or to be the only ones to understand beauty. It is not our ambition to dictate others what they should like or how they should live their lives. Our projects are a synonym a common search for ideal solutions with our partners mirroring their personalities and lifestyles.

We consider the absence of specific expression our asset. Whatever we do, we always rely on a deep local analysis and respect of the genius loci. In our view, architecture should build on the strengths of the site and eliminate its weaknesses. We take pride on searching for innovative solutions and do our best to see things without any prejudice.

Bei der Gestaltung von Projekten fördern wir den Austausch mit Partnern, die unsere Werte und Ansichten teilen. Wir geben nicht vor, alles zu wissen oder die Einzigen zu sein, die Schönheit verstehen. Es ist nicht unser Ziel, anderen vorzuschreiben, was sie sich wünschen oder wie sie ihr Leben leben sollen. Unsere Projekte sind ein Synonym für die gemeinsame Suche nach optimalen Lösungen mit unseren Partnern, die ihre Persönlichkeit und ihren Lebensstil widerspiegeln.

Wir betrachten das Fehlen eines spezifischen Ausdrucks als unseren Vorteil. Was auch immer wir tun, wir verlassen uns immer auf eine tiefe lokale Analyse und den Respekt vor dem genius loci. Unserer Meinung nach sollte die Architektur auf den Stärken des Standorts aufbauen und seine Schwächen beseitigen. Wir sind stolz auf die Suche nach innovativen Lösungen und tun unser Bestes, um die Dinge vorurteilsfrei zu sehen.

Lors de la conception de projets, nous encourageons la discussion avec des partenaires qui partagent nos valeurs et nos points de vue. Nous ne prétendons pas tout savoir ou être les seuls à comprendre la beauté. Notre ambition n'est pas de dicter aux autres ce qu'ils aimeraient ou comment ils devraient vivre leur vie. Nos projets sont synonymes d'une recherche commune de solutions idéales avec nos partenaires reflétant leur personnalité et leur mode de vie.

Nous considérons l'absence d'expression spécifique comme notre atout. Quoi que nous fassions, nous nous appuyons toujours sur une analyse locale approfondie et sur le respect du génie local. Selon nous, l'architecture doit s'appuyer sur les forces du site et éliminer ses faiblesses. Nous sommes fiers de chercher des solutions innovantes et nous faisons de notre mieux pour voir les choses sans aucun préjugé.

Cuando diseñamos proyectos, fomentamos la discusión con los socios que comparten nuestros valores y puntos de vista. No pretendemos saberlo todo ni ser los únicos en entender la belleza. No es nuestra ambición dictar a otros lo que les gustaría o cómo deberían vivir sus vidas. Nuestros proyectos son sinónimo de una búsqueda común de soluciones ideales que reflejan la personalidad y estilo de vida de los clientes.

Consideramos que la ausencia de una expresión específica es nuestra ventaja. Hagamos lo que hagamos, siempre nos basamos en un profundo análisis local y en el respeto del genio de las gentes del lugar. En nuestra opinión, la arquitectura debe basarse en los puntos fuertes del sitio en el que se construye, eliminando sus puntos débiles. Nos enorgullecemos de buscar soluciones innovadoras y hacemos todo lo posible para contemplar las cosas sin prejuicios.

Architect: Mgr. arch. Igor Lichý,
Ing. arch. Tomáš Šebo,
Ing. arch. Drahan Petrovic,
Ing. arch. Katarína Uhnáková,
Ing. arch. Emanuel Zatlukaj.

Investor: ITB Development and
Imagine Development

General contractor: Me&Co

Statics: Konstrukt+

Land area: 2206 m²

Utility area: 6504,51 m²

Building area: 1868 m²

Building volume: 25 750 m³

N° of flats: 75

Beginning of building designing:
November 2009

**Completion of building
designing:** August 2011

General contractor: Me&Co

Photo credits: © Dano Veselský,
© Olja Triaska Stefanovic,
© Lubo Stacho

Awards:
Slovak Apartment Block 2015

The architectural concept of Nový háj is based on two essential factors:
Firstly, a direct reaction to its location in Petržalka, the largest housing complex of precast concrete panels in Central Europe, which is a relic of the communist era. The building's two towers make the most of their visual contact with the nearby woods and park, and each apartment is facing two façades.
The second factor is the active participation of the residents in the architectural conception of the building. Its flexible design and the architectural language used allow clients to choose the size and location of their windows and balconies without compromising the coherence of the whole. The result of this approach is an authentic architecture that reflects the real life of real people.

Das architektonische Konzept von Nový háj basiert auf zwei wesentlichen Faktoren:
Erstens, eine direkte Reaktion auf die Lage in Petržalka, dem größten Wohnkomplex aus Betonfertigteilen in Mitteleuropa, der ein Relikt aus der kommunistischen Zeit ist. Die beiden Türme des Gebäudes nutzen den Blickkontakt zu den nahegelegenen Wäldern und Parks, und jede Wohnung hat zwei Fassaden.
Der zweite Faktor ist die aktive Beteiligung der Bewohner an der architektonischen Gestaltung des Gebäudes. Das flexible Design und die Architektursprache ermöglichen es dem Kunden, die Größe und Lage seiner Fenster und Balkone zu wählen, ohne die Kohärenz des Ganzen zu beeinträchtigen. Das Ergebnis dieses Ansatzes ist eine authentische Architektur, die das reale Leben der realen Menschen im Inneren widerspiegelt.

RESIDENTIAL BUILDING NOVÝ HÁJ
BRATISLAVA, SLOVAKIA

Le concept architectural de Nový háj repose sur deux facteurs essentiels :
Tout d'abord, une réaction directe à son emplacement à Petržalka, le plus grand complexe résidentiel de panneaux préfabriqués en béton d'Europe centrale, qui est un vestige de l'ère communiste. Les deux tours de l'immeuble profitent au maximum de leur contact visuel avec les bois et le parc voisins, et chaque appartement fait face à deux façades.
Le deuxième facteur est la participation active des résidents à la conception architecturale du bâtiment. Son design flexible et son langage architectural permettent aux clients de choisir la taille et l'emplacement de leurs fenêtres et balcons sans compromettre la cohérence de l'ensemble. Le résultat de cette approche est une architecture authentique qui reflète la vie réelle des gens à l'intérieur.

El concepto arquitectónico de Nový háj se basa en dos factores esenciales:
En primer lugar, una reacción directa frente a su ubicación en Petržalka, el mayor conjunto de viviendas de paneles prefabricados de hormigón en Europa Central, que constituye una reliquia de la era comunista. Las dos torres del edificio sacan el máximo provecho de su contacto visual con los bosques y el parque cercanos, y cada apartamento goza de orientación hacia dos fachadas.
El segundo factor es la participación activa de los residentes en la concepción arquitectónica del edificio. Su diseño flexible y el lenguaje arquitectónico empleado permiten que los clientes puedan elegir el tamaño y la ubicación de sus ventanas y balcones sin comprmeter la coherencia del conjunto. El resultado de este enfoque es una arquitectura auténtica que refleja la vida real de personas reales en su interior.

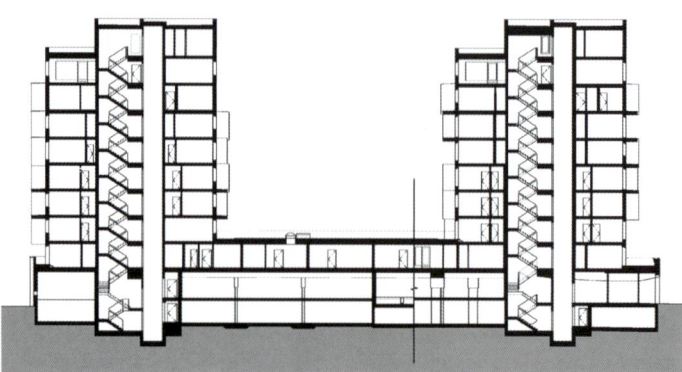

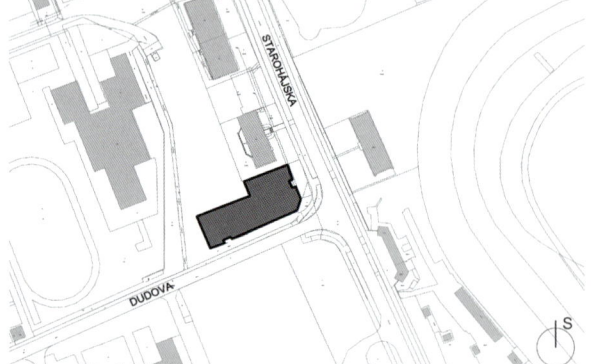

Site plan

Section

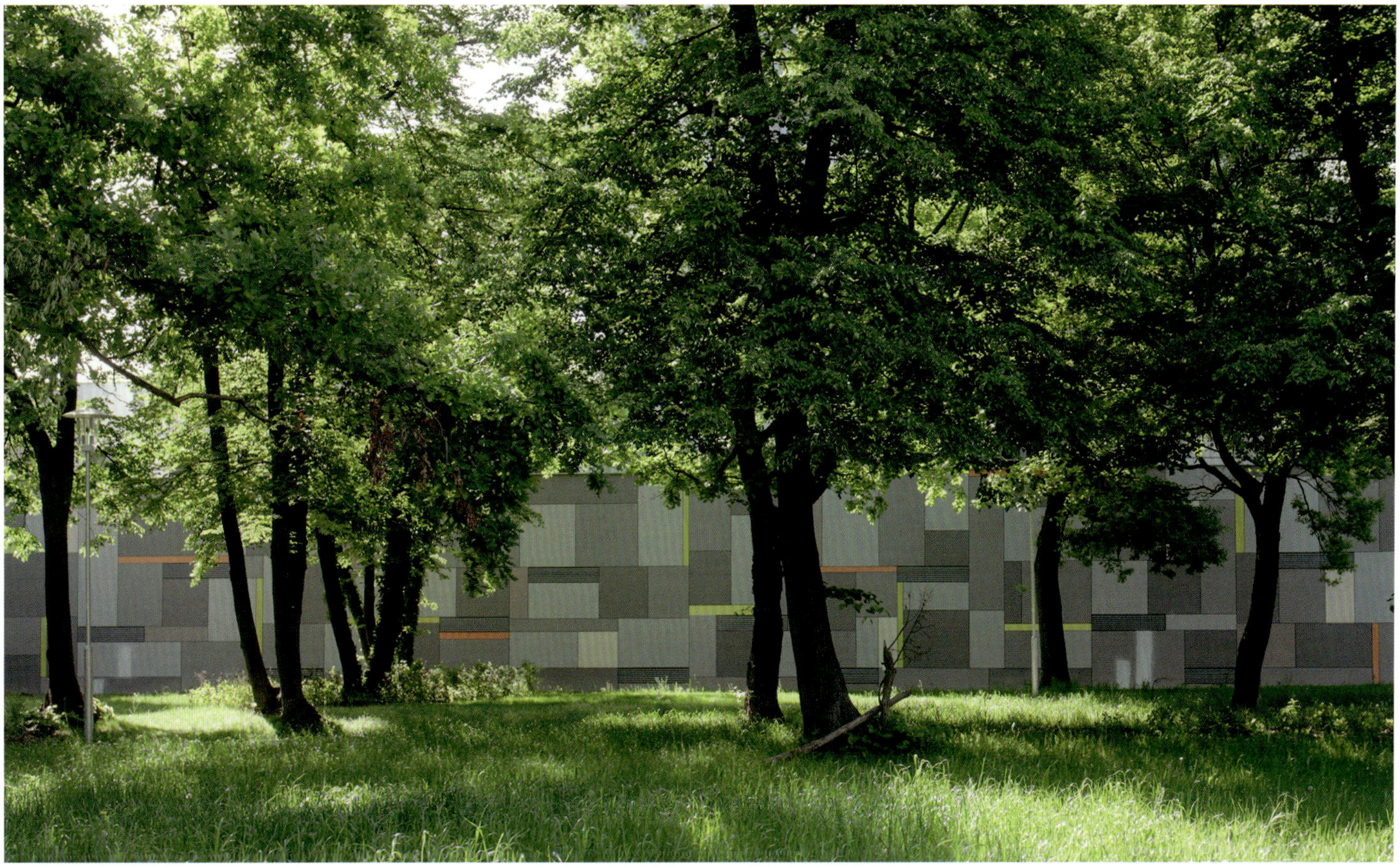

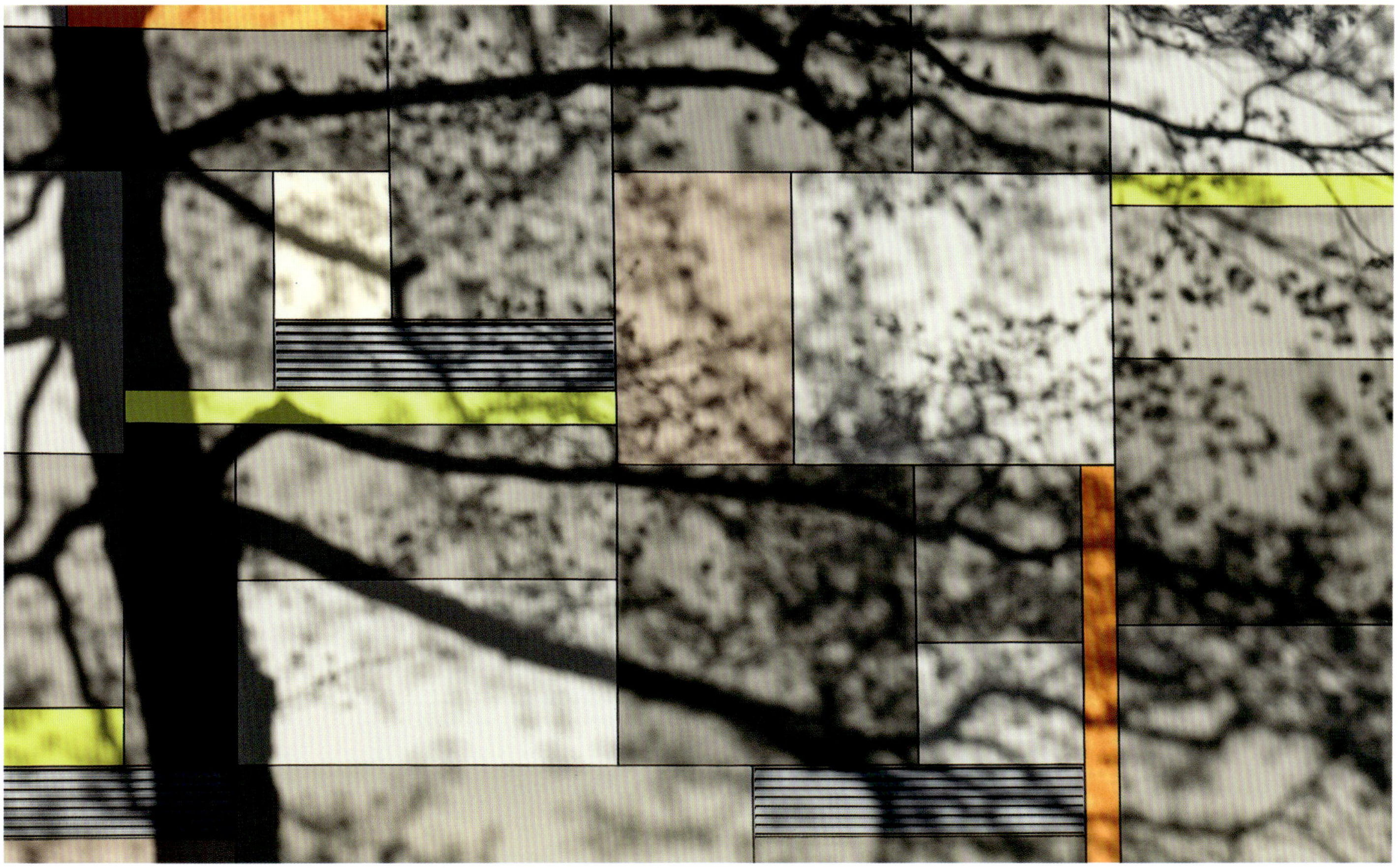

East elevation

North elevation

▦ Windows and loggias position before client's changes

■ Windows and loggias position after client's changes

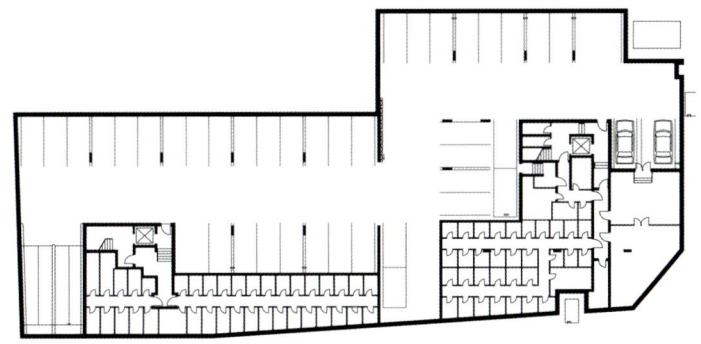

Lower ground floor plan

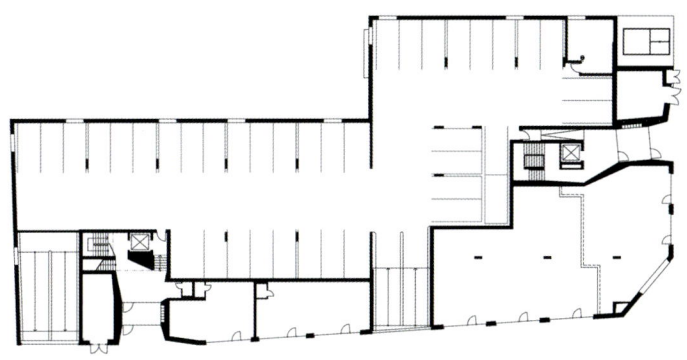

Ground floor plan

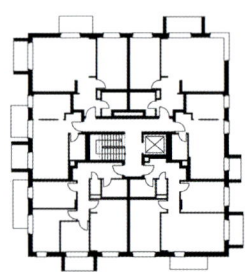

Third floor plan

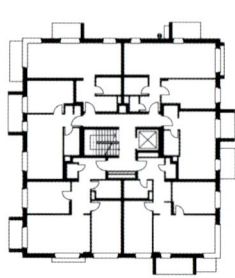

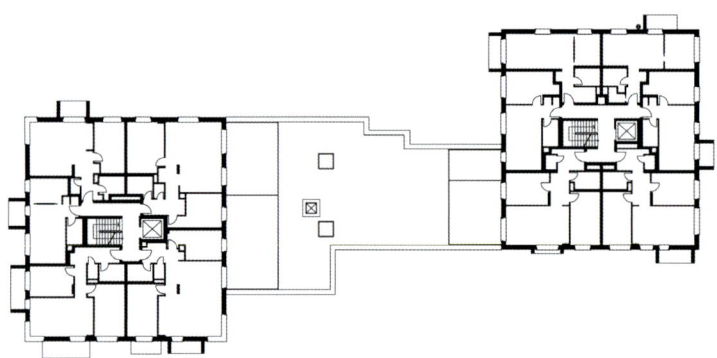

Second floor plan

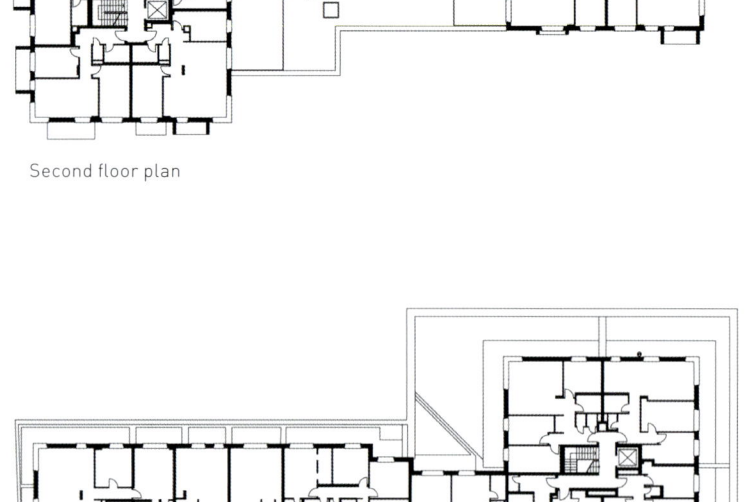

First floor plan

ADNBA

http://www.adnba.ro

ADNBA was established in 2003 in Bucharest, by Andrei Șerbescu and Adrian Untaru, later joined by Bogdan Brădățeanu. The work of our practice is characterised by our attempt to search for the right balance between experiment and experience in the complex and delicate landscape of contemporary life.

ADNBA's work has been several times nominated for the European Prize for Contemporary Architecture Mies van der Rohe Awards, for which it was also shortlisted within the last 40 projects in 2019 and 2015. It was also the winner of the Milan Zlokovic award for the best architectural achievement in the Balkan Region in 2015, a finalist at the World of Architecture Festival Awards in 2014, the winner of the Romanian National Architecture Biennale in the same year, and of the Bucharest Architecture Annual in 2014, 2017 and 2018. In 2016, the office won the first prize at the Romanian Building Awards and the East Centric Architecture Triennale Award, and were also part of the main exhibition at the Venice Architecture Biennale in 2016.

ADNBA wurde 2003 in Bukarest von Andrei Șerbescu und Adrian Untaru gegründet, später von Bogdan Brădățeanu Die Arbeit unseres Studios ist geprägt von dem Versuch, die richtige Balance zwischen Erfahrung und Experiment in der komplexen und heiklen Landschaft des zeitgenössischen Lebens zu finden.

Die Arbeit von ADNBA wurde mehrfach für den Mies van der Rohe European Prize for Contemporary Architecture nominiert, für den sie auch in den letzten 40 Projekten 2019 und 2015 in die engere Wahl kam. Es war auch der Gewinner des Mailänder Zlokovic-Preises für die beste architektonische Leistung auf dem Balkan im Jahr 2015, Finalist der World of Architecture Festival Awards 2014, Gewinner der Nationalen Architekturbiennale Rumäniens im selben Jahr und des Bukarester Architekturjahres 2014, 2017 und 2018. Im Jahr 2016 gewann das Büro den ersten Preis bei den Rumänischen Baupreisen und dem Triennale Eastern Central Architecture Award und war auch Teil der Hauptausstellung der Architekturbiennale in Venedig 2016.

ADNBA a été fondée en 2003 à Bucarest par Andrei Șerbescu et Adrian Untaru, rejoints plus tard par Bogdan Brădățeanu Le travail de notre atelier se caractérise par la recherche du juste équilibre entre expérience et expérience dans le paysage complexe et sensible de la vie contemporaine.

L'œuvre de l'ADNBA a été nominée à plusieurs reprises pour le Prix européen d'architecture contemporaine Mies van der Rohe, pour lequel elle a également été présélectionnée dans les 40 derniers projets en 2019 et 2015. Elle a également été lauréate du prix Milan Zlokovic pour la meilleure réalisation architecturale dans la région des Balkans en 2015, finaliste aux World of Architecture Festival Awards en 2014, lauréate de la Biennale nationale d'architecture de Roumanie la même année et de la Bucarest Architecture Annual en 2014, 2017 et 2018. En 2016, le bureau a remporté le premier prix des Prix roumains de la construction et le Prix triennal d'architecture du Centre-Est, et a également participé à l'exposition principale de la Biennale d'architecture de Venise en 2016.

ADNBA fue fundada en 2003 en Bucarest, por Andrei Șerbescu y por Adrian Untaru, a los que posteriormente se unió Bogdan Brădățeanu El trabajo de nuestro estudio se caracteriza por el intento de encontrar el equilibrio adecuado entre la experiencia y el experimento en el complejo y delicado paisaje de la vida contemporánea.

La obra de ADNBA ha sido nominada en varias ocasiones al Premio Europeo de Arquitectura Contemporánea Premios Mies van der Rohe, para el que también ha sido preseleccionada en los últimos 40 proyectos en 2019 y 2015. También fue el ganador del premio Milan Zlokovic al mejor logro arquitectónico de la región de los Balcanes en 2015, finalista en los World of Architecture Festival Awards en 2014, ganador de la Bienal Nacional de Arquitectura de Rumania en el mismo año y del Bucarest Architecture Annual en 2014, 2017 y 2018. En 2016, la oficina ganó el primer premio en los Premios Rumanos de la Construcción y el Premio Trienal de Arquitectura Centrica del Este, y también formó parte de la exposición principal en la Bienal de Arquitectura de Venecia en 2016.

URBAN SPACES 1'/DOGARILOR 26-30 HOUSING

Architecture and design coordination: ADNBA

Developer: Salzburg Investment Group SA

Project management: Salzburg Investment Group SA, Vision Property Partner

Authors: Andrei Şerbescu, Adrian Untaru, Claudiu Forgaci, Valentina Ţigâră, Bogdan Brădăţeanu, Simina Ignat

Number of units: 77 apartments, 2 ateliers/shops

Total built area: 8.537 m²

Design and construction period: 2011 – 2014

Photo credits:
© Cosmin Dragomir

Awards
- 2016 Romanian Building Awards, winner
- 2016 East Centric Architecture Triennale, Bucharest, winner
- 2016 East Centric Arhitext Awards, shortlisted
- 2015 Mies Van der Rohe Award, shortlisted
- 2015 "Milan Zlokovic" Award, first prize
- 2014 National Biennale of Architecture Bucharest, Housing category, first prize
- 2014 Architecture Annual Bucharest, Housing category, first prize
- 2014 World Architecture Festival, Housing category, shortlisted

MORA RESIDENTIAL BUILDING

Place: 17bis, Dr. Grigore Mora Street, Bucharest, Romania

Architecture and design coordination: ADNBA

Developer: private

Project management: Epstein PM&Consulting

Authors: Adrian Untaru, Andrei Şerbescu, Bogdan Brădăţeanu, Marius Dumitraşcu, Ruxandra Bardaş, Carmen Petrea

Photo credits: © Cosmin Dragomir

Number of units: 5 apartments

Total built area: 2020 m²

Design and construction period: 2011 - 2014

Awards
- 2014 Mies van der Rohe Awards, nominated
- 2014 National Biennale of Architecture Bucharest, Housing category, nominated

In response to the densification of the central area of Bucharest, the project tries to integrate into a puzzle of new and old buildings of different typologies and scales. The intervention, structured in two volumes, seeks to reproduce the porosity and depth of the plots in the area and attempts to capture part of the collage aspect of the surroundings. The exterior volume has a permeable ground floor that opens the building towards the street and a façade that mediates between the alignment required by municipal regulations and the fragmentation of the surrounding urban fabric.

The 77 residential units that make up the project are of different sizes and typologies and are designed with a flexibility that allows two or more units to be connected horizontally or vertically. The apartments are complemented with several exterior and interior common spaces.

Als Reaktion auf die Verdichtung des zentralen Bereichs von Bukarest versucht das Projekt, sich in ein Puzzle von Neu- und Altbauten unterschiedlicher Typologien und Größenordnungen zu integrieren. Die Intervention, die in zwei Teile gegliedert ist, zielt darauf ab, die Porosität und Tiefe der Parzellen in dem Gebiet zu reproduzieren und versucht, einen Teil des Collage-Aspektes der Umgebung zu erfassen. Das Außenvolumen weist ein durchlässiges Erdgeschoss auf, das das Gebäude zur Straße hin öffnet, und eine Fassade, die zwischen der von der Gemeindeordnung geforderten Ausrichtung und der Fragmentierung des umgebenden Stadtgefüges vermittelt.

Die 77 Wohneinheiten, aus denen sich das Projekt zusammensetzt, sind unterschiedlich groß und typisiert sowie mit einer Flexibilität konzipiert, die es ermöglicht, zwei oder mehr Einheiten horizontal oder vertikal zu verbinden. Die Wohnungen werden durch mehrere gemeinsame Außen- und Innenräume ergänzt.

URBAN SPACES
1'/DOGARILOR 26-30 HOUSING
BUCAREST, ROMANIA

En réponse à la densification de la zone centrale de Bucarest, le projet tente d'intégrer un puzzle de bâtiments nouveaux et anciens de différentes typologies et échelles. L'intervention, structurée en deux volumes, cherche à reproduire la porosité et la profondeur des parcelles de la zone et tente de capter une partie de l'aspect collage de l'environnement. Le volume extérieur est composé d'un rez-de-chaussée perméable qui ouvre le bâtiment vers la rue et d'une façade qui fait le lien entre l'alignement requis par la réglementation municipale et la fragmentation du tissu urbain environnant.

Les 77 unités résidentielles qui composent le projet sont de tailles et de typologies différentes et sont conçues avec une flexibilité qui permet de relier deux ou plusieurs unités horizontalement ou verticalement. Les appartements sont complétés par plusieurs espaces communs extérieurs et intérieurs.

Como respuesta a la densificación del área central de Bucarest, el proyecto trata de integrarse en un rompecabezas de edificios nuevos y antiguos de diferentes tipologías y escalas. La intervención, estructurada en dos volúmenes, busca reproducir la porosidad y la profundidad de las parcelas de la zona e intenta capturar parte del aspecto de "collage" de los alrededores. El volumen exterior tiene una planta baja permeable que abre el edificio hacia la calle y una fachada que media entre la alineación requerida por la normativa municipal y la fragmentación del tejido urbano circundante.

Las 77 unidades residenciales que componen el proyecto son de diferentes tamaños y tipologías y están diseñadas con una flexibilidad que permite conectar horizontal o verticalmente dos o más unidades. Los apartamentos se complementan con varios espacios comunes exteriores e interiores.

Fifth floor plan

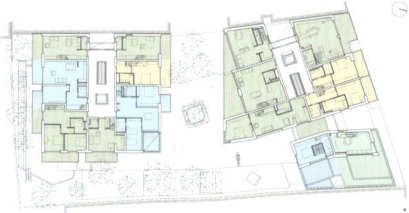

Fourth floor plan

Third floor plan

First floor plan

Ground floor plan

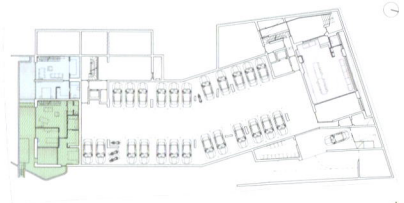

Basement floor plan

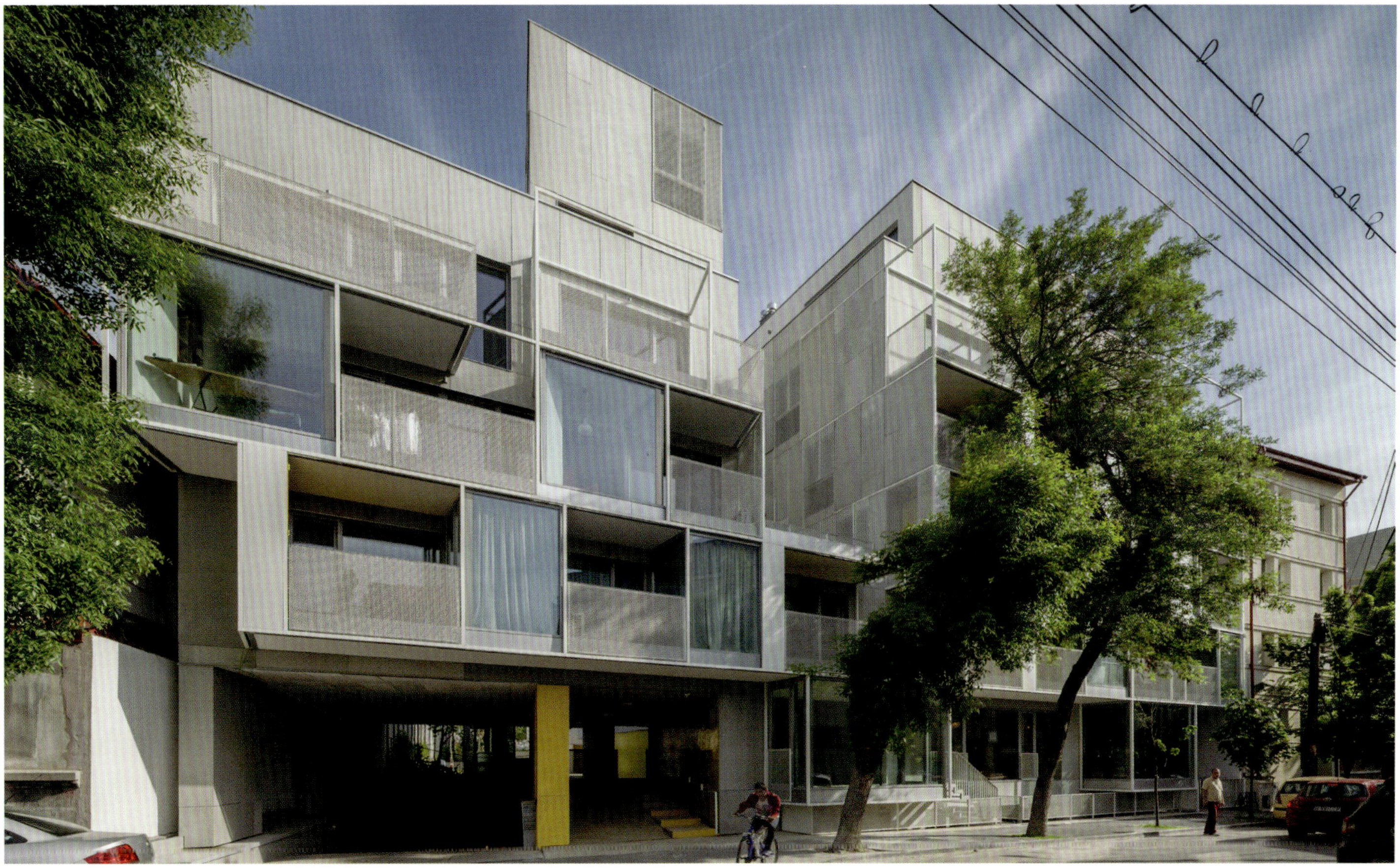

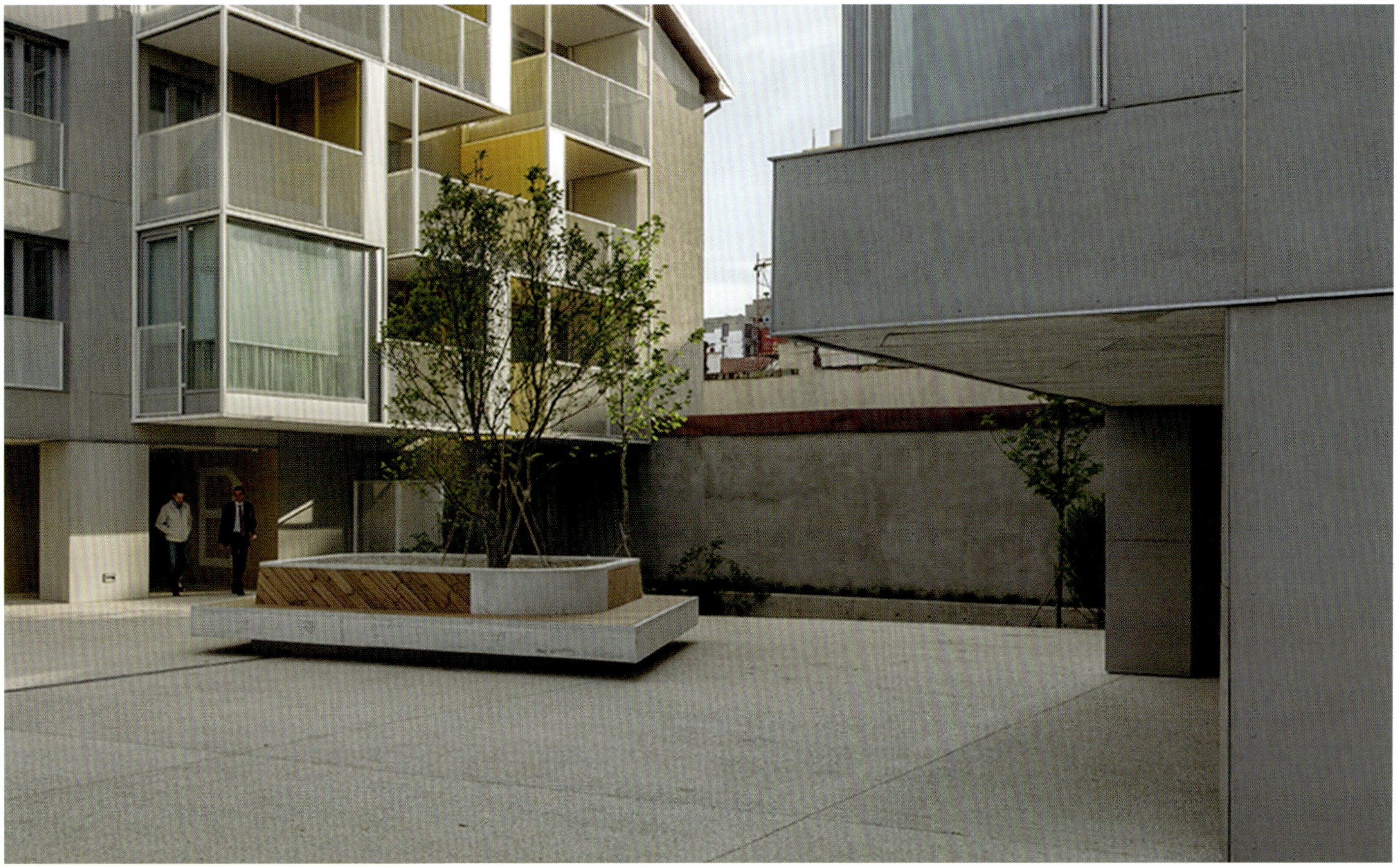

Site plan

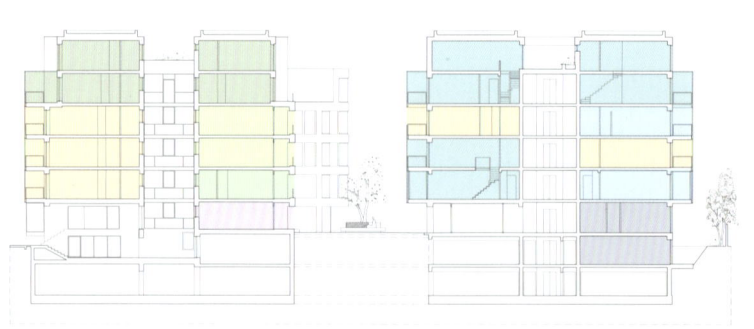

Building section

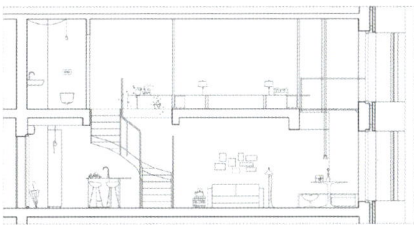

Duplex apartment. Section

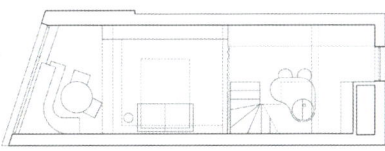

Duplex apartment. First floor

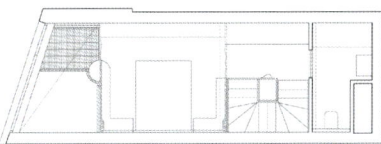

Duplex apartment. Ground floor

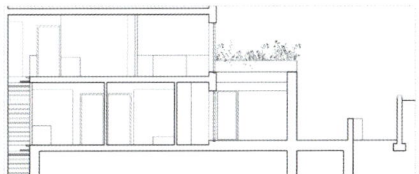

Duplex apartment. Section

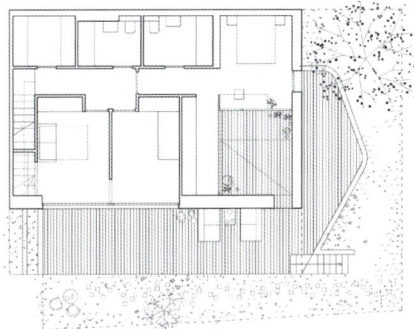

Duplex apartment. First floor

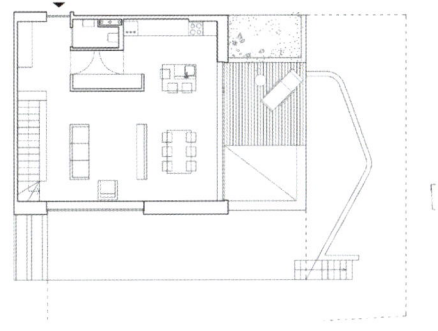

Duplex apartment. Ground floor

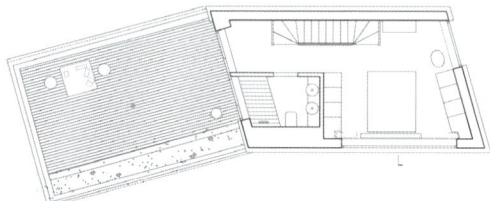

Studio top floor plan

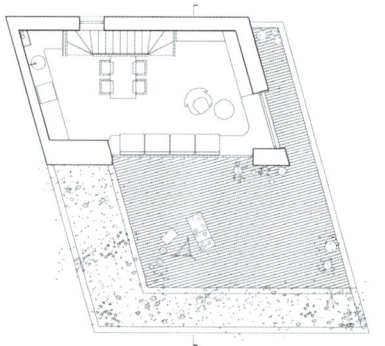

Studio fourth floor plan

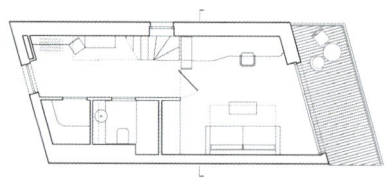

Studio third floor plan

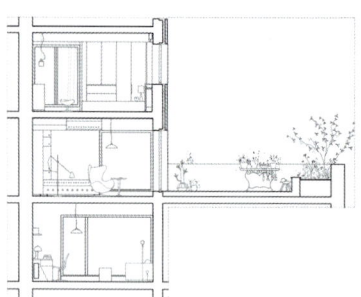

Section

Located in a historic area of the city centre, this urban village tries to preserve the architectural values of the area against recent interventions that have devalued its particular elegance and nobility. The dignity of the villa is highlighted by the exterior covering of light and matt limestone that covers the entire envelope and confers a monolithic but luminous image. The design of the construction details presents the façade as a simple light layer and not as a structural configuration with volume. The composition of the façade is subordinated to the needs of the interior common areas, with large south-facing openings and deep terraces that provide privacy and protection from the sun. The different configurations of windows and terraces allow for various degrees and types of relationships between the interior space and the surroundings.

In einem historischen Viertel des Stadtzentrums gelegen, versucht dieses städtische Dorf, die architektonischen Werte des Gebietes gegen die jüngsten Interventionen zu bewahren, die seine besondere Eleganz und Vornehmheit beeinträchtigt haben. Die Würde der Villa wird durch die äußere Hülle aus hellem und mattem Kalkstein unterstrichen, die die gesamte Hülle bedeckt und ein monolithisches, aber leuchtendes Bild erzeugt. Die Gestaltung der Konstruktionsdetails stellt die Fassade als einfache Lichtspur und nicht als strukturelle Konfiguration mit Volumen dar. Die Zusammensetzung der Fassade ist den Bedürfnissen der inneren Gemeinschaftsräume untergeordnet, mit großen Öffnungen nach Süden und tiefen Terrassen, die Privatsphäre und Sonnenschutz bieten. Die verschiedenen Konfigurationen der Fenster und Terrassen ermöglichen verschiedene Grade und Arten von Beziehungen zwischen dem Innenraum und der Umgebung.

MORA RESIDENTIAL BUILDING
BUCAREST, ROMANIA

Situé dans un quartier historique du centre-ville, ce village urbain s'efforce de préserver les valeurs architecturales du quartier contre les interventions récentes qui ont dévalué son élégance et sa noblesse particulières. La dignité de la villa est soulignée par le revêtement extérieur en calcaire clair et mat qui recouvre toute l'enveloppe et confère une image monolithique, mais lumineuse. La conception des détails de construction présente la façade comme une simple couche de lumière et non comme une configuration structurelle avec volume. La composition de la façade est subordonnée aux besoins des parties communes intérieures, avec de grandes ouvertures orientées au sud et des terrasses profondes qui offrent intimité et protection contre le soleil. Les différentes configurations de fenêtres et de terrasses permettent différents degrés et types de relations entre l'espace intérieur et l'environnement.

Ubicada en un área histórica del centro de la ciudad, esta villa urbana trata de preservar los valores arquitectónicos de la zona frente a recientes intervenciones que han devaluado su particular elegancia y nobleza. La dignidad de la villa es remarcada por el recubrimiento exterior de piedra caliza clara y mate que cubre toda la envolvente y que confiere una imagen monolítica pero luminosa. El diseño de los detalles constructivos presenta la fachada como una simple capa ligera y no como una configuración estructural con volumen. La composición de la fachada se subordina a las necesidades de las zonas comunes interiores, con grandes aberturas orientadas al sur y profundas terrazas que aportan privacidad y protección frente al sol. Las diferentes configuraciones de ventanas y terrazas permiten varios grados y tipos de relaciones entre el espacio interior y el entorno.

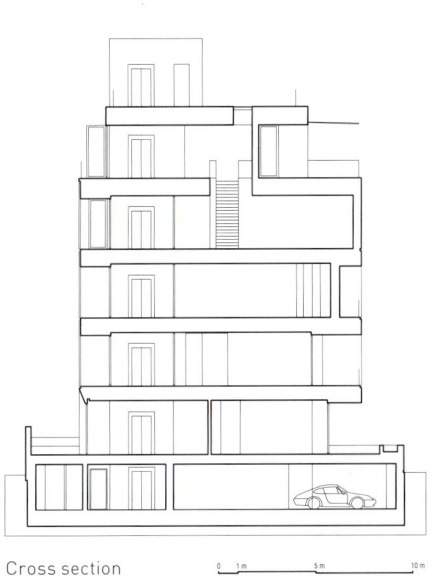

Cross section

0 1 m   5 m   10 m

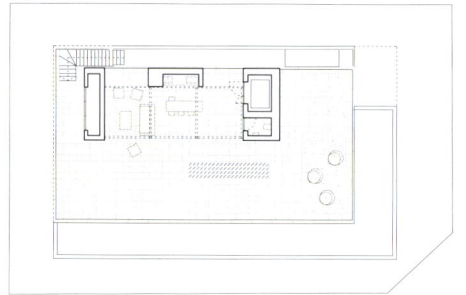

Terrace plan

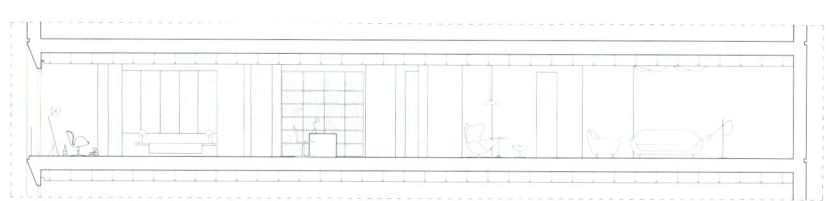

Detailed apartment section

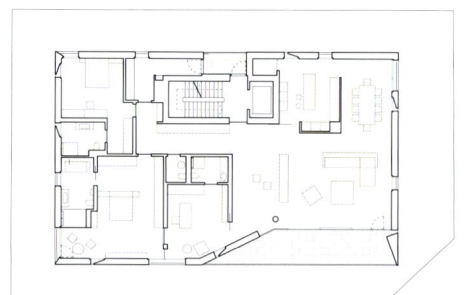

Second floor plan

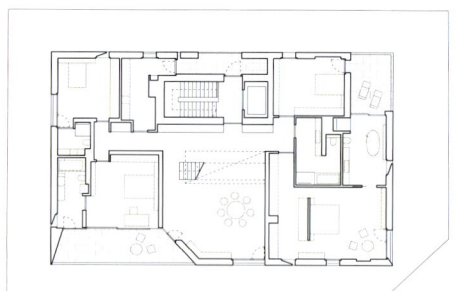

Third floor plan

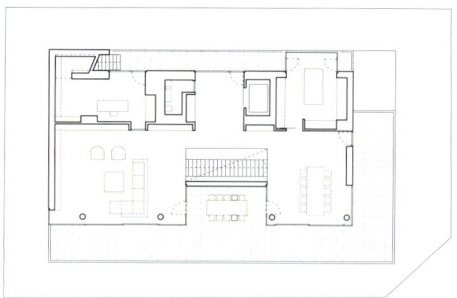

Fourth floor plan

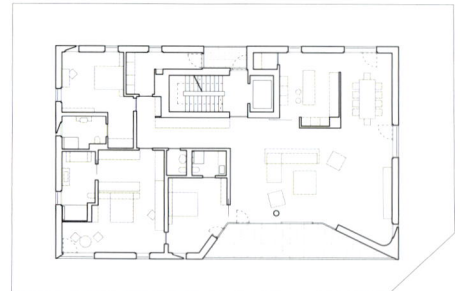

First floor plan

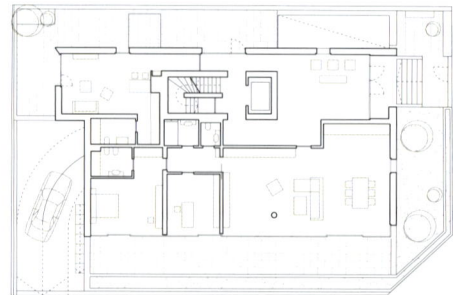

Ground floor plan

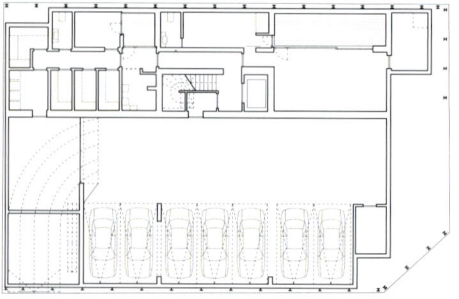

Basement plan

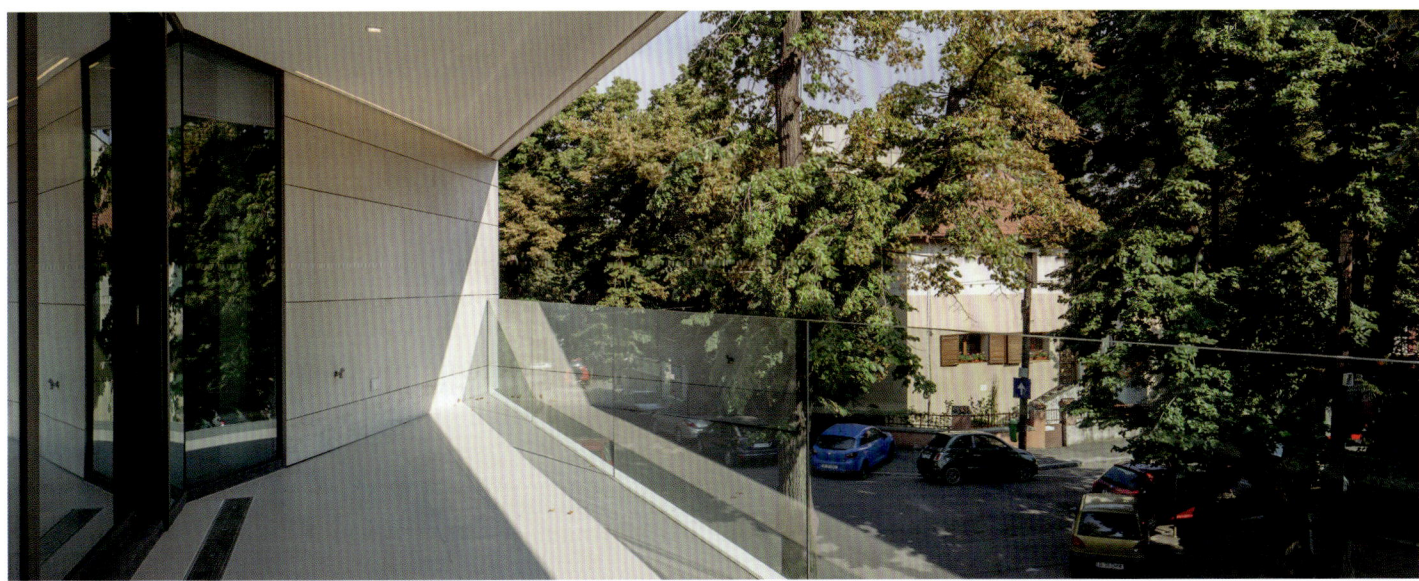

BERNARD BÜHLER

http://www.bernard-buhler.com/

We devote a major part of our work to the design and construction of social housing and are very sensitive to projects that give the opportunity to qualifier- requalifier a place.
The treatment of the privacy of homes and their relationship to collective and public spaces as a factor of success and appropriation, the optimization of surfaces, the maximum functionality in minimum surfaces are issues that structure our projects. In general, it is important to us to propose:
A playful architecture. In the constraints related to social housing (budget, surfaces, regulations) find loopholes that remain economical by working on colour, a particular staging of openings... work on everything that is too connoted social housing. Afin to offer atypical, personalized housing... find realistic inventiveness, economic optical effects... to change an often trivialized perception.
Each project is considered as a signal, an element qualifiant a context.

Wir widmen einen großen Teil unserer Arbeit der Planung und dem Bau von Sozialwohnungen und sind sehr sensibel für Projekte, die die Möglichkeit bieten, einen Platz zu requalifizieren.
Der Umgang mit der Privatsphäre von Wohnungen und deren Beziehung zu kollektiven und öffentlichen Räumen als Erfolgs- und Aneignungsfaktor, die Optimierung von Oberflächen, maximale Funktionalität bei minimalen Oberflächen sind Themen, die unsere Projekte strukturieren. Im Allgemeinen ist es uns wichtig, dass wir einen Vorschlag machen:
Eine spielerische Architektur. In den Einschränkungen des sozialen Wohnungsbaus (Budget, Flächen, Vorschriften) gibt es Schlupflöcher, die bei der Arbeit an Farben, einer bestimmten Inszenierung von Eröffnungen wirtschaftlich bleiben ... Arbeit an allem, was sozialer Wohnungsbau ist, der zu konnotiert ist ... bietet atypischen und personalisierten Wohnungsbau ... schärfen den Erfindungsreichtum, wirtschaftliche optische Effekte ... um eine oft trivialisierte Wahrnehmung zu verändern.
Jedes Projekt wird als Signal, als qualifizierendes Element eines Kontextes betrachtet.

Nous consacrons une part majeur de notre travail à la conception et la construction de logements sociaux et sommes très sensibles aux projets qui donnent l'occasion de qualifier- requalifier un lieu.
Le traitement de l'intimité des logements et leurs relations aux espaces collectifs et publics comme facteur de réussite et d'appropriation, l'optimisation des surfaces, la fonctionnalité maximum dans des surfaces minimum sont des problématiques qui structurent nos projets. De manière générale il nous tient à cœur de proposer :
Une architecture ludique. Dans les contraintes liées au logement social (budget, surfaces, réglementation) trouver des échappatoires qui restent économiques par un travail sur la couleur, une mise en scène particulière des ouvertures... travailler sur tout ce qui est trop connoté logement social. Afin d'offrir des logements atypiques, personnalisés... trouver de l'inventivité réaliste, des effets d'optique économiques... pour changer une perception souvent banalisée.
Chaque projet est envisagé comme un signal, un élément qualifiant un contexte.

Dedicamos gran parte de nuestro trabajo al diseño y construcción de viviendas sociales y somos muy sensibles a los proyectos que dan la oportunidad de recalificar un lugar.
El tratamiento de la privacidad de los hogares y su relación con los espacios colectivos y públicos como factor de éxito y apropiación, la optimización de superficies, la máxima funcionalidad en superficies mínimas son cuestiones que estructuran nuestros proyectos. En general, es importante para nosotros proponer:
Una arquitectura lúdica. En las limitaciones relacionadas con la vivienda social (presupuesto, superficies, normativa) se encuentran lagunas que siguen siendo económicas al trabajar sobre el color, una escenificación particular de las aperturas... trabajar sobre todo lo que es vivienda social demasiado connotada... ofrecer viviendas atípicas y personalizadas... agudizar la inventiva, los efectos ópticos económicos... para cambiar una percepción a menudo trivializada.
Cada proyecto es considerado como una señal, un elemento cualificador de un contexto.

Architect and manager:
Bernard Bühler,
Nº 5, Marie Bühler

Project function: 87 social
collective housings + 2 stores
+ parking in basement

Site area: 1458 m²

Building area: 996 m²

Gross built area: 6000 m² (housings
+ 2 stores)

Photo credits:
© Sergio Grazia photograph

Completion year: January 2017

Lead architects:
Bernard Bühler / Marie Bühler

FULTON

The building benefits from a very beautiful location along the Austerlitz quay, facing the Seine. Consisting of a base that features two distinct buildings in R+11 via an urban fault, the project echoes its immediate environment.
The height graduations of the base mark the project in relation to its direct context.
The fault seems to sculpt the built masses of the two emerging volumes. The project evokes an impression of successive erosions that carve the inner body of the block buildings. Thus dug in depth, the induced volumes reveal a brilliant and vibrant materiality composed of glass products. The shapes of the buildings provide diagonal views, avoiding the relationship of frontality or simplicity vis-à-vis. These folded shapes continuously redirect the views, opening up ideal perspectives on the Seine.

Das Gebäude profitiert von einer sehr schönen Lage am Austerlitzer Kai gegenüber der Seine. Das Projekt besteht aus einer Basis, die zwei verschiedene Gebäude in R+11 über einen städtischen Fehler aufweist und spiegelt die unmittelbare Umgebung wider.
Die Höhenabstufungen der Basis markieren das Projekt in Bezug auf seinen direkten Kontext. Der Fehler scheint die gebauten Massen der beiden entstehenden Volumen zu formen. Das Projekt erweckt den Eindruck von aufeinanderfolgenden Erosionen, die den Innenkörper der Blockgebäude zerlegen. Die induzierten Volumen zeigen eine brillante und lebendige Materialität aus Glasprodukten. Die Formen der Gebäude bieten diagonale Ansichten und vermeiden so das Verhältnis von Frontalität oder Einfachheit gegenüber. Diese gefalteten Formen lenken die Blicke kontinuierlich um und eröffnen ideale Perspektiven auf die Seine.

FULTON
PARIS, FRANCE

Le bâtiment bénéficie d'un très bel emplacement le long du quai d'Austerlitz, face à la Seine. Constitué d'un socle qui met en scène deux bâtiments distincts en R+11 par l'intermédiaire d'une faille urbaine, le projet fait écho à son environnement proche.
Les graduations de hauteur du socle inscrivent le projet en rapport avec son contexte direct.
La faille semble sculpter les masses bâties des deux volumes émergents. Le projet évoque une impression d'érosions successives qui taillent le corps intérieur des bâtiments plots. Ainsi creusé en profondeur, les volumes induits font apparaitre une matérialité brillante et vibrante composées de produits verriers. Les formes des bâtiments dégagent des vues diagonales, évitant ainsi le rapport de frontalité ou de simple vis-à-vis. Ces formes pliées réorientent continuellement les vues, ouvrent des perspectives idéales sur la Seine.

El edificio se beneficia de una preciosa ubicación a lo largo del muelle de Austerlitz, frente al Sena. Compuesto por una base que presenta dos edificios distintos en R+11 a través de una falla urbana, el proyecto se hace eco de su entorno inmediato.
Las graduaciones de altura de la base marcan el proyecto en relación a su contexto.
La falla parece esculpir las masas construidas de los dos volúmenes emergentes. El proyecto evoca una impresión de sucesivas erosiones que tallan el cuerpo interior de los edificios. Así, excavados en profundidad, los volúmenes inducidos revelan una materialidad brillante y vibrante compuesta de productos de vidrio. Las formas de los edificios proporcionan vistas diagonales, evitando así la relación de frontalidad o simplicidad frente a ellos. Estas formas re direccionan continuamente las vistas, abriendo bonitas perspectivas sobre el río Sena.

Site plan

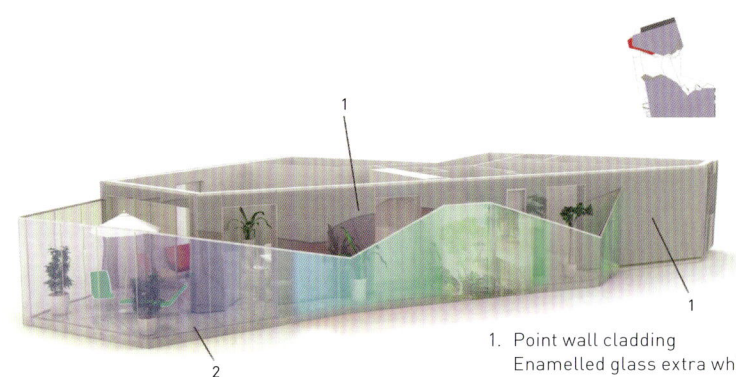

Balcony + apartment view

1. Point wall cladding
   Enamelled glass extra white
2. Dichroic glass
   (SCHOTT Narima® color effect)

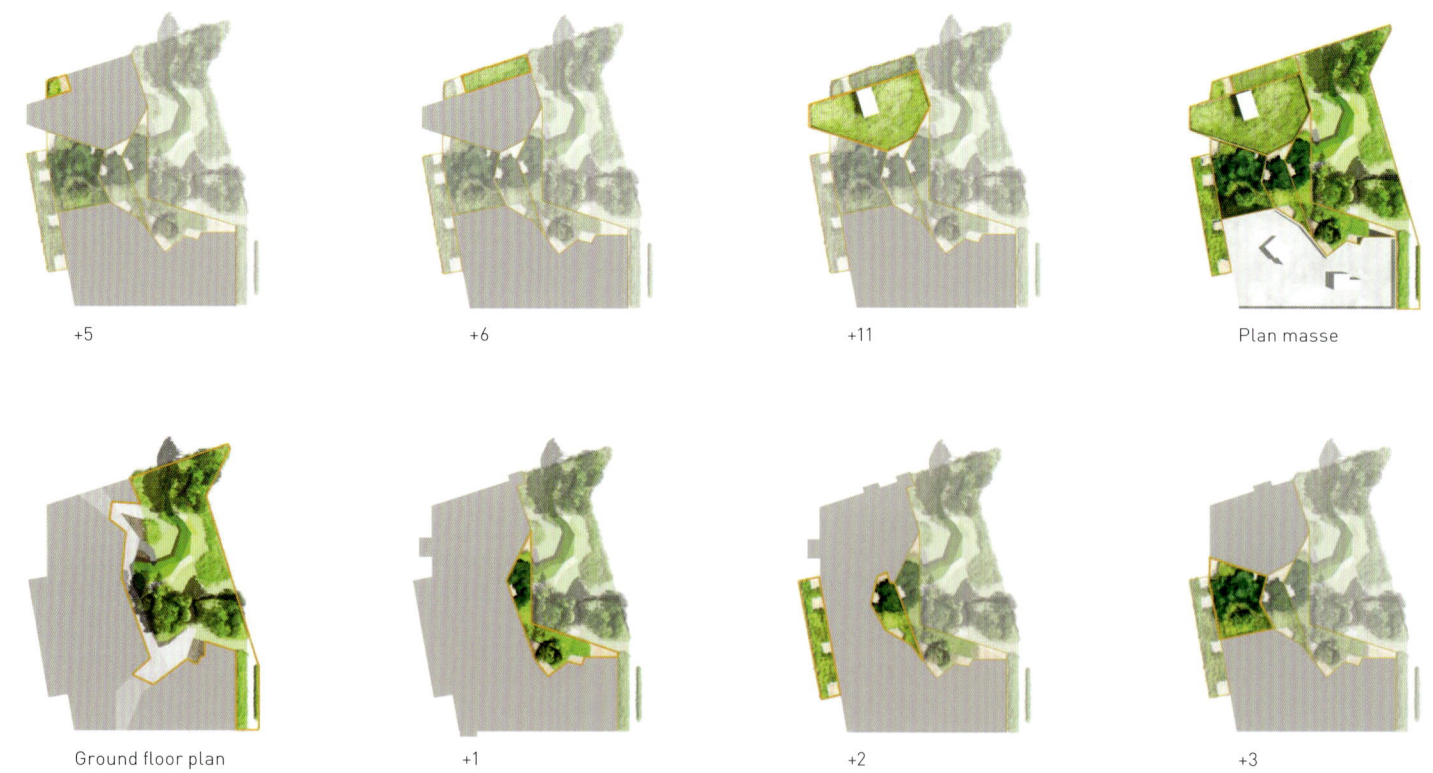

+5

+6

+11

Plan masse

Ground floor plan

+1

+2

+3

Landscaping

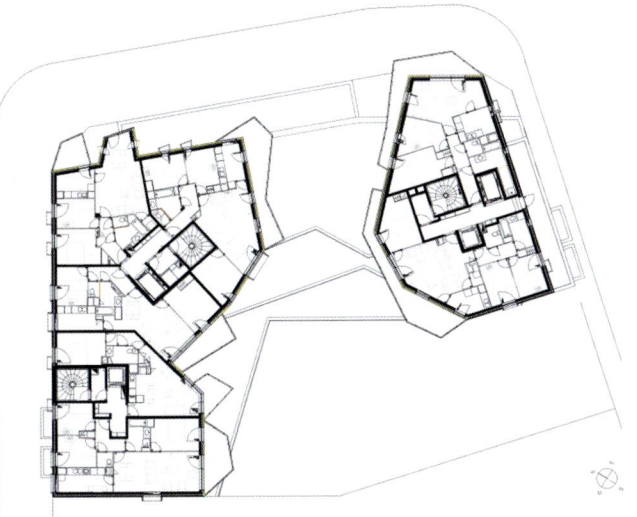

Sixth floor plan

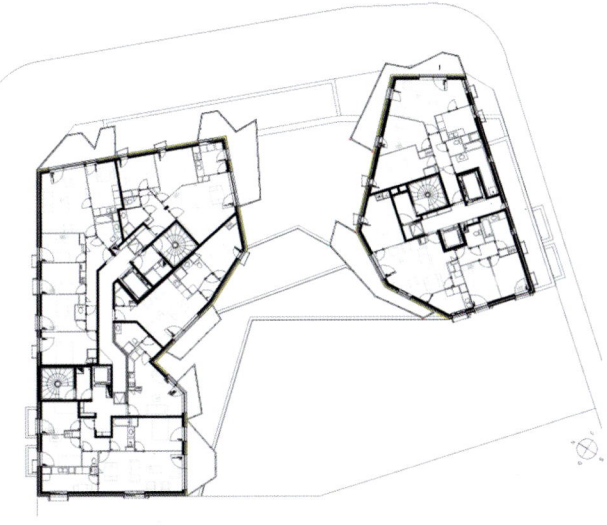

Eleventh floor plan

Second floor plan

Third floor plan

Ground floor plan

First floor plan

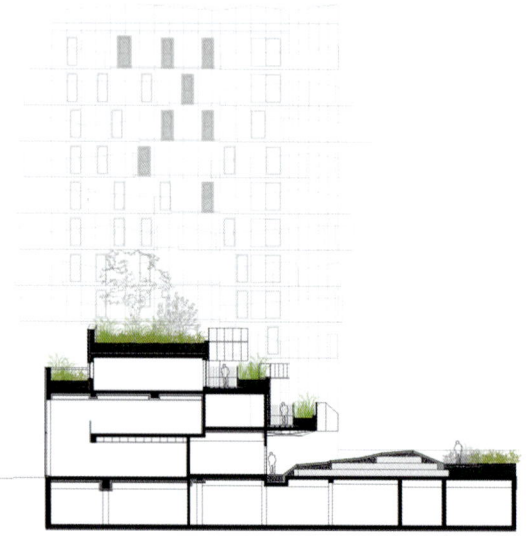

Section

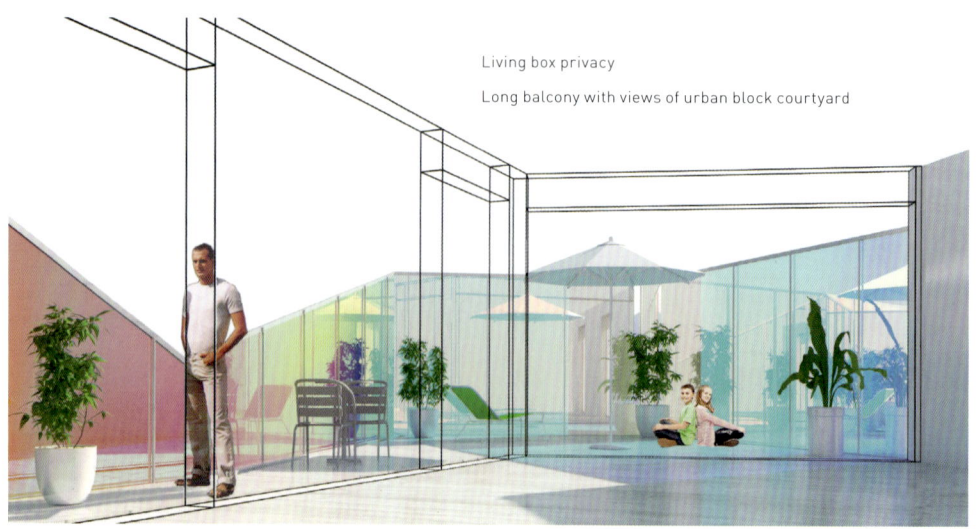

Living box privacy

Long balcony with views of urban block courtyard

Balcony view

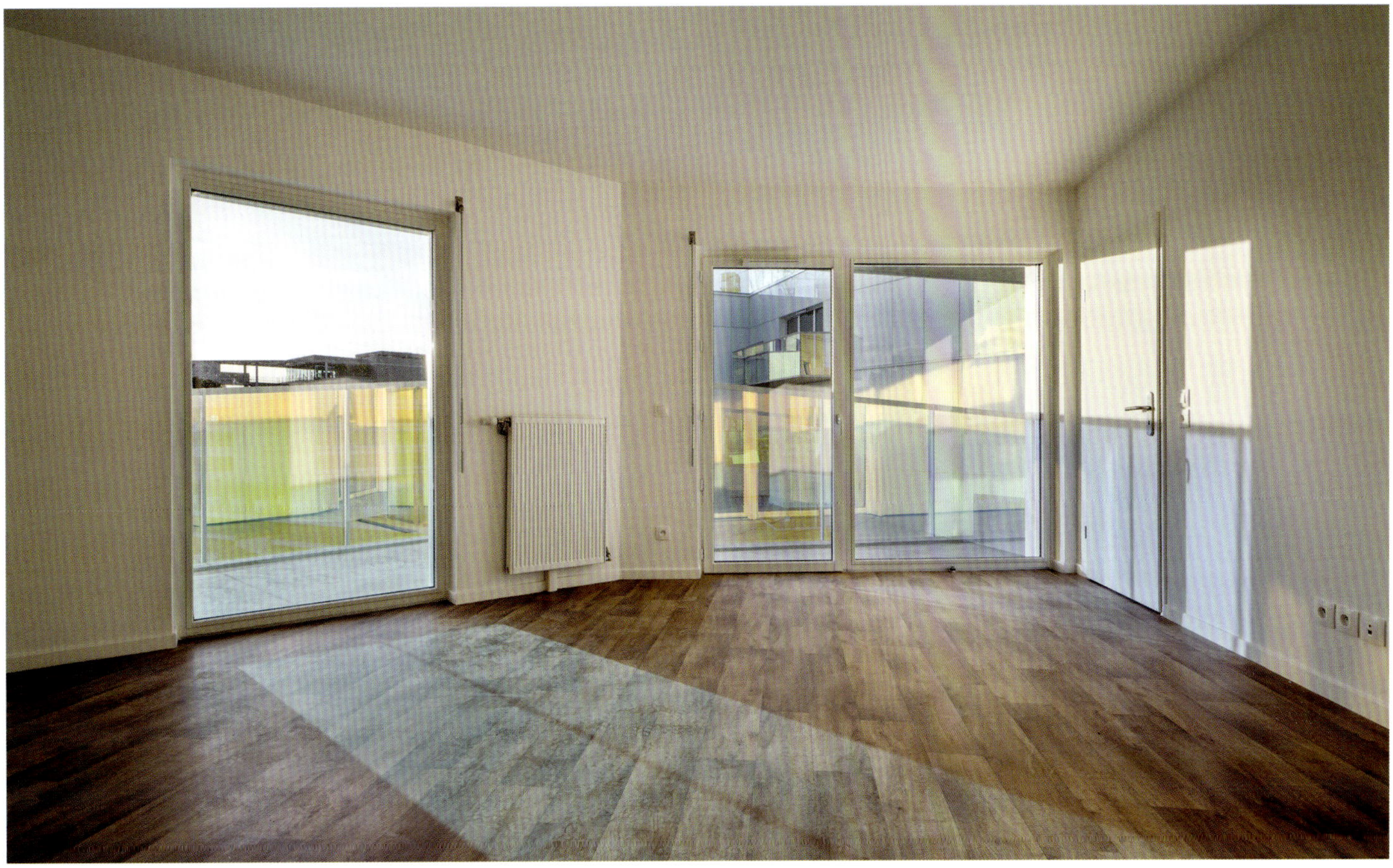

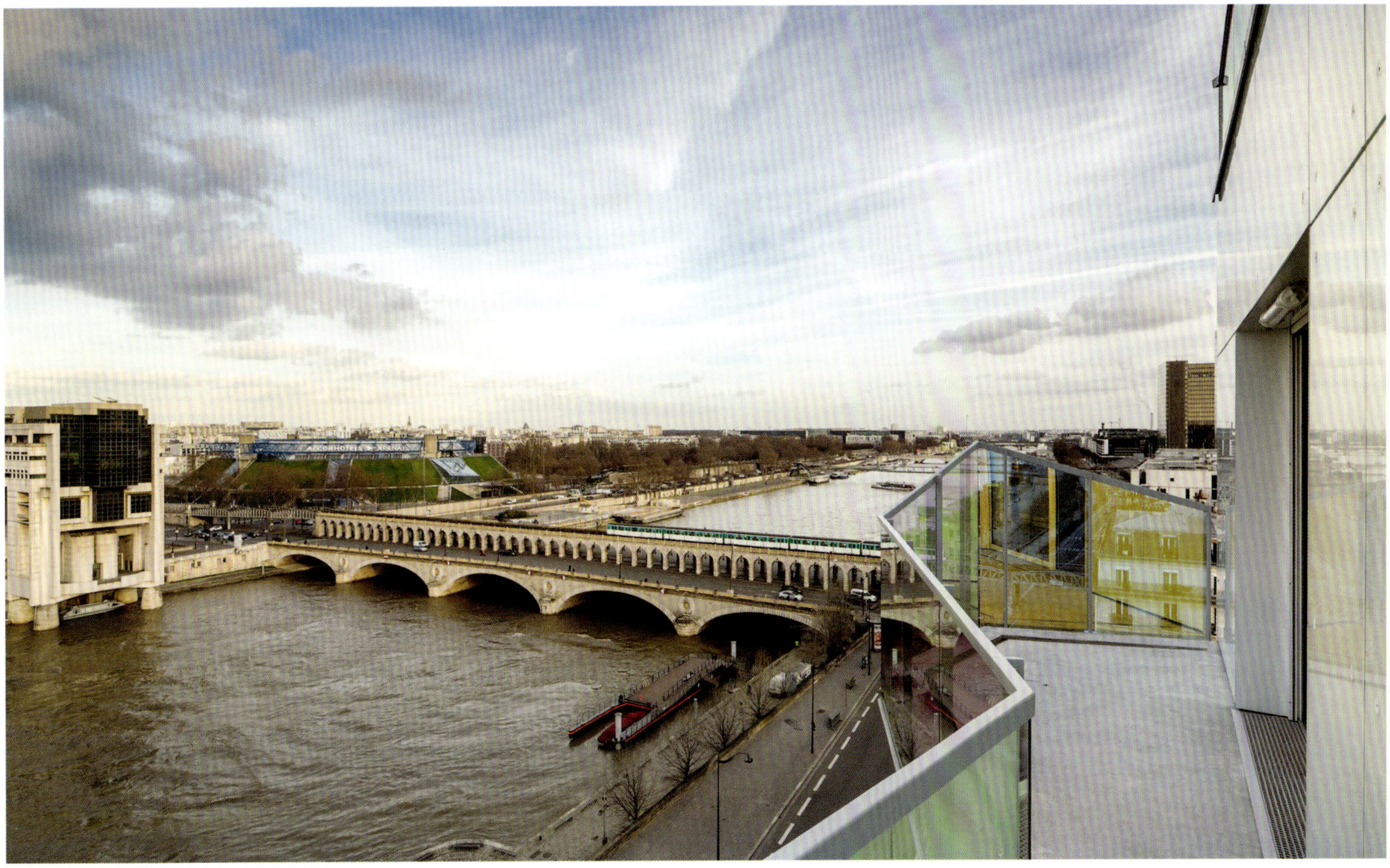

BIAGIONI / PECORARI ARQUITECTOS

www.biagionipecorari.com.ar

Biagioni / Pecorari is an Architectural studio based in the city of Santa Fe, Argentina, which since 1998 has been developing projects that cover a wide range of programmes and scales, from single-family and collective dwellings to highly complex buildings and urban projects based on a constant reflection on the quality of the habitable space and an expression linked to the constructive fact.

Their works have been awarded and published in different media. In parallel to their projecs, they work as professors and researchers in Architecture, Project Theory and Morphology, in addition to actively participating in project competitions, and activities of discussion and dissemination of architectural culture.

Biagioni / Pecorari ist ein Architekturstudio mit Sitz in der Region Stadt Santa Fe, Argentinien, die seit 1998 Projekte entwickelt, die ein breites Spektrum an Programmen und Größenordnungen abdecken, von Ein- und Mehrfamilienhäusern bis hin zu hochkomplexen Gebäuden und städtischen Projekten, die auf einer ständigen Reflexion über die Qualität des Wohnraums und einem mit der konstruktiven Tatsache verbundenen Ausdruck basieren.

Seine Arbeiten wurden ausgezeichnet und in verschiedenen Medien veröffentlicht. Parallel zu ihrer Projektarbeit sind sie als Professoren und Forscher in den Bereichen Architektur, Projekttheorie und Morphologie tätig, außerdem nehmen sie aktiv an Projektwettbewerben und Aktivitäten zur Diskussion und Verbreitung der Architekturkultur teil.

Biagioni / Pecorari est un studio d'architecture basé dans la région de l'Atlantique.

La ville de Santa Fe, Argentine, qui depuis 1998 développe des projets qui couvrent un large éventail de programmes et d'échelles, allant des maisons individuelles et collectives aux bâtiments très complexes et aux projets urbains basés sur une réflexion constante sur la qualité de l'espace habitable et une expression liée au fait constructif.

Ses œuvres ont été récompensées et publiées dans différents médias. Parallèlement à leur travail de projet, ils travaillent comme professeurs et chercheurs en Architecture, Théorie de projet et Morphologie, en plus de participer activement à des concours de projets, des activités de discussion et de diffusion de la culture architecturale.

Biagioni / Pecorari es un estudio de Arquitectura radicado en la ciudad de Santa Fe, Argentina, que desde 1998 desarrolla proyectos que abarcan una amplia gama de programas y escalas, desde viviendas unifamiliares y colectivas hasta edificios de alta complejidad y proyectos urbanos en base a una constante reflexión en torno a la calidad del espacio habitable y a una expresión vinculada al hecho constructivo.

Sus trabajos han sido premiados y publicados en diferentes medios. En paralelo a su labor proyectual, se desempeñan como profesores e investigadores en Arquitectura, Teoría de proyecto y Morfología, además de participar activamente en concursos de proyecto, y actividades de discusión y divulgación de cultura arquitectónica.

CASTELLI BUILDING

Location: Castelli and Tacuarí, Santa Fe, Argentina

Covered surface: 362 m²

Project: 2013

Construction: 2014-2015

Project and site management: Architect Gabriel Biagioni, Architect Sergio Pecorari

Collaborators: Architect Virginia Aranda, Architect Nestor Mancini, Architect Ramiro Sosa, Architect Lucía Izquierdo, Architect Sabrina Perisinotto, Mats Bakken

Structural engineering: Ing. Gustavo Perini

Builder: Constructora RIO SRL

Photo credits: © Ramiro Sosa

Awards:
In 2017, the Castelli Building won the First Prize (High Density Multifamily Housing Category) in the Competition 21st Century Built Architecture of the Architects Association of Santa Fe.

BUILDING ON TALCAHUANO STREET

Location: Talcahuano and Obispo Boneo, Santa Fe, Argentina

Covered surface: 468 m²

Project: 2010

Construction: 2011-2012

Project and site management: Architect Gabriel Biagioni, Architect Sergio Pecorari

Collaborators:
Arq. Matías Gabrielloni, Arq. Virginia Aranda

Structural engineering: Ing. Rudy Grether, Ing. Fernanda Carrasco

Builder: Constructora RIO SRL

Photo credits: © Federico Cairoli

Awards:
Talcahuano Building has obtained the Second Prize (Low Density Multifamily Housing Category) in the Contest "CAPSF/FADEA Award Built Work 2015".

The building owes its form to a recent regulation that increases the edificability of the area without limiting the height. In a small corner plot, the volume complies with the obligatory withdrawals to the fronts and the projects towards the interior of the block, which allow to obtain a height that takes advantage of the views. The slenderness of the small tower adds a new typology to the neighbourhood, where individual dwellings and small horizontal buildings predominate.

The programme combines a ground floor with two bedrooms and a patio, three floors with one-bedroom apartments and a duplex on the last two levels, with a social floor and a private area that includes a multifunctional space.

To the west, a blind façade controls the sunshine and integrates an elevator whose volume houses the water tank and a staircase as part of the urban space.

Das Gebäude verdankt seine Physiognomie einer neuen Verordnung, die die Bebaubarkeit der Fläche erhöht, ohne die Höhe einzuschränken. In einem kleinen Eckgrundstück entspricht das Volumen den obligatorischen Rückzügen zu den Fronten und den Vorsprüngen zum Inneren des Blocks, die es ermöglichen, eine Höhe zu erreichen, die die Aussicht nutzt. Die Schlankheit des kleinen Turms verleiht dem Quartier, in dem einzelne Wohnungen und kleine horizontale Gebäude dominieren, eine neue Typologie.

Das Programm kombiniert ein Erdgeschoss mit zwei Schlafzimmern und Terrasse, drei Stockwerke mit Einzimmerwohnungen und ein Duplex in den letzten beiden Stockwerken, mit einer Gemeinschafts-Etage und einer privaten Etage, die einen multifunktionalen Raum beinhaltet. Im Westen steuert eine Blindfassade die Sonneneinstrahlung und integriert einen Aufzug, dessen Volumen den Wassertank und eine Treppe als Teil des Stadtraums beherbergt.

CASTELLI BUILDING
CASTELLI AND TACUARÍ, SANTA FE, ARGENTINA

Le bâtiment doit sa physionomie à une réglementation récente qui augmente la constructibilité de l'espace sans en limiter la hauteur. Dans un petit coin de terrain, le volume est conforme aux retraits obligatoires vers les façades et aux projets vers l'intérieur du bloc, qui permettent d'obtenir une hauteur qui profite des vues. La minceur de la petite tour ajoute une nouvelle typologie au quartier, où prédominent les habitations individuelles et les petits bâtiments horizontaux.

Le programme combine un rez-de-chaussée avec deux chambres et un patio, trois étages avec des appartements d'une chambre à coucher et un duplex sur les deux derniers niveaux, avec un étage social et un étage privé qui comprend un espace multifonctionnel.

A l'ouest, une façade aveugle contrôle l'ensoleillement et intègre un ascenseur dont le volume abrite le réservoir d'eau et un escalier considéré comme faisant partie de l'espace urbain.

El edificio debe su fisonomía a una reciente normativa que aumenta la edificabilidad de la zona sin limitar la altura. En una pequeña parcela en esquina, el volumen se conforma con los retiros obligatorios a los frentes y los proyectuales hacia el interior de la manzana, que permiten obtener una altura que aprovecha las vistas. La esbeltez de la pequeña torre incorpora una nueva tipología al barrio, donde predominan las viviendas individuales y los pequeños edificios horizontales.

El programa combina una planta baja de dos dormitorios y patio, tres pisos con departamentos de un dormitorio y un dúplex en los últimos dos niveles, con una planta social y una privada que incluye un espacio multifuncional.

Hacia el oeste, una fachada ciega controla el asoleamiento e integra un ascensor cuyo volumen alberga el tanque de agua y una escalera vista como parte del espacio urbano.

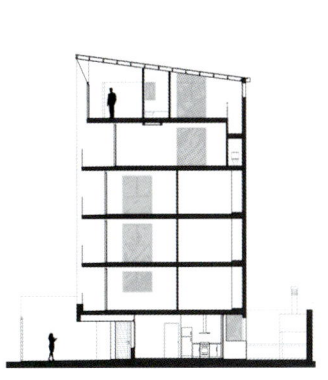

Longitudinal section

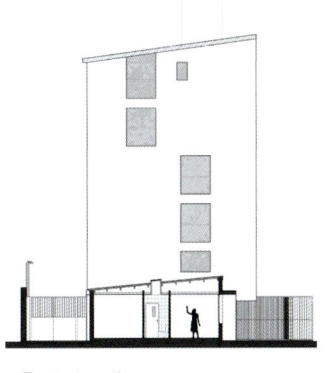

East elevation

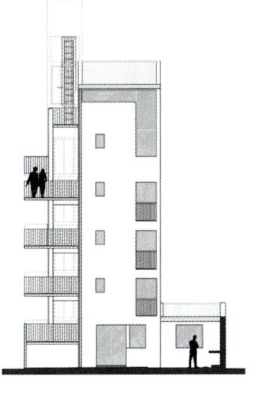

West elevation

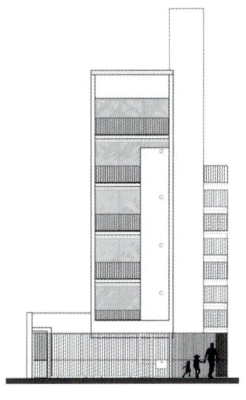

South elevation

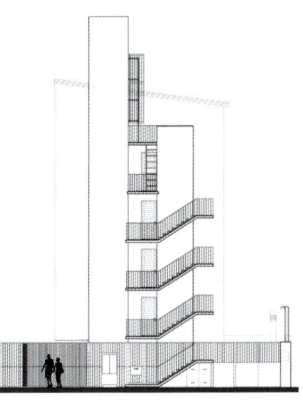

North elevation

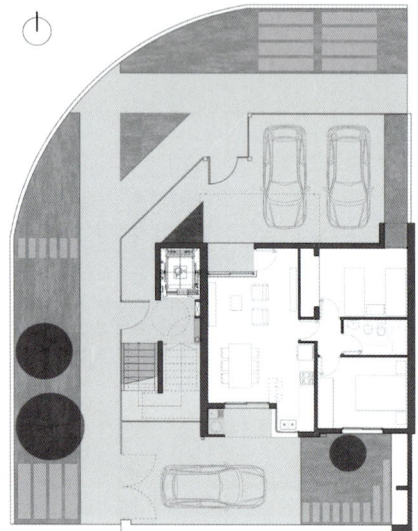

Ground floor plan

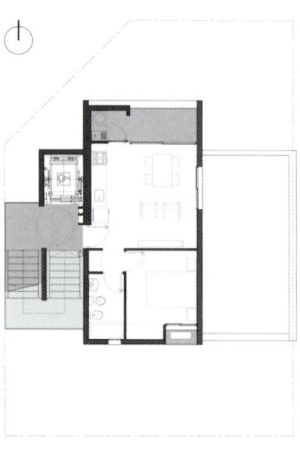

First, second and third floors plan

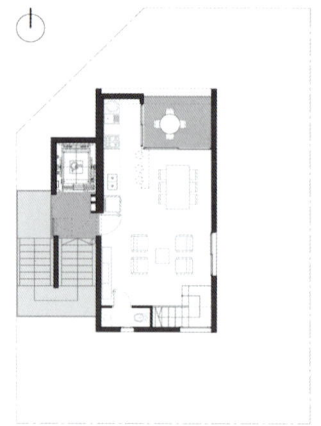

Fourth floor plan

Fifth floor plan

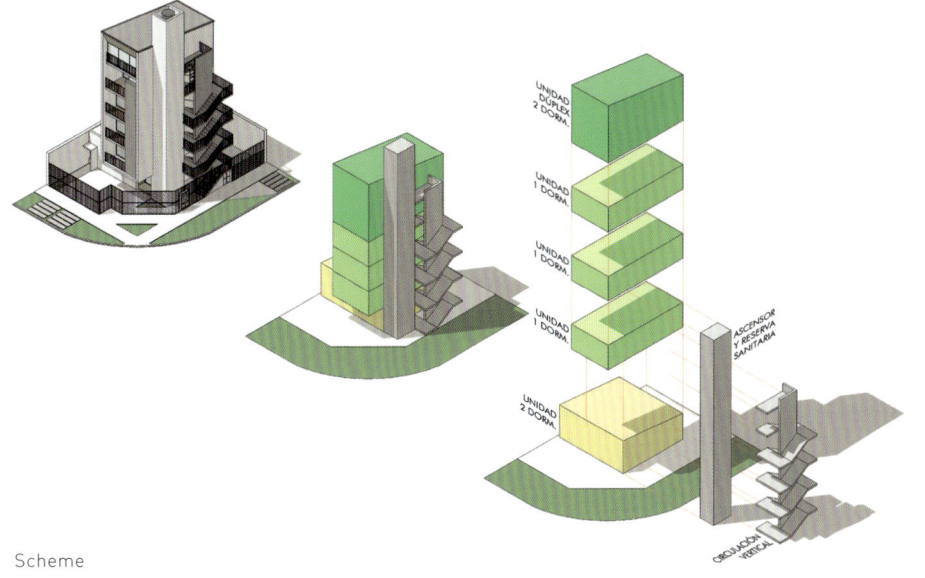

Scheme

The work is located in the district of Guadalupe, a garden-city sector that is currently being occupied by young people and university students. A project research on collective housing in this environment originated typological variants that conceive common areas as continuity of the urban space. Stairs, walkways and open halls function as a spatial transition in contact with the street. In this case, the layout and shape of the apartments are the result of taking advantage of a pre-existing ground-floor dwelling; this units were located within their walls and the upper units were arranged according to the inherited silhouette. The walls treated with white plaster unify new with old and contrast with the iron and wood treatment of the circulation elements.

Die Arbeit befindet sich im Stadtteil Guadalupe, einem ehemaligen Quintensektor und späteren Nachbarschaftsgarten, der derzeit von Jugendlichen und Studenten genutzt wird. In einem Projekt zur Erforschung des kollektiven Wohnens in diesem Umfeld entstanden typologische Varianten, die gemeinsame Räume als Kontinuität des urbanen Raumes begreifen. Treppen, Laufstege und offene Achsen fungieren als räumlicher Übergang im Kontakt mit der Straße. In diesem Fall sind Grundriss und Form der Wohnungen das Ergebnis der Nutzung einer bereits bestehenden Erdgeschosswohnung; die Erdgeschosseinheiten befanden sich in einem kastenförmigen Volumen und die Obergeschosse wurden entsprechend der ererbten Silhouette angeordnet. Mit weißem Putz behandelte Wände vereinen das Neue mit dem Alten und kontrastieren mit der Eisen- und Holzbehandlung der Zirkulationselemente.

BUILDING ON TALCAHUANO STREET
TALCAHUANO AND OBISPO BONEO, SANTA FE, ARGENTINA

L'œuvre est située dans le quartier de Guadalupe, un ancien secteur de cinquièmes et plus tard quartier-jardin qui est actuellement occupé par des jeunes et des étudiants universitaires. Un projet de recherche sur le logement collectif dans cet environnement a donné naissance à des variantes typologiques qui conçoivent les espaces communs comme continuité de l'espace urbain. Les escaliers, passerelles et axes ouverts fonctionnent comme une transition spatiale en contact avec la rue. Dans ce cas, la disposition et la forme des appartements sont le résultat de l'utilisation d'une habitation préexistante au rez-de-chaussée ; les unités du rez-de-chaussée étaient situées dans un volume en forme de boîte et les unités supérieures étaient disposées en fonction de la silhouette héritée. Les murs traités avec du plâtre blanc unifient le neuf avec l'ancien et contrastent avec le traitement en fer et en bois des éléments de circulation.

La obra se sitúa en el barrio de Guadalupe, un antiguo sector de quintas y más tarde barrio-jardín que actualmente está siendo ocupado por jóvenes y universitarios. Una investigación proyectual sobre la vivienda colectiva en este entorno originó variantes tipológicas que conciben los espacios comunes como continuidad del espacio urbano. Escaleras, pasarelas y palieres abiertos funcionan como transición espacial en contacto con la calle. En este caso, la disposición y forma de los departamentos son el resultado del aprovechamiento de una vivienda en planta baja prexistente; las unidades de planta baja se ubicaron dentro de su caja muraria y las unidades superiores se dispusieron en función de la silueta heredada. Las paredes tratadas con revoques blancos unifican lo nuevo con lo viejo y contrastan con el tratamiento de hierro y madera de los elementos de circulación.

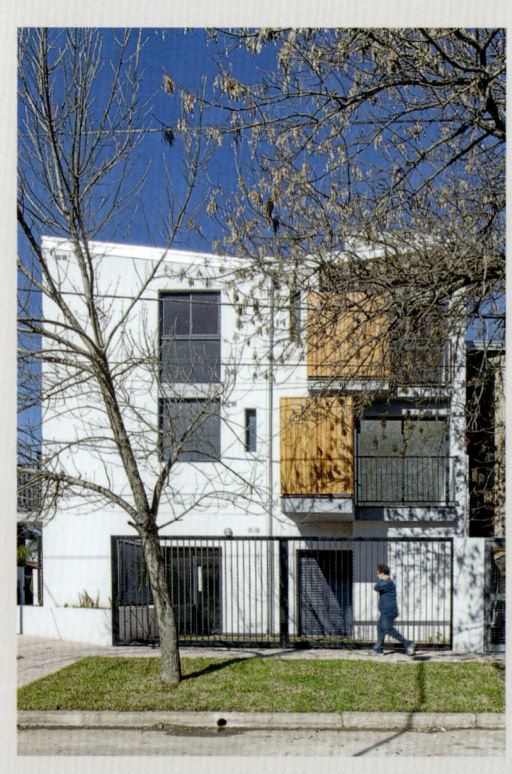

Obispo Boneo Street elevation

Talcahuano Street elevation

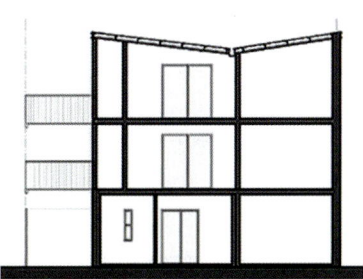

Section A-A

Section B-B

Pre-existing one storey house

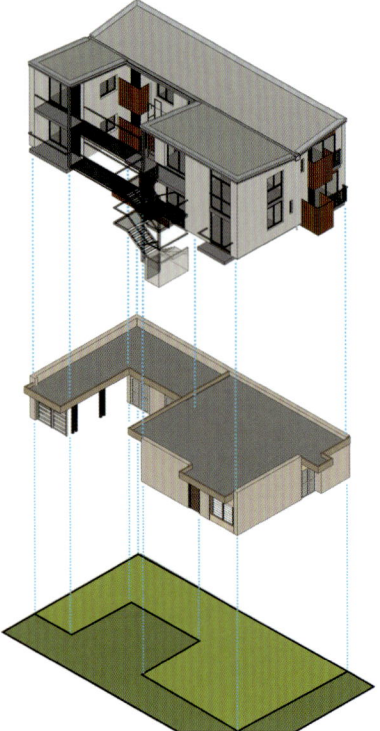

Scheme

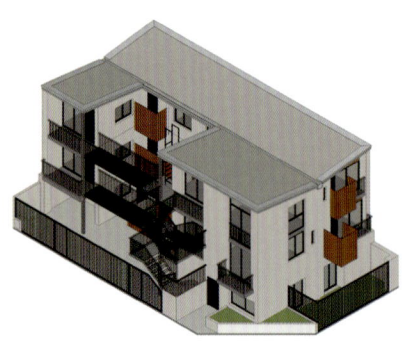

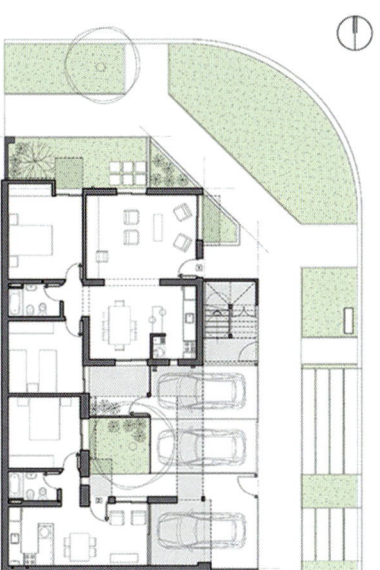

Ground floor plan

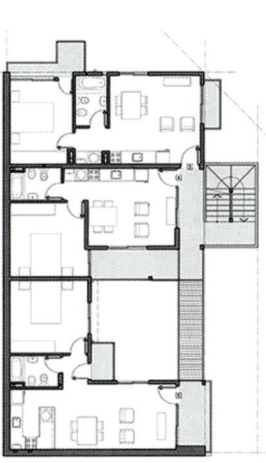

First floor plan

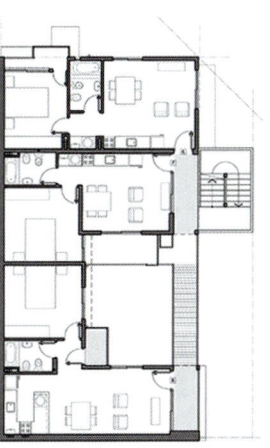

Second floor plan

BIG-BJARKE INGELS GROUP

http://www.big.dk

BIG is a Copenhagen, New York and London based group of architects, designers, urbanists, landscape professionals, interior and product designers, researchers and inventors. The office is currently involved in a large number of projects throughout Europe, North America, Asia and the Middle East. BIG's architecture emerges out of a careful analysis of how contemporary life constantly evolves and changes. Not least due to the influence from multicultural exchange, global economical flows and communication technologies that all together require new ways of architectural and urban organization. We believe that in order to deal with today's challenges, architecture can profitably move into a field that has been largely unexplored. A pragmatic utopian architecture that steers clear of the petrifying pragmatism of boring boxes and the naïve utopian ideas of digital formalism. Like a form of programmatic alchemy we create architecture by mixing conventional ingredients such as living, leisure, working, parking and shopping. By hitting the fertile overlap between pragmatic and utopia, we architects once again find the freedom to change the surface of our planet, to better fit contemporary life forms.

BIG ist eine Gruppe von Architekten, Designern, Urbanisten, Landschaftsplanern, Innenarchitekten, Produktdesignern und Forschern mit Sitz in Kopenhagen, New York und London. Das Büro ist derzeit an einer Vielzahl von Projekten in Europa, Nordamerika, Asien und dem Mittleren Osten beteiligt. Die Architektur von BIG entsteht aus einer sorgfältigen Analyse, wie sich das zeitgenössische Leben ständig weiterentwickelt und verändert. Wir glauben, dass die Architektur, um den heutigen Herausforderungen gerecht zu werden, gewinnbringend in ein Feld vordringen kann, das noch weitgehend unerforscht ist. Eine pragmatische utopische Architektur, die sich vom versteinernden Pragmatismus langweiliger Kisten und den naiven utopischen Ideen des digitalen Formalismus fernhält. Wie eine Form der programmatischen Alchemie schaffen wir Architektur, indem wir konventionelle Zutaten wie Wohnen, Freizeit, Arbeiten, Parken und Einkaufen miteinander verbinden. Indem wir Architekten die fruchtbare Überschneidung zwischen Pragmatismus und Utopie treffen, finden wir Architekten wieder einmal die Freiheit, die Oberfläche unseres Planeten zu verändern, um uns den heutigen Lebensformen besser anzupassen.

BIG est un groupe d'architectes, de designers, d'urbanistes, de professionnels du paysage, de designers d'intérieur, de designers et de chercheurs basé à Copenhague, New York et Londres. Le bureau est actuellement impliqué dans un grand nombre de projets en Europe, en Amérique du Nord, en Asie et au Moyen-Orient. L'architecture de BIG émerge d'une analyse attentive de la façon dont la vie contemporaine évolue et change constamment. Nous pensons que pour faire face aux défis d'aujourd'hui, l'architecture peut évoluer de manière rentable dans un domaine largement inexploré. Une architecture utopique pragmatique qui évite le pragmatisme pétrifiant des boîtes ennuyeuses et les idées utopiques naïves du formalisme numérique. Comme une forme d'alchimie programmatique, nous créons l'architecture en mélangeant des ingrédients conventionnels tels que la vie, les loisirs, le travail, le stationnement et le shopping. En frappant le chevauchement fertile entre le pragmatisme et l'utopie, nous, architectes, retrouvons la liberté de changer la surface de notre planète, pour mieux l'adapter aux formes de vie contemporaines.

BIG es un grupo de arquitectos, diseñadores, urbanistas, profesionales del paisaje, diseñadores de interiores e investigadores con sede en Copenhague, Nueva York y Londres. Actualmente, la oficina está involucrada en un gran número de proyectos en Europa, Norteamérica, Asia y Oriente Medio. La arquitectura de BIG surge de un cuidadoso análisis de cómo la vida contemporánea evoluciona y cambia constantemente. Creemos que para hacer frente a los retos actuales, la arquitectura puede moverse de forma rentable en un campo que ha sido en gran medida inexplorado. Una arquitectura pragmática que se aleja de las líneas aburridas y de las ideas utópicas del formalismo digital. Como una forma de alquimia programática, creamos arquitectura mezclando ingredientes convencionales como la vida, el ocio, el trabajo, el aparcamiento y las compras. Al golpear el fértil espacio entre lo pragmático y lo utópico, los arquitectos encontramos una vez más la libertad de cambiar la superficie de nuestro planeta, para encajar mejor las formas de vida contemporáneas.

VIA 57 WEST

Name: VIA 57 WEST

Date: 2016

Program: Housing

Status: Completed

Size: 77202 m²

Project type: Direct Commission

Client: The Durst Organization

Collaborators: SLCE Architects, Starr Whitehouse, Thornton Tomasetti, Dagher Engineering, Langan Engineering, Hunter Roberts, Enclos, Philip Habib & Assoc, Vidaris Inc, Nancy Packes, Van Deusen & Assoc, Cerami & Assoc, CPP, AKRF, Glessner Group, Brandston Partnership Inc

Partners in Charge: Bjarke Ingels, Thomas Christoffersen, Beat Schenk

Project Architect: David Brown

Project leader, interiors: David Brown

Project manager, interiors: Beat Schenk

Photo credits: © Iwan Baan, Nic Lehoux

Awards: 2015 P/A Progressive Architecture Citation Award, 2012 NYAIA Merit Award Future Award

DORTHEAVEJ RESIDENCE

Date: 2018

Size: 6800 m²

Project type: Commission

Client: LEJERBO

Collaborators: MOE

Location text: Copenhagen, DK

Awards: Danish Architect Associations Lille Arne Award, 2018

Partners in Charge: Bjarke Ingels, Finn Nørkjær

Project managers: Ole Elkjær-Larsen, Per Bo Madsen

Photo credits: © Rasmus Hjortshoj

VIA 57 West is a hybrid between the European perimeter block and Manhattan's traditional skyscraper. The contrast between its elevated northeast corner and the remaining 3 low corners generates views from the central courtyard toward the Hudson River and allows for abundant entry of sunlight. Its shape changes according to the viewer's point of view: the pyramid that appears from the adjacent motorway becomes a spectacular glass needle from West 58th Street. The courtyard, inspired by the Copenhagen's classic urban oasis, is visible from the street and connects with the vegetation of neighbouring Hudson River Park. The slope of the building is a transition between the low buildings to the south and the high residential towers to the north of the site. The striking sloping roof is a simple ruled surface perforated by south-facing terraces.

Die VIA 57 West ist ein Hybrid zwischen dem europäischen Perimeterblock und Manhattans traditionellem Wolkenkratzer. Der Kontrast zwischen der hohen nordöstlichen Ecke und den restlichen 3 niedrigen Ecken erzeugt einen Blick vom zentralen Innenhof auf den Hudson River und ermöglicht den Blick in die untergehende Sonne. Je nach Blickwinkel des Betrachters ändert sich die Form: Die Pyramide, die man von der angrenzenden Autobahn aus sieht, wird zu einer spektakulären Glasnadel von der West 58th Street aus. Der Innenhof, inspiriert von der klassischen Stadtoase Kopenhagens, ist von der Straße aus sichtbar und verbindet sich mit der Vegetation des benachbarten Hudson River Park. Der Hang des Gebäudes stellt einen Übergang zwischen den niedrigen Gebäuden im Süden und den hohen Wohntürmen im Norden des Geländes dar. Das auffällige Schrägdach ist eine einfach regulierte Fläche, die von nach Süden ausgerichteten Terrassen durchbrochen wird.

VIA 57 WEST
MANHATTAN, NEW YORK, USA

Le VIA 57 West est un hybride entre le bloc périphérique européen et le gratte-ciel traditionnel de Manhattan. Le contraste entre son angle nord-est élevé et les trois coins bas restants offre une vue de la cour centrale vers le fleuve Hudson et permet une entrée abondante du soleil couchant. Sa forme change selon le point de vue du spectateur : la pyramide qui apparaît de l'autoroute adjacente devient une spectaculaire aiguille de verre de West 58th Street. La cour intérieure, inspirée de l'oasis urbaine classique de Copenhague, est visible de la rue et est reliée à la végétation du parc voisin du fleuve Hudson. La pente du bâtiment représente une transition entre les bâtiments bas au sud et les hautes tours résidentielles au nord du site. Le toit incliné attire l'attention par sa surface simple et régulée, perforée par des terrasses orientées plein sud.

VIA 57 West es un híbrido entre el bloque perimetral europeo y el rascacielos tradicional de Manhattan. El contraste entre su elevada esquina noreste y las 3 esquinas bajas restantes genera vistas desde el patio central hacia el río Hudson y permite una abundante entrada del sol de poniente. Su forma cambia según el punto de vista del espectador: la pirámide que aparece desde la autopista contigua deviene una espectacular aguja de cristal desde la calle West 58th. El patio, inspirado en el clásico oasis urbano de Copenhague, es visible desde la calle y conecta con la vegetación del vecino Hudson River Park. La pendiente del edificio supone una transición entre los edificios bajos situados al sur y las altas torres residenciales situadas al norte del lugar. El llamativo techo inclinado es una superficie reglada simple perforada por terrazas orientadas hacia el sur.

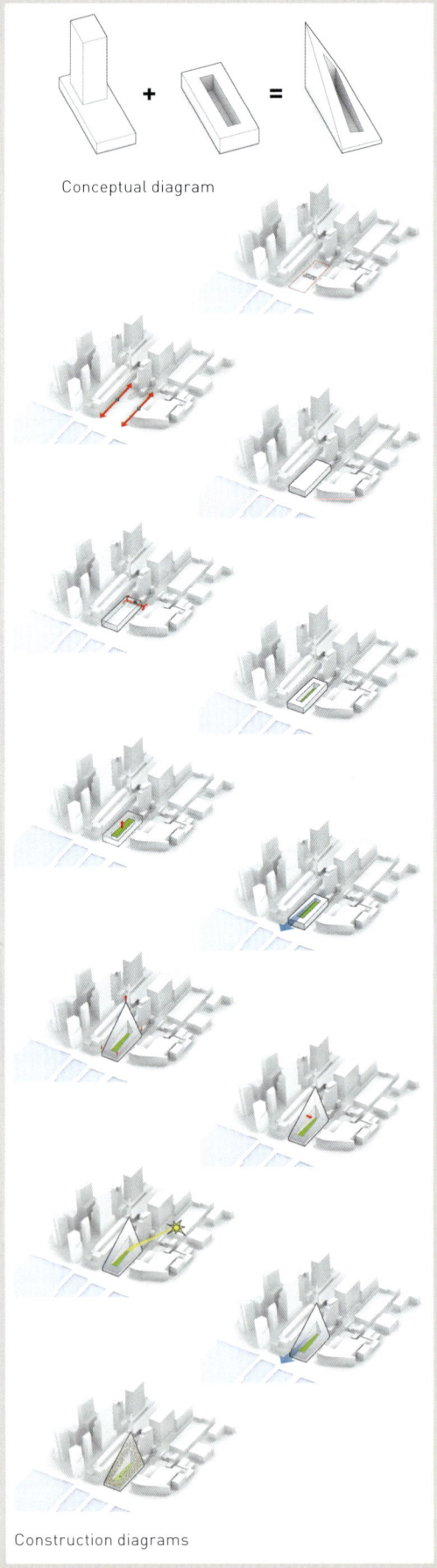

Conceptual diagram

Construction diagrams

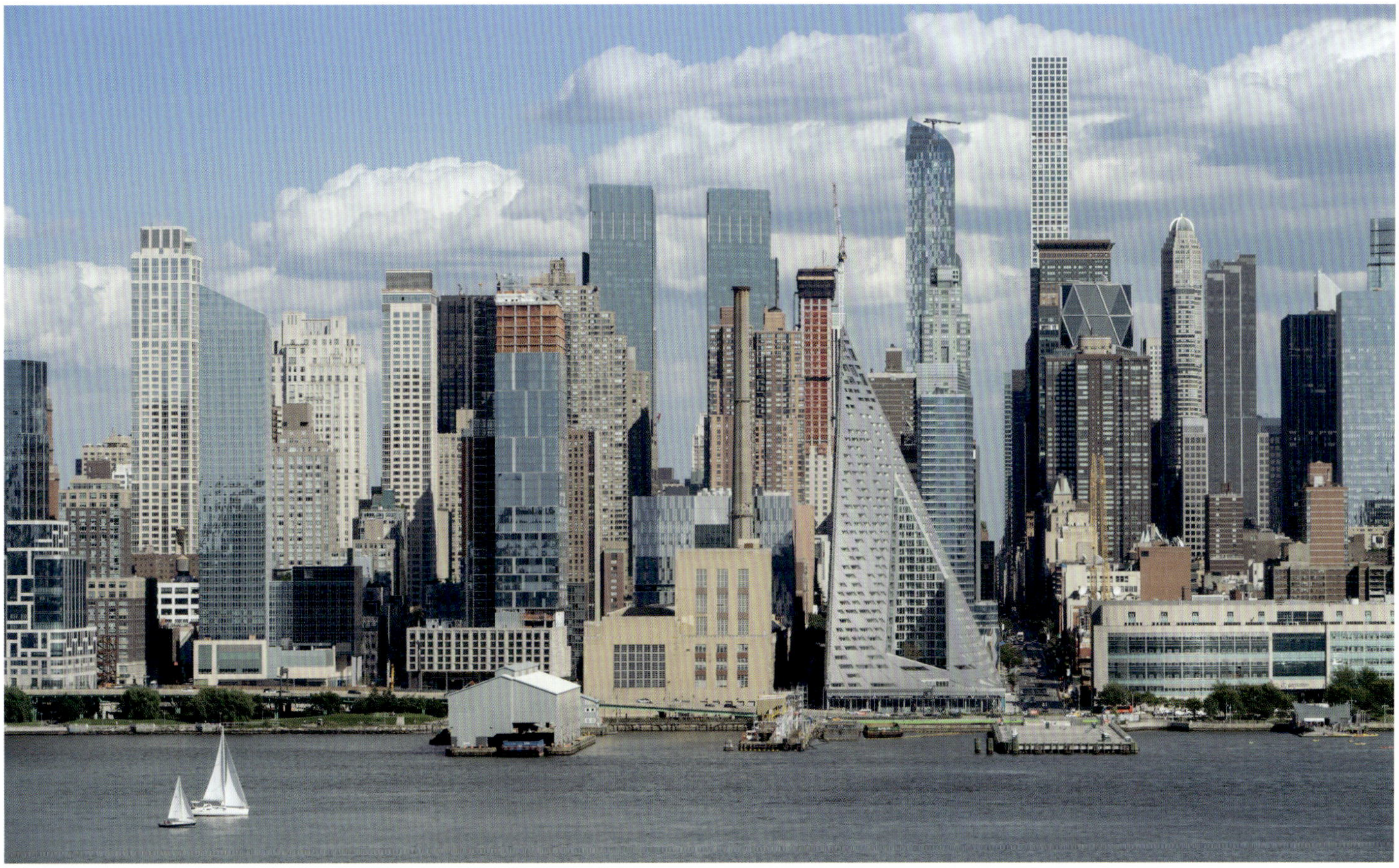

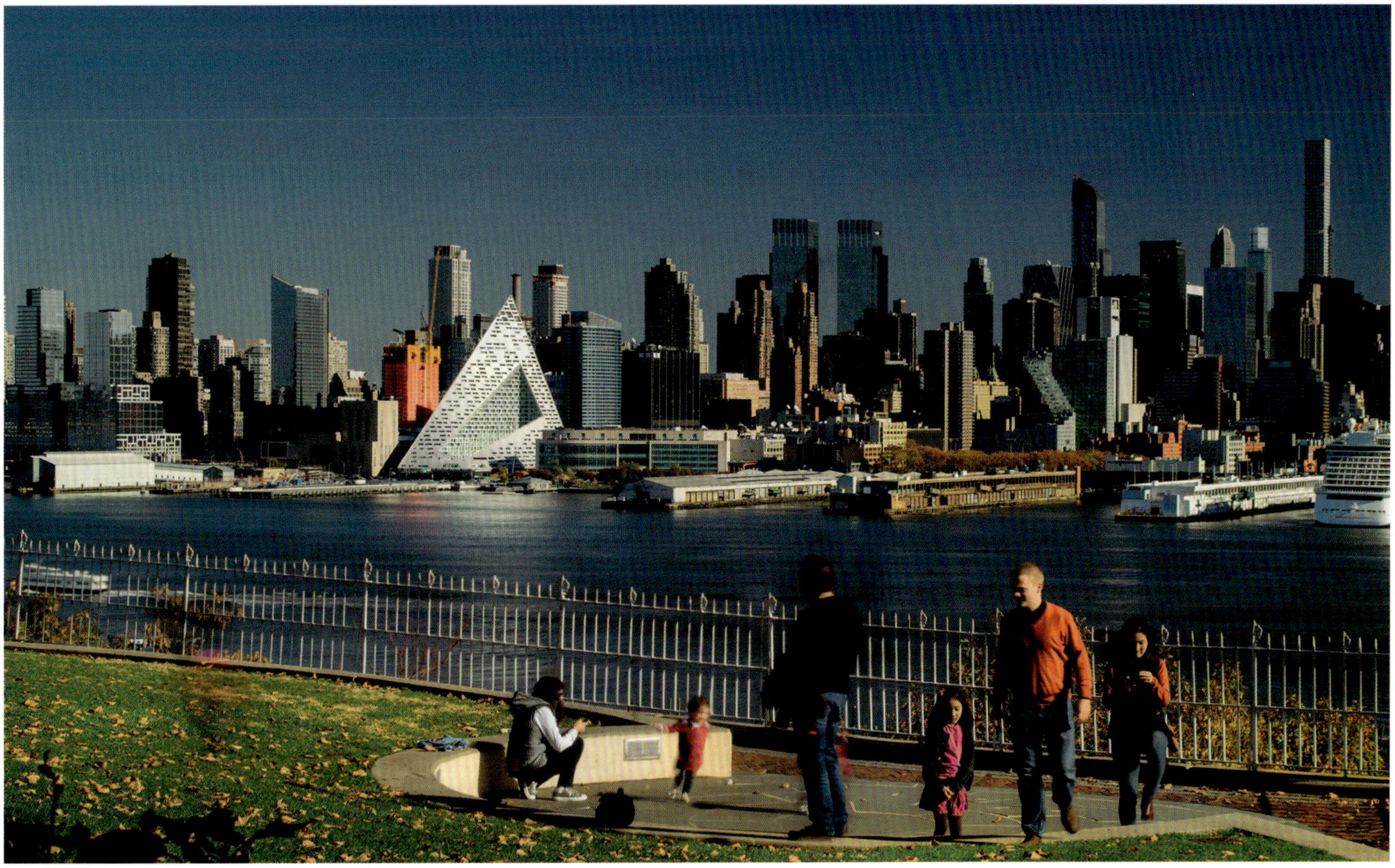

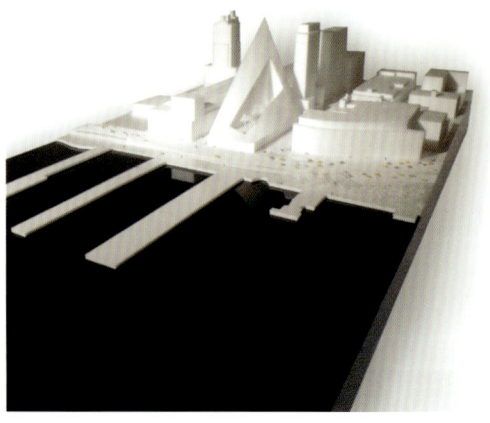

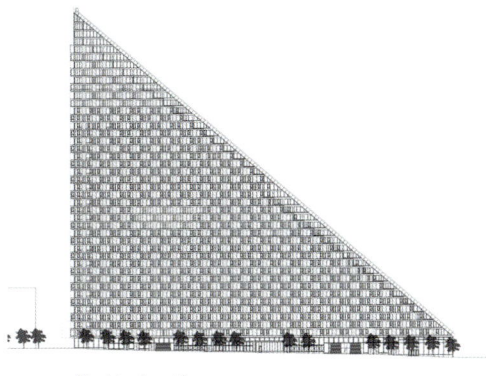

North elevation

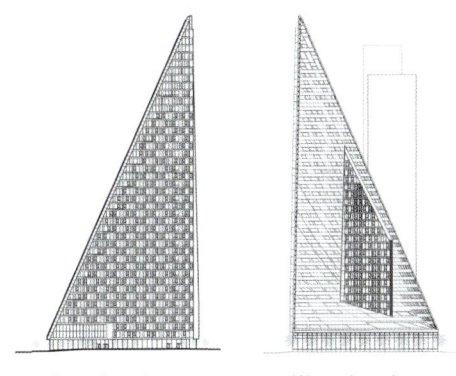

Fast elevation

West elevation

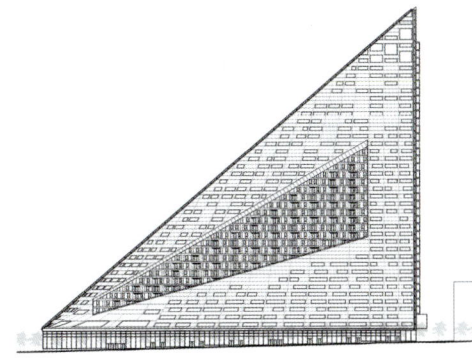

South elevation

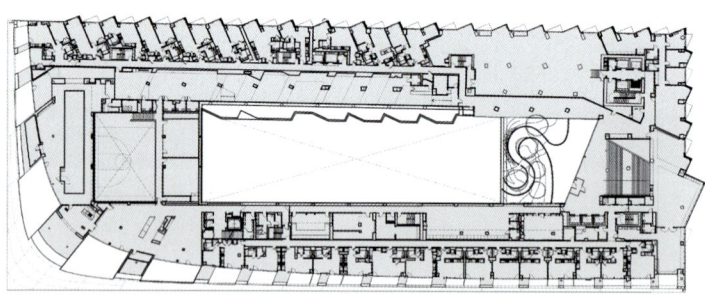

Second floor plan

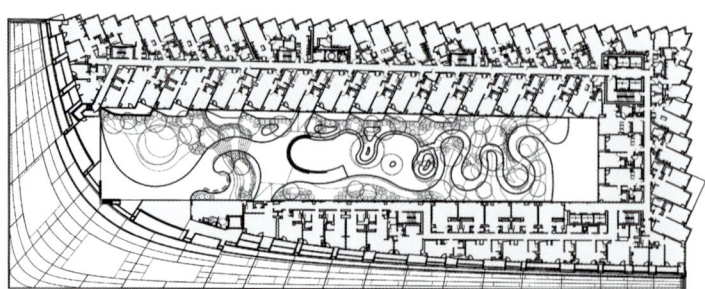

Fourth floor plan

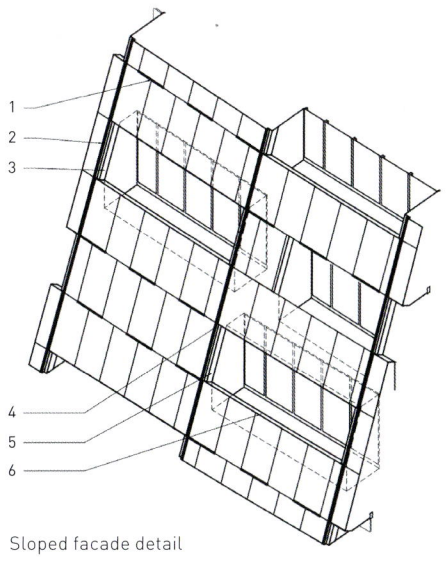

Sloped facade detail

1. Snow stop with weephole
2. Window washing track
3. SST fascia
4. Leader for track drainage
5. GFRC wall panel
6. GFRC handrail

The project consists of 66 affordable housing born in collaboration with the non-profit association Lejerbo. The building represents a 5-storey porous wall that meanders around warehouses and industrial buildings and gently curves in its centre, creating a public square towards the street on the south side and a more enclosed green area to the north. The construction system is based on a checkered pattern formed by repetition and stacking of the accommodation modules, which creates a small terrace for each dwelling and gives depth to the south façade. The materials used are simple, with predominant use of wood and concrete in light tones. The façades are clad with long wooden planks that underline the structure of the building modules and alternate their direction to highlight the checkered pattern.

Das Projekt besteht aus 66 erschwinglichen Wohnungen und ist aus der Zusammenarbeit mit dem gemeinnützigen Verein Lejerbo entstanden. Das Gebäude stellt eine 5-geschossige poröse Wand dar, die sich um Lager- und Industriegebäude schlängelt und sich in ihrer Mitte sanft wölbt, wodurch ein öffentlicher Platz zur Straße hin auf der Südseite und ein geschlossenerer Grünbereich im Norden geschaffen wird. Das Bausystem basiert auf einem Schachbrettmuster, das sich aus der Wiederholung und Stapelung der Wohnmodule ergibt, für jede Wohnung eine kleine Terrasse schafft und der Südfassade Tiefe verleiht. Die verwendeten Materialien sind einfach, wobei überwiegend Holz und Beton in hellen Farbtönen verwendet werden. Die Fassaden sind mit langen Holzbohlen verkleidet, die die modulare Struktur des Gebäudes unterstreichen und ihre Richtung ändern, um das karierte Muster hervorzuheben.

DORTHEAVEJ RESIDENCE
COPENHAGEN, DENMARK

Le projet comprend 66 logements abordables et est né d'une collaboration avec l'association à but non lucratif Lejerbo. Le bâtiment représente un mur poreux de 5 étages qui serpente autour des entrepôts et des bâtiments industriels et s'incurve doucement en son centre, créant une place publique vers la rue du côté sud et un espace vert plus fermé au nord. Le système de construction est basé sur un motif en damier formé par la répétition et l'empilement des modules d'habitation, ce qui crée une petite terrasse pour chaque logement et donne de la profondeur à la façade sud. Les matériaux utilisés sont simples, avec une utilisation prédominante du bois et du béton dans des tons clairs. Les façades sont revêtues de longues planches de bois qui soulignent la structure modulaire du bâtiment et alternent leur direction pour mettre en valeur le motif en damier.

El proyecto consta de 66 viviendas asequibles y nace de la colaboración con la asociación sin ánimo de lucro Lejerbo. El edificio representa un muro poroso de 5 plantas de altura que serpentea en un entorno de almacenes y edificios industriales y que se curva suavemente en su centro, creando una plaza pública hacia la calle en el lado sur y una zona verde más cerrada hacia el norte. El sistema constructivo se basa en un patrón a cuadros formado por la repetición y el apilamiento de los módulos de alojamiento, que crea una pequeña terraza para cada vivienda y da profundidad a la fachada sur. Los materiales utilizados son sencillos, con uso predominante de la madera y el hormigón en tonos claros. Las fachadas se revisten con largos tablones de madera que subrayan la estructura de módulos del edificio y que alternan su dirección para resaltar el patrón a cuadros.

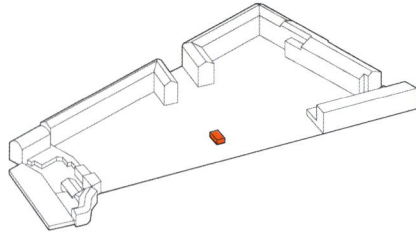

MODULE. The project is generated from a simple prefab structure.

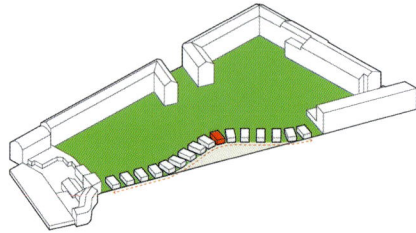

CURVE. The element is repeated along a curve. The system defines a courtyard for the urban block and introduces a public square towards the street.

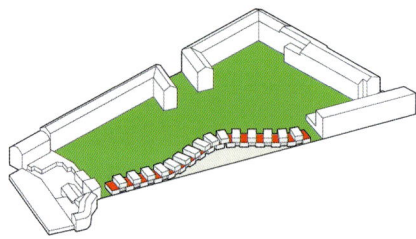

STARK. The element is stacked along the curve creating interstitial spaces that face yard and square.

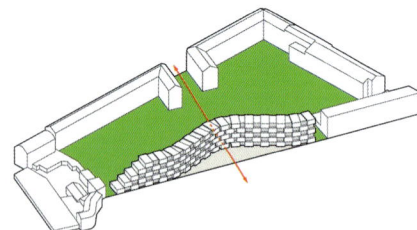

POROSITY. The building is raised to the height of the surroundings. A passage at the ground level allows public flow between square and yard.

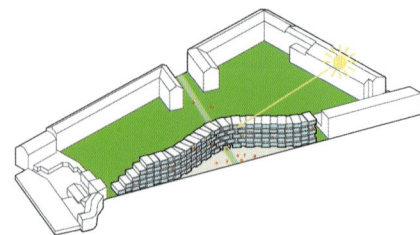

SOCIAL REALM. The system combines a valuable public space with social housing units optimally oriented.

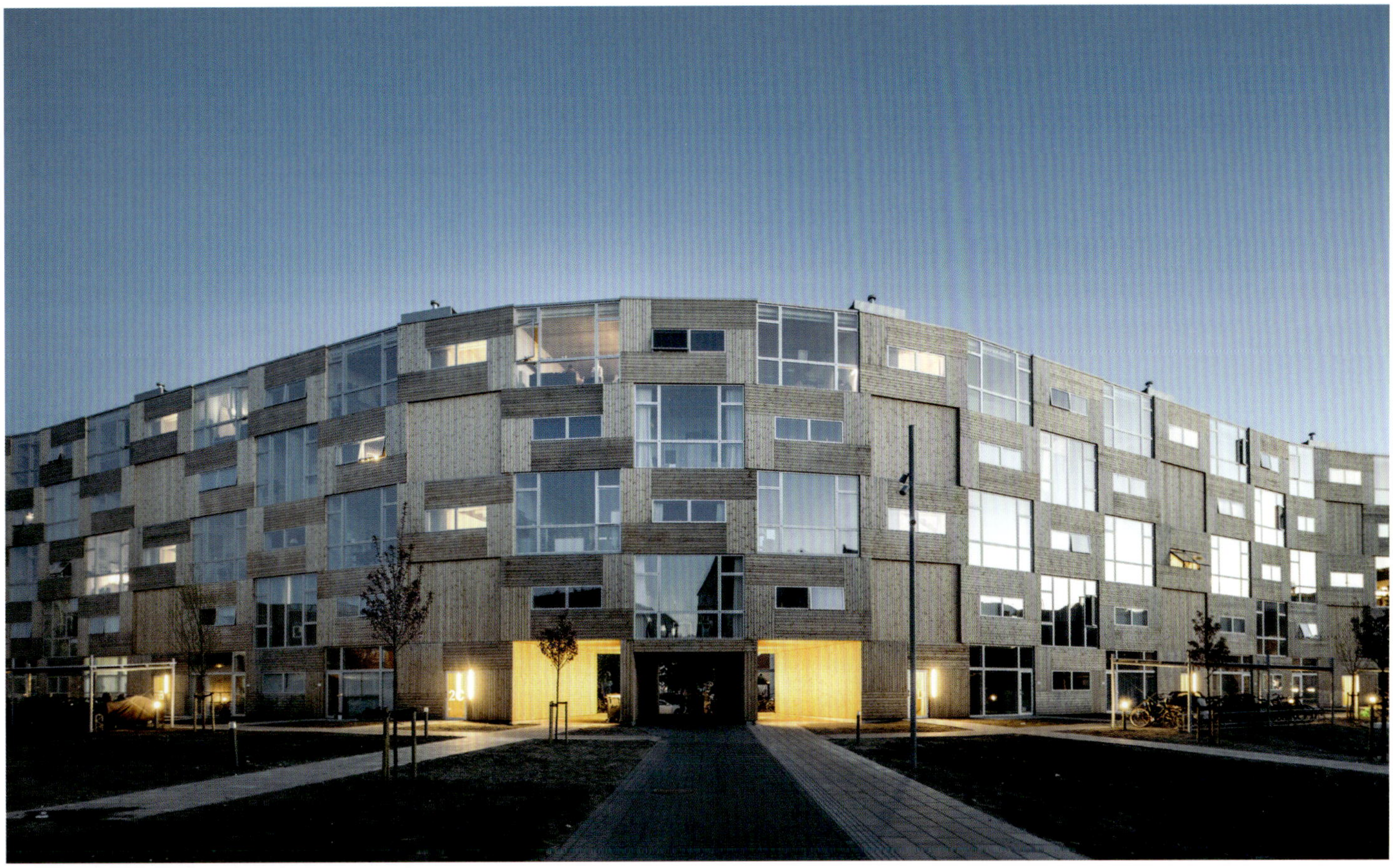
2C

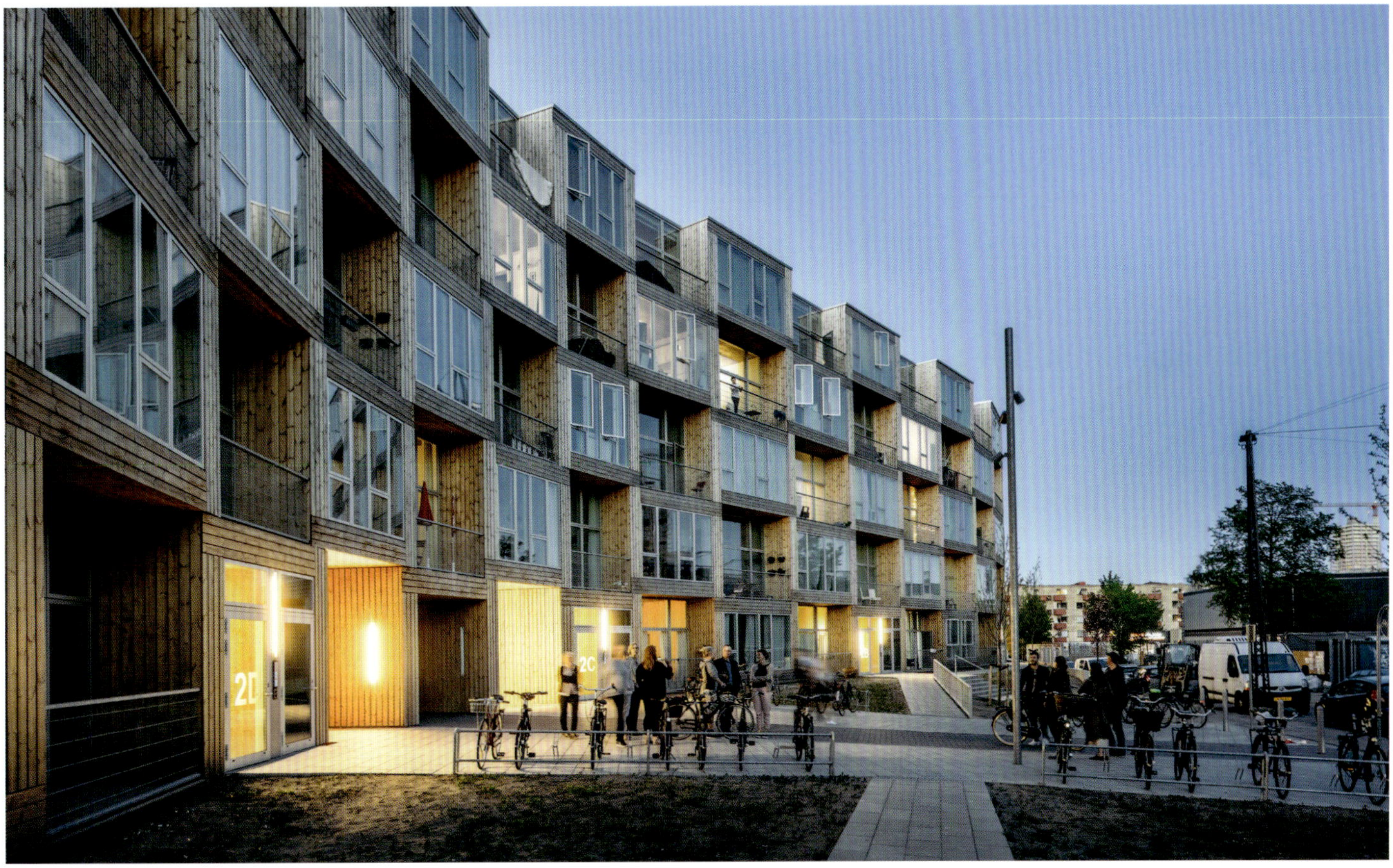
2D

North elevation

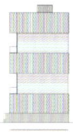

East elevation

West elevation

South elevations

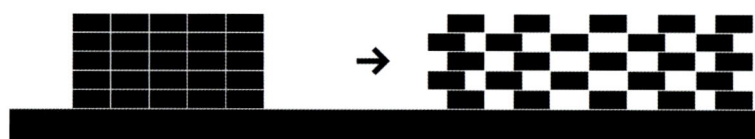

Concept diagram

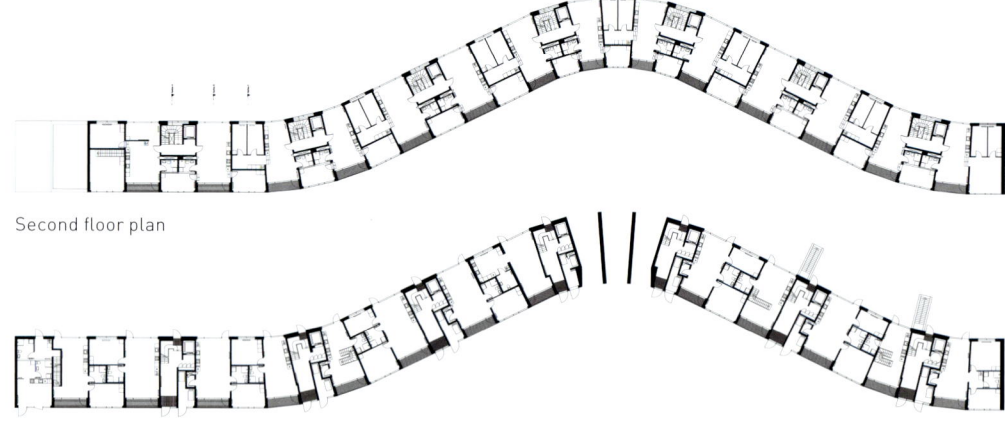

Second floor plan

Ground floor plan

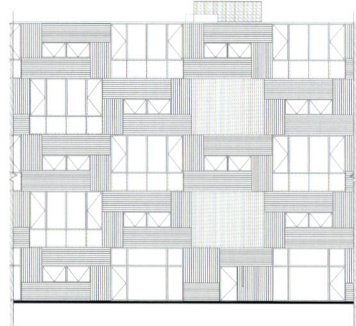

North elevation detail

South elevation detail

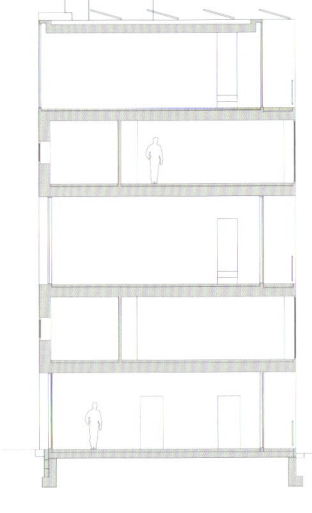
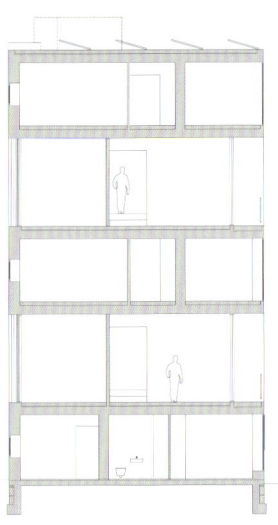

Sections

BOGEVISCHS BUERO

www.bogevisch.de

bogevischs buero was founded in 1996 by architects Ritz Ritzer and Rainer Hofmann.

Any project, any competition entry, any feasibility study we engage in becomes a quest for the essence of what we have established with our clients as the key issues. We love shapes and materials and we also love to explore new ways of applying them to our buildings. The core of our doing, however, focuses somewhere else. Out of the design strategy we develop a sort of recipe. There is seldom a preconceived form rather a kind of backbone. Form happens as a result of this core and the strategic recipe. We do not strive for the New or Fashionable. The New never stays new for long, forms stay seldom fashionable forever. Buildings stay. A good recipe and a good strategy can be communicated and understood in times to come.

bogevischs buero offers services in all scales ranging from urban planning to single object planning and from strategic concept outline to coordinated detailed planning in actual size.

Jedes Projekt, jeder Wettbewerb, an dem wir uns beteiligen, wird zu einer – im besten Falle erfolgreichen – Suche nach Innen, nach den Punkten, die wir im Projekt, in der Aufgabenstellung, im Dialog mit Bauherrn und Nutzern abstecken. Form und Oberflächen interessieren uns sehr und wir sind fasziniert von alternativen Möglichkeiten des Materialeinsatzes. Was unsere Projekte jedoch viel mehr auszeichnet, ist eine Art Rezeptur, die aus einem Prozess heraus entsteht. Die scheinbar darin liegende Weichheit ist in Zeiten von unendlichen und nicht mehr enden wollenden Planungsvorgaben und DIN-Vorschriften eine Art Wundertüte. Diese scheinbare Weichheit darf aber nicht mit einer Formlosigkeit verwechselt werden, eher entsteht im Prozess eine Art Rückgrat, das allmählich seine Form findet. Unser Interesse gilt weniger dem Neuen oder Modischen. Das Neue ist ja selten lange neu, Formen überholen sich.

bogevischs buero bietet Dienstleistungen in allen Größenordnungen, von der Stadtplanung bis zur Planung einzelner Objekte, von der strategischen Konzeptskizze bis zur in Realgröße koordinierten Detailplanung.

bogevischs buero a été fondé en 1996 par les architectes Ritz Ritzer et Rainer Hofmann.

Tout projet, toute participation à un concours, toute étude de faisabilité à laquelle nous participons devient une recherche de l'essence de ce que nous avons établi avec nos clients. Nous aimons les formes et les matériaux et nous aimons aussi explorer de nouvelles façons de les appliquer à nos bâtiments. Cependant, le cœur de nos actions est différent. A partir de la stratégie de conception, nous développons une recette. Il existe rarement une forme préconçue, mais une sorte de colonne vertébrale. La forme est le résultat de ce noyau et de la recette stratégique. Nous ne recherchons ni le Nouveau ni le Moderne. Le Nouveau ne reste jamais longtemps, les formes sont rarement à la mode pour toujours. Les bâtiments restent. Une bonne recette et une bonne stratégie peuvent être communiquées et comprises dans les temps à venir.

bogevischs buero offre des services à toutes les échelles, de l'urbanisme à la planification d'objets individuels et de l'esquisse du concept stratégique à la planification détaillée coordonnée en taille réelle.

bogevischs buero fue fundada en 1996 por los arquitectos Ritz Ritzer y Rainer Hofmann.

Cualquier proyecto, cualquier participación en un concurso, cualquier estudio de viabilidad en el que participemos, se convierte en una búsqueda de la esencia de lo que hemos establecido con nuestros clientes. Nos encantan las formas y los materiales y también nos gusta explorar nuevas formas de aplicarlos a nuestros edificios. Sin embargo, el núcleo de nuestras acciones es diferente. A partir de la estrategia de diseño desarrollamos una receta. Rara vez hay una forma preconcebida, sino una especie de columna vertebral. La forma es el resultado de este núcleo y de la receta estratégica.

No nos esforzamos por lo Nuevo o por lo Moderno. Lo nuevo nunca permanece por mucho tiempo, las formas rara vez están de moda para siempre. Los edificios se quedan. Una buena receta y una buena estrategia pueden ser comunicadas y entendidas en los tiempos venideros.

Name of the client:
Wohnbaugenossenschaft wagnis eG

Name of the architect:
Joint venture bogevischs buero architekten & stadtplaner GmbH / SHAG Schindler Hable Architekten GbR (design stages 1-5)

Design stages 6-9:
SHAG Schindler Hable Architekten GbR with Architekturbüro Christian Köhler

Duration of design and construction: 2012-2015

Net floor area:
9590 m²/ 138 Appartments

Energy performance certificate rating: Passive House

Building area (m²): 20.275 m²

Photo credits:
© Michael Heinrich, Munich

Awards:
- "Ehrenpreis für guten Wohnungsbau 2018" der Stadt München
- "Honorable Award" of the City of Munich
- The DAM (Deutsches Architektur Museum) Award for Architecture in Germany 2018
- Award of the DGNB (German Sustainable Building Council) 2017- Prize Sustainable Building
- Nominated for the "Deutscher Bauherrenpreis 2018"
- Awarded with the "Deutschen Städtebaupreis 2016"
- Award of the "Deutscher Landschaftsarchitektur-Preis 2017"

The project is located in the district of Domagkpark and was developed together with its future inhabitants. The planning allowed few restrictions on the design of the buildings and placed them around patios and passages forming open communal spaces.

The complex consists of five buildings, the upper floors of which are connected to each other by bridges that create a unique landscape of elevated gardens. The ground floors house community rooms, workshops, offices and open spaces for the activities of residents and the neighbourhood.

wagnisART is a certified passive building with heat recovery ventilation, built with a hybrid system of reinforced concrete load-bearing walls and a suspended timber façade. The reduction in parking space due to a mobility concept underlines the sustainability of the project.

Das Projekt befindet sich im Stadtteil Domagkpark und wurde gemeinsam mit seinen zukünftigen Bewohnern entwickelt. Die Planung erlaubte nur wenige Einschränkungen bei der Gestaltung der Gebäude und legte sie um Terrassen und Durchgänge, die Gemeinschaftsräume bilden, die öffentlich zugänglich sind.

Der Komplex besteht aus fünf Gebäuden, deren obere Stockwerke durch Brücken miteinander verbunden sind, die eine einzigartige Landschaft mit Hochgärten bilden. Im Erdgeschoss befinden sich Gemeinschaftsräume, Werkstätten, Büros und Freiflächen für Wohn- und Nachbarschaftsaktivitäten.

wagnisART ist ein zertifiziertes Passivhaus mit Wärmerückgewinnung, gebaut mit einem Hybridsystem aus Stahlbeton-Tragwänden und abgehängter Fassade. Die Reduzierung der Parkplätze durch ein Mobilitätskonzept unterstreicht die Nachhaltigkeit des Projekts.

COOPERATIVE HOUSING COMPLEX WAGNISART
MUNICH, GERMANY

Le projet est situé dans le quartier de Domagkpark et a été développé avec ses futurs habitants. La planification permettait peu de restrictions sur la conception des bâtiments et les plaçait autour de patios et de couloirs formant des espaces communautaires ouverts sur l'environnement.

Le complexe se compose de cinq bâtiments dont les étages supérieurs sont reliés entre eux par des ponts qui créent un paysage unique de jardins surélevés. Le rez-de-chaussée abrite des salles communautaires, des ateliers, des bureaux et des espaces ouverts pour les activités des résidents et du quartier.

wagnisART est un bâtiment passif certifié avec ventilation à récupération de chaleur, construit avec un système hybride de murs porteurs en béton armé et façade suspendue. La réduction de l'espace de stationnement due à un concept de mobilité souligne la durabilité du projet.

El proyecto se sitúa en el distrito de Domagkpark y fue desarrollado conjuntamente con sus futuros habitantes. El planeamiento permitió pocas restricciones en el diseño de los edificios y situarlos alrededor de patios y pasajes formando espacios comunitarios abiertos al entorno.

El complejo consta de cinco edificios, cuyas plantas superiores se conectan entre sí a través de puentes generadores de un paisaje único de jardines elevados. Las plantas bajas albergan salas comunitarias, talleres, oficinas y espacios abiertos, destinados a las actividades de los residentes y del vecindario.

wagnisART es un edificio pasivo certificado con ventilación de recuperación de calor, construido con un sistema híbrido de muros de carga hormigón armado y fachada suspendida. La reducción del espacio de estacionamiento por un concepto de movilidad subraya la sostenibilidad del proyecto.

Location map

Site plan

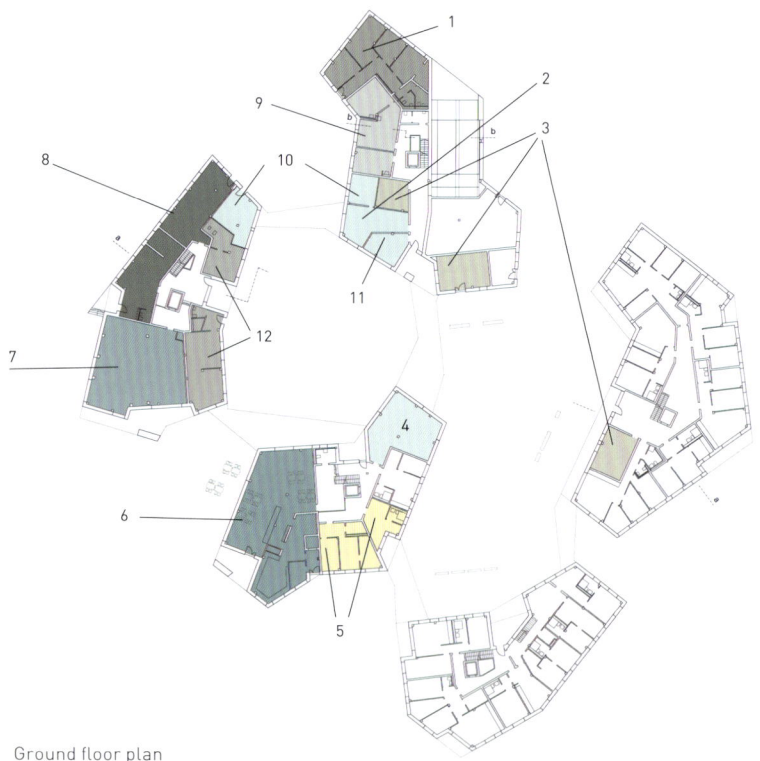

Ground floor plan

Type floor plan

1. Office spaces
2. Common laundry
3. Bicycle and buggy room
4. Community room
5. Guest apartments
6. Cafe
7. Event space
8. Medical treatment rooms
9. Workshops
10. Community studio
11. Common sewing room
12. Artist studios

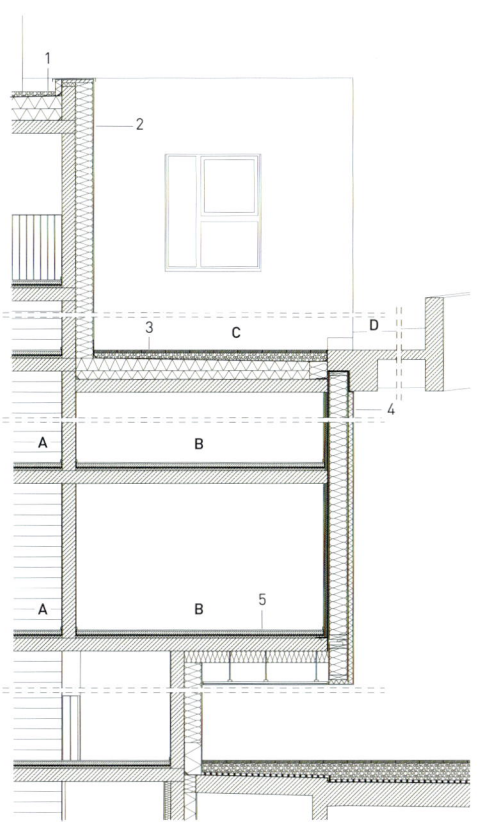

A. Stairwell
B. Apartment
C. Roof terrace
D. Bridge

1. Roof construction
   - ≥ 40 mm grit
   - 5 mm protection mat
   - 5 mm 2nd layer of bitumen seal
   - 3 mm 1st layer of bitumen seal
   - 300 mm (on average) gradient insulation
   - 3 mm vapor barrier
   - 220 mm reinforced concrete

2. Construction of exterior wall reinforced concrete
   - 15 mm plaster
   - 280 mm mineral insulation
   - 10 mm glue
   - 220 mm reinforced concrete
   - 15 mm plaster

3. Construction of roof terrace
   - 50 mm factory flagstone, concrete
   - ≥ 40 mm grit
   - 5 mm protection mat
   - 5 mm 2nd layer of bitumen seal
   - 3 mm 1st layer of bitumen seal
   - 300 mm (on average) gradient insulation
   - 3 mm vapor barrier
   - 220 mm reinforced concrete

4. Construction of exterior wall timber frame
   - 15 mm plaster
   - 60 mm mineral insulation
   - 5 mm glue
   - 30 mm 2 layers of gypsum fiber board as fire protection
   - 300 mm timber frame, infill mineral insulation
   - 30 mm 2 layers of gypsum fiber board as fire protection
   - 0,5 mm vapor barrier
   - 60 mm installation layer, infill mineral insulation
   - 25 mm 2 layers of plaster board

5. Floor construction
   - 10mm parquet
   - 50 mm cement screed
   - 0,2 mm PE film
   - 20 mm impact sound insulation
   - 60 mm EPS insulation, compensation layer
   - 0,2 mm PE film
   - 220 mm reinforced concrete
   - 200 mm mineral insulation
   - 335 mm ceiling substructure
   - 10 mm fiber cement board
   - 15 mm plaster

Facade section

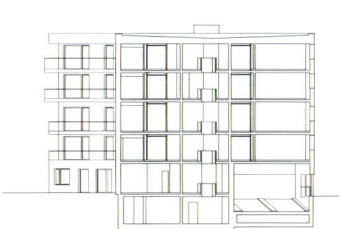

Transversal section

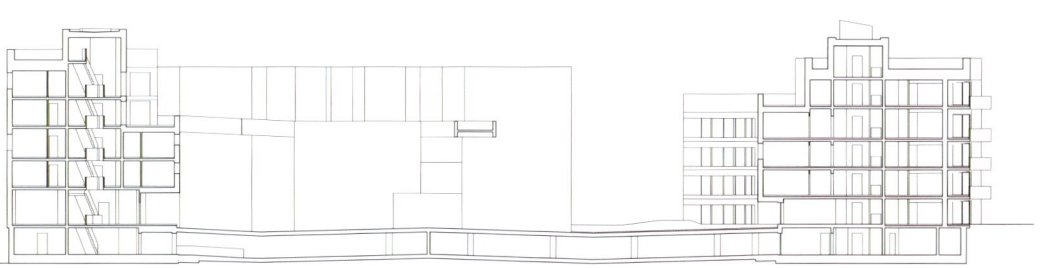

Section A-A

CHRIST.CHRIST. ASSOCIATED ARCHITECTS

www.christ-christ.cc

Christ.Christ. associated architects is a supra-regionally active company for architecture and interior architecture with its headquarters in Wiesbaden.

The projects executed by the office range from administration and industrial buildings, to the construction of residences and villas and right up to interior architecture and shopfitting.

Our office is the decisive member of an interdisciplinary network consisting of architects, structural engineers, electrical engineers, specialist planners for technical building equipment, fire safety experts, construction physicists, geologists and landscape architects. Together with these partners, we act as experienced and competent contacts for building owners during the development and execution of projects.

Projects by Christ.Christ. associated architects have been internationally published and received multiple awards.

Christ.Christ. associated architects ist ein überregional tätiges Unternehmen für Architektur und Innenarchitektur mit Sitz in Wiesbaden. Es wurde 1898 von Karl Christ Sen. gegründet und wird heute in der vierten Generation von Roger Christ geführt. Die vom Büro realisierten Projekte reichen von Verwaltungs- und Industriegebäuden über den Bau von Wohnungen und Villen bis hin zur Innenarchitektur und dem Ladenbau.

Unser Büro ist das maßgebliche Mitglied eines interdisziplinären Netzwerkes bestehend aus Architekten, Tragwerksplanern, Elektroingenieuren, Fachplanern für die technische Gebäudeausstattung, Brandschutzsachverständigen, Bauphysikern, Geologen und Landschaftsarchitekten. Zusammen mit diesen Partnern stehen wir bei der Entwicklung und Durchführung von Projekten dem Bauherrn als erfahrener und kompetenter Ansprechpartner zur Verfügung.

Christ.Christ. associated architects Projekte wurden international publiziert und vielfach ausgezeichnet.

Christ.Christ. associated architects est une entreprise d'architecture et d'architecture d'intérieur basée à Wiesbaden, active au niveau national. Elle a été fondée en 1898 par Karl Christ Sen. et est aujourd'hui dirigée par Roger Christ, quatrième génération. Les projets réalisés par le bureau vont des bâtiments administratifs et industriels à la construction d'appartements et de villas, en passant par l'aménagement intérieur et l'aménagement de magasins.

Notre bureau est le membre clé d'un réseau interdisciplinaire composé d'architectes, d'ingénieurs en structure, d'ingénieurs électriciens, de planificateurs techniques de bâtiments, d'experts en protection incendie, de physiciens du bâtiment, de géologues et d'architectes paysagers. Avec ces partenaires, nous sommes à la disposition du client en tant que partenaire expérimenté et compétent pour le développement et la réalisation de projets.

Les projets d'architectes associés Christ.Christ. ont été publiés à l'échelle internationale et ont reçu de nombreux prix.

Christ.Christ. es una empresa de arquitectura e interiorismo con sede en Wiesbaden. Fue fundada en 1898 por Karl Christ Sen. y ahora es administrada por la cuarta generación por Roger Christ. Los proyectos realizados van desde edificios administrativos e industriales hasta la construcción de apartamentos y villas, pasando por el diseño de interiores y el equipamiento deesapcios comerciales.

Nuestra oficina es el miembro clave de una red interdisciplinaria compuesta por arquitectos, ingenieros estructurales, ingenieros eléctricos, planificadores técnicos de edificios, expertos en protección contra incendios, físicos de edificios, geólogos y arquitectos paisajistas. Junto con estos socios, estamos a disposición del cliente como un socio experimentado y competente para el desarrollo e implementación de proyectos.

Los proyectos de los arquitectos asociados Christ.Christ. han sido publicados internacionalmente y han recibido numerosos premios.

RESIDENTIAL BUILDING AM HEILIGENSTOCK

Location: Wiesbaden, Germany

Client: Pered GmbH, Wiesbaden

Completion: 06/2014

Living Space: 442 m²

Construction costs:
1.080.000 € net (type of costs 300+400+500)

Procedure type:
Direct Commission

Number of apartments: 4

Number of underground parking lots: 4

Team: Roger Christ, Christiane Bolesta (Project Management), Julia Christ

Typology: Residential Buildings

Status: Built

Year: 2014

Photo credits:
© Thomas Herrmann, Stuttgart

Awards:
- Johann-Wilhelm-Lehr-Plakette 2018
- German Design Award 2016 - Special Mention
- Iconic Award 2015 - Winner
- The International Architecture Award 2015

RESIDENTIAL BUILDING SPOHRSTRASSE

Location: Wiesbaden, Germany

Client: Private

Completion: 10/2015

Living space: 647 m²

Procedure type:
Direct Commission

Number of apartements: 4

Number of underground parking lots: 6

Team:
Roger Christ, Christiane Bolesta (Project Management)

Typology: Residential Buildings

Status: Built

Year: 2016

Photo credits:
© Thomas Herrmann, Stuttgart

Awards:
Build Architecture Award 2017

RESIDENTIAL BUILDINGS CHRISTIAN-MORGENSTERN-STRASSE

Location:
Christian-Morgenstern-Straße 1a + b, 7a + b
65201 Wiesbaden, Schierstein
Germany

Client: GWW Wiesbadener Wohnbaugesellschaft mbH, Wiesbaden

Completion: 12/2016

Floor area: 3.394 m²

Construction costs: 3.290.000 € net (type of costs 300 + 400)

Procedure type:
Direct Commission

Number of apartements: 16

Number of parking lots: 48

Team: Roger Christ, Julia Christ, Sascha Daum, Laura Lehmacher

Typology: Residential Buildings

Status: Built

Year: 2016

Photo credits:
© Thomas Herrmann, Stuttgart

Awards:
- The International Architecture Award 2018
- Johann-Wilhelm-Lehr-Plakette 2018
- Iconic Awards 2018 - Selection
- FIABCI Prix d'Excellence Germany - Official Selection 2018
- DAM Award 2019 - nominated

The residential building Am Heiligenstock is located in a villa-style residential area featuring relatively homogeneous development.
The building extends across three floors, whereby all the bedrooms of all the apartments are accommodated on the middle floor. The living areas are either located on the ground floor or on the top floor, and they all have a protruding open area.
The four apartments are nested inside the building shell as L-shaped rooms so that, in spite of the density of the development, they permit a maximum of privacy through the layout and orientation.
The building, which is realised in a clear language of form, reacts to the existing developments and the construction elements typically found in this residential area, but interprets them in contemporary form.

Das Wohnhaus Am Heiligenstock liegt in einem villenartigen Wohngebiet mit einer verhältnismäßig homogenen Bebauung.
Das Gebäude erstreckt sich über drei Ebenen, wobei im mittleren Geschoss sämtliche Schlafräume aller Wohnungen untergebracht sind. Die Wohnräume befinden sich entweder im Erd- oder Dachgeschoss und haben jeweils einen vorgelagerten Freibereich.
Die vier Wohnungen sind als L-förmige Raumkörper innerhalb der Gebäudehülle so ineinander verschachtelt, dass sie trotz der dichten Bebauung durch ihre Anordnung und Orientierung ein Maximum an Privatsphäre erlauben.
Der in einer klaren Formensprache realisierte Bau reagiert auf die vorhandene Bebauung und die in dem Wohngebiet typischen Bauelemente, interpretiert diese aber in einer zeitgenössischen Form.

RESIDENTIAL BUILDING AM HEILIGENSTOCK
WIESBADEN, GERMANY

L'immeuble d'habitation Am Heiligenstock est situé dans un quartier résidentiel de style villa avec un développement relativement homogène.
L'immeuble s'étend sur trois étages, toutes les chambres de tous les appartements étant situées à l'étage central. Les pièces à vivre sont situées soit au rez-de-chaussée, soit au dernier étage, et elles ont toutes une partie ouverte en saillie.
Les quatre appartements sont imbriqués à l'intérieur de l'enveloppe du bâtiment sous la forme de pièces en forme de L, de sorte que, malgré la densité du développement, ils permettent un maximum d'intimité grâce à leur disposition et leur orientation.
Le bâtiment, réalisé dans un langage clair des formes, réagit aux développements existants et aux éléments de construction typiques de ce quartier résidentiel, mais les interprète sous une forme contemporaine.

El edificio de viviendas Am Heiligenstock se encuentra en una zona residencial de estilo „chalet" con un desarrollo relativamente homogéneo.
El edificio se extiende a lo largo de tres plantas, por lo que los dormitorios de todos los apartamentos se alojan en la planta media. Las zonas de estar están situadas en la planta baja o en el último piso, y todas ellas tienen acceso a una zona abierta.
Los cuatro apartamentos están anidados en el interior del edificio como habitaciones en forma de L, de modo que, a pesar de la densidad de la urbanización, permiten un máximo de privacidad a través de la distribución y la orientación.
El edificio, realizado en un lenguaje formal claro, reacciona a los desarrollos existentes y a los elementos constructivos típicos de esta zona residencial, pero los interpreta en forma contemporánea.

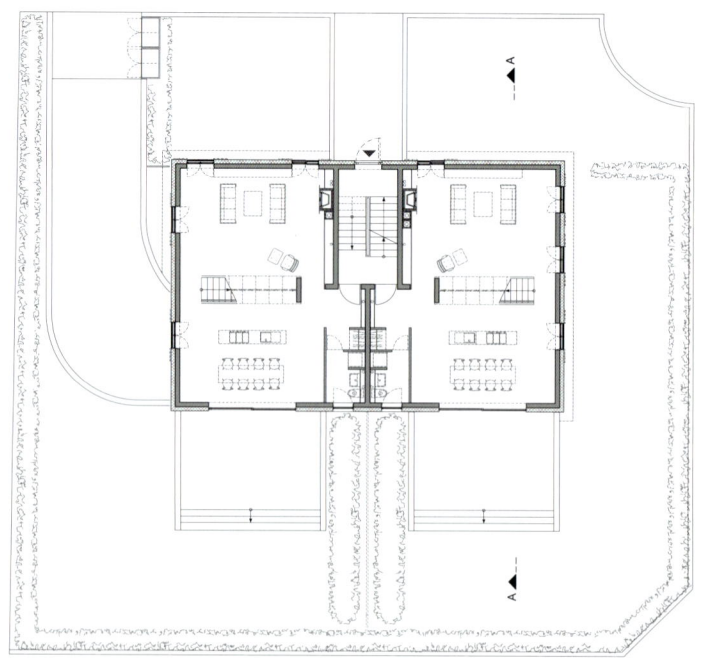

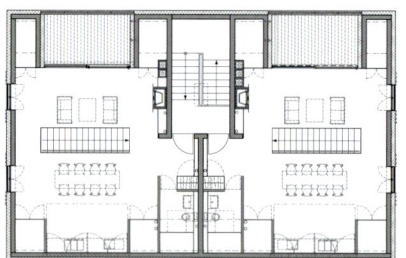

Second floor plan

First floor plan

Ground floor plan

The residential building on Spohrstraße is located in a villa-style residential area featuring relatively homogeneous development.

In the residential area, an over-regulative development plan has been imposed with specifications that extend to almost all areas. In addition to the regular defined specifications laid down in a development plan, the aspect ratio of the base area, the type of façade (punctuated façade), the aspect ratio of the window formats, the number of window formats, the permitted overall window area, a symmetrical façade structure, plaster as façade material, light-coloured to muted façade paint shades and the form and number of the façade projections are determined here.

Within this constrictive corset of specifications, a striking symbol of radical minimalism has been achieved which, however, is imbued with charm through its materiality, colouration and details.

Das Wohnhaus Spohrstraße liegt in einem villenartigen Wohngebiet mit einer verhältnismäßig homogenen Bebauung.

In dem Wohngebiet gilt ein überregulierender Bebauungsplan mit Festsetzungen in nahezu allen Bereichen. Zusätzlich zu den üblich definierten Festsetzungen eines Bebauungsplans werden in diesem das Seitenverhältnis der Grundfläche, der Fassadentyp (Lochfassade), das Seitenverhältnis der Fensterformate, die Anzahl der Fensterformate, die zulässige gesamte Fensterfläche, eine symmetrische Fassadengliederung, Putz als Fassadenmaterial, helle bis gedeckte Fassadenfarben und die Form und Anzahl der Fassadenversprünge festgesetzt.

Verwirklicht wurde innerhalb dieses engen Korsetts an Vorgaben ein markantes Zeichen eines radikalen Minimalismus, welches aber durch seine Materialität, Farbgebung und Detaillierung reizvoll wird.

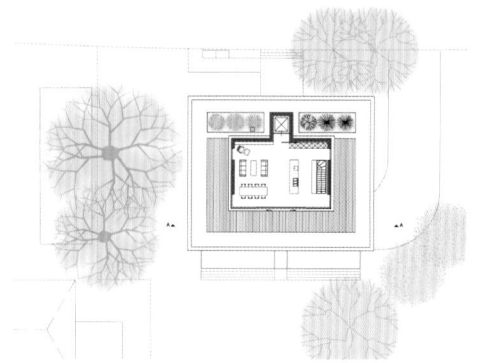

Second floor plan

RESIDENTIAL BUILDING SPOHRSTRASSE
WIESBADEN, GERMANY

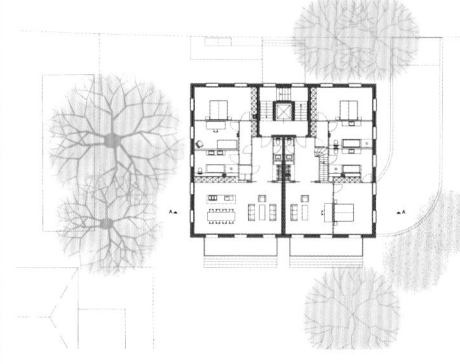

First floor plan

L'immeuble d'habitation de la Spohrstraße est situé dans un quartier résidentiel de style villa, relativement homogène.

Dans la zone résidentielle, un plan de développement surréglementaire a été imposé avec des spécifications qui s'étendent à presque toutes les zones. Outre les spécifications régulièrement définies dans un plan d'aménagement, le rapport d'aspect de la surface de base, le type de façade (façade ponctuée), le rapport d'aspect des formats de fenêtres, le nombre de fenêtres, la surface totale autorisée des fenêtres, une structure de façade symétrique, le plâtre comme matériau de façade, les teintes claires à atténuées des peintures de façade et la forme et le nombre des projections de façade sont déterminés.

Dans ce corset de cahier des charges contraignant, un symbole frappant de minimalisme radical a été réalisé, mais il est empreint de charme par sa matérialité, sa coloration et ses détails.

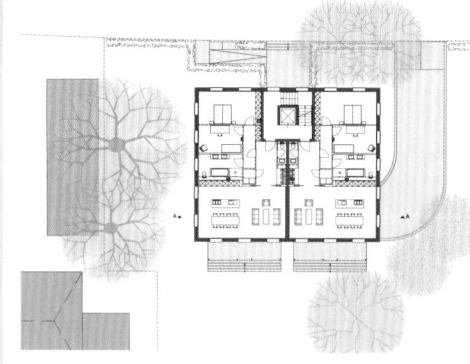

Ground floor plan

El edificio de viviendas en Spohrstraße se encuentra en una zona residencial de estilo de montaña con un desarrollo homogéneo.

En la zona residencial se ha impuesto un plan de desarrollo excesivamente regulado con especificaciones que se extienden a casi todas las áreas. Además de estas especificaciones definidas en un plan de desarrollo, se determinan la relación de aspecto de la superficie base, el tipo de fachada, los formatos y número de ventanas, la superficie total permitida, la estructura simétrica de la fachada, el yeso como material a utilizar, las tonalidades de pintura (color claro tenue), así como la forma y el número de los salientes de la fachada.

Dentro de este constrictivo corsé de especificaciones, se ha logrado un llamativo símbolo de minimalismo radical que, sin embargo, está impregnado de encanto por su materialidad, colorido y detalles.

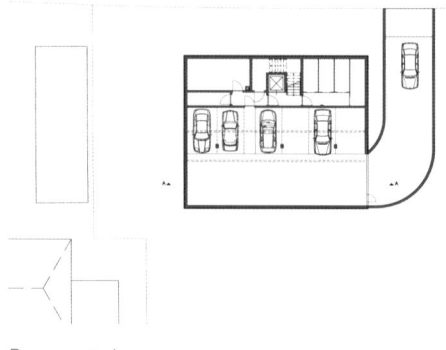

Basement plan

Site plan

Section

Detached single-family homes are still considered the most attractive form of living in Germany and across most parts of the world. And yet, the related urban sprawl is leading to severe traffic congestion combined with major infrastructure and mobility problems, and to increased destruction of the natural landscape.

For this reason, high-quality concentration is a central strategy for correcting the disadvantages of urban sprawl. The aim was to erect a residential building which has a high residential density, but does not lose the living quality of a single-family home with a garden and garage. The residential building shown here are new constructions comprising two almost identical apartment buildings featuring eight residential units each. Due to the open multi-storey car park on the ground floor, the apartments are suspended over the landscape.

Das freistehende Einfamilienhaus gilt nach wie vor als die attraktivste Wohnform in Deutschland und in großen Teilen der Welt. Doch führt die damit verbundene Zersiedelung zu einer starken Verkehrsbelastung verbunden mit hohen Infrastruktur- und Mobilitätsproblemen und zur weiteren Zerstörung der Naturlandschaft.

Daher ist die qualitätsvolle Verdichtung eine zentrale Strategie, um die durch die Zersiedelung entstehenden Nachteile zu korrigieren. Ziel war es, Wohngebäude zu errichten, welche eine hohe Wohndichte aufweisen, aber die Wohnqualität des Einfamilienhauses mit Garten und Garage nicht verlieren.

Bei den gezeigten Wohngebäuden handelt es sich um den Neubau von zwei nahezu identischen Mehrfamilienhäusern mit jeweils acht Wohnungen. Durch die offene Parkgarage im Erdgeschoss schweben die Wohnungen über der Landschaft und sind abgehoben von der angrenzenden Straße.

RESIDENTIAL BUILDINGS
CHRISTIAN-MORGENSTERN-STRASSE
WIESBADEN, SCHIERSTEIN, GERMANY

Les maisons unifamiliales individuelles sont toujours considérées comme la forme de vie la plus attrayante en Allemagne et dans la plupart des régions du monde. Pourtant, l'étalement urbain qui s'ensuit entraîne de graves embouteillages combinés à d'importants problèmes d'infrastructure et de mobilité, ainsi qu'une destruction accrue du paysage naturel.

C'est pourquoi la concentration de haute qualité est une stratégie centrale pour corriger les inconvénients de l'étalement urbain. L'objectif était de construire un bâtiment d'habitation à haute densité résidentielle, sans pour autant perdre la qualité de vie d'une maison unifamiliale avec jardin et garage.

L'immeuble d'habitation présenté ici est une construction neuve composée de deux immeubles d'appartements presque identiques, comprenant chacun huit unités d'habitation. Grâce au parking ouvert à plusieurs étages au rez-de-chaussée, les appartements sont suspendus au-dessus du paysage.

Las casas unifamiliares se siguen considerando la forma más atractiva de vivir en Alemania y en la mayor parte del mundo. Sin embargo, la expansión urbana relacionada está provocando una grave congestión del tráfico, combinada con importantes problemas de infraestructura y movilidad, y una mayor destrucción del paisaje natural.

Por esta razón, la concentración de alta calidad es una estrategia central para corregir las desventajas de la expansión urbana. El objetivo era construir un edificio de alta densidad residencial, pero que no pierda la calidad de vida de una vivienda unifamiliar con jardín y garaje. El edificio de viviendas que aquí se muestra es de nueva construcción y consta de dos edificios de apartamentos casi idénticos con ocho unidades residenciales cada uno. Gracias al aparcamiento abierto de varios pisos en la planta baja, los apartamentos están suspendidos sobre el paisaje.

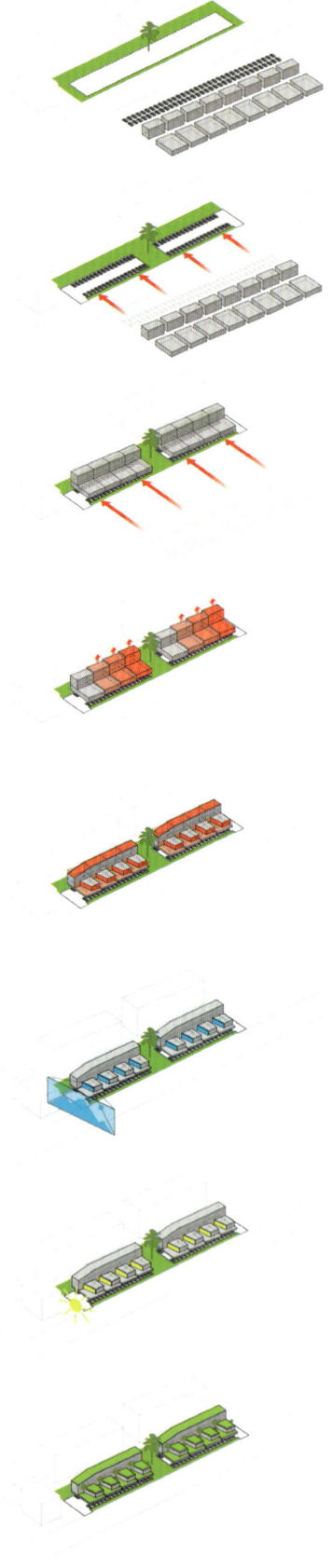

Construction diagrams

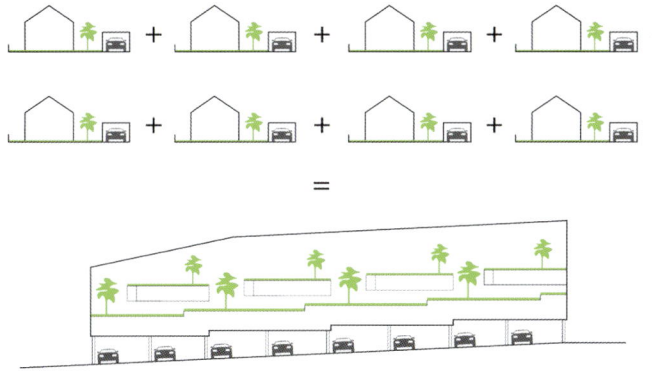

Concept diagram

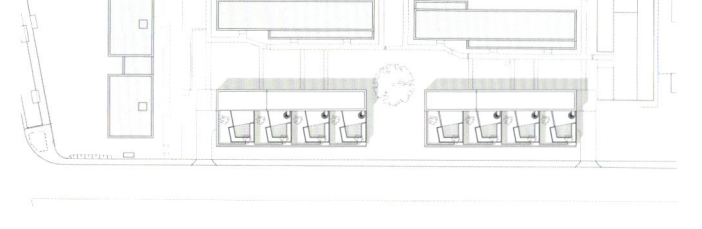

Site plan

First floor plan

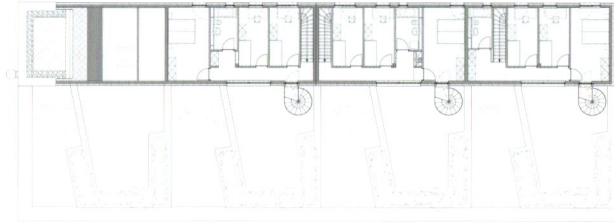

Third floor plan

Ground floor plan

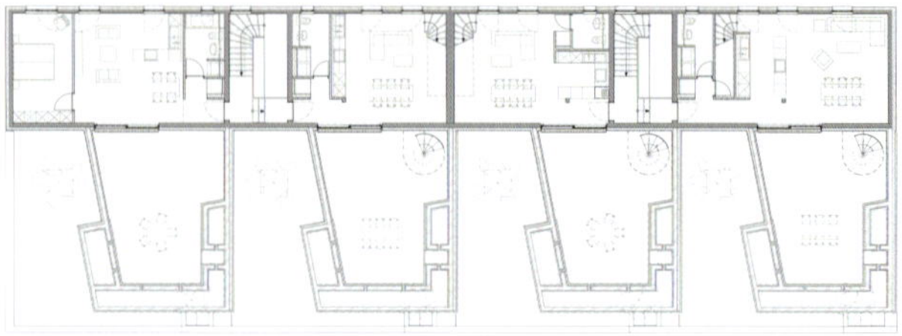

Second floor plan

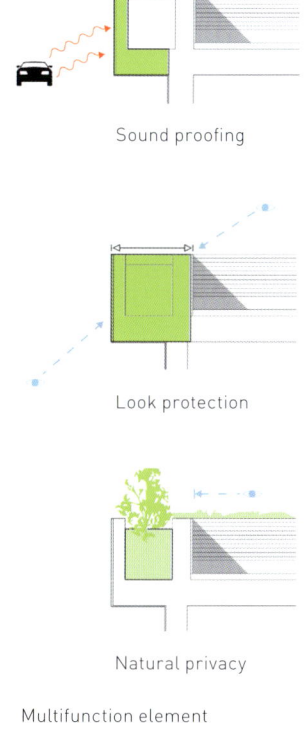

Sound proofing

Look protection

Natural privacy

Multifunction element

FRANTZEN et al ARCHITECTEN

www.frantzen.nl

The thread that links our work is not an esthetic signature but our approach of each individual commission as a unique project. Rather than imposing a more or less consistent corporate architectural handwriting on each project we aim to fit our projects to each specific context.

Although the credits are often attributed to the principal architect a building is by definition the result of extensive teamwork. Therefore our office is called FRANTZEN et al, et al meaning "et alteri", "and others". We really value cooperating with building consultants and often team up together with other architectural firms to get the job done.

Besides working for institutional and private clients since 2002 we started developing projects at our own risk and expense in 2005. In 2009 we founded Lemniskade Projects to develop sustainable and flexible residential buildings with solid wood structures. In 2018 this company was awarded the Golden Pyramid, the Dutch state prize for excellence in commissioning architecture.

Der Leitfaden unserer Arbeit ist nicht eine ästhetische Haltung, sondern die Herangehensweise an jeden Auftrag als ein einzigartiges Projekt. Anstatt jedem Projekt einen mehr oder weniger konsistenten Architektur-Corporate-Style aufzuzwingen, ist es unser Ziel, die Projekte an jeden Kontext anzupassen.

Obwohl die Anerkennung oft dem Hauptarchitekten zugeschrieben wird, ist ein Gebäude per Definition das Ergebnis einer umfangreichen Teamarbeit. Deshalb heißt unser Büro FRANTZEN et al, „et al", was „et alteri", „und andere" bedeutet. Wir schätzen die Zusammenarbeit mit technischen Beratern und arbeiten oft mit anderen Architekturbüros zusammen, um den Auftrag auszuführen.

Neben der Arbeit für institutionelle und private Kunden seit 2002 haben wir 2005 mit der Entwicklung eigener Projekte begonnen, in denen wir Risiken eingehen und die Kosten tragen. Im Jahr 2009 haben wir Lemniskade Projects gegründet, um nachhaltige und flexible Wohngebäude mit Massivholzstrukturen zu entwickeln. Im Jahr 2018 erhielt das Unternehmen die Goldene Pyramide, den niederländischen Staatspreis für herausragende Leistungen im Bereich der Architektur.

Le fil conducteur de notre travail n'est pas une posture esthétique, mais l'approche de chaque commande comme un projet unique. Plutôt que d'imposer à chaque projet un style architectural et corporatif plus ou moins cohérent, notre objectif est d'adapter les projets à chaque contexte.

Bien que les crédits soient souvent attribués à l'architecte principal, un bâtiment est, par définition, le résultat d'un long travail d'équipe. C'est pourquoi notre bureau s'appelle FRANTZEN et al, « et al », qui signifie « et alteri », « et autres ». Nous apprécions la collaboration avec des consultants techniques et nous travaillons souvent en partenariat avec d'autres cabinets d'architectes pour mener à bien cette mission.

En plus de travailler pour des clients institutionnels et privés depuis 2002, nous avons commencé à développer nos propres projets en 2005 ; des projets dans lesquels nous prenons les risques et assumons les coûts. En 2009, nous avons fondé Lemniskade Projects pour développer des bâtiments résidentiels durables et flexibles avec des structures en bois massif. En 2018, l'entreprise a reçu la Pyramide d'or, le prix d'État néerlandais pour l'excellence dans les commandes architecturales.

El hilo conductor de nuestro trabajo no es una postura estética, sino el enfoque de cada encargo como un proyecto único. En lugar de imponer un estilo arquitectónico-corporativo más o menos consistente en cada proyecto, nuestro objetivo es adaptar los proyectos a cada contexto.

Aunque los créditos se atribuyen a menudo al arquitecto principal, un edificio es, por definición, el resultado de un extenso trabajo en equipo. Por lo tanto, nuestra oficina se llama FRANTZEN et al, «et al», que significa «et alteri», «y otros». Valoramos la colaboración con los consultores técnicos y amenudo nos asociamos con otras firmas de arquitectos para realizar el encargo.

Además de trabajar para clientes institucionales y privados desde 2002, comenzamos a desarrollar proyectos propios en 2005; proyectos en los que somos nosotros quien corre los riesgos y asume los costes. En 2009 fundamos Lemniskade Projects para desarrollar edificios residenciales sostenibles y flexibles con estructuras de madera maciza. En 2018 esta empresa fue galardonada con la Pirámide de Oro, el premio estatal holandés a la excelencia en el encargo de arquitectura.

Program: work-living housing

Location: Amsterdam

Partner in charge: Tom Frantzen

Team: Karel van Eijken, Laura Reinders

Design – completion: 2009– 2016

Client: Lemniskade Projects (Tom Frantzen & Claus Oussoren)

Contractor: Hillen & Roosen

Gross floor area: 5,209 m²

Lettable floor area: 4,295 m²

Photo credits: © Luuk Kramer, © Isabel Nabuurs

Awards:
- 2018: first prize Golden Pyramid
- 2018: first prize "Sustainable Building Award 2018", The Dutch Sustainable Building Awards
- 2017: first prize 'WAN residential awards 2016
- 2017: "Green Good Design Award", The European Centre for Architecture Art Design and Urban Studies and The Chicago Athenaeum
- 2017: honourable mention "BNA building of the Year"
- 2017: nomination "Amsterdamse Nieuwbouw Prijs"
- 2017: nomination Amsterdam Architecture Prize
- 2016: nomination 'Zuiderkerkprijs 2016; the best housing block of Amsterdam
- 2016: nomination ARC16 innovation award PATCH22, Amsterdam

Program: Elderly housing and healthcare centre

Location: Amsterdam

Partner in charge: Tom Frantzen

Team: Karel van Eijken, Stephan Schülecke, Felix Reiter, Jasper Hermans, Laura Reinders, Gertjan Rohaan

Technical elaboration: INBO Woudenberg, Piet van der ploeg, Roy Wallet, Martijn van den Hoek

Urban planner: DRO Amsterdam, Irene Klarenbeek

Design – completion: 2004/08 – 2011

Client: De Key/De Principaal, Amsterdam

Contractor: BOT Bouw, Heerhugowaard

Gross floor area: 17,108 m²

Lettable floor area: 14,086 m²

Photo credits: © Roos Aldershoff

Awards:
- 2011: first prize 'Zuiderkerkprijs 2011; the best housing block of Amsterdam
- 2011: first prize 'VKG architecture award 2011' De Keyzer, Amsterdam

DE KEYZER HOUSING AND HEALTHCARE CENTRE

Patch 22 is a sustainable building thanks to its energy efficiency, the use of renewable materials and the great functional flexibility offered by its design. The structure and facades are built with timber and the 4m high levels can be functionally reconverted without affecting the structure or the facilities, that are diverted to the central core. The floors enter and leave the façade plane in a playful way and can be distributed as lofts of up to 540 m² with large balconies, as eight smaller apartments or as an open office space that occupies the entire floor thanks to the lack of structural division. All apartment layouts are custom designed for their owners. The building is equipped with multiple sustainable measures, such as a roof full of photovoltaic panels, the reuse of rainwater or the CO_2 neutral generation of heat through pellet boilers.

Patch 22 ist ein nachhaltiges Gebäude, dank seiner Energieeffizienz, dem Einsatz erneuerbarer Materialien und der hohen funktionalen Flexibilität seines Designs. Seine Struktur und seine Fassaden sind aus Holz gebaut und seine 4 m hohen Stock können ihre Nutzung und Verteilung wiederherstellen, ohne die Struktur oder die Einrichtungen zu beeinträchtigen, die horizontal zu einem zentralen Kern umgeleitet werden. Die Etagen betreten und verlassen spielerisch die Fassadenebene und können als Lofts von bis zu 540 m² mit großen Balkonen, als acht kleinere Wohnungen oder als offene Büroflächen aufgeteilt werden, die aufgrund der fehlenden baulichen Trennung die gesamte Etage einnehmen. Alle Wohnungsgrundrisse werden nach Maß für ihre Besitzer entworfen. Das Gebäude ist mit mehreren nachhaltigen Maßnahmen ausgestattet, wie z. B. einem Dach voller Photovoltaikmodule, der Wiederverwendung von Regenwasser oder der Wärmeerzeugung durch Pelletkessel.

PATCH22
AMSTERDAM, NETHERLANDS

Patch 22 est un bâtiment durable grâce à son efficacité énergétique, à l'utilisation de matériaux renouvelables et à la grande flexibilité fonctionnelle offerte par sa conception. Sa structure et ses façades sont construites en bois et ses plantes, d'une hauteur de 4 m, peuvent reconvertir leur utilisation et leur distribution sans affecter la structure ou les installations, dérivées horizontalement vers un noyau central. Les étages entrent et sortent de la façade de manière ludique et peuvent être distribués sous forme de lofts jusqu'à 540 m² avec de grands balcons, de huit appartements plus petits ou de bureaux ouverts qui occupent tout l'étage grâce à l'absence de division structurelle. Tous les plans d'appartements sont conçus sur mesure pour leurs propriétaires. Le bâtiment est équipé de multiples mesures durables, telles qu'un toit plein de panneaux photovoltaïques, la réutilisation de l'eau de pluie ou la production de chaleur par des chaudières à pellets.

Patch 22 es un edificio sostenible gracias a su eficiencia energética, el uso de materiales renovables y la gran flexibilidad funcional que ofrece su diseño. Su estructura y sus fachadas están construidas con madera y sus plantas, de 4 m de altura libre, pueden reconvertir su uso y su distribución sin afectar a la estructura ni a las instalaciones, desviadas horizontalmente hacia un núcleo central. Las plantas entran y salen del plano de fachada de forma lúdica y se pueden distribuir como *lofts* de hasta 540 m² con grandes balcones, como ocho apartamentos más pequeños o como espacio de oficina abierto que ocupa toda la planta gracias a la falta de división estructural. Todas las plantas de los apartamentos son diseñadas a la medida de sus propietarios. El edificio está dotado de múltiples medidas sostenibles, como una cubierta llena de paneles fotovoltaicos, la reutilización de agua de lluvia o la generación de calor mediante calderas de *pellets*.

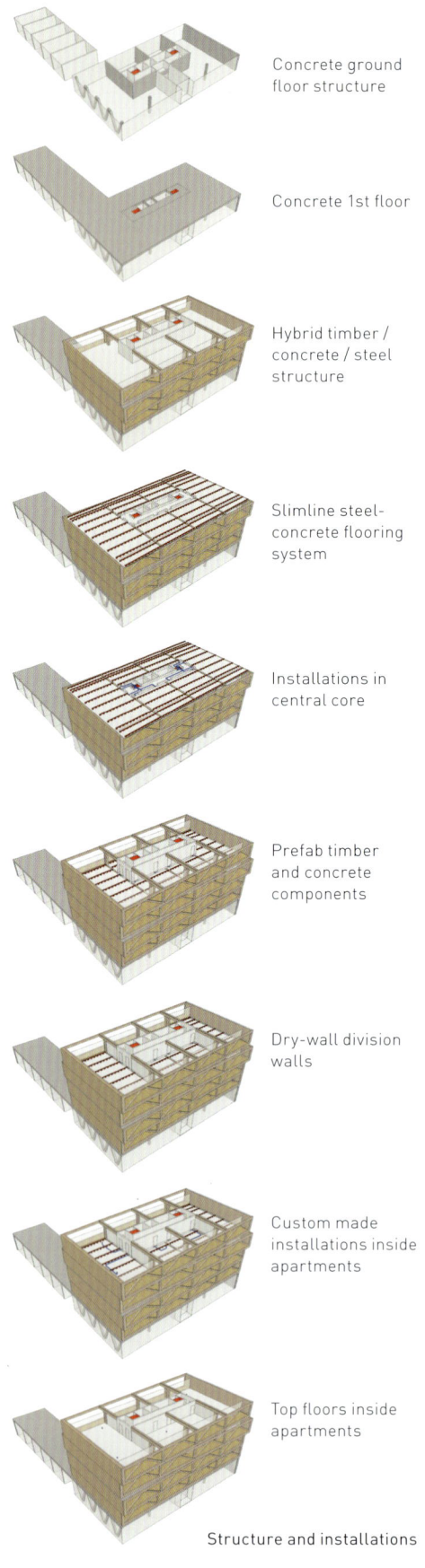

Concrete ground floor structure

Concrete 1st floor

Hybrid timber / concrete / steel structure

Slimline steel-concrete flooring system

Installations in central core

Prefab timber and concrete components

Dry-wall division walls

Custom made installations inside apartments

Top floors inside apartments

Structure and installations

West elevation

South elevation

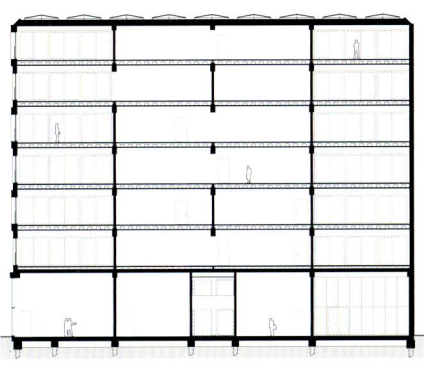

Section C

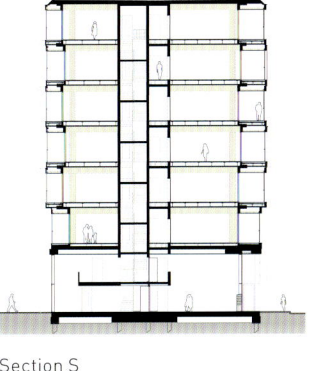

Section S

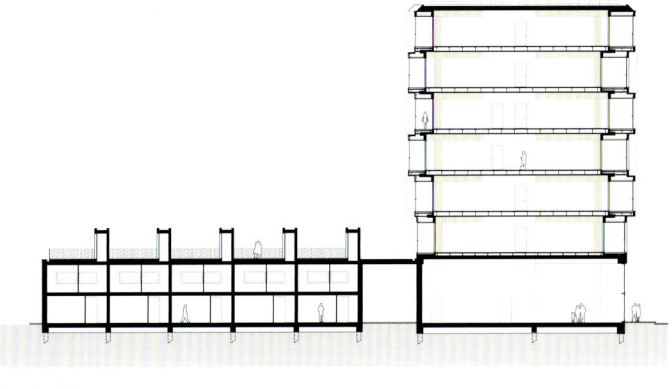

Section R

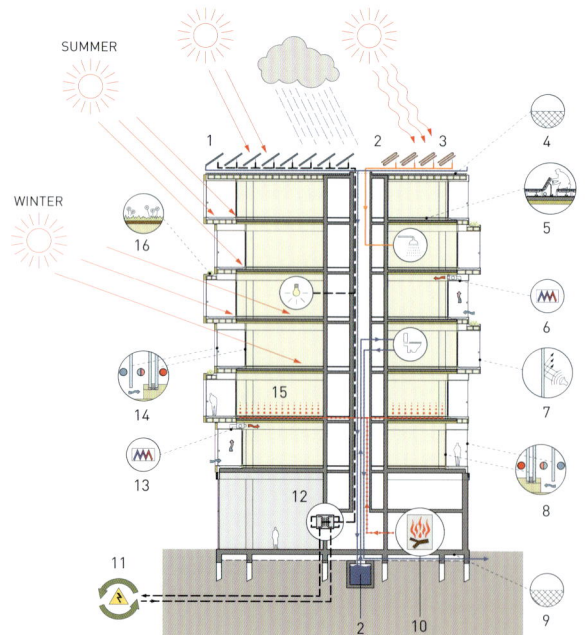

SUMMER

WINTER

1. Solar cells
2. Rainwater collection
3. Solar collectors
4. Insulation thermal resistance value=7
5. Removable underfloor heating panels for access to pipework and cabling
6. Heat exchanger unit
7. Single glazing noise barrier
8. Climate-protected loggia with single + double glazing
9. Insulation thermal resistance value=5
10. Pellet stove
11. Surplus electricity is stored in electricity grid
12. Transformer
13. Heat exchanger unit
14. Climate-protected loggia with single + double glazing
15. Underfloor heating
16. Sedum roof covering

Installation scheme

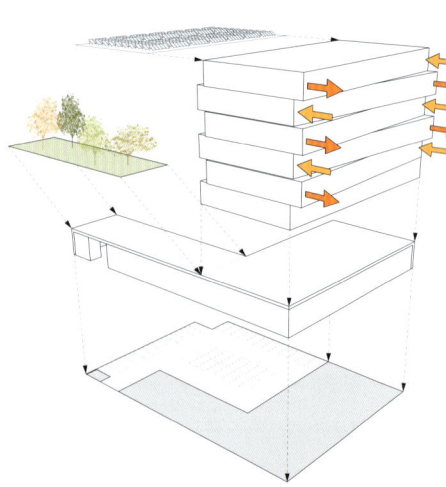

Design concept

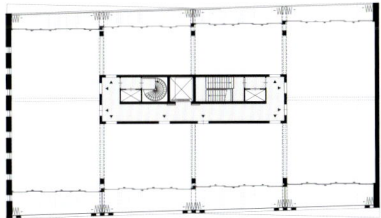

Typical floorplan

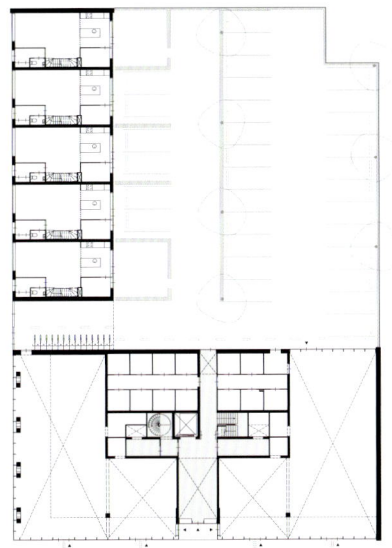

Ground floor plan

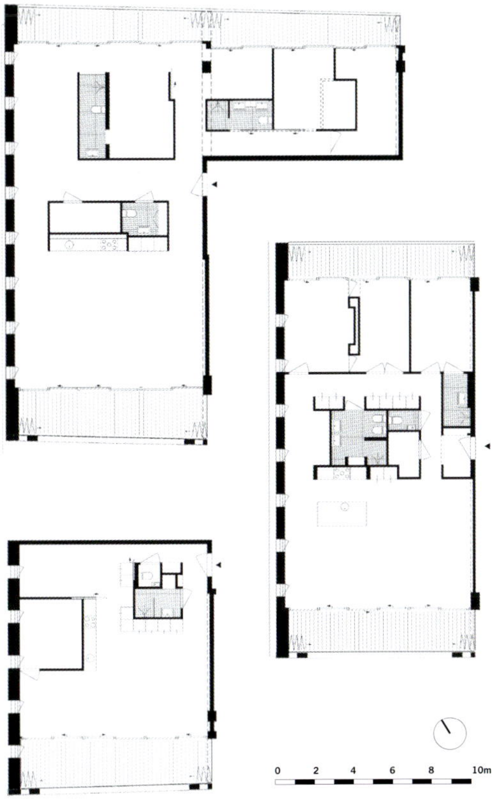

Custom designed apartment layouts

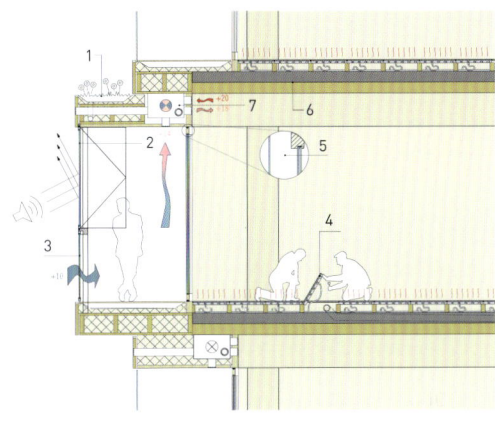

Section concept

1. Low-maintenance sedum roof
2. Glass can be opened for cleaning from the inside
3. Rear facade with soundproofed single glazing
4. Removable underfloor heating tiles ensure continued access to pipework and cabling
5. Insulating double glazing + single glazing in loggia
6. Slimline hollow floor
7. CO_2 controlled heat recovery unit

The project replaces the historic Dubbeltjespanden building on Czaar Petersraat, adapting Amsterdam's 19th century architecture to a new residential building. The limited depth of the site generated a scheme with two pairs of light courtyards, accessed by an elevator and a staircase. Perimeter corridors around the courtyards give access to the shallow, L-shaped apartments. The project includes a psychogeriatric centre in the centre of the block, healthcare related premises on the ground floor and parking and storage rooms in the basement. The design is inspired by the symmetrical silhouette, the composition of the façades with shop windows and vertical frames, and the bricks and colours of the Dubbeltjespanden, but integrates these traditional elements in a rational contemporary scheme that is not nostalgic.

Das Projekt ersetzt das historische Dubbeltjespanden-Gebäude auf Czaar Petersraat und passt die Amsterdamer Architektur des 19. Jahrhunderts an ein neues Wohngebäude an. Die begrenzte Tiefe des Geländes, das über einen Aufzug und eine Treppe zugänglich ist, erzeugte ein Schema mit zwei Paaren von Lichthöfen. Das Projekt umfasst ein psychogeriatrisches Zentrum in der Mitte des Blocks, Geschäftsräume im Erdgeschoss sowie Park- und Lagerräume im Untergeschoss. Das Design ist inspiriert von der symmetrischen Silhouette, der Komposition der Fassaden mit Schaufenstern und Vertikalrahmen sowie den Ziegeln und Farben des Dubbeltjespanden, integriert diese traditionellen Elemente aber in ein rationales und nicht nostalgisches zeitgenössisches Konzept.

DE KEYZER HOUSING AND HEALTHCARE CENTRE
AMSTERDAM, NETHERLANDS

Le projet remplace le bâtiment historique Dubbeltjespanden sur Czaar Petersraat, en adaptant l'architecture du 19e siècle d'Amsterdam à un nouveau bâtiment résidentiel. La profondeur limitée du site a généré un schéma avec deux paires de patios de lumière, auxquels on accède par un ascenseur et un escalier. Des couloirs périphériques autour des patios donnent accès aux appartements peu profonds en L. Le projet comprend un centre psychogériatrique au centre de l'immeuble, des locaux commerciaux au rez-de-chaussée et des espaces de stationnement et de rangement au sous-sol. Le design s'inspire de la silhouette symétrique, de la composition des façades avec vitrines et cadres verticaux, des briques et des couleurs du Dubbeltjespanden, mais il intègre ces éléments traditionnels dans un schéma contemporain rationnel et non nostalgique.

El proyecto reemplaza el histórico edificio Dubbeltjespanden situado en la calle Czaar Petersraat, adaptando de forma contemporánea la arquitectura del siglo XIX de Ámsterdam a un nuevo edificio de viviendas. La limitada profundidad del solar generó un esquema con dos pares de patios de luz, a los que se accede mediante un ascensor y una escalera. Pasillos perimetrales situados alrededor de los patios dan acceso a los apartamentos, poco profundos y en forma de L. El proyecto incluye un centro psicogeriátrico en el centro del bloque, locales comerciales en planta baja y aparcamientos y trasteros en el sótano. El diseño se inspira en la silueta simétrica, la composición de las fachadas con escaparates y marcos verticales, y los ladrillos y los colores de la Dubbeltjespanden, pero integra estos elementos tradicionales en un esquema contemporáneo racional y no nostálgico.

"Dubbeltjespanden", the previous building on the site

Site plan

Elevations

Sections

Fourth floor plan

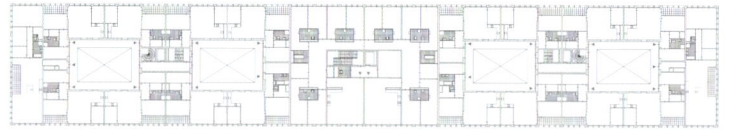

Second floor plan

Ground floor plan

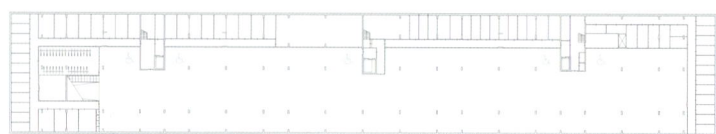

Basement floor plan

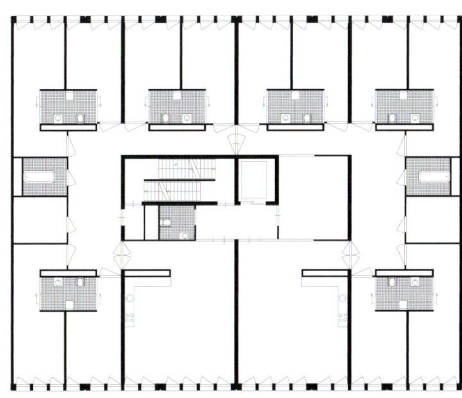

Two groups of psycho-geriatric residents

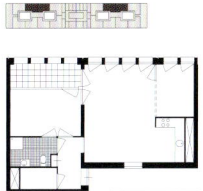

Dwelling type R
(social sector) 70 m²

Dwelling type S
82 m²

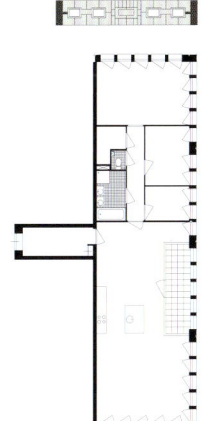

Dwelling type T
135 m²

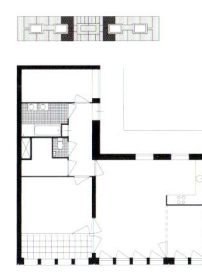

Dwelling type S
90 m²

Dwelling type X
83 m²

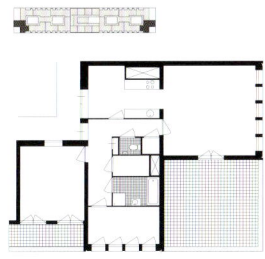

Dwelling type Y
102 m²

GROUPWORK

http://groupwork.uk.com

GROUPWORK are an employee ownership trust studio in which all collaborators are equal partners with engineers, landscape architects and other designers joining on specific projects. These have varied from private houses, residential and office buildings, arts centres, infrastructure bridges and metro stations. The two featured projects Barretts Grove and Clerkenwell Close have been recognized by the RIBA Stirling and EU Mies van Der Rohe jury. Barretts Grove investigates contemporary equivalent of London's C18th and C19th mass housing, spacious with some idiosyncratic and tactile details here and there but inexpensive and fast to mass produce. Clerkenwell Close aims to be bespoke and site specific with both historical visual and structural technological references of the long vanished C11th Norman abbey. Together they illustrate the practices core philosophy, Explore – Restore – Ignore, allowing good or poor context to drive material, structure and compositional for narratives.

GROUPWORK ist eine Mitarbeiter-Truststudie, bei der alle Mitarbeiter gleichberechtigte Partner von Ingenieuren, Landschaftsarchitekten und anderen Designern sind, die sich an konkreten Projekten beteiligen. Sie haben Privat-, Wohn- und Geschäftshäuser, Kunstzentren, Infrastrukturbrücken und U-Bahn-Stationen umgebaut. Die beiden vorgestellten Projekte Barretts Grove und Clerkenwell Close wurden von der Jury aus RIBA Stirling und EU Mies van Der Rohe ausgezeichnet. Barretts Grove untersucht das zeitgenössische Äquivalent der Londoner Massenwohnungen des 17. und 19. Jahrhunderts, geräumig, mit einigen eigenwilligen und taktilen Details, aber billig und schnell zu bauen. Clerkenwell Close zielt darauf ab, eine spezifische Studie mit historischen, visuellen und strukturellen Bezügen zur inzwischen nicht mehr existierenden Normandieabtei zu sein. Gemeinsam veranschaulichen sie die zentrale Philosophie des Studios, Exploring - Restoring - Ignoring, die es dem Kontext ermöglicht, Material, Struktur und Zusammensetzung ihrer architektonischen Erzählungen voranzutreiben.

GROUPWORK est une étude sur la confiance des employés dans laquelle tous les collaborateurs sont des partenaires égaux avec les ingénieurs, les architectes paysagistes et autres concepteurs qui participent à des projets spécifiques. Ils ont rénové des maisons privées, des immeubles résidentiels et des bureaux, des centres d'art, des ponts d'infrastructure et des stations de métro. Les deux projets présentés, Barretts Grove et Clerkenwell Close, ont été reconnus par le jury de RIBA Stirling et EU Mies van Der Rohe. Barretts Grove étudie l'équivalent contemporain des habitations de masse londoniennes des XVIIe et XIXe siècles, spacieuses et avec quelques détails idiosyncrasiques et tactiles, mais bon marché et rapides à construire. Clerkenwell Close se veut une étude spécifique avec des références historiques, visuelles et structurelles à l'ancienne abbaye de Normandie. Ensemble, ils illustrent la philosophie centrale de l'atelier, Exploration - Restauration - Ignorer, permettant au contexte de guider le matériau, la structure et la composition de leurs récits architecturaux.

GROUPWORK es un estudio de confianza de los empleados en el que todos los colaboradores son socios en igualdad de condiciones con los ingenieros, arquitectos paisajistas y otros diseñadores que se unen en proyectos específicos. Estos han remodelado casas privadas, edificios residenciales y de oficinas, centros de arte, puentes de infraestructura y estaciones de metro. Los dos proyectos presentados, Barretts Grove y Clerkenwell Close, han sido reconocidos por el jurado de RIBA Stirling y EU Mies van Der Rohe. Barretts Grove investiga el equivalente contemporáneo de las viviendas en masa de los siglos XVII y XIX de Londres, espaciosas, con algunos detalles idiosincrásicos y táctiles, pero baratas y rápidas de construir. Clerkenwell Close pretende ser un estudio específico con referencias históricas, visuales y estructurales de la desaparecida abadía de Normandía. Juntos ilustran la filosofía central del estudio, Explorar - Restaurar - Ignorar, permitiendo que el contexto impulse el material, la estructura y la composición de sus narrativas arquitectónicas.

15 CLERKENWELL CLOSE

Project address:
15 Clerkenwell Close,
London, EC1R 0AA

Use: Office and Residential

Gross internal area: 2,000 m²

Contract value: £4.65 m
(excluding land costs and fees)

Contract type:
Phase 1 – JCT Traditional, Phase
2 – D+B

Occupation date: 23rd Nov 2017

Architect practice:
GROUPWORK + Amin Taha
Architects

Project team:
Dominic Kacinskas, Alex Cotterill,
Amin Taha

Client: 15CC Limited, Amin Taha

Phase 1 contractor:
JB Structures (Shell + Core)

Phase 2:
Ecore Construction (Fit Out)

Photo credits:
© Timothy Soar

BARRETTS GROVE

Start on site: 20.02.15

Completion: 20.05.16

Gross internal floor area:
635 sqm GIA

**Form of contract or procurement
route:** JCT Design+Build

Construction cost: £ 1.27 m

Construction cost per m²:
£1,983 /m²

Architect groupwork:
Dale Elliott (Project Architect),
Sam Douek (Assistant Architect),
Nerissa Yeung (Assistant
Architect), Amin Taha (Senior
Architect)

Executive architect: GROUPWORK

Client: Cobstar Developments

Project manager: GROUPWORK

CDM coordinator: Syntegra

Approved building inspector:
MLM

Main contractor:
Ecore Construction Ltd

Cad software used: Mixed

Annual Co₂ emissions:
16.84 kg/m²

Photo credits: © Timothy Soar

The aim of the project was to build an apartment and office building with open-plan floors, free of pillars, on a plot of land that formed part of a former Norman abbey from the 11th century. The limestone construction system used in the abbey, introduced by the Normans in the country, inspired the development of the project. The use of limestone blocks with a structural function in the façade, in which quarry work and even fossils are visible, and of archaeological components integrated into the design, gives the building a better and broader sense of context than many recent buildings. The intervention helps to explain and disseminate the poetic possibilities inherent in the structural and aesthetic qualities of all the materials that make up the vocabulary of all architectural languages.

Ziel des Projekts war es, auf einem Grundstück, das Teil einer ehemaligen normannischen Abtei aus dem 11. Jahrhundert war, ein Wohn- und Geschäftshaus mit offenen stützenfreien Etagen zu errichten. Das in der Abtei verwendete Kalksteinbausystem, das von den Normannen des Landes eingeführt wurde, inspirierte die Entwicklung des Projekts. Die Verwendung von Kalksteinblöcken mit struktureller Funktion in der Fassade, in denen Steinbrucharbeiten und sogar Fossilien sichtbar sind, und von archäologischen Komponenten, die in das Design integriert sind, verleiht dem Gebäude ein besseres und breiteres Kontextgefühl als viele jüngere Gebäude. Die Intervention trägt dazu bei, die poetischen Möglichkeiten zu erklären und zu verbreiten, die den strukturellen und ästhetischen Qualitäten aller Materialien innewohnen, welche das Vokabular aller Architektursprachen ausmachen.

15 CLERKENWELL CLOSE
LONDON, UNITED KINGDOM

L'objectif du projet était de construire un immeuble d'appartements et de bureaux à aire ouverte, sans piliers, sur un terrain qui faisait partie d'une ancienne abbaye normande du XIe siècle. Le système de construction en calcaire utilisé dans l'abbaye, introduit par les Normands dans le pays, a inspiré le développement du projet. L'utilisation de blocs de calcaire ayant une fonction structurelle dans la façade, dans lesquels sont visibles des carrières et même des fossiles, et d'éléments archéologiques intégrés dans la conception, donne au bâtiment un sens du contexte meilleur et plus large que celui de nombreux bâtiments récents. L'intervention permet d'expliquer et de diffuser les possibilités poétiques inhérentes aux qualités structurelles et esthétiques de tous les matériaux qui composent le vocabulaire de toutes les langues architecturales.

El objetivo del proyecto fue levantar un edificio de apartamentos y oficinas de plantas diáfanas, libres de pilares, en un solar que formaba parte de una desaparecida abadía normanda del siglo XI. El sistema de construcción con piedra caliza empleado en la abadía, introducido por los normandos en el país, sirvió de inspiración para desarrollar el proyecto. El uso de bloques de piedra caliza con función estructural en la fachada, en los que son visibles el trabajo de cantera e incluso los fósiles, y de componentes arqueológicos integrados en el diseño, otorga al edificio un mejor y más amplio sentido de contexto que muchas edificaciones recientes. La intervención contribuye a explicar y difundir las posibilidades poéticas inherentes a las cualidades estructurales y estéticas de todos los materiales que conforman el vocabulario de todos los lenguajes arquitectónicos.

Site plan

Elevation

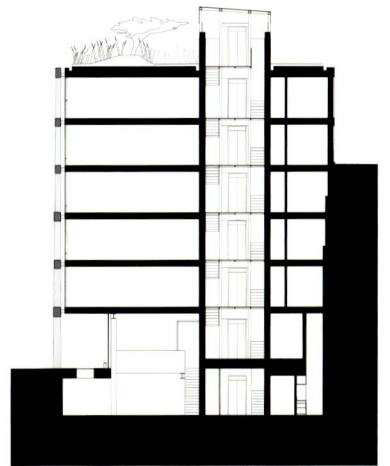

Section

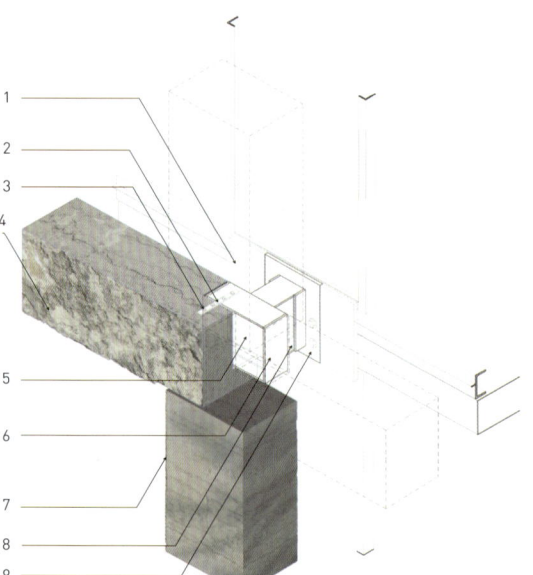
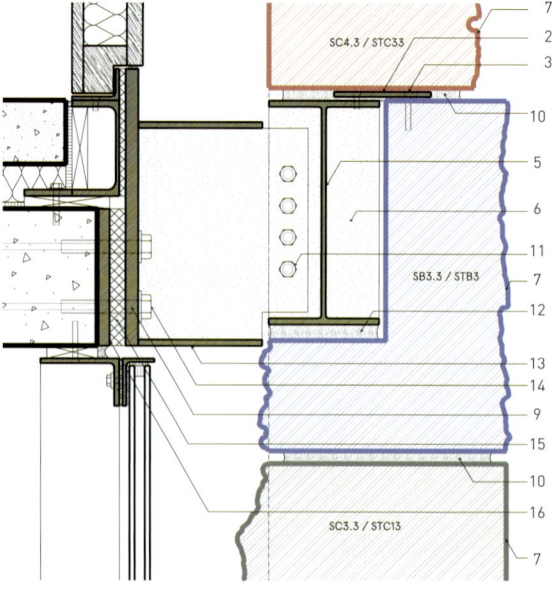

1. 45 mm galvanised MS cassette filled with insulation and bonded to floor slab edge painted black
2. 150 mm galvanised steel strap between UB and stone lintel
3. Strap fixed to stone lintel and UB with countersunk galvanised bolts to SE details
4. Limestone lintel see stone schedule for details and coding
5. 356 x 171 x 45 kg galvanised UB with 10 mm end plates all exposed faces painted black
6. 10 mm galvanised MS end plate welded to UB painted black
7. Limestone column see stone schedule for details and coding
8. 356 x 171 x 45 kg galvanised UB all exposed faces paited black
9. 20 mm 356 x 171 x 45 kg galvanised MS plate welded to back of floor slab UB painted black
10. 20 mm mortar between column and lintel to SE details
11. 4no. M16 bolts fixed through tab in stone connection UB and floor slab UB
12. 25 mm approx levelling mortar to achieve level UB in stone lintel cutout
13. 356 x 171 x 45 kg galvanised UB all exposed faces painted black
14. 2no. M20 bolts fixed through tab in floor connection UB into floor slab plate cast in place
15. 25 mm black nylon thermal separator between cast in fixing plate and stone connection plate
16. 20 mm. galvanised MS fixing plate cast into floor slab fixing plate tied into floor slab rebar painted black to SE details

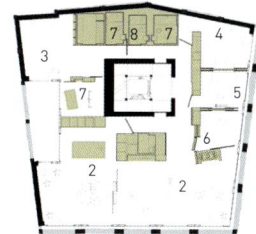

Fifth floor plan

1. Living room
2. Kitchen
3. Master bedroom
4. Bedroom 2
5. Bedroom 3
6. Study
7. Ensuite
8. Bathroom

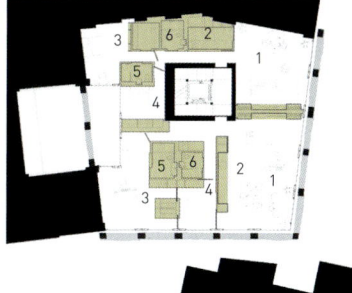

Second floor plan

1. Living room
2. Kitchen
3. Master bedroom
4. Bedroom 2
5. Ensuite
6. Bathroom

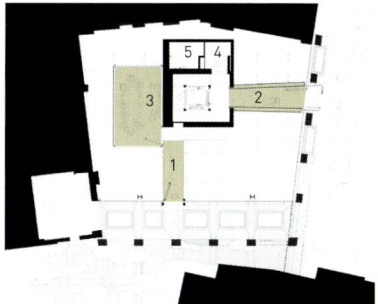

Ground floor plan

1. Office bridge
2. Residential bridge
3. Meeting box
4. Concierge
5. Accesible WC

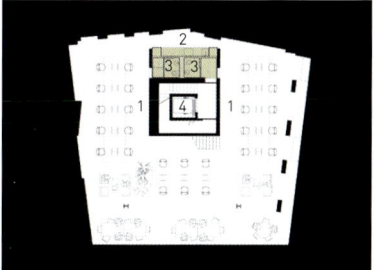

Lower ground floor

1. Office
2. Kitchen
3. WC
4. Lift

Barretts Grove is located in Stoke Newington and accommodates six flats on a small brown-field garage workshop site. Set between a Victorian terrace and Edwardian redbrick school it echoes the tall gables of the school and standalone 'villa' architype of the Victorian terrace. Built from cross laminated timber the structure is left exposed internally allowing its material finish to drive the character of the architecture, with the exterior using brick as an expressed nonstructural but protective perforated screen. Large wicker screened balconies are offset in elevation to allow residents to communicate with neighbours above and below.

In einer typisch viktorianischen Straße mit gemauerten Stadthäusern gelegen, erinnert die äußere Zusammensetzung dieses 6er-Wohnhauses an die beiden umliegenden Gebäude. Ein perforiertes rotes Ziegelsieb bedeckt die gesamte Baugruppe, einschließlich des Daches, und drückt seinen schützenden, aber nicht strukturellen Charakter aus. Das Raster der großen Öffnungen an den Fassaden unterstreicht die Stärke der Form trotz ihrer Schlankheit. Die langen Balkone aus Weidengeflecht, die von den Öffnungen zur Straße hängen, sind abwechselnd angeordnet und schaffen Raum für soziale Beziehungen zwischen Nachbarn verschiedener Stockwerke. Der kreuzweise Holzaufbau mit sichtbaren Arbeitsfugen, mit denen das Gebäude errichtet wurde, bleibt im Inneren offen und ist auch in den Details im häuslichen Bereich präsent, was den Charakter der Architektur unterstreicht.

BARRETTS GROVE
LONDON, UNITED KINGDOM

Situé sur une rue victorienne typique de maisons de ville en briques, la composition extérieure de cet immeuble de 6 appartements fait écho aux deux bâtiments qui l'entourent. Un écran de brique rouge perforé recouvre l'ensemble, y compris le toit, exprimant sa nature protectrice, mais non structurelle. La grille de grandes ouvertures sur les façades souligne la force de la forme malgré sa finesse. Les longs balcons en osier qui s'accrochent aux ouvertures de la rue créent alternativement un espace de relations sociales entre les voisins des différents étages. La superstructure en bois lamellé-collé avec des joints de construction visibles uti-lisée pour ériger le bâtiment est exposée à l'intérieur et est également présente dans les détails à l'échelle domestique, renforçant ainsi le caractère de l'architecture.

Situado en una típica calle victoriana de casas adosadas de ladrillo, la composición exterior de este edificio de 6 apartamentos se hace eco de las dos edificaciones que lo rodean. Una pantalla perforada de ladrillo rojo recubre todo el conjunto, incluida la cubierta, expresando su naturaleza protectora pero no estructural. La retícula de grandes aberturas de las facha-das subraya la fortaleza de la forma a pesar de su esbeltez. Los largos balcones de malla de mimbre que cuelgan de las aberturas a la calle se disponen de forma alterna creando un espacio de relación social entre los vecinos de diferentes plantas. La superestructura de ma-dera laminada cruzada con juntas de construcción visibles utilizada para levantar el edificio se deja expuesta en el interior y se hace presente también en los detalles a escala doméstica, impulsando el carácter de la arquitectura.

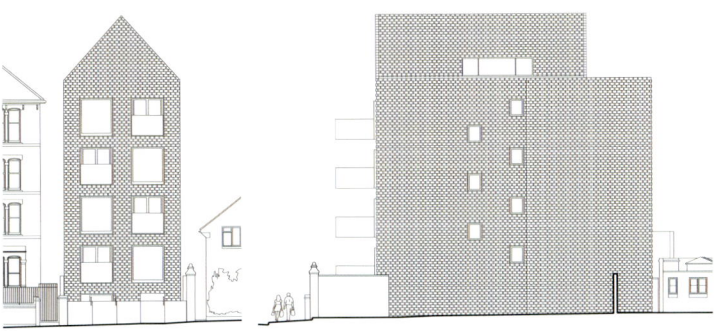

Elevations

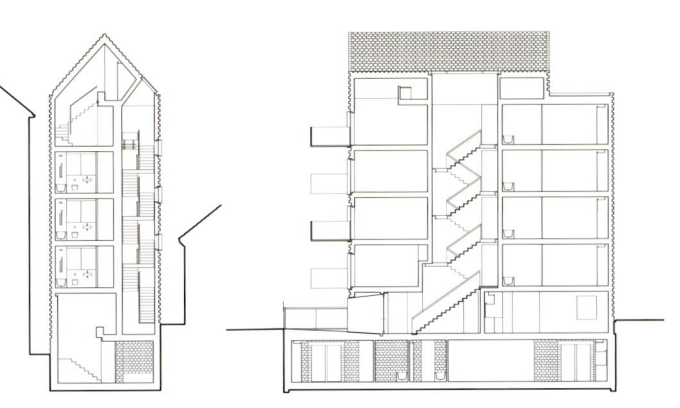

Elevations

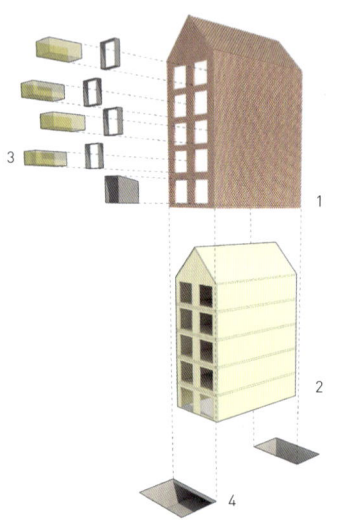

1. Perforated brick cladding
2. Cross laminated timber structure
3. Wicker balconies
4. Light wells

Exploded axonometry

Basement plan. Unit 1

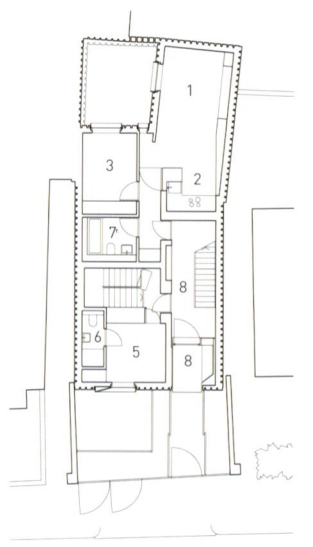

Ground floor plan. Unit 1 / 2

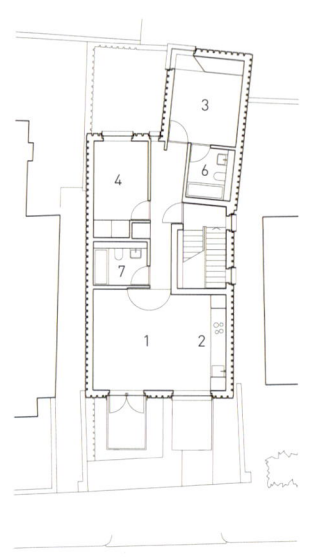

First floor plan. Unit 3

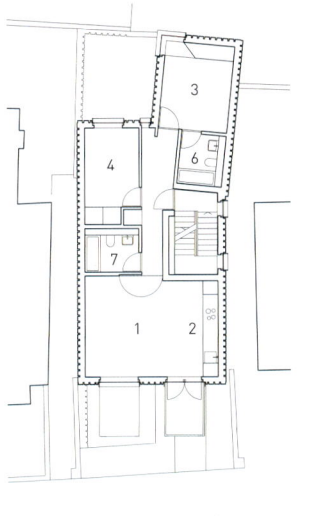

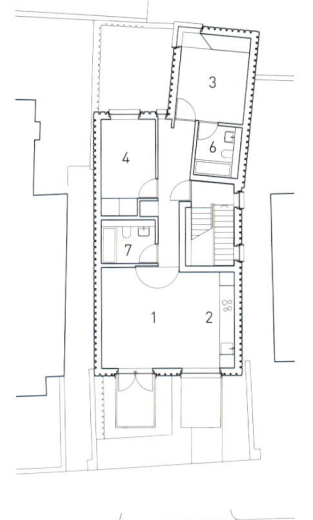

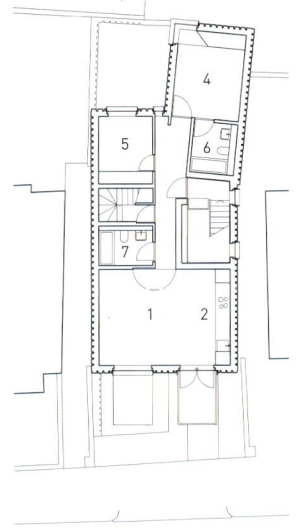

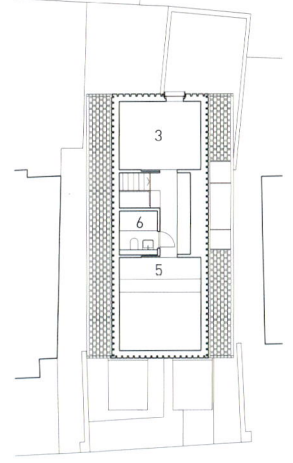

Second floor plan. Unit 4

Third floor plan. Unit 5

Fourth floor main plan. Unit 6

Fourth floor mezzanine plan.
Unit 6

1. Living room
2. Kitchen
3. Master bedroom
4. Bedroom 2
5. Bedroom 3 / study
6. En suite
7. Bathroom
8. Entry lobby

JORGE HERNÁNDEZ DE LA GARZA

www.hernandezdelagarza.com

Graduated from Universidad La Salle de Mexico. In 1999 he won the Architectonic Composition Award Ing. Alberto J. Pani. In 2002 Studied Design at AA The Architectural Association in London, England. In 2005 is finalist of the Icons of Design Awards with Los Amates house. In autumn of 2006 wins the Icons of Design Awards with the project of Vladimir Kaspe Cultural Centre, and also this year is finalist of the Interior Design Award with the project Showroom Comex. In 2007 was selected as one of the 44 international firms for the Young Architects Annual Event in Spain. In this same year was part of the 101 Most Exciting New Architects In Wallpaper London. In 2008 The College of Architecture of Mexico City gives him the first mention of Young Architects under 40 years old. His works have been published in Tokyo, England, Spain, Portugal, Brazil, Korea, Ukraine, Russia, Argentina, Italy, Germany and México.

Jorge Hernandez de la Garza ist Absolvent der La Salle University in Mexiko. 1999 erhielt er den Preis für Architekturkomposition Ing. Alberto J. Pani. Er studierte Design an der AA The Architectural Association in London. Im Jahr 2005 ist er Finalist des Icons of Design Award mit Casa Los Amates. Im Jahr 2006 gewann er den Icons of Design Award für das Projekt des Vladimir Kaspé Cultural Center und ist Finalist des National Interior Design Award für den Comex Showroom. Im Jahr 2007 wurde er als eines von 44 internationalen Büros für das Young Architects Annual Event in Spanien und als einer der 101 erfolgreichsten Young Architects in Wallpaper London ausgewählt. Im Jahr 2008 verlieh ihm das College of Architects of Mexico die erste Auszeichnung Young Architects under 40 years old. Im Jahr 2015 erhält er mit dem Amsterdamer Gebäude den Cemex-Preis. Seine Werke wurden in Japan, England, Spanien, Deutschland, Portugal, Brasilien, Korea, der Ukraine, Russland, Argentinien, Italien, Deutschland und Mexiko veröffentlicht.

Jorge Hernandez de la Garza est diplômé de l'Université La Salle au Mexique. En 1999, il a remporté le prix de composition architecturale Ing. Alberto J. Pani. Il a étudié le design à AA The Architectural Association à Londres. En 2005, il est finaliste du prix Icons of Design Award avec Casa Los Amates. En 2006, il a remporté le prix Icons of Design Award pour le projet du Centre culturel Vladimir Kaspé et été finaliste au National Interior Design Award pour le Comex Showroom. En 2007, il a été sélectionné comme l'un des 44 cabinets internationaux pour l'événement annuel des jeunes architectes en Espagne et comme l'un des 101 jeunes architectes les plus performants de Wallpaper London. En 2008, le Collège des Architectes du Mexique lui a décerné la première mention Jeune Architecte de moins de 40 ans. En 2015, il remporte le prix Cemex avec le bâtiment d'Amsterdam. Ses œuvres ont été publiées au Japon, en Angleterre, en Espagne, en Allemagne, au Portugal, au Brésil, en Corée, en Ukraine, en Russie, en Argentine, en Italie, en Allemagne et au Mexique.

Jorge Hernández de la Garza es graduado por la Universidad La Salle de México. En 1999 gana el premio a la composición arquitectónica Ing. Alberto J. Pani. Cursa estudios de Diseño en AA The Architectural Association en Londres. En el 2005 es finalista del Premio Iconos del Diseño con la Casa Los Amates. En el 2006 gana el Premio Iconos del Diseño por el proyecto del Centro Cultural Vladimir Kaspé y es finalista en el Premio Nacional de Interiorismo por el Showroom Comex. En el 2007 es seleccionado como una de las 44 firmas internacionales para El Young Architects Annual Event en España y como parte de los 101 Arquitectos Jóvenes más exitosos en Wallpaper Londres. En el 2008 el colegio de arquitectos de México le otorga la primera mención Jóvenes Arquitectos menores de 40 años. En el 2015 Gana el Premio Cemex con el Edificio Amsterdam. Sus obras han sido publicadas en Japón, Inglaterra, España, Alemania, Portugal, Brasil, Corea, Ucrania, Rusia, Argentina, Italia, Alemania y México.

Design team:
Alin Gamboa, Miguel Angel Loyola,
Octavio Alvarado,
Isabel Hernández

Real state development:
Grupo Desarrollador FG2

Structural design:
Miguel Angel Arriaga

Engineering: Mauricio Gutierrez

Photo credits:
© Jorge Hernández de la Garza

AMSTERDAM 75

Amsterdam 75 is located in the Colonia Hipódromo in Mexico City in a rectangular area where the intervention consisted of resolving 5 apartments of different types and an additional house which is inside an old house catalogued by the National Institute of Fine Arts.

The architectural program was resolved in two large volumes in the form of concrete boxes which are oriented towards the tree-lined avenue, managing to frame the best views towards the immediate context.

A penthouse is located in the last two levels and has a double height that articulates the public spaces of the house in its two floors.

At the back of the property, the building is tucked into its western façade with terraces that generate solar protection and take advantage of the views towards the Parque España

Amsterdam 75 befindet sich in der Colonia Hipódromo in Mexiko City in einem rechteckigen Gebiet, in dem die Intervention bestand 5 verschiedene Sektionen und ein zusätzliches Haus, das sich in einem alten Haus befindet, das vom National Institute of Fine Arts katalogisiert wurde, zu lösen.

Das Architekturprogramm wurde in zwei großen Volumen in Form von scheinbaren Betonboxen gelöst, die sich an der von Bäumen gesäumten Allee orientieren und so die besten Blicke auf den unmittelbaren Kontext ermöglichen.

Ein Dachgeschoss befindet sich in den letzten beiden Stockwerken und hat eine doppelte Höhe, die die öffentlichen Räume des Hauses artikuliert.

Auf der Rückseite des Grundstücks befindet sich die Westfassade des Gebäudes, mit Terrassen, die Sonnenschutz bieten und den Blick auf den España-Park nutzen.

AMSTERDAM 75
HIPÓDROMO, MÉXICO D.F

Amsterdam 75 est situé dans la Colonia Hipódromo à Mexico dans une zone rectangulaire où l'intervention a consisté à résoudre 5 départements de différents types, et une maison supplémentaire qui est à l'intérieur d'une ancienne maison cataloguée par l'Institut National des Beaux Arts.

Le programme architectural a été résolu en deux grands volumes sous la forme de boîtes apparentes en béton orientées vers l'avenue bordée d'arbres, ce qui a permis d'encadrer les meilleures vues vers le contexte immédiat.

Un grenier est situé sur les deux derniers étages et a une double hauteur qui articule les espaces publics de la maison.

A l'arrière de la propriété, le bâtiment est encastré dans sa façade ouest avec des terrasses qui génèrent une protection solaire et profitent de la vue sur le Parque España.

Ámsterdam 75 está ubicado en la Colonia Hipódromo de la Ciudad de México en un terreno rectangular en donde la intervención consistió en resolver 5 departamentos de diferentes tipologías y una vivienda adicional la cual se encuentra en el interior de una antigua casa catalogada por el Instituto Nacional de Bellas Artes.

El programa arquitectónico se resolvió en dos grandes volúmenes a manera de cajas de concreto aparente las cuales están orientadas hacia la avenida arbolada logrando así enmarcar las mejores vistas hacia el contexto inmediato.

Un penthouse se encuentra en los dos últimos niveles y cuenta con una doble altura que articula los espacios públicos de la vivienda en sus dos niveles.

En la parte posterior del predio el edificio se remete en su fachada poniente con terrazas que generan protección solar y que aprovechan las vistas hacia el parque España.

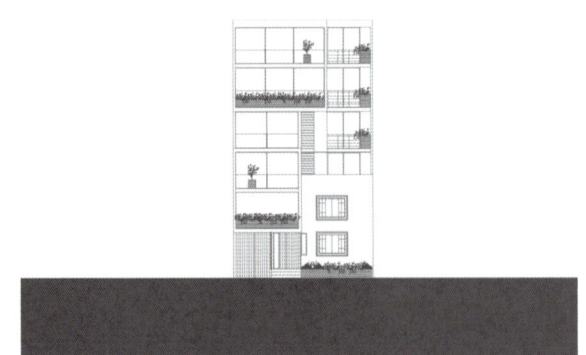

Front elevation

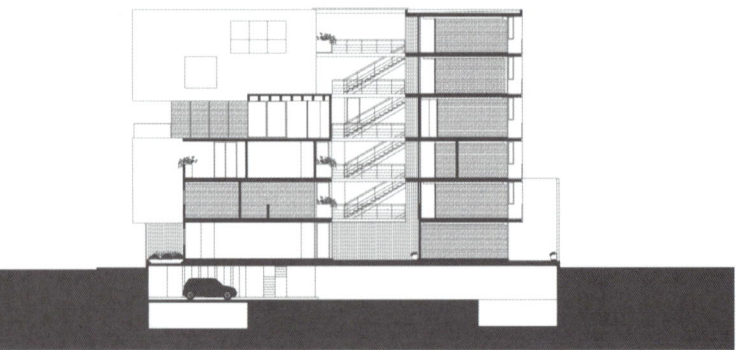

Longitudinal section

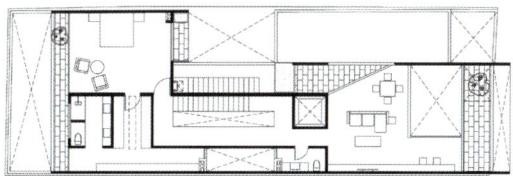

Sixth floor plan

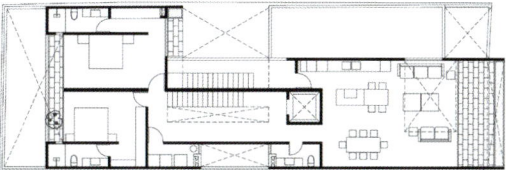

Fifth floor plan

Fourth floor plan

Third floor plan

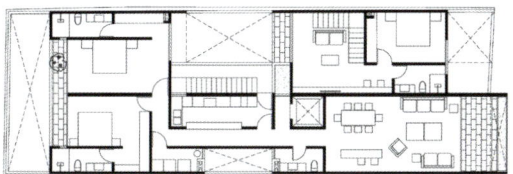

Second floor plan

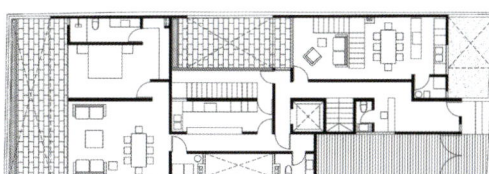

Ground floor plan

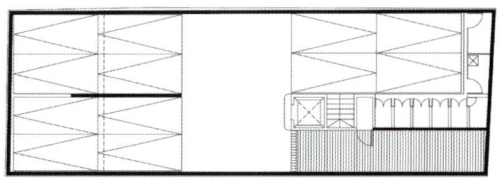

Parking plan

LEPPANEN ANKER
ARQUITECTURA

leppanenanker.com

Leppanen Anker was founded in 2012 by Aaron Leppanen and Gabriela Anker. The studio has experience in residential, commercial, cultural, educational and health care projects in both the public and private sectors. Leppanen Anker specializes in creating architectural spaces that consider the needs of their clients under their economic, environmental, cultural and contextual influences. Their work is based on a parametric digital design process that allows multiple solutions to predetermined problems and improves the efficiency of the design and construction process. The integration of digital technology with manual techniques of local work has resulted in sculptural projects that drive the advancement of possibilities in terms of construction in the country. The inspiration for their designs comes mainly from nature and the local environment, always seeking maximum energy efficiency.

Leppanen Anker wurde 2012 von Aaron Leppanen und Gabriela Anker gegründet. Das Unternehmen verfügt über Erfahrung in Projekten im Bereich Wohnen, Gewerbe, Kultur, Bildung und Gesundheitswesen im öffentlichen und privaten Sektor. Leppanen Anker ist spezialisiert auf die Schaffung von architektonischen Räumen, die die Bedürfnisse ihrer Kunden unter wirtschaftlichen, ökologischen, kulturellen und kontextuellen Einflüssen berücksichtigen. Seine Arbeit basiert auf einem parametrischen digitalen Entwurfsprozess, der mehrere Lösungen für vorgegebene Probleme ermöglicht und die Effizienz des Entwurfs- und Konstruktionsprozesses verbessert. Die Integration der digitalen Technologie in die manuellen Techniken regionaler Arbeit hat zu skulpturalen Projekten geführt, die wiederum die Weiterentwicklung der Baumöglichkeiten im Land vorantreiben. Die Inspiration für seine Entwürfe kommt vor allem aus der Natur und der lokalen Umgebung, immer auf der Suche nach maximaler Energieeffizienz.

Leppanen Anker a été fondé en 2012 par Aaron Leppanen et Gabriela Anker. Le cabinet possède de l'expérience dans des projets résidentiels, commerciaux, culturels, éducatifs et de soins de santé dans les secteurs public et privé. Leppanen Anker se spécialise dans la création d'espaces architecturaux qui tiennent compte des besoins de leurs clients, sous leurs influences économiques, environnementales, culturelles et contextuelles. Son travail est basé sur un processus de conception numérique paramétrique qui permet des solutions multiples à des problèmes prédéterminés, et améliore l'efficacité du processus de conception et de construction. L'intégration de la technologie numérique avec les techniques manuelles du travail local a donné lieu à des projets sculpturaux qui, à leur tour, conduisent à l'avancement des possibilités de construction dans le pays. L'inspiration pour ses créations vient principalement de la nature et de l'environnement local, toujours à la recherche d'une efficacité énergétique maximale.

Leppanen Anker fue fundada en el 2012 por Aaron Leppanen y Gabriela Anker. El estudio tiene experiencia en proyectos residenciales, comerciales, culturales, educativos y de atención médica, tanto en el sector público como en el privado. Leppanen Anker se especializa en la creación de espacios arquitectónicos que consideran las necesidades de sus clientes, bajo sus influencias económicas, ambientales, culturales y contextuales. Su trabajo se basa en un proceso de diseño digital paramétrico que permite dar soluciones múltiples a problemas predeterminados y mejora la eficiencia del proceso de diseño y construcción. La integración de la tecnología digital con técnicas manuales de trabajo local ha dado como resultado proyectos escultóricos que a su vez impulsan al avance de las posibilidades en cuanto a la construcción en el país. La inspiración para sus diseños proviene principalmente de la naturaleza y el entorno local, buscando siempre la máxima eficiencia energética.

Architects:
Leppanen Anker Arquitectura,
Uribe & Schwarzkopf

Interior design:
Uribe & Schwarzkopf

Developer, owner and builder:
Uribe & Schwarzkopf

Architectural team:
Uribe & Schwarzkopf,
Leppanen Anker Arquitectura

Design: April 2013

Work started: October 2014

Completion: October 2016

Height: 59 m

Surface: 15,000 m² (5 basements.
14 upper floors plus terrace)

Construction: Uribe &
Schwarzkopf, MIRACIELO S.A.

Photo credits:
© Bicubik Photo

Awards:
- 2018 German Design Awards,
  Winner
- 2017 Iconic Awards, Winner
- 2017 A' Design Awards,
  Gold winner
- 2017 Architizer A + Award,
  Special mention
- 2017 WAN Facade Awards,
  Finalist
- 2018 Council on Tall Buildings
  and Urban Habitat Awards,
  Finalist: Best Tall Building:
  Americas Region
- Archdaily's Building of the Year
  Awards 2018, Finalist

GAIA BUILDING

The Gaia building stands as a new landmark in the capital of Ecuador. Its 15 floors house shops, offices and homes on the 9 upper levels, and are crowned by a green roof visually connected to the Andes. Being the first new construction in the area, its design attempts to combine the various existing and new elements through a movement that generates a play of light and shadow. The deep perimeter balconies reduce solar gain inside and prevent large glass openings from damaging the passive and controlled climate of the rooms.
The façade consists of prefabricated GFRC panels, reusable and with an easy and efficient installation. Its construction process was based on a system of repetitive patterns that reduced the number of moulds used.

Das Gaia-Gebäude liegt an einem wichtigen Knotenpunkt der Stadt und ist ein neues Wahrzeichen der Hauptstadt Ecuadors. Auf 15 Stockwerken befinden sich Geschäfte, Büros und in den 9 Obergeschossen Wohnungen, gekrönt von einem grünen Dach, das optisch mit den Anden verbunden ist. Als erster Neubau in diesem Bereich versucht das Design, die verschiedenen vorhandenen und neuen Elemente durch eine Bewegung zu kombinieren, die ein Spiel von Licht und Schatten erzeugt. Tiefe Randbalkone reduzieren die Sonneneinstrahlung im Innenbereich und verhindern, dass große Glasöffnungen das passive kontrollierte Raumklima beeinträchtigen.
Die Fassade besteht aus vorgefertigten GFRC-Platten, die wiederverwendbar sowie einfach und effizient zu installieren sind. Der Konstruktionsprozess basiert auf einem System sich wiederholender Muster, das die Anzahl der verwendeten Formen reduziert.

GAIA BUILDING
QUITO, ECUADOR

Situé à un carrefour important de la ville, le bâtiment Gaia est un nouveau point de repère dans la capitale de l'Equateur. Ses 15 étages abritent des commerces, des bureaux et des logements sur les 9 niveaux supérieurs, et sont couronnés par un toit vert visuellement relié aux Andes. Etant la première nouvelle construction dans la région, sa conception tente de combiner les différents éléments existants et nouveaux à travers un mouvement qui génère un jeu d'ombre et de lumière. Les balcons périmétriques profonds réduisent le gain solaire intérieur et empêchent les grandes ouvertures vitrées d'endommager le climat passif et contrôlé des pièces.
La façade est constituée de panneaux préfabriqués en GFRC, réutilisables et faciles et efficaces à installer. Son processus de construction était basé sur un système de modèles répétitifs qui réduisait le nombre de moules utilisés.

Ubicado en una importante intersección de la ciudad, el edificio Gaia se erige como un nuevo hito de la capital de Ecuador. Sus 15 plantas albergan comercios, oficinas y viviendas en los 9 niveles superiores, y están coronadas por una cubierta verde conectada visualmente con los Andes. Al ser la primera construcción nueva de la zona, su diseño intenta combinar los diversos elementos existentes y nuevos a través de un movimiento que genera un juego de luces y sombras. Los profundos balcones perimetrales reducen la ganancia solar en el interior y evitan que las grandes aberturas de vidrio perjudiquen el clima pasivo y controlado de las estancias.
La fachada se compone de paneles prefabricados de GFRC, reutilizables y de instalación fácil y eficiente. Su proceso constructivo se basó en un sistema de patrones repetitivos que redujo la cantidad de moldes utilizados.

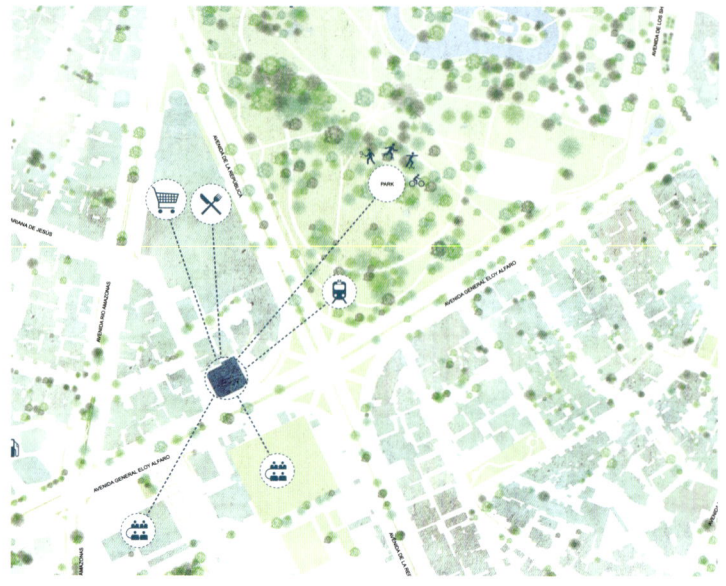

Site plan

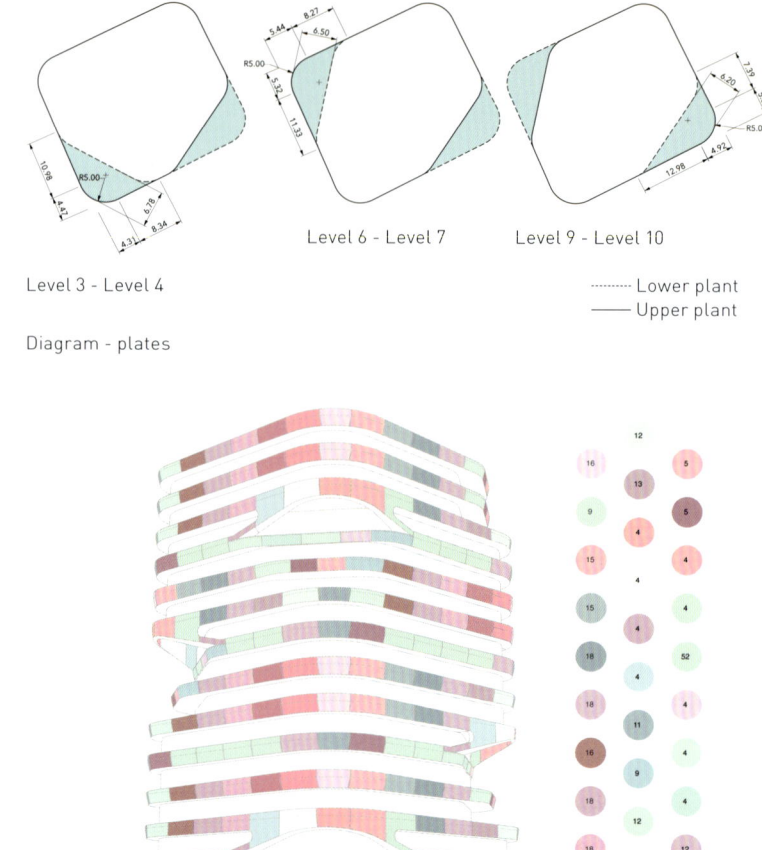

Diagram - plates

Level 3 - Level 4

Level 6 - Level 7

Level 9 - Level 10

···· Lower plant
—— Upper plant

Diagram - panels

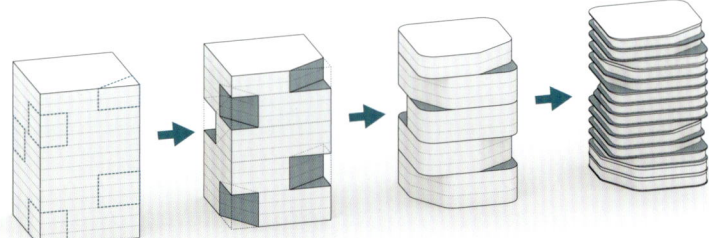

Concept diagram

Front elevation

Left elevation

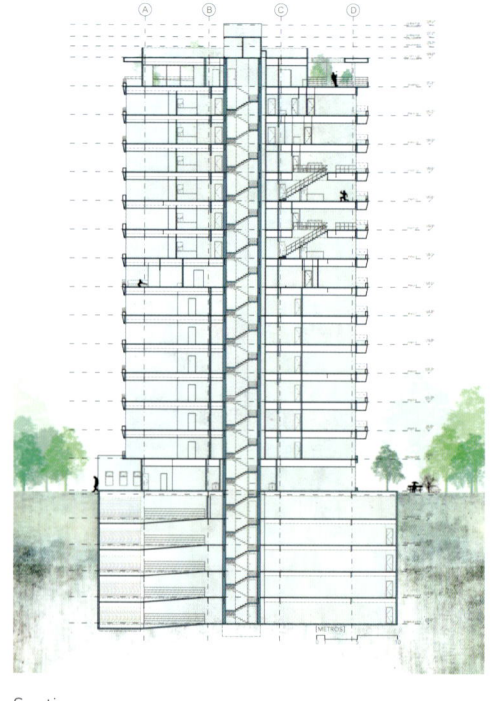

Section

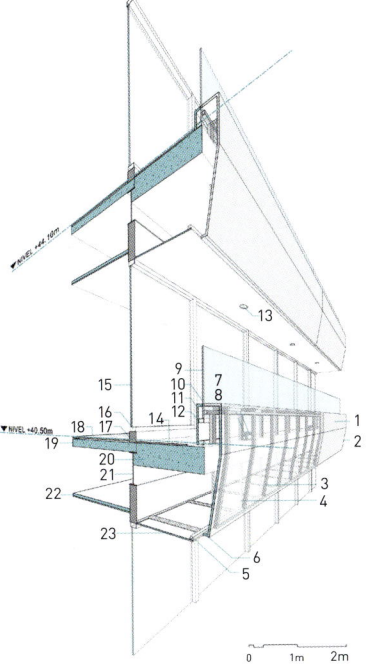

Construction detail

1. Prefabricated gfrc panel (glass fiber reinforced concrete)
2. Elastomeric sealant between grfc plates
3. Reinforcement ribs anchored in grfc profile metallic box 50 x 25 mm e = 2 mm
4. Ribbed rod cast into concrete slab
5. Metal drawer profile welded to ribbed rod for false ceiling support and bottom anchorage of gfrc panel.
6. Dripper
7. Gfrc panel anchorage metal box profile bolted to metal plate
8. Metal plate e=5mm bolted to reinforced concrete slab @ 2m
9. Tempered glass handrail e = 15 mm Anchored to metal perimeter structure and insulated with elastomeric sealant
10. Metallic perimetral profile of gfrc panel anchor bolted to metallic floor plate for flexible connection
11. Exterior gypsum paneling with a waterproofing finish
12. Metallic perimetral profile for dry paneling anchorage
13. Outdoor lighting
14. Finishing of exterior floor with fall to Sumidero
15. Tempered glass 8mm
16. Aluminium profile 40 x 100 mm
17. Kerb block 15cm with fall to outside
18. Interior floor finish
19. Slab with collaborating plate 15 cm
20. Reinforced concrete slab 20 cm
21. Loading beam type i 500 x 160 mm
22. Indoor gypsum panel
23. Exterior gypsum panel

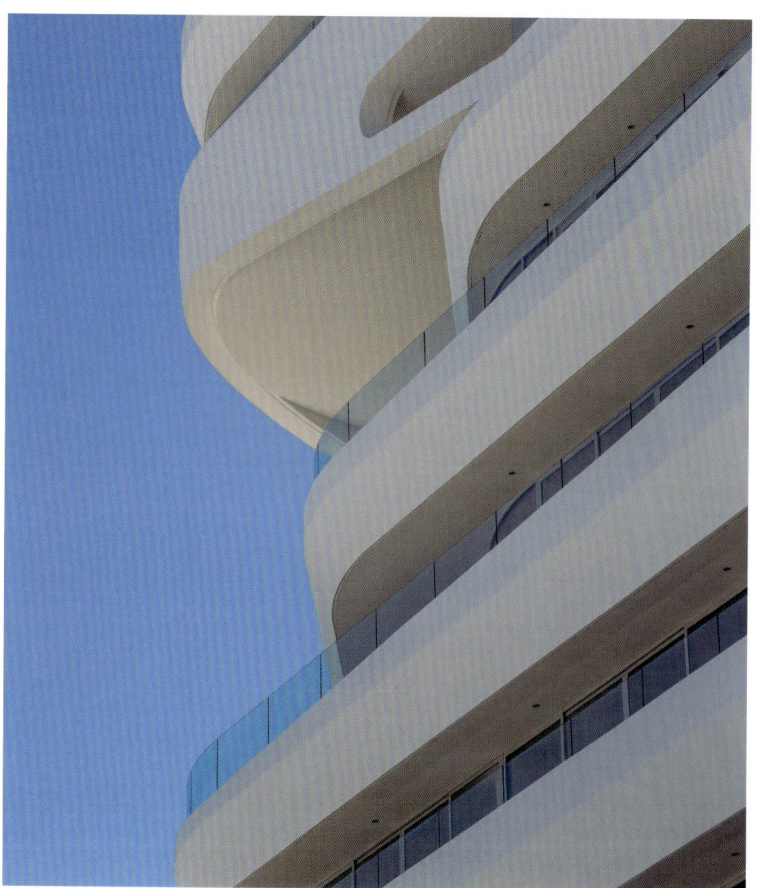

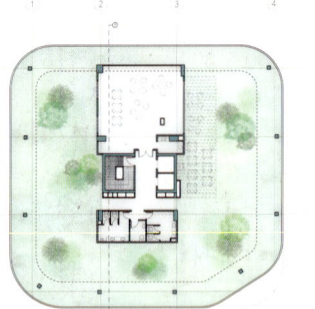

Roof plan

Typical residential floor

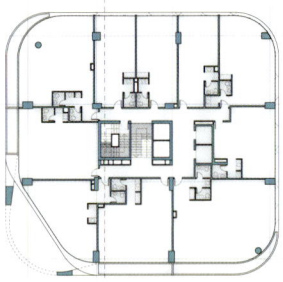

Typical office floor

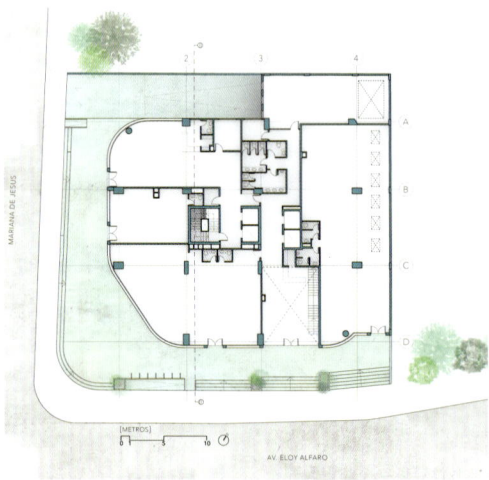

Ground floor

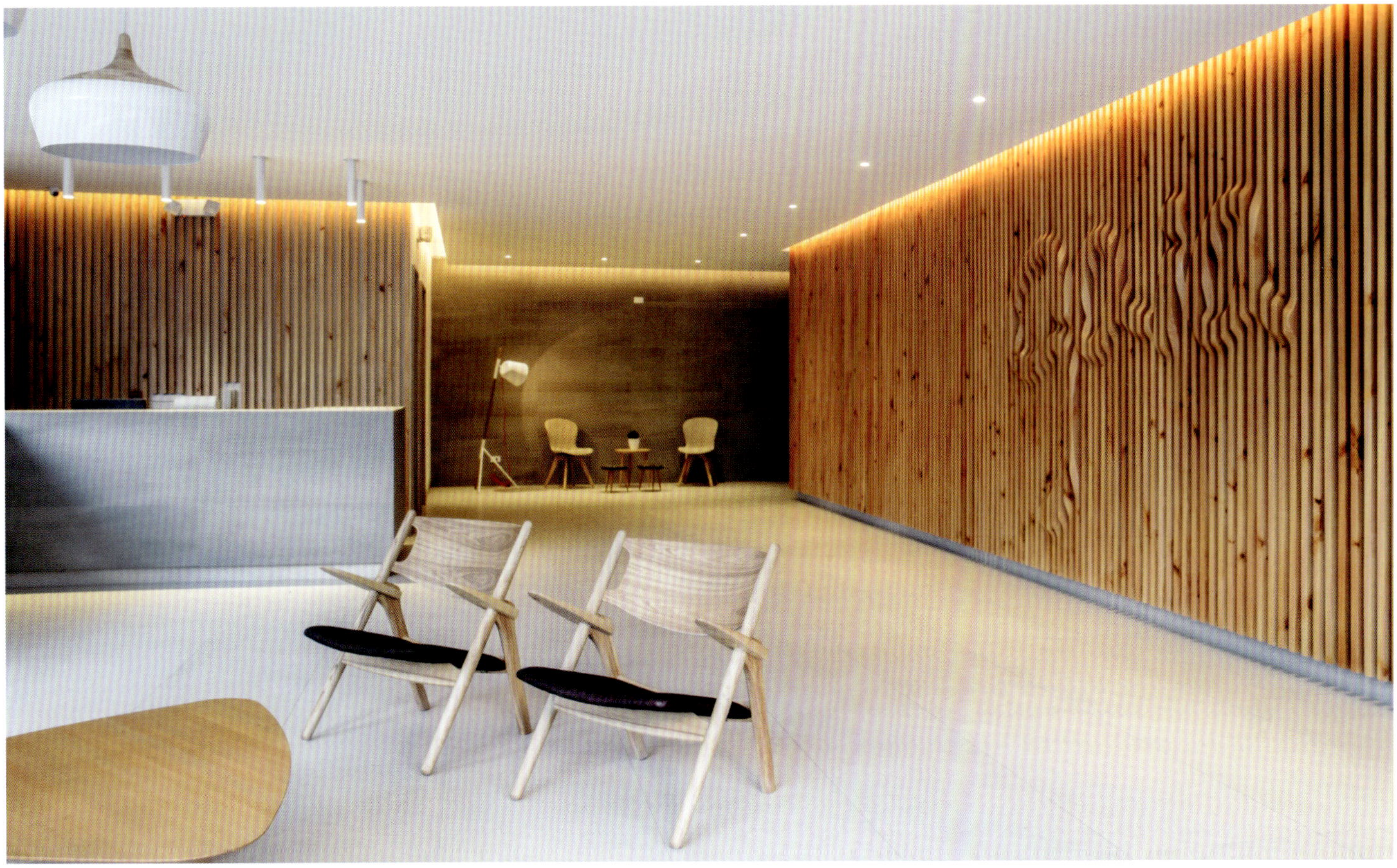

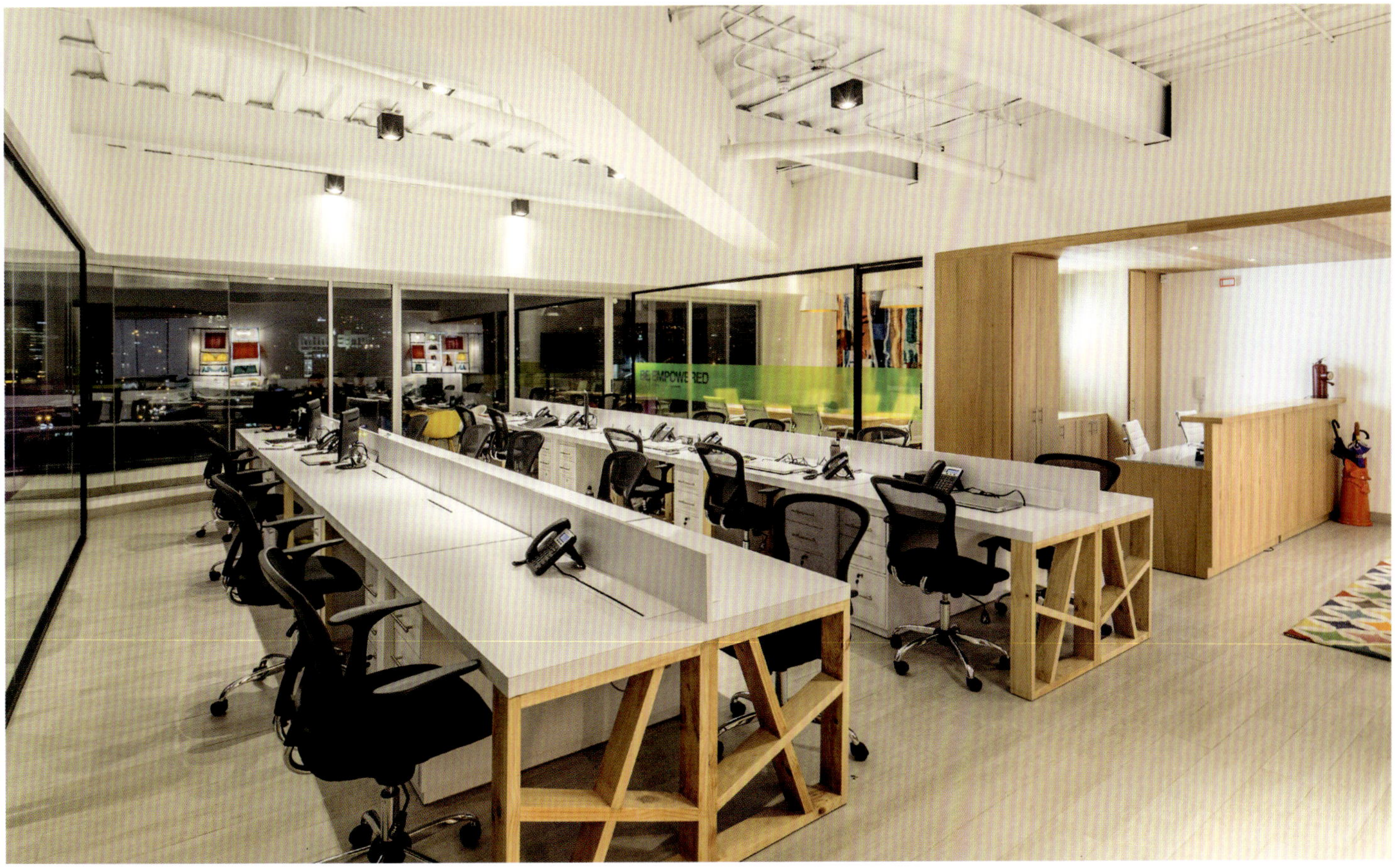
BE EMPOWERED

MAISON EDOUARD FRANÇOIS

www.edouardfrancois.com

Edouard François, a former student of the Ecole Nationale des Beaux-Arts de Paris and the Ecole Nationale des Ponts et Chaussées, created his own architecture, town planning, and design agency in 1998. In 2011, he was named Designer of the Year and the Royal Institute of British Architects elected him an honorary international member for his contribution to architecture. In 2012, the French Ministry of Culture and Communication awarded him the grade of Chevalier of the Order of Arts and Letters. His work on sustainable architecture led The Financial Times to dub him "The Hero of Green Architecture" in 2011.

In 2012, he gave new impetus to his agency, which became the Maison Edouard François. Comprising an international team of architects to whom he has passed on his philosophy and expertise, Maison Edouard François develops sustainable, unique, and innovative projects, all specifically established in relation to their geographic, economic, social, historical, and environmental context.

Edouard François, ehemaliger Schüler der Ecole Nationale des Beaux-Arts in Paris und der Ecole Nationale des Ponts et Chaussées, gründete 1998 seine eigene Architektur-, Städtebau- und Designagentur. Im Jahr 2011 wurde er zum Designer des Jahres gewählt und vom Royal Institute of British Architects als internationales Ehrenmitglied für seinen Beitrag zur Architektur ausgezeichnet. Im Jahr 2012 verlieh ihm das französische Ministerium für Kultur und Kommunikation den Rang eines Ritters des Ordens für Kunst und Literatur. Seine Arbeit an nachhaltiger Architektur führte dazu, dass die Financial Times ihn 2011 „The Hero of Green Architecture" nannte.

Im Jahr 2012 gab er seinem Atelier, das zum Maison Edouard François wurde, neue Impulse. Das Maison Edouard François, das von einem internationalen Architektenteam gebildet wird, dem es seine Philosophie und Erfahrung vermittelt hat, entwickelt nachhaltige, einzigartige und innovative Projekte, die alle speziell nach ihrem geographischen, wirtschaftlichen, sozialen, historischen und ökologischen Kontext erstellt wurden.

Edouard François, ancien élève de l'Ecole Nationale des Beaux-Arts de Paris et de l'Ecole Nationale des Ponts et Chaussées, a créé son propre bureau d'architecture, d'urbanisme et de design en 1998. En 2011, il a été nommé Designer of the Year et a été choisi par le Royal Institute of British Architects comme membre honoraire international pour sa contribution à l'architecture. En 2012, le Ministère de la Culture et de la Communication lui décerne le titre de Chevalier de l'Ordre des Arts et des Lettres. Son travail sur l'architecture durable a conduit le Financial Times à le surnommer « The Hero of Green Architecture » en 2011.

En 2012, il donne un nouvel élan à son atelier qui devient la Maison Edouard François. Formée d'une équipe internationale d'architectes à qui elle a transmis sa philosophie et son expérience, la Maison Edouard François développe des projets durables, uniques et innovants, tous spécifiquement établis en fonction de leur contexte géographique, économique, social, historique et environnemental.

Edouard François, antiguo alumno de la Ecole Nationale des Beaux-Arts de París y de la Ecole Nationale des Ponts et Chaussées, creó su propia agencia de arquitectura, urbanismo y diseño en 1998. En 2011 fue nombrado Diseñador del Año y el Royal Institute of British Architects lo eligió miembro honorario internacional por su contribución a la arquitectura. En 2012, el Ministerio de Cultura y Comunicación francés le otorgó el grado de Caballero de la Orden de las Artes y las Letras. Su trabajo sobre arquitectura sostenible llevó a The Financial Times a apodarlo «El Héroe de la Arquitectura Verde» en 2011.

En 2012, dio un nuevo impulso a su estudio, que se convirtió en la Maison Edouard François. Formada por un equipo internacional de arquitectos a los que ha transmitido su filosofía y su experiencia, Maison Edouard François desarrolla proyectos sostenibles, únicos e innovadores, todos ellos específicamente establecidos en función de su contexto geográfico, económico, social, histórico y medioambiental.

Program: Design and construction of four residential buildings (18, 8, 10, and 6 stories), nursery and retail.

Client: Paris Habitat DPOs

Team:
Maison Edouard François, base (landscape architect), École De Breuil (landscape architect), Arcoba, Arcadis (engineering)

Area: 13830 m² net floor area

Competition: 2010

Construction permit: 2012

Delivery: 2016

Photo credits:
© Pierre L'Excellent

TOWER OF BIODIVERSITY

One of the objectives of the project was to answer questions about the relationship between building height and sustainability. The main building of this complex is a tower covered with plants of wild natural areas. This tower is a sowing tool that allows the wind to spread seeds in the environment, thus regenerating urban biodiversity. The moiré patterns of its titanium cladding give it a subtle and fluctuating character and contribute to creating an image that distils a "green" aura to the Parisian urban landscape. The landscaping strategy is developed in three stages, corresponding to the three speeds of growth of the plants envisaged in the action. The vegetal façade extends towards the interior of the block, where the complex's set of buildings envelops a quiet and protected garden.

Eines der Ziele des Projekts war es, Fragen zum Zusammenhang zwischen Gebäudehöhe und Nachhaltigkeit zu beantworten. Das Hauptgebäude dieses Komplexes ist ein Turm, der mit Pflanzen aus wilden Naturgebieten bedeckt ist. Dieser Turm fungiert als Säwerkzeug, das es dem Wind ermöglicht, Saatgut in der Umwelt zu verbreiten und so die städtische Biodiversität zu regenerieren. Die Moiré-Muster der Titanverkleidung verleihen ihr einen subtilen und schwankenden Charakter und tragen dazu bei, ein Bild zu schaffen, das eine „grüne" Aura in die Pariser Stadtlandschaft destilliert. Die Strategie der Landschaftsgestaltung wird in drei Phasen entwickelt, die den drei Wachstumsgeschwindigkeiten der in der Aktion vorgesehenen Pflanzen entsprechen. Die vegetative Fassade erstreckt sich zum Inneren des Blocks, wo der Gebäudekomplex des Komplexes einen ruhigen und geschützten Garten umgibt.

TOWER OF BIODIVERSITY
PARIS, FRANCE

L'un des objectifs du projet était de répondre à des questions sur la relation entre la hauteur des bâtiments et la durabilité. Le bâtiment principal de ce complexe est une tour couverte de plantes d'espaces naturels sauvages. Cette tour est un outil de semis qui permet au vent de répandre des graines dans l'environnement, régénérant ainsi la biodiversité urbaine. Les motifs moirés de son revêtement en titane lui confèrent un caractère subtil et fluctuant et contribuent à créer une image qui distille une aura « verte » dans le paysage urbain parisien. La stratégie d'aménagement paysager se développe en trois étapes, correspondant aux trois vitesses de croissance des plantes envisagées dans l'action. La façade végétale s'étend vers l'intérieur de l'immeuble, où l'ensemble des bâtiments du complexe enveloppe un jardin calme et protégé.

Uno de los objetivos del proyecto fue responder a las dudas que suscita la relación entre la altura de los edificios y la sostenibilidad. El edificio principal de este complejo es una torre recubierta de plantas de áreas naturales silvestres. Esta torre se erige en una herramienta para sembrar que permite que el viento esparza semillas en el entorno, regenerando así la biodiversidad urbana. Los patrones de moiré de su revestimiento de titanio le dan un carácter sutil y fluctuante y contribuyen a crear una imagen que destila un áura «verde» al paisaje urbano parisino. La estrategia de paisajismo se desarrolla en tres etapas, correspondientes a las tres velocidades de crecimiento de las plantas previstas en la actuación. La fachada vegetal se prolonga hacia el interior de la manzana, donde el conjunto de edificios del complejo envuelven un jardín tranquilo y protegido.

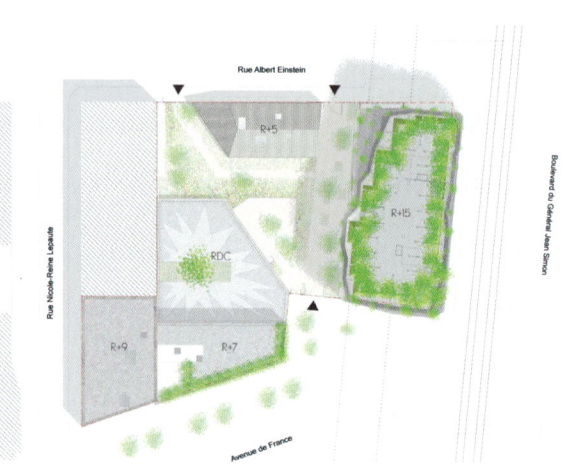

Site plan

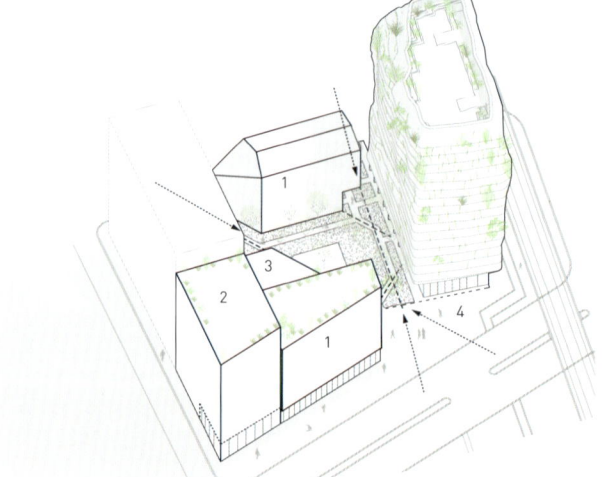

Axonometry with plants

1. Housing
2. Young worker's hostel
3. Crèche
4. Shopping area

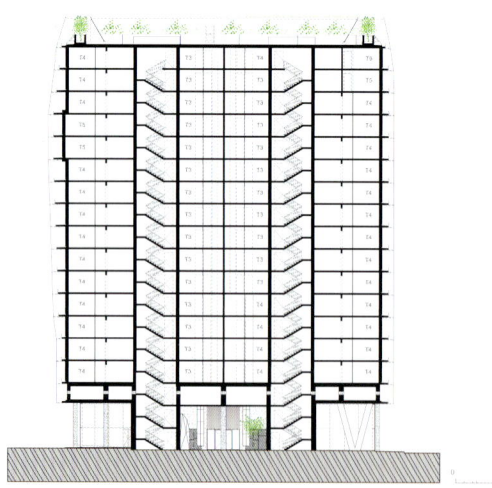

Longitudinal section

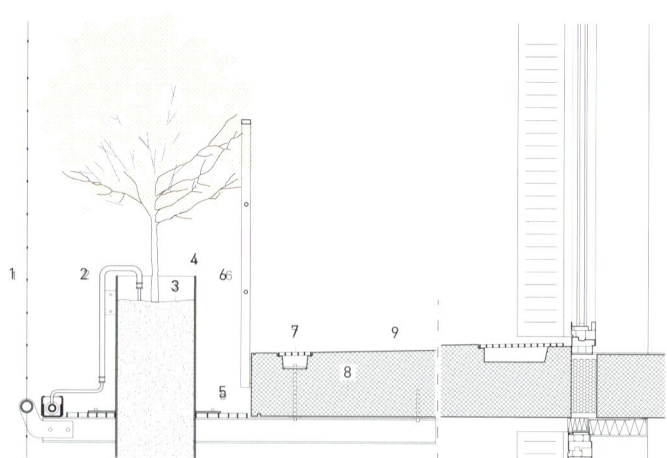

Construction detail

1. Stainless steel net
2. Watering system
4. Stainless steel tube
   Green support
3. Soil

5. Maintenance footbridge
6. Separating balustrade
7. Rainwater collection
8. Concrete balcony
9. Impermeability

Elevation

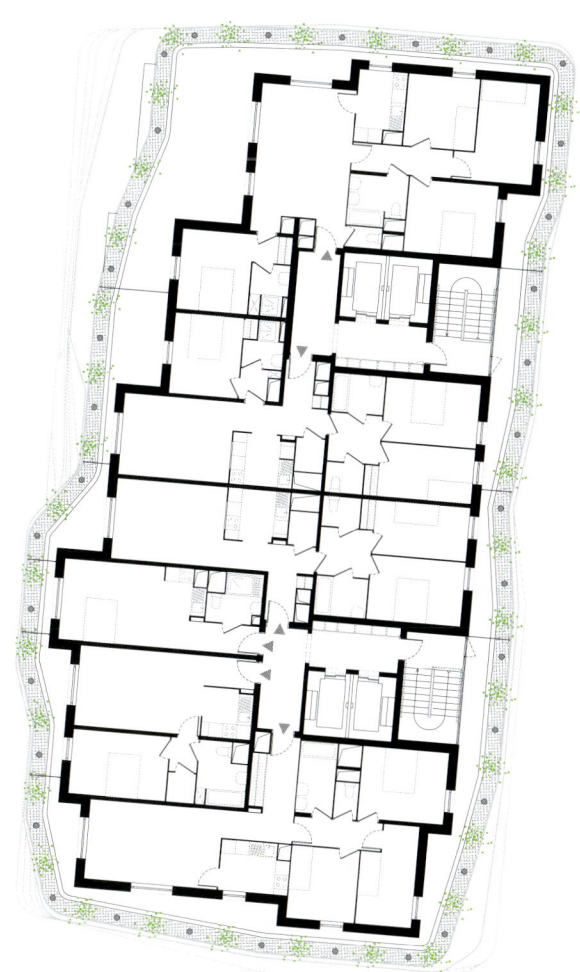

15 th floor plan

MCEA | ARQUITECTURA
NAOS ARQUITECTOS

www.manuelcostoya.com / www.naos.es / www.davidfrutos.com

MCEA Architecture is based in Murcia and began its activity in 2008. The studio is made up of a multidisciplinary team that develops Architecture and Urbanism projects of different scales and uses that range from single-family homes to large public facilities.

Manuel Costoya is an architect graduated by ETSA A Coruña since 2004, completing his training at the School of Architecture of La Villette (Paris) and the Higher Technical School of Architecture of the Polytechnic University of Madrid, where he has studied the Diploma of Advanced Studies.

The NAOS Architecture Studio is based in A Coruña and is directed by Santiago González García (director), Paula Costoya Carro, Mónica Fernández Garrido and Miguel Porras Gestido. Since 1991 it has been developing projects in both the public and private spheres, with the aim of offering unique and innovative proposals linked to the idea of environmental integration, quality and flexibility.

MCEA Architecture hat seinen Sitz in Murcia und begann seine Tätigkeit 2008. Das Studio besteht aus einem multidisziplinären Team, das Architektur- und Städtebauprojekte unterschiedlicher Größenordnungen entwickelt, die vom Einfamilienhaus bis hin zu großen öffentlichen Einrichtungen reichen.

Manuel Costoya ist seit 2004 bei ETSA A Coruña diplomierter Architekt und absolvierte seine Ausbildung an der School of Architecture von La Villette (Paris) und der Higher Technical School of Architecture der Polytechnischen Universität Madrid, wo er das Diploma of Advanced Studies absolvierte.

Das Architekturstudio NAOS hat seinen Hauptsitz in A Coruña und wird von Santiago González García (Direktor), Paula Costoya Carro, Mónica Fernández Garrido und Miguel Porras Gestido geleitet. Seit 1991 entwickelen sie Projekte im öffentlichen und privaten Bereich mit dem Ziel, einzigartige und innovative Vorschläge im Zusammenhang mit der Idee des Einbeziehens von Umweltaspekten, Qualität und Flexibilität anzubieten.

MCEA Architecture est basée à Murcie et a commencé son activité en 2008. Le studio est composé d'une équipe multidisciplinaire qui développe des projets d'architecture et d'urbanisme de différentes échelles, allant de la maison unifamiliale aux grands équipements publics.

Manuel Costoya est architecte diplômé de l'ETSA A Coruña depuis 2004, il a terminé sa formation à l'École d'architecture de La Villette (Paris) et à l'École technique supérieure d'architecture de l'Université polytechnique de Madrid, où il a étudié le diplôme d'études supérieures.

Le Studio d'Architecture NAOS a son siège à La Corogne et est dirigé par Santiago González García (directeur), Paula Costoya Carro, Mónica Fernández Garrido et Miguel Porras Gestido. Depuis 1991, il développe des projets tant dans le domaine public que privé, dans le but d'offrir des propositions uniques et innovantes liées à l'idée d'intégration environnementale, de qualité et de flexibilité.

MCEA | Arquitectura tiene su sede en Murcia y comienza su actividad en el año 2008. El estudio esá compuesto por un equipo multidisciplinar que desarrolla proyectos de Arquitectura y Urbanismo de distintas escalas y usos que incluyen desde viviendas unifamiliares hasta grandes equipamientos públicos.

Manuel Costoya es arquitecto titulado por la ETSA A Coruña desde el año 2004, completando su formación en la Escuela de Arquitectura de La Villette (París) y la Escuela Técnica Superior de Arquitectura de la Universidad Politécnica de Madrid, en la que ha cursado el Diploma de Estudios Avanzados.

El Estudio de Arquitectura NAOS tiene su sede en A Coruña y está dirigido por Santiago González García (director), Paula Costoya Carro, Mónica Fernández Garrido y Miguel Porras Gestido. Desde 1991 desarrolla proyectos tanto en el ámbito público como en el privado, con el objetivo de ofrecer propuestas singulares e innovadoras, vinculadas a la idea de integración ambiental, calidad y flexibilidad.

Architect: MCEA | ARCHITECTURE
NAOS 04 ARCHITECTS

Location: Avda. Juan Carlos I,
39-49. Lorca, Spain

Year: 2016

Built area (m²): 23.802 m²

Photo credits:
© David Frto Architecture
Photography

Construction:
DRAGADOS / TECOPSA

Awards:
- XIV Spanish Biennial of
  Architecture and Urbanism,
  selected work

- Best work of 2017 by ArchDaily,
  nomination

RECONSTRUCTION OF RESIDENCIAL SAN MATEO

The project is located in the old Residencial San Mateo, one of the most emblematic buildings of Lorca, demolished by the pathologies derived from the earthquake of May 11, 2011. Following the guidelines of the competition called for its reconstruction, the project maintains the central space open to the Avenida Juan Carlos I and a structure of ownership equal to that of the original building. The final result is the result of a participatory process that incorporated all the owners and was reflected in the final project, with 45 different types of housing. This process is also reflected in the façade by means of an ordered system of shutters in which the individual will modifies the general composition, thus obtaining an image of the building in permanent change and adapted at each moment to the individual needs.

Das Projekt befindet sich in der alten Residencial San Mateo, einem der emblematischsten Gebäude Lorcas, das durch die vom Erdbeben am 11. Mai 2011 verursachten Erschütterungen zerstört wurde. In Anlehnung an die Richtlinien des Wettbewerbs, der für die Rekonstruktion ausgeschrieben wurde, erhält das Projekt den zentralen Raum, der der Juan Carlos I Avenue offen steht, und eine eigentümliche Struktur, die der des ursprünglichen Gebäudes entspricht. Das Endergebnis ist das eines partizipativen Prozesses, der alle Eigentümer einbezog und sich im Endprojekt mit 45 verschiedenen Wohnformen widerspiegelte. Dieser Prozess spiegelt sich auch in der Fassade wider, indem ein geordnetes System von Fensterläden verwendet wird, in dem der Einzelne die allgemeine Zusammensetzung ändert und so ein Bild des Gebäudes in permanenter Veränderung erhält und zu jedem Zeitpunkt an die individuellen Bedürfnisse angepasst wird.

RECONSTRUCTION OF
RESIDENCIAL SAN MATEO
LORCA, ESPAÑA

Le projet est situé dans l'ancien Residencial San Mateo, l'un des bâtiments les plus emblématiques de Lorca, démoli par les pathologies dérivées du séisme du 11 mai 2011. Suivant les lignes directrices du concours demandé pour sa reconstruction, le projet maintient l'espace central ouvert sur l'avenue Juan Carlos I et une structure de propriété égale à celle du bâtiment d'origine. L'aboutissement est le résultat d'un processus participatif qui a intégré tous les propriétaires et a été reflété dans le projet final, avec 45 types de logements différents. Ce processus se reflète également dans la façade au moyen d'un système ordonné de volets dans lequel l'individu modifie la composition générale, obtenant ainsi une image du bâtiment en évolution permanente et adaptée à chaque instant aux besoins individuels.

El proyecto se sitúa en el ámbito del antiguo Residencial San Mateo, una de las edificaciones más emblemáticas de Lorca, demolida por las patologías derivadas del terremoto del 11 de mayo de 2011. Siguiendo las directrices del concurso convocado para su reconstrucción, el proyecto mantiene el espacio central abierto a la avenida Juan Carlos I y una estructura de la propiedad igual a la de la edificación original. El resultado final es fruto de un proceso participativo que incorporó a todos los propietarios y que se reflejó en el proyecto definitivo, con 45 tipologías diferentes de vivienda. Este proceso se refleja también en la fachada mediante un sistema ordenado de contraventanas en el que la voluntad individual modifica la composición general, obteniendo así una imagen de la edificación en permanente cambio y adaptada en cada momento a las necesidades individuales.

Site plan

Floor plans

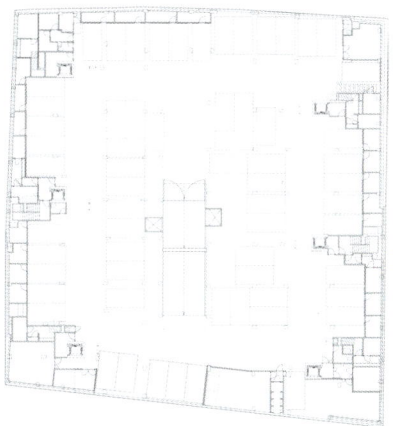

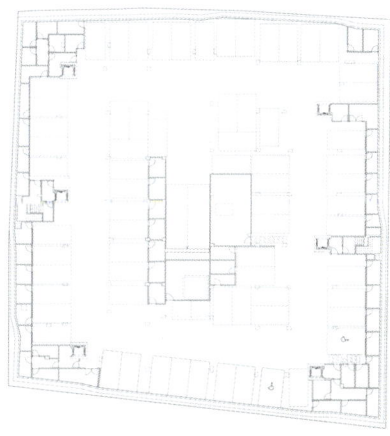

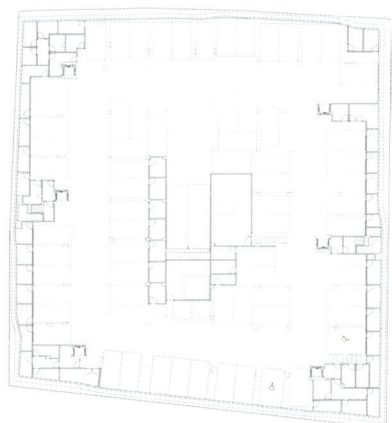

Floor plans

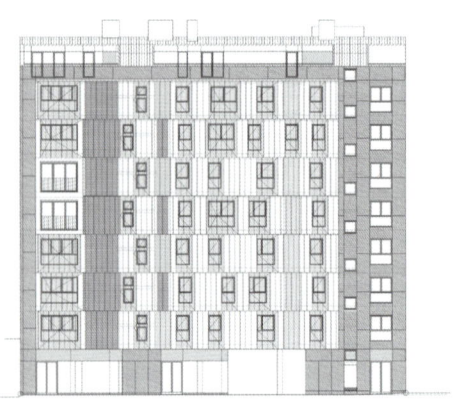

Elevations

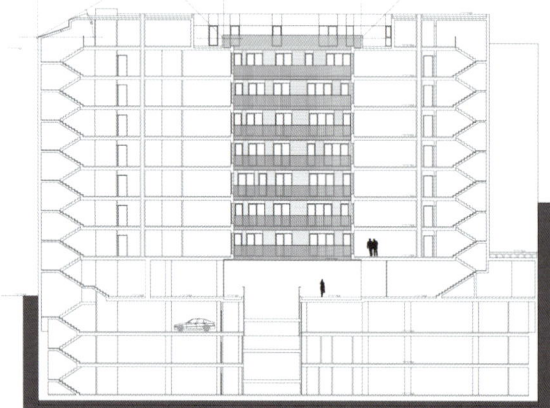

Transversal section

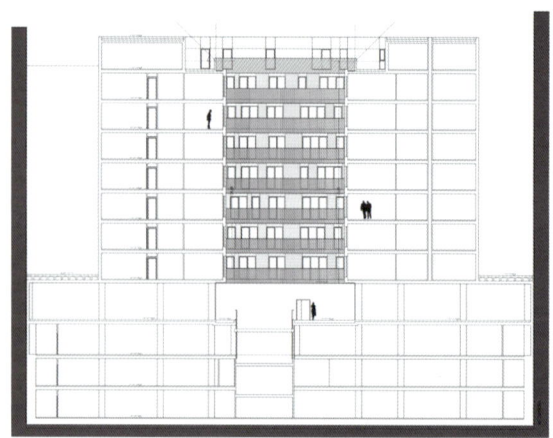

Transversal section

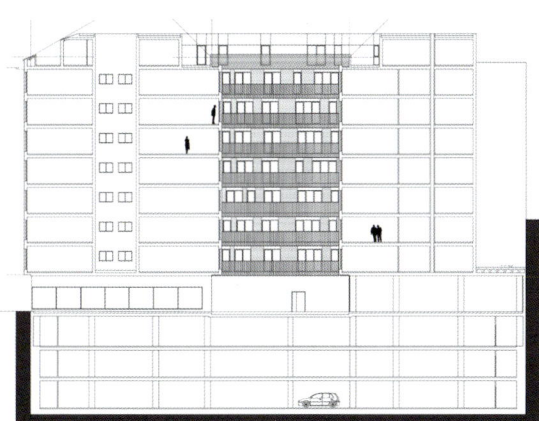

Transversal section

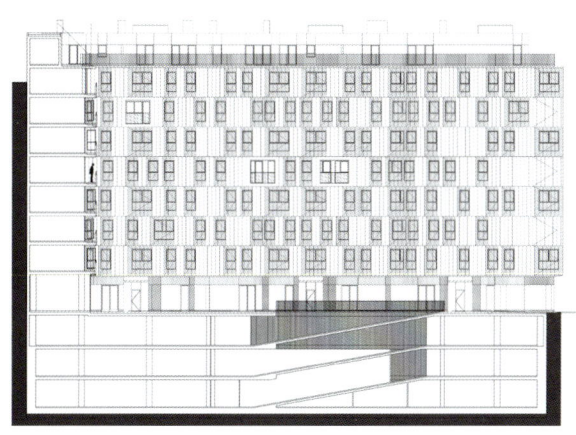

Longitudinal section

NERMA LINSBERGER

www.nermalinsberger.com

Vienna-based NERMA LINSBERGER ZTGMBH was founded in 2010. Inspired by a variety of global influences, the firm uses research and curiosity to innovate and create the best possible solutions. The approach is open-minded, analytical and pragmatic, leading to designs that have meaning and purpose but often go against the grain of conventionality. The result is buildings of outstanding quality, especially in the social housing sector. By thinking outside the box, the firm creates sustainable designs, as well as atmospheric environments for residents and the surrounding urban setting.

Nerma Linsberger, Arch.Mag.arch.
Born in Sarajevo, Bosnia and Herzegovina.
1993 - 1997 Study of architecture at Akademie of Fine Arts Vienna
Masterclass Prof.Timo Pentillä and Prof.Massimiliano Fuksas
2007 - 2010 ICNL Architektur with Innocad Architecure
2010 NERMA LINSBERGER ZTGMBH
2016 - 2018 Member of Quality Advisory Board Upper Austria
2017 Univerisity Lecturer at TU Vienna

NERMA LINSBERGER ZTGMBH mit Sitz in Wien wurde 2010 gegründet. Inspiriert von einer Vielzahl globaler Einflüsse, nutzt das Unternehmen Forschung und Neugierde, um Innovationen zu entwickeln und die besten Lösungen zu schaffen. Der Ansatz ist offen, analytisch und pragmatisch und führt zu Entwürfen, die Sinn und Zweck haben, aber oft im Widerspruch zur Konventionalität stehen. Das Ergebnis sind Gebäude von ausgezeichneter Qualität, insbesondere im Bereich des sozialen Wohnungsbaus. Das Unternehmen entwickelt nachhaltige Designs sowie Umgebungen für die Bewohner und die umliegende städtische Umwelt.

Nerma Linsberger, Arch.Mag.arch.
Geboren in Sarajevo, Bosnien und Herzegowina.
1993 - 1997 Studium der Architektur an der Akademie der Bildenden Künste in Wien
Meisterkurs Prof. Timo Pentillä und Prof. Massimiliano Fuksas
2007 - 2010 ICNL Architektur mit Innocad Architecure
2010 NERMA LINSBERGER ZTGMBMBH
2016 - 2018 Mitglied des Österreichischen Qualitätsbeirats
2017 Univ. Lektorin an der Technischen Universität Wien

NERMA LINSBERGER ZTGMBH, basée à Vienne, a été fondée en 2010. Inspirée par une variété d'influences mondiales, l'entreprise utilise la recherche et la curiosité pour innover et créer les meilleures solutions. L'approche est ouverte, analytique et pragmatique, et conduit à des conceptions qui ont un sens et un but, mais qui vont souvent à l'encontre des conventions. Il en résulte des bâtiments d'excellente qualité, notamment dans le secteur du logement social. L'entreprise crée des conceptions durables ainsi que des environnements pour les résidents et l'environnement urbain environnant.

Nerma Linsberger, Arch.Mag.arch.arch.
Né en à Sarajevo, Bosnie-Herzégovine.
1993 - 1997 Etudes d'architecture à l'Académie des Beaux-Arts de Vienne
Masterclass Prof.Timo Pentillä et Prof.Massimiliano Fuksas
2007 - 2010 ICNL Architektur avec Innocad Architecure
2010 NERMA LINSBERGER ZTGMBH
2016 - 2018 Membre du conseil consultatif autrichien de la qualité
2017 Professeur à l'Université Polytechnique de Vienne

NERMA LINSBERGER ZTGMBH, con sede en Viena, fue fundada en 2010. Inspirada por una variedad de influencias globales, la empresa utiliza la investigación y la curiosidad para innovar y crear las mejores soluciones. El enfoque es abierto, analítico y pragmático, y conduce a diseños que tienen sentido y propósito, pero que a menudo van en contra de la convencionalidad. El resultado son edificios de excelente calidad, especialmente en el sector de la vivienda social. La firma crea diseños sostenibles, así como ambientes para los residentes y el entorno urbano circundante.

Nerma Linsberger, Arch.Mag.arch.
Nacida en Sarajevo, Bosnia y Herzegovina.
1993 - 1997 Estudio de Arquitectura en la Academia de Bellas Artes de Viena
Masterclass Prof.Timo Pentillä y Prof.Massimiliano Fuksas
2007 - 2010 ICNL Architektur con Innocad Architecure
2010 NERMA LINSBERGER ZTGMBH
2016 - 2018 Miembro del Consejo Asesor de Calidad de Austria
2017 Profesor de la Universidad Politécnica de Viena

SAKURA

Type: social housing

Location: Vienna, Austria

Space: 12.500 m²

Start of construction: 2014

Completion: 2016

General contractor: Traunfellner

Photo credits:
© Thomas Hernerbichler,
© Andreas Buchberger,
© Daniel Hawelka

Awards:
- AAP American Architecture Prize 2016 (New York, USA) SAKURA Social Housing on Brünner Straße

- IDA Interantional Design Award 2016 (Los Angeles, USA) SAKURA Social Housing on Brünner Straße

- German Design Award 18 (Germany) - SAKURA Social Housing on Brünner Straße

- If Design Award 2018 (Hannover, Germany) - SAKURA Social Housing on Brünner Straße

MÜHLGRUND

Type: Social housing

Location: Vienna, Austria

Floor space: 11,000 m²

Status: On site

Year: 2011–2016

Photo credits:
© Thomas Hennerbichler,
© Daniel Hawelka

Awards
- Schorsch 2017 (Vienna) M GRUND Social Housing Mühlgrund

- Architizer A+ Award Finalist 2017 (New York, USA) – M GRUND Social Housing Mühgrund

- AAP American Architecture Prize 2017 (New York, USA) M GRUND Social Housing Mühlgrund

- Best architects 19 (Düsseldorf, Germany) - M grund Social Housing Mühlgrund

- German Design Award 2019 for M GRUND Social Housing Mühlgrund

- If Design Award 2019

The façade of this social housing complex reflects the link between the Viennese Florids-dorf district and the Katsushika district in Tokyo. Located precisely on Katsushikastraße, the building stands out for the large, stylised cherry blossoms, known in Japanese as sakura, unfolded in the metal veil that surrounds the whole. This pixelated sakura gives a glimpse of the daily activity of the inhabitants, offering a colourful and vivid image behind the silver-grey lacquered flowers. The ground plan of the building makes the most of the surface of the site by means of folds that create an interior courtyard and a 20-metre high atrium with impressive views of Katsushikastraße. This atrium, supported by expressive inclined columns, becomes a meeting place for neighbors to chat and gather.

Die Fassade dieses sozialen Wohnkomplexes spiegelt die Verbindung zwischen dem Wiener Stadtteil Floridsdorf und dem Stadtteil Katsushika in Tokio wider. Genau an der Katsushika-straße gelegen, zeichnet sich das Gebäude durch die großen stilisierten Kirschblüten aus, die im Japanischen als Sakura bekannt sind und sich im Metallschleier entfalten, der das Ensem-ble umgibt. Diese pixelige Sakura gibt einen Einblick in die tägliche Aktivität der Bewohner und bietet ein buntes und lebendiges Bild hinter den silbergrau lackierten Blumen. Der Grundriss des Gebäudes maximiert die Fläche des Geländes durch Linien, die einen Innenhof und ein 20 Meter hohes Atrium mit beeindruckendem Blick auf die Katsushikastraße bilden. Dieses Atrium, das von ausdrucksstarken geneigten Säulen getragen wird, wird zum Treffpunkt für die Nachbarn zum Treffen und Plaudern.

SAKURA
VIENNA, AUSTRIA

La façade de ce complexe de logements sociaux reflète le lien entre le quartier viennois de Floridsdorf et le quartier Katsushika à Tokyo. Situé précisément dans la Katsushikastraße, le bâtiment se distingue par de grandes fleurs de cerisier stylisées, connues en japonais sous le nom de sakura, dépliées dans le voile métallique qui entoure l'ensemble. Cette sakura pixélisée permet d'entrevoir l'activité quotidienne des habitants, offrant une image colorée et vivante derrière les fleurs laquées gris argent. Le plan du bâtiment maximise la surface du site grâce à des plis qui créent une cour intérieure et un atrium de 20 mètres de haut avec une vue impressionnante sur la Katsushikastraße. Cet atrium, soutenu par des colonnes inclinées expressives, devient un lieu de rencontre où les voisins peuvent discuter et se rencontrer.

La fachada de este conjunto de viviendas sociales es un reflejo de la vinculación del distri-to vienés de Floridsdorf con el distrito de Katsushika, en Tokio. Situado precisamente en la Katsushikastraße, el edificio llama la atención por las grandes y estilizadas flores de cerezo, llamadas en japonés sakura, desplegadas en el velo de metal que envuelve el conjunto. Esta sakura pixelada permite entrever la actividad cotidiana de los habitatantes, ofreciendo una imagen colorida y viva tras las flores lacadas de color gris plata. La forma en planta del edificio aprovecha al máximo la superficie del solar mediante pliegues que crean un patio interior y un atrio de 20 metros de altura con impresionantes vistas hacia la Katsushikastraße. Este atrio, sustentado por unas expresivas columnas inclinadas, se convierte en lugar de encuentro de los vecinos para charlar y reunirse.

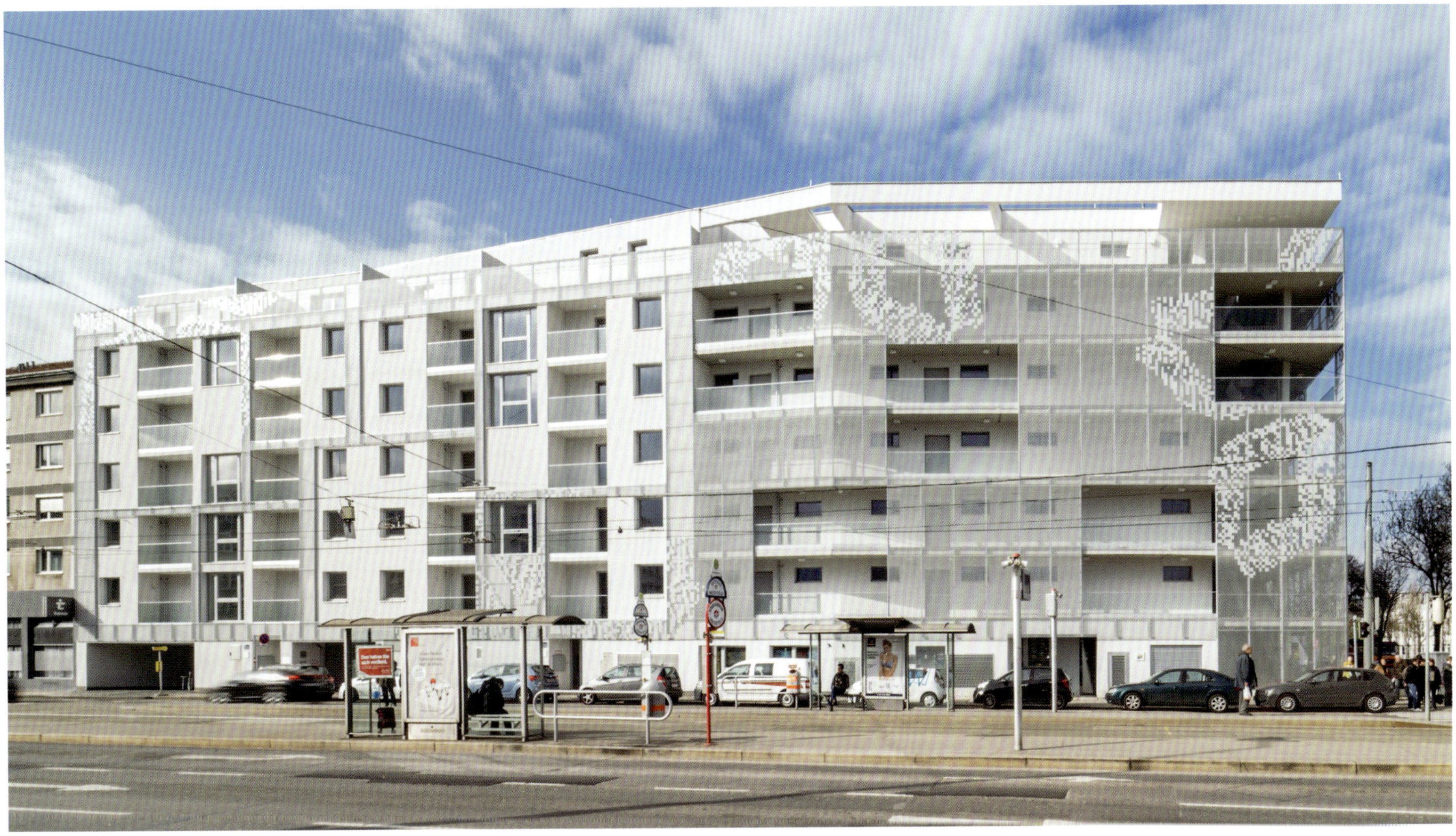

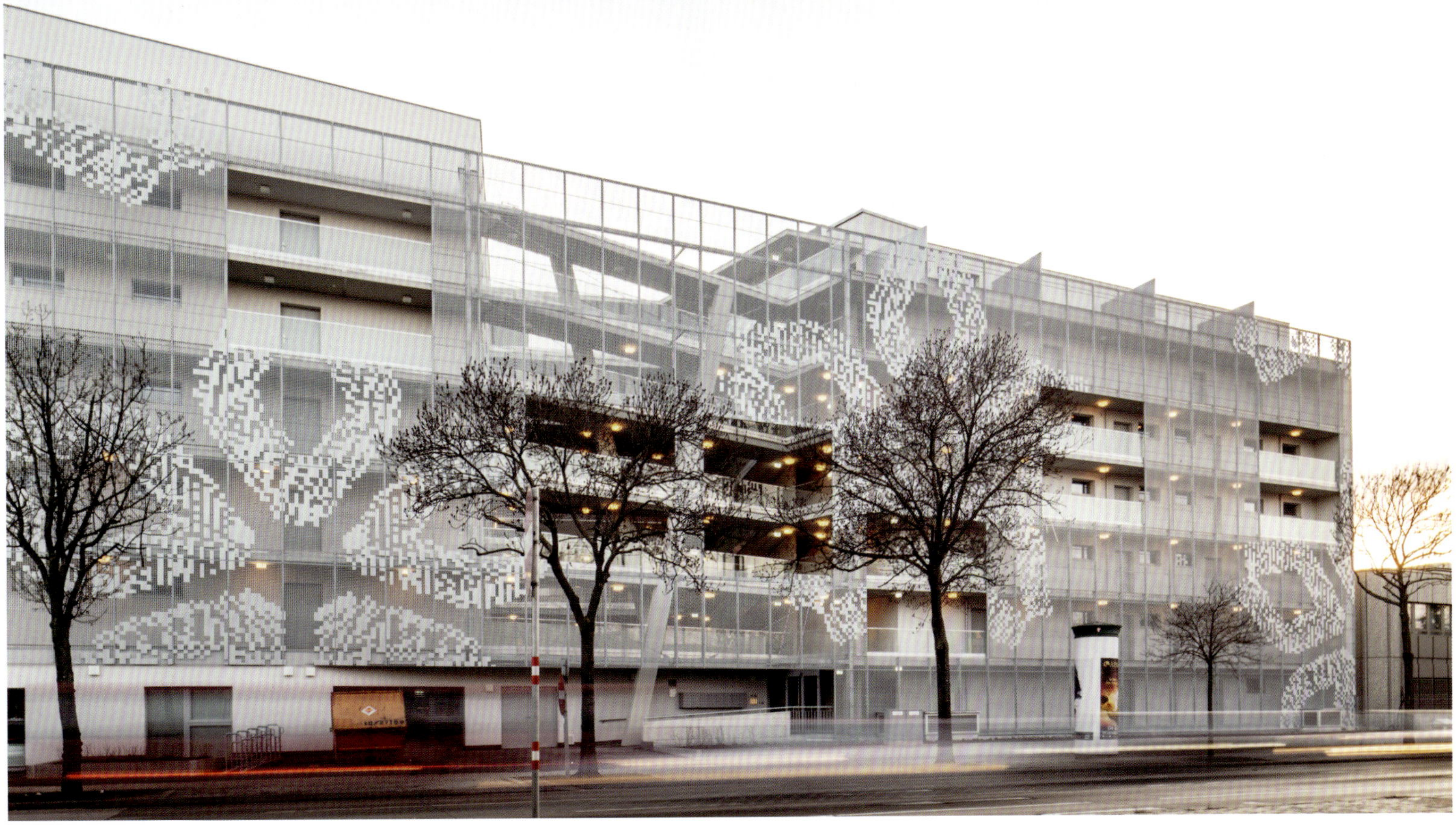

Attic floor plan

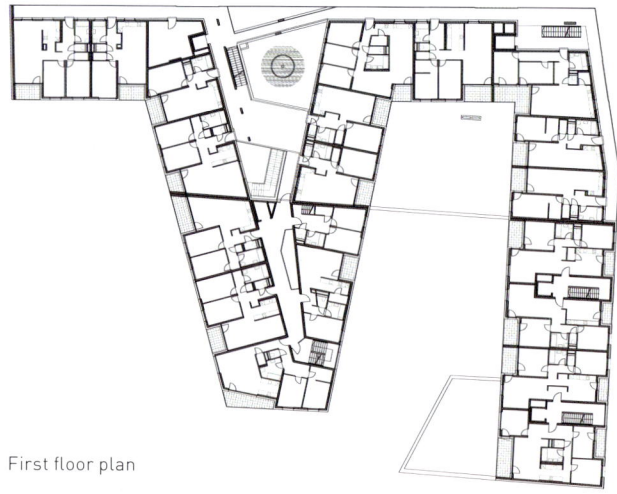

First floor plan

Ground floor plan

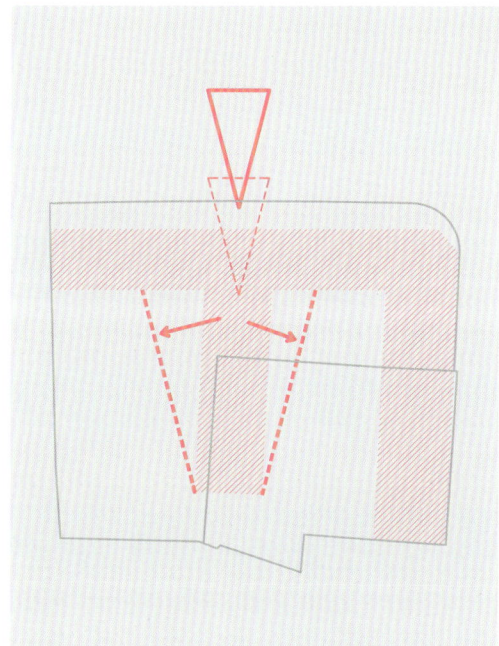

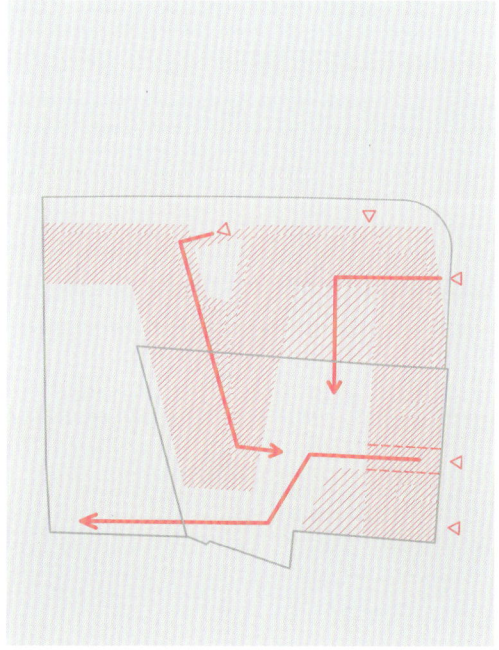

Concept diagram

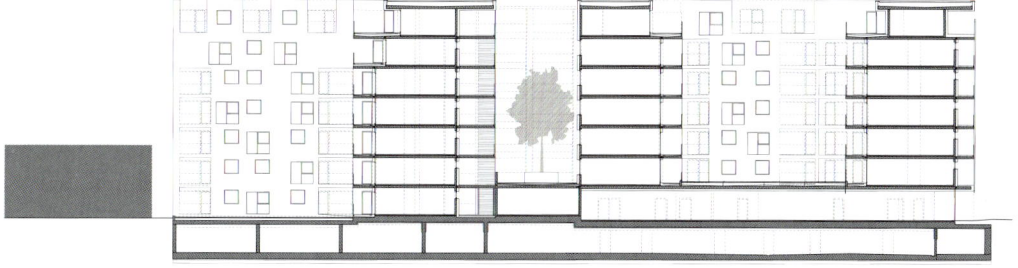

Section

The introverted structure of this group of social dwellings is a response to its heterogeneous environment. The project defines clear boundaries on the north, east and west sides, whose façades dialogue with the surrounding urban space, and opens up towards the wide south-facing spaces. The dynamic modular structure used accommodates different types of housing, compact and with great use of space. The project promotes social interaction through the design of elements such as porticoes, staircases or connecting corridors and through community spaces, gardens and patios that strengthen the residents' sense of identification with their housing complex. Accommodation of disadvantaged social groups in the supervised housing apartments on the ground floor seeks to establish stronger community bonds and reduce prejudice.

Die introvertierte Struktur dieser Gruppe Sozialwohnungen ist eine Antwort auf ihr heterogenes Umfeld. Das Projekt definiert klare Grenzen auf der Nord-, Ost- und Westseite, deren Fassaden mit dem umgebenden Stadtraum in Dialog stehen, und öffnet sich zu den breiten nach Süden gerichteten Räumen. Der dynamische modulare Aufbau ermöglicht die Unterbringung verschiedener Gehäusetypen, kompakt und platzsparend. Das Projekt fördert die soziale Interaktion durch die Gestaltung von Elementen wie Portikus, Treppen oder Verbindungsgängen sowie durch Gemeinschaftsräume, Gärten und Terrassen, die die Identifikation der Bewohner mit ihrer Wohnanlage stärken. Die Unterbringung benachteiligter sozialer Gruppen in den betreuten Wohnungen im Erdgeschoss zielt darauf ab, stärkere Gemeinschaftsbeziehungen herzustellen und Vorurteile abzubauen.

MÜHLGRUND
VIENNA, AUSTRIA

La structure introvertie de ce groupe de logements sociaux est une réponse à son environnement hétérogène. Le projet définit des limites claires au nord, à l'est et à l'ouest, dont les façades dialoguent avec l'espace urbain environnant et s'ouvrent vers les grands espaces exposés au sud. La structure modulaire dynamique utilisée permet d'accueillir différents types de logements, compacts et avec une grande utilisation de l'espace. Le projet favorise l'interaction sociale par la conception d'éléments tels que des portiques, des escaliers ou des couloirs de liaison, ainsi que des espaces communautaires, des jardins et des patios qui renforcent le sentiment d'identification des résidents à leur complexe de logements. L'hébergement des groupes sociaux défavorisés dans les appartements de logements supervisés du rez-de-chaussée vise à renforcer les liens communautaires et à réduire les préjugés.

La estructura introvertida de este conjunto de viviendas sociales es una respuesta a su entorno heterogéneo. El proyecto define unos límites claros en los lados norte, este y oeste, cuyas fachadas dialogan con el espacio urbano circundante, y se abre hacia los amplios espacios orientados a sur. La dinámica estructura modular utilizada acomoda diversas tipologías de vivienda, compactas y con gran aprovechamiento del espacio. El proyecto fomenta la interacción social a través del diseño de elementos como pórticos, escaleras o pasillos de conexión y a través de espacios comunitarios, jardines y patios que fortalecen el sentido de identificación de los residentes con su complejo de viviendas. El alojamiento de grupos sociales desfavorecidos en los apartamentos de vivienda tutelada de la planta baja busca establecer vínculos comunitarios más sólidos y reducir los prejuicios.

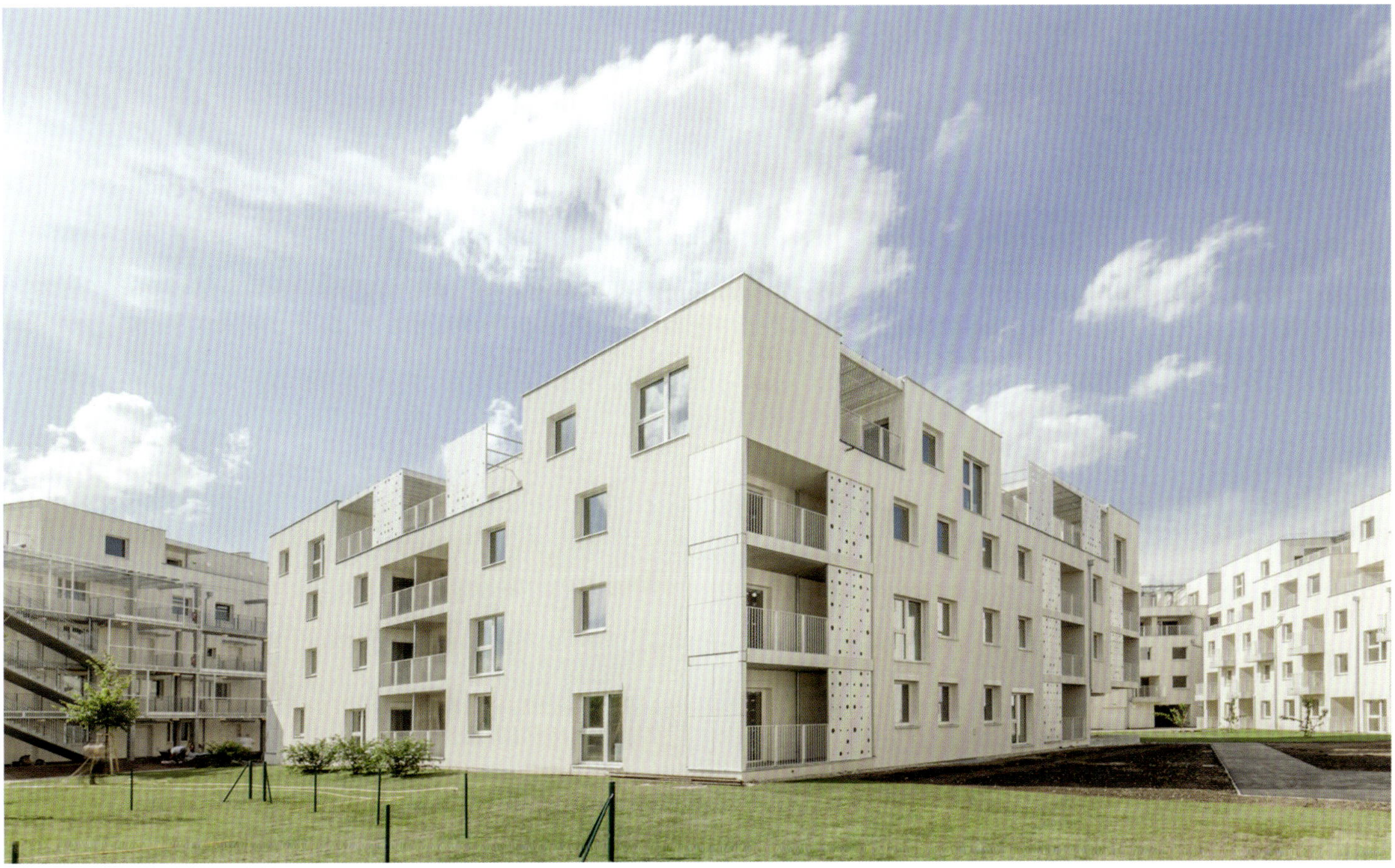

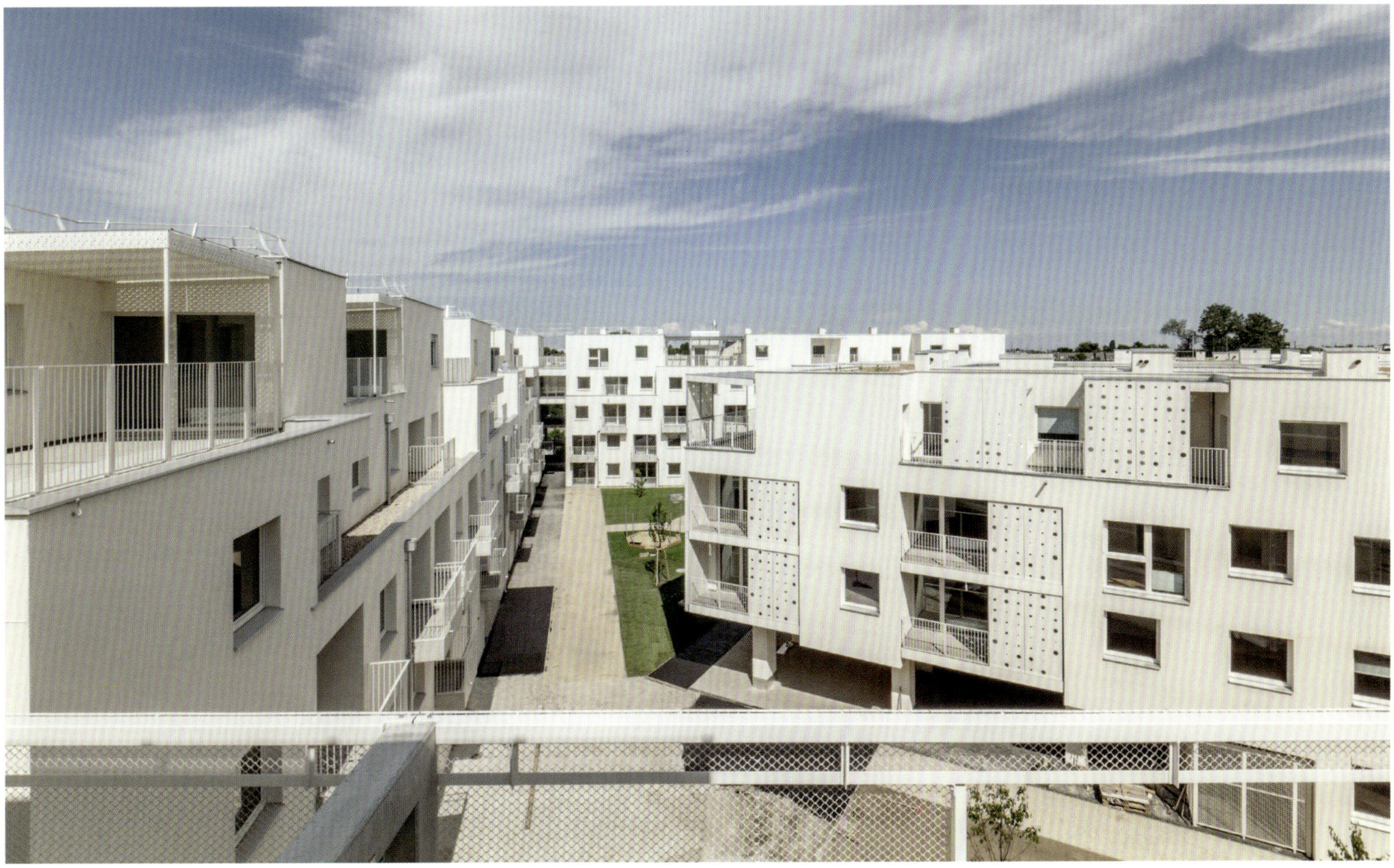

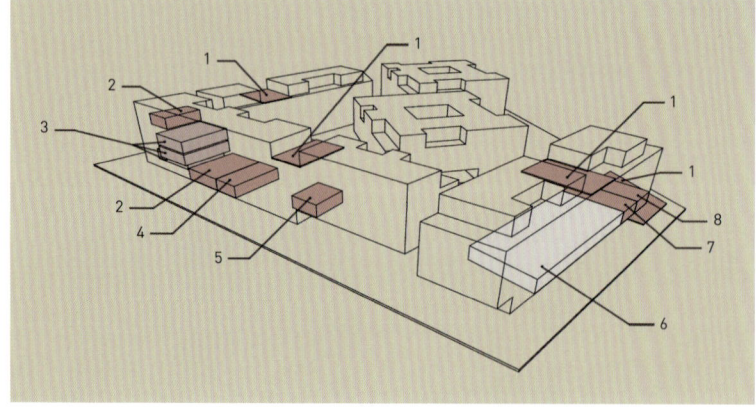

Community sketches

1. Community terrace
2. Community room
3. Zumietbare ateliers
4. Laundry
5. Workshop
6. Supervised flat share
7. Community kitchen
8. Children's playroom

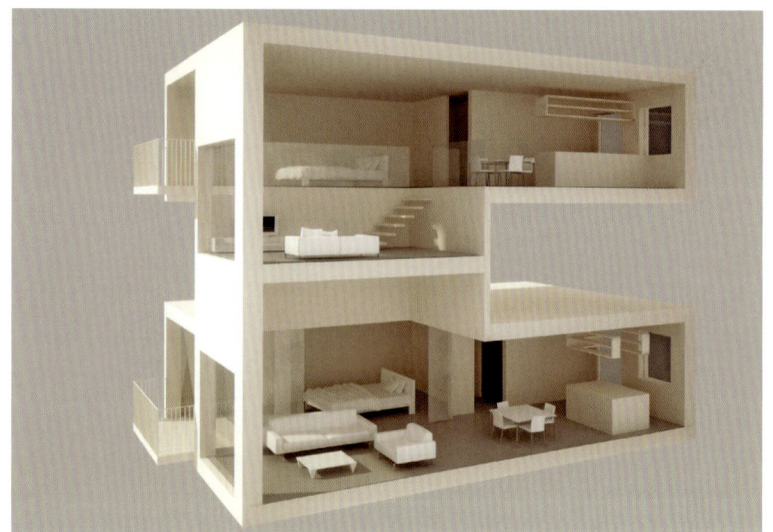

Apartments model

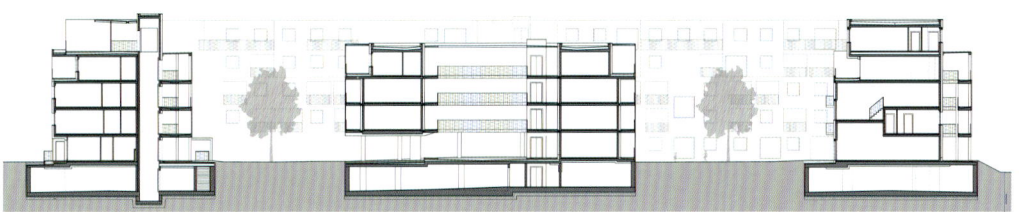

Section

Ground floor plan

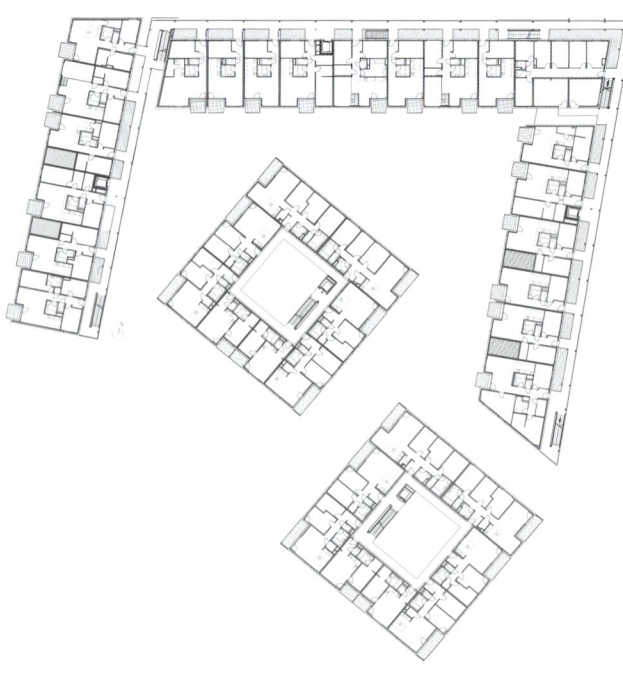

First floor plan

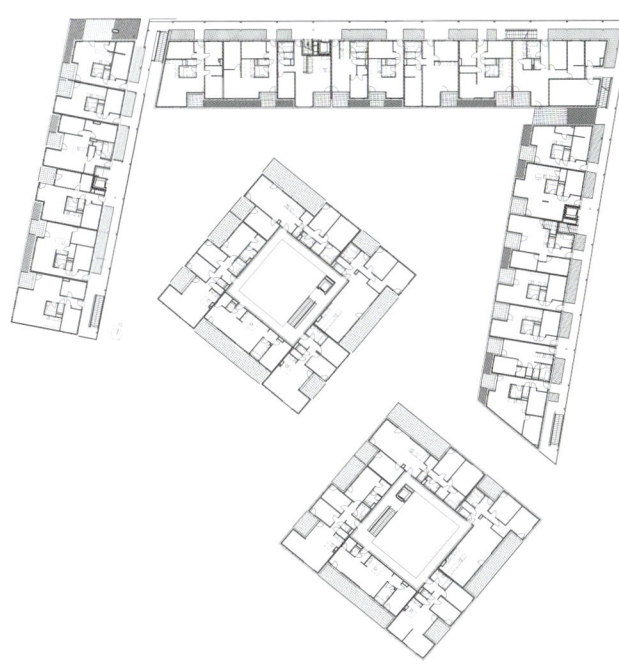

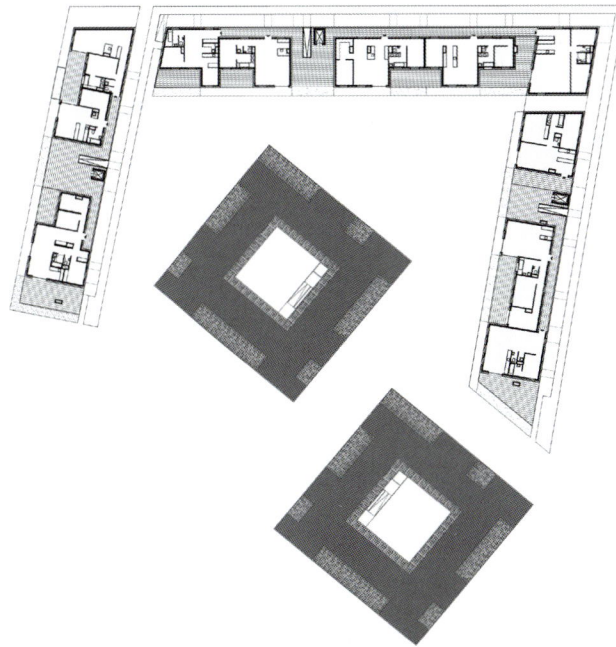

First attic floor plan

Second attic floor plan

OLGOO

www.olgooco.com

Mehran Khoshroo was born in Mashhad, northwest Iran, and studied at Shahid Beheshti University, one of the most prestigious in the country. After finishing his studies, he began his career and in 2005 established his own company, Olgoo. The office had as its main objective the participation in various architectural awards and marked the beginning of a new stage in Mehran's career.

It can be said that the main characteristic of Mehran's work is his ability to work in different fields and his ability to design buildings of different typologies. For this reason, he has been honored with various awards both within and outside his country. In 2018, his System Warehouse project was included in the final round of the World Architecture Festival.

Mehran Khoshroo wurde in Mashhad im Nordwesten des Iran geboren und studierte an der Shahid Beheshti Universität, einer der renommiertesten des Landes. Nach Abschluss seines Studiums begann er seine Karriere und gründete 2005 sein eigenes Unternehmen, Olgoo. Das Hauptziel des Büros war die Teilnahme an mehreren Architekturpreisen und markierte den Beginn einer neuen Phase in Mehrans Karriere.

Es ist festzuhalten, dass das Hauptmerkmal von Mehrans Arbeit seine Fähigkeit ist, in verschiedenen Bereichen zu arbeiten und Gebäude mit unterschiedlichen Typologien zu entwerfen. Aus diesem Grund wurde er mit verschiedenen Auszeichnungen innerhalb und außerhalb seines Landes geehrt. Im Jahr 2018 wurde sein Projekt System Warehouse in die Endrunde des World Architecture Festival aufgenommen.

Mehran Khoshroo est né à Mashhad, dans le nord-ouest de l'Iran, et a étudié à l'Université Shahid Beheshti, l'une des plus prestigieuses du pays. Après avoir terminé ses études, il a commencé sa carrière et, en 2005, il a fondé sa propre entreprise, Olgoo. L'objectif principal du bureau était la participation à plusieurs prix d'architecture et a marqué le début d'une nouvelle étape dans la carrière de Mehran.

On peut dire que la caractéristique principale du travail de Mehran est sa capacité à travailler dans différents domaines et sa capacité à concevoir des bâtiments de différentes typologies. C'est pour cette raison qu'il a reçu de nombreuses distinctions à l'intérieur et à l'extérieur de son pays. En 2018, son projet System Warehouse a été inclus dans la phase finale du Festival Mondial d'Architecture.

Mehran Khoshroo nació en Mashhad, en el noroeste de Irán, y estudió en la Universidad Shahid Beheshti, una de las más prestigiosas del país. Tras acabar sus estudios, comenzó su carrera y en 2005 estableció su propia compañía, Olgoo. La oficina tenía como pricipal objetivo la participación en diversos premios de arquitectura y marcó el inicio una nueva etapa en la carrera de Mehran.

Se puede decir que la principal característica del trabajo de Mehran es su capacidad para trabajar en diferentes campos y su destreza para diseñar edificios de diferentes tipologías. Por esta razón, ha sido honrado con diversos premios dentro y fuera de su país. En 2018, su proyecto System Warehouse fue incluido en la ronda final del World Architecture Festival.

Architect's firm: Olgoo Office

Contact e-mail:
mehrankhoshroo@yahoo.com

Lead architects:
Mehran Khoshroo

Completion year: 2016

Gross built area: 38,000m²

Function: Residential

Site area (plottage): 6,400 m²

Covered area: 38,000 m²

Total floor area (=gross area):
1,950 m²

Photo credits:
© Mohammad Hassan Ettefagh

Completed date: 2016

Design team:
Almara Melkomian, Mehdi
Atashbar, Amir Masoud Nafisi,
Adel Ataei, Soudabe Qorbani,
Nastaran Namvar, Tannaz
Khoshroo, Ni-loofar Esmaeili,
Reyhane Miraftab, Sepide
Ghabelzede, Amir Hossein
Mohebi, Torang Asadi,
Hashem Karimi

ZAFERANIYE GARDEN COMPLEX

This 64-unit residential complex located in a 6500 m² garden in northern Tehran promotes interaction between nature and city life. The footprint of the building tries to preserve the existing vegetation and the composition of its façade, based on a volumetric game with wooden boxes from 2 to 5 floors high, creates terraces with trees and plants that create microclimates and provide privacy to the houses. A rainwater recovery system allows the abundant development of this vegetation on the balconies and on the communal roof, which also includes a viewpoint, an orchard and a meeting area. The project avoids repeating the compositional schemes of the neighbouring height typologies and confers on the green layer of vegetation the range of main material of the façade, which it endows with a dynamic appearance.

Die 64 Wohneinheiten umfassende Wohnanlage in einem 6.500 m² großen Garten im Norden Teherans fördert die Interaktion zwischen Natur und Stadtleben. Der Grundriss des Gebäudes versucht, die bestehende Vegetation und die Komposition seiner Fassade zu erhalten, die auf einem volumetrischen Spiel mit Zellen aus Holz von 2 bis 5 Stockwerken Höhe basiert sowie Terrassen mit Bäumen und Pflanzen einzurichten, die Mikroklima erzeugen und den Häusern Privatsphäre bieten. Ein Regenwasserrückgewinnungssystem ermöglicht die üppige Entwicklung dieser Vegetation auf den Balkonen und auf dem Gemeinschaftsdach, zu dem auch ein Aussichtspunkt, ein Obstgarten und ein Besprechungsraum gehören. Das Projekt vermeidet es, die Kompositionsschemata der benachbarten Typologien in der Höhe zu wiederholen und verleiht der grünen Schicht der Vegetation die Bandbreite des Hauptmaterials der Fassade, dem es einen dynamischen Aspekt verleiht.

ZAFERANIYE GARDEN COMPLEX
TEHRAN, IRAN

Ce complexe résidentiel de 64 logements situé dans un jardin de 6 500 m² au nord de Téhéran favorise l'interaction entre la nature et la vie urbaine. L'empreinte du bâtiment tente de préserver la végétation existante et la composition de sa façade, basée sur un jeu volumétrique avec des caisses en bois de 2 à 5 étages de hauteur, crée des terrasses avec des arbres et des plantes qui créent des microclimats et offrent une intimité aux maisons. Un système de récupération des eaux pluviales permet le développement abondant de cette végétation sur les balcons et sur le toit communal, qui comprend également un belvédère, un verger et une salle de réunion. Le projet évite de répéter les schémas de composition des typologies voisines en hauteur et confère à la couche verte de la végétation la gamme de matériau principal de la façade, à laquelle il donne un aspect dynamique.

Este complejo residencial de 64 viviendas ubicado en un jardín de 6.500 m² de la zona norte de Teherán promueve la interacción entre la naturaleza y la vida de la ciudad. La huella del edificio intenta preservar la vegetación existente y la composición de su fachada, basada en un juego volumétrico con cajas de madera de 2 a 5 pisos de altura, crea terrazas con árboles y plantas que crean microclimas y aportan privacidad a las viviendas. Un sistema de recuperación de agua de lluvia permite el desarrollo abundante de esta vegetación en los balcones y en la cubierta comunitaria, que incluye también un mirador, un huerto y una zona de reunión. El proyecto evita repetir los esquemas compositivos de las tipologías en altura vecinas y confiere a la capa verde de la vegetación el rango de material principal de la fachada, a la que dota de un aspecto dinámico.

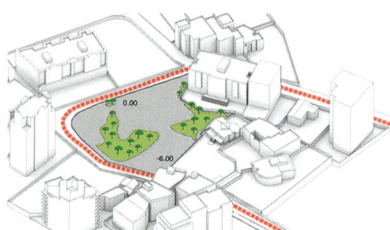

Access and landscape

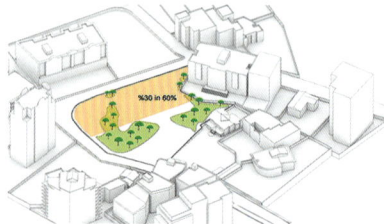

Occupation

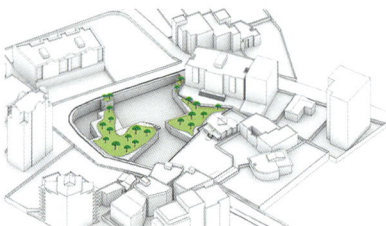

Excavation

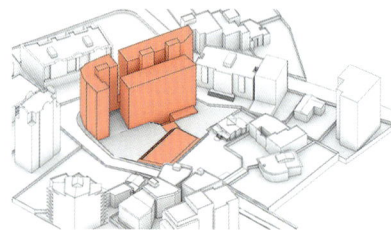

Primitive mass

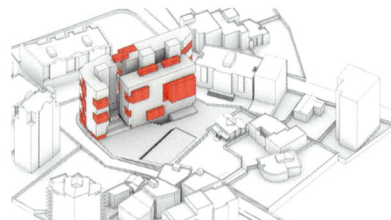

Extrusion

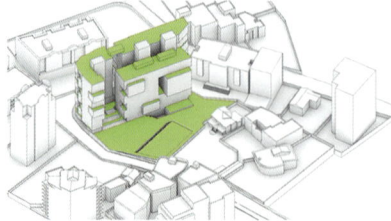

Outdoor living

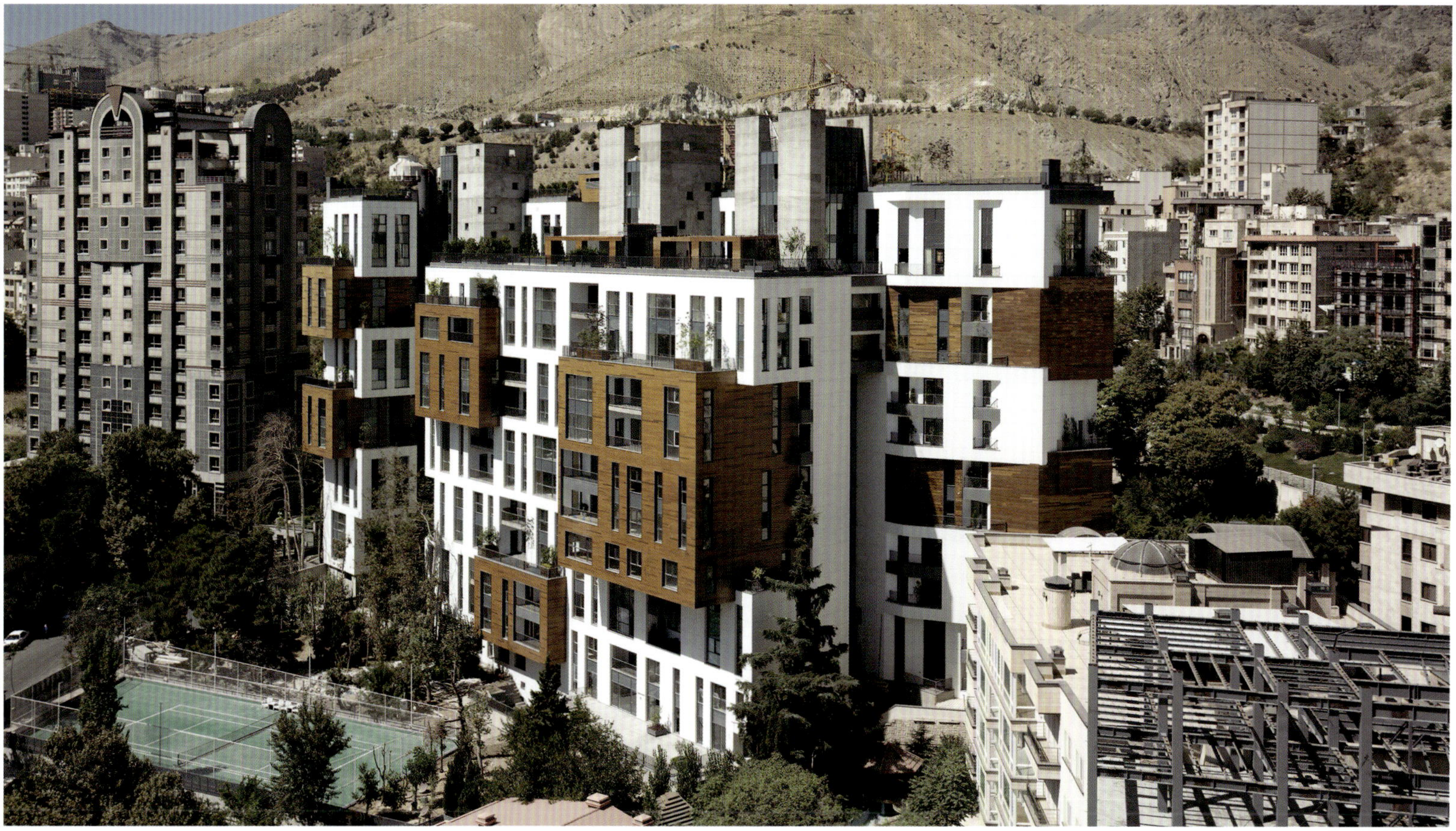

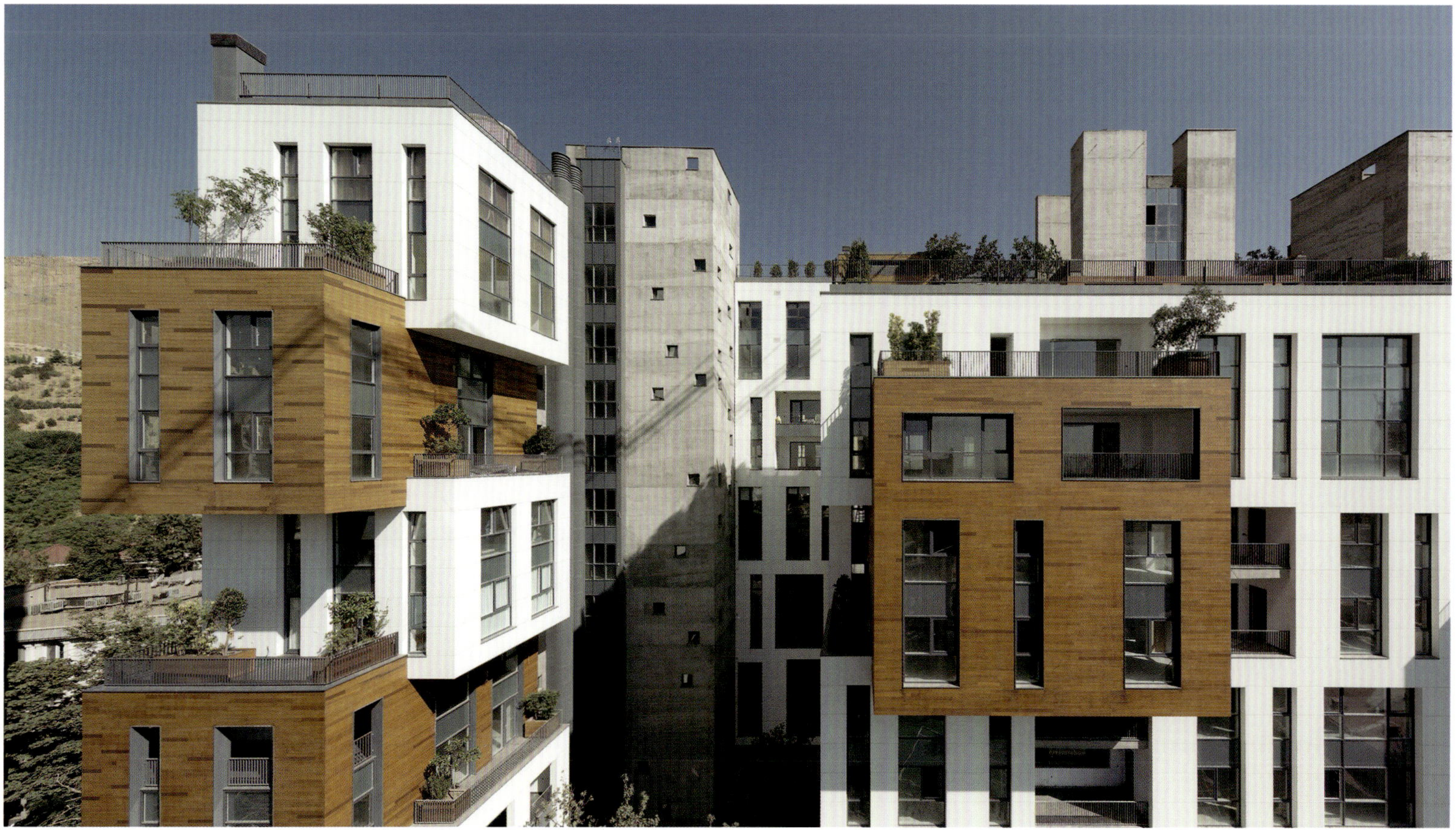

Site plan

East elevation

West elevation

South elevation

North elevation

Section B-B

Section A-A

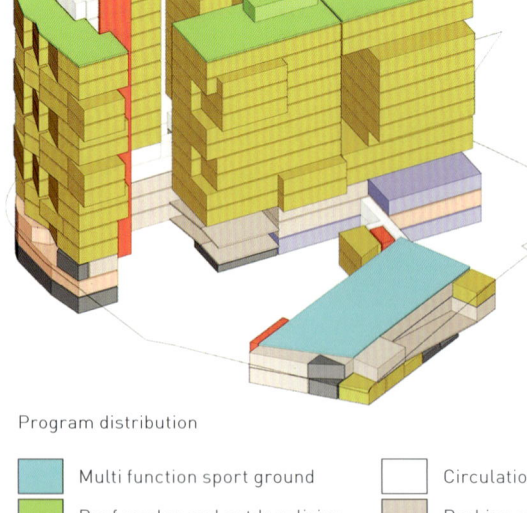

Program distribution

▦	Multi function sport ground	▢	Circulation
▦	Roof garden and outdoor living	▦	Parking area and access ramps
▦	Residential units	▦	M.E.P. zone
▦	Staircase	▦	Private stores
▢	Elevators	▦	Common services (sport hall & ceremony hall)

Plan 11

Plan 10

Plan 03

Plan 00

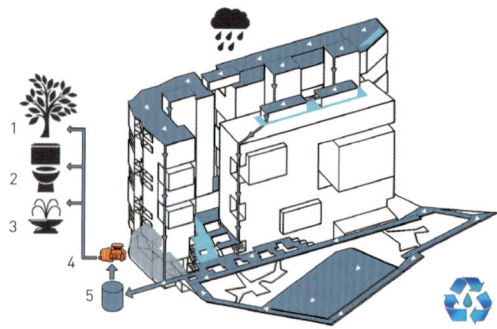

Rainwater recycling diagram

1. Green plants
2. Toilets
3. Water surface
4. Plumbing
5. Water tank

Materials

Privacy and green layer

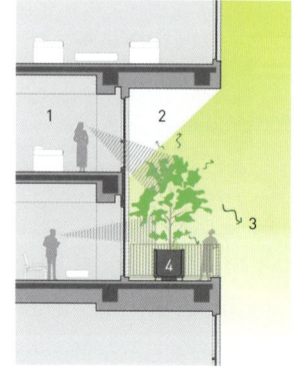

1. In
2. Out
3. Microclimate condition around the tree
4. Min height of soil 90 cm.

Green balconies diagram

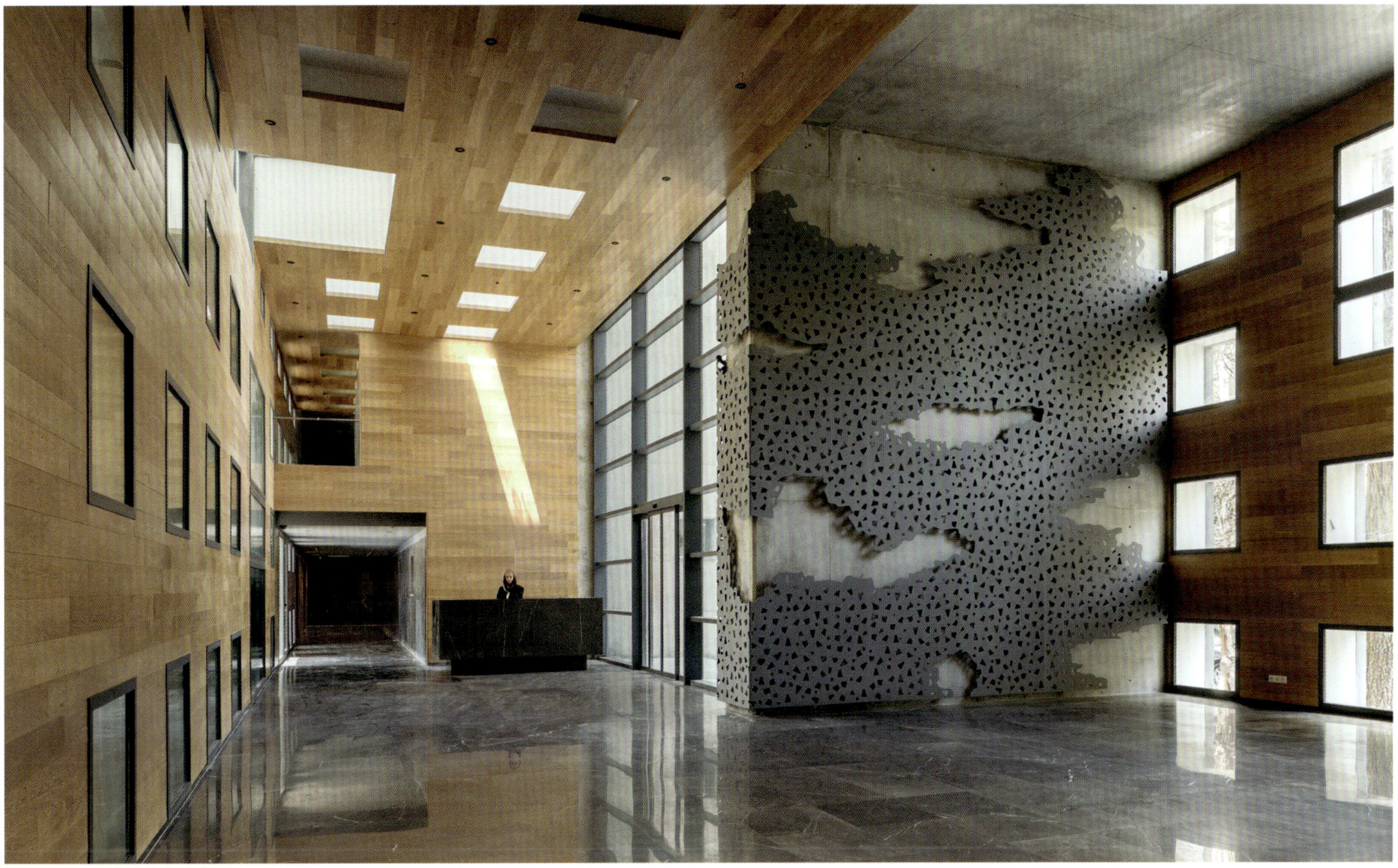

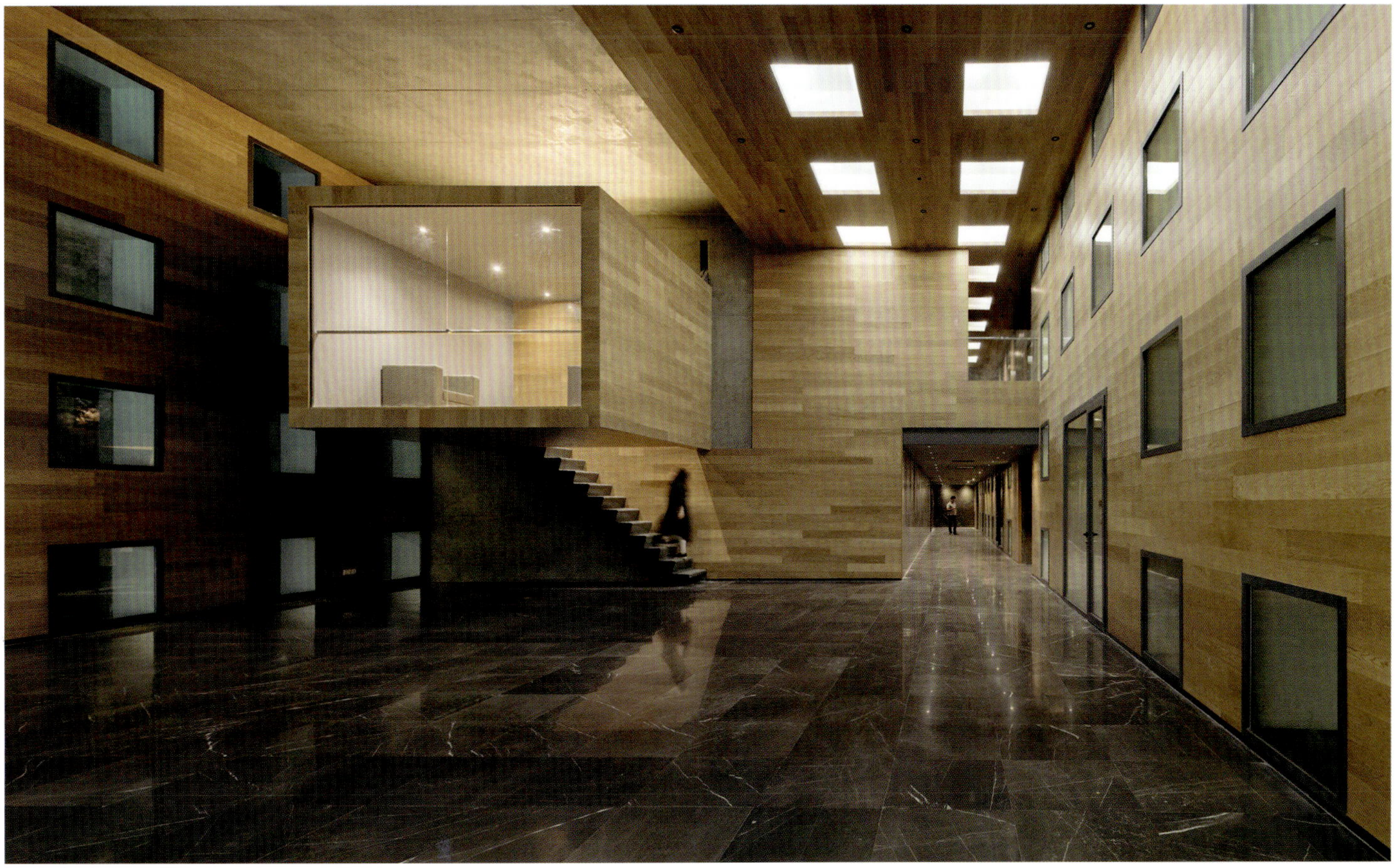

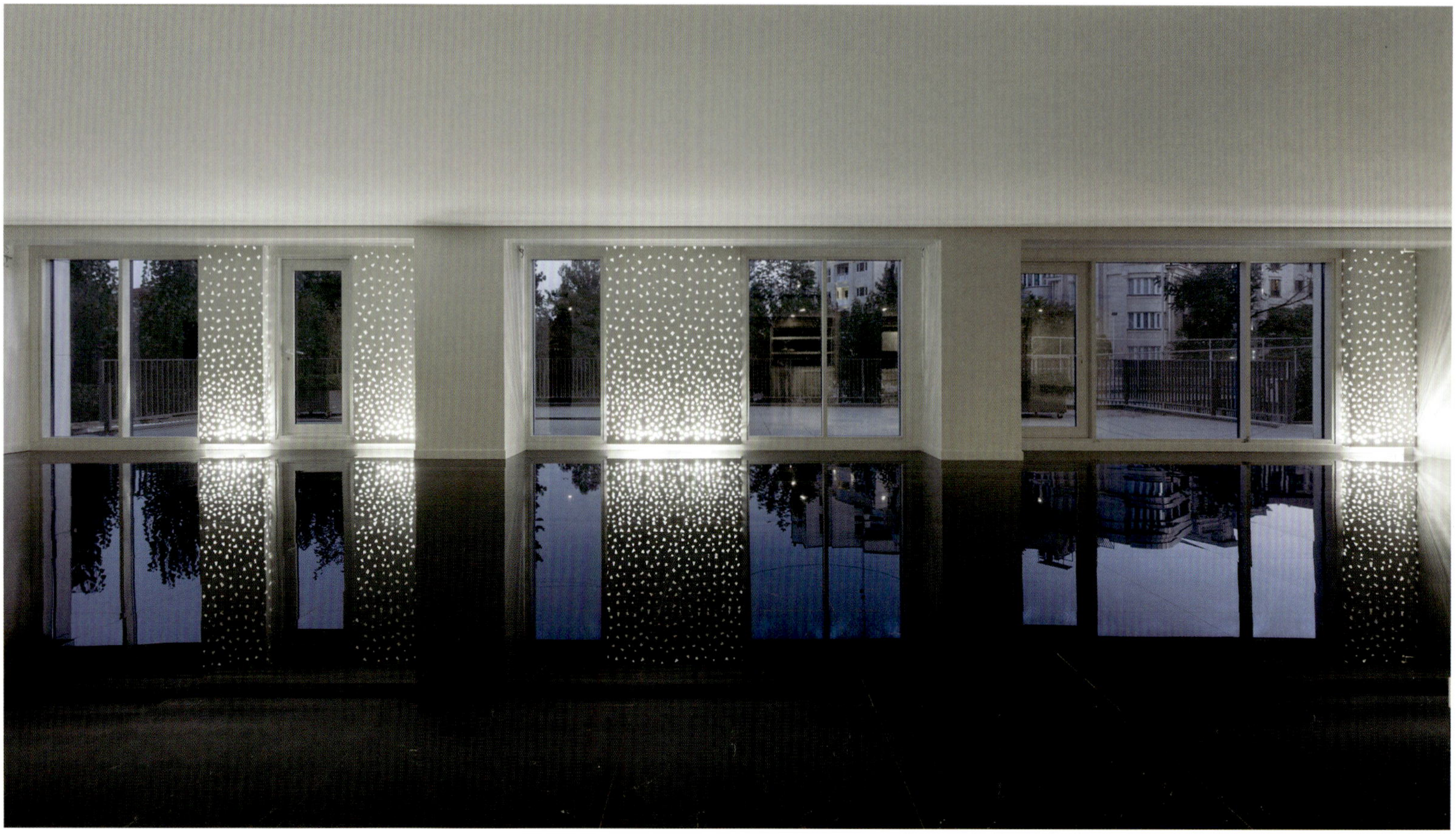

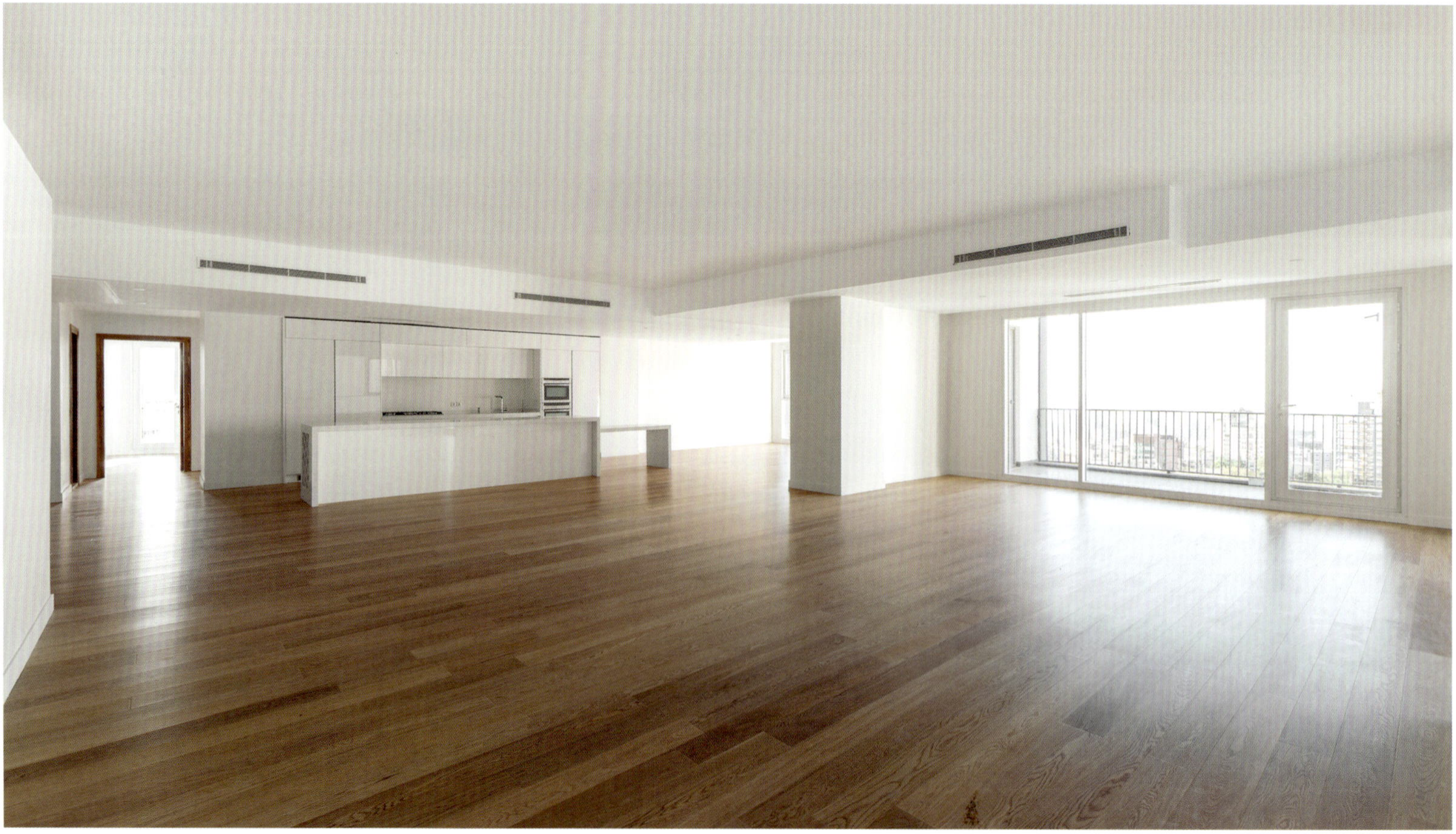

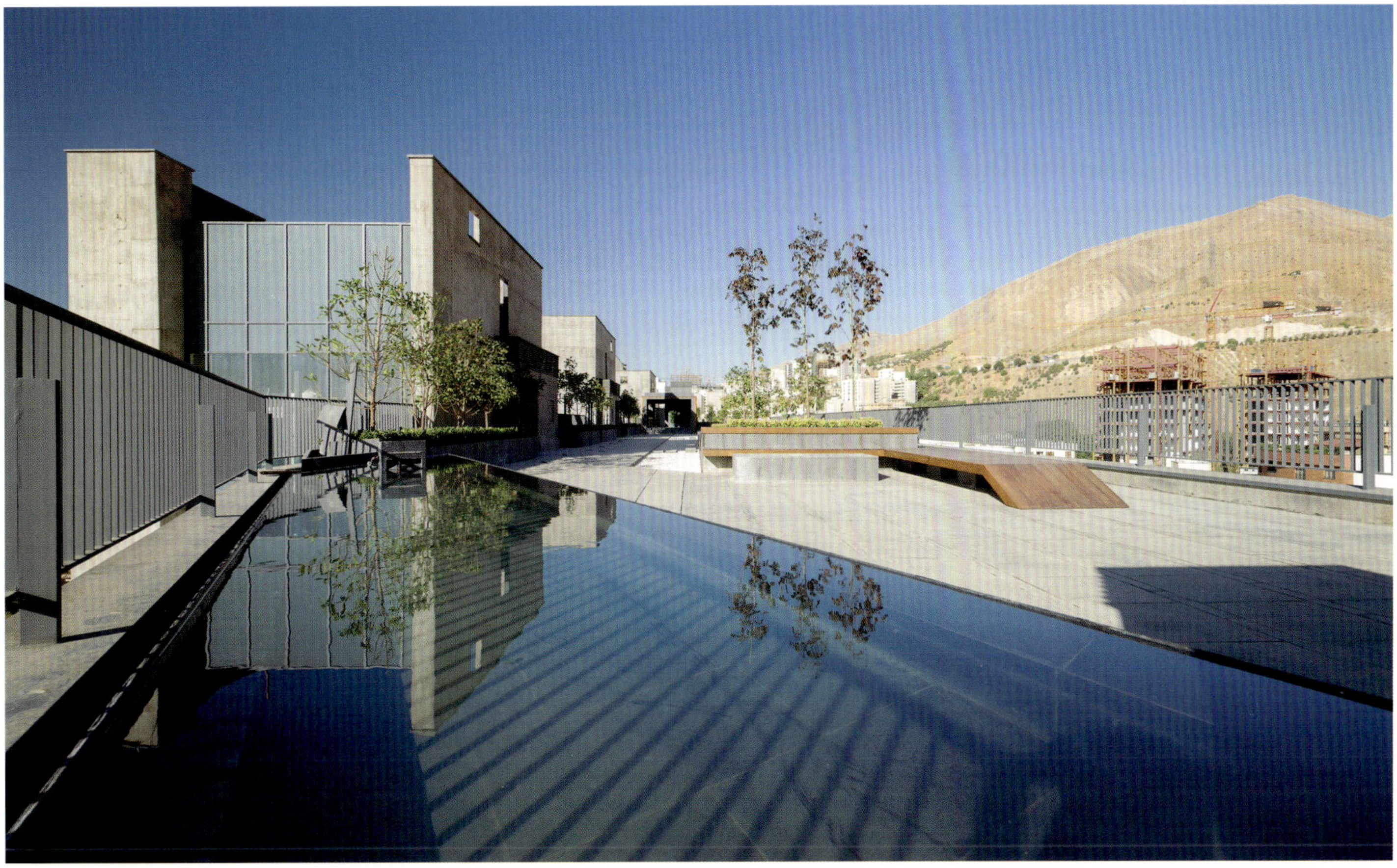

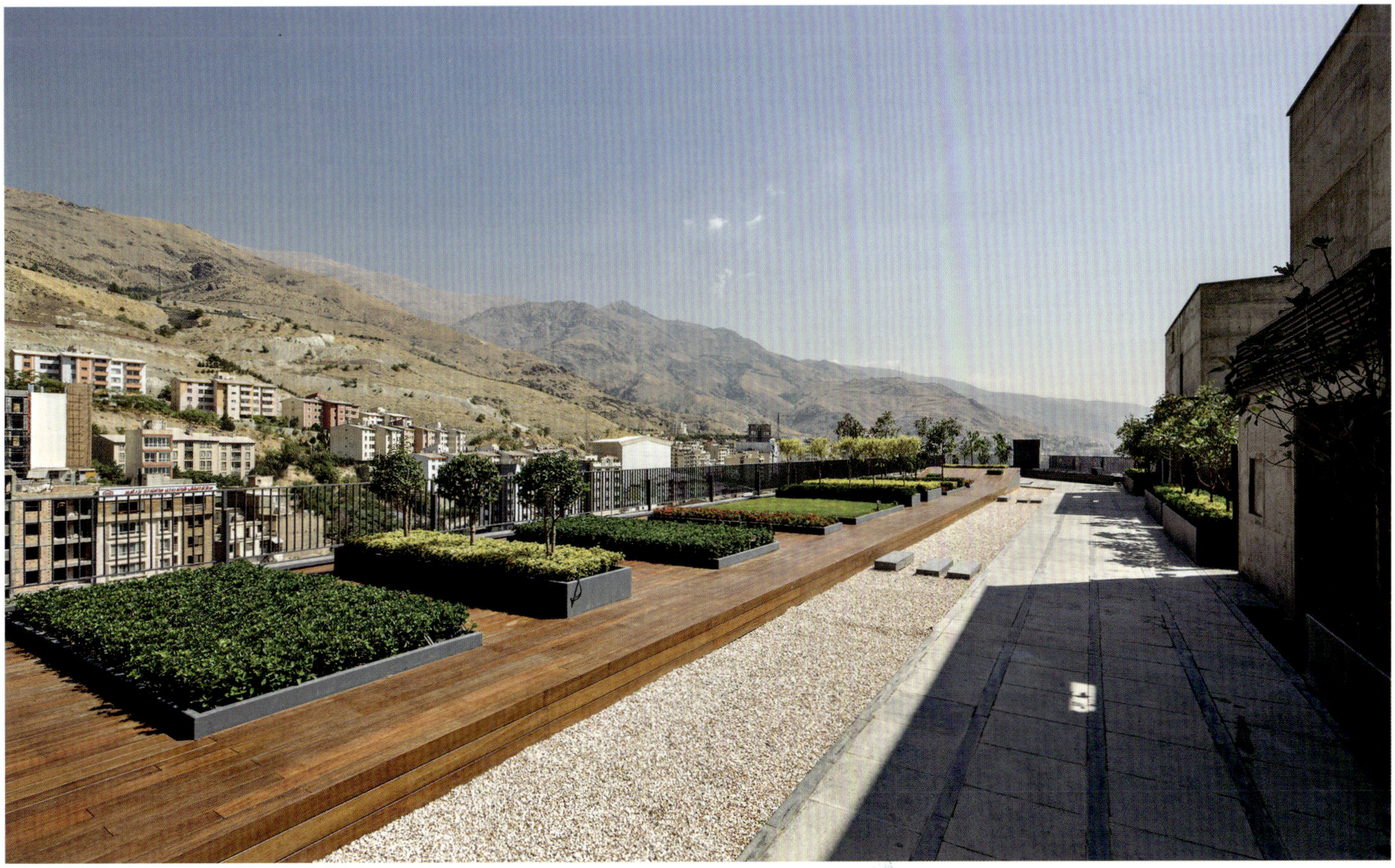

PAVE ARCHITECTS

www.pavearchitects.com

PAVE Architects, led by Pave Mikkonen, is a high-profile design office from Finland specialized in creating innovative and comprehensive architecture and interior design – all with their very own twist and without compromises on aesthetics.

PAVE Architects aspires to create unique buildings and sustainable environments, high in terms of quality, ambiance and architecture, carried out with a cost-conscious and responsible service of the client. The open-minded, unprejudiced attitude, as well as the bold questioning of well-established ideas and solutions, is the core for creating and reaching new, better designs. The relationship between buildings in their broader context, such as the local conditions and environment, gives each project an individual starting point. Therefore, with PAVE Architects, each project becomes unique as the designs stem from a clean slate. Thus, the office doesn't really have a distinct style, as each design is individually tailored to meet the clients' needs – by true professionals of the field.

PAVE Architects unter der Leitung von Pave Mikkonen ist ein hochkarätiges Designbüro, das sich auf die Entwicklung innovativer und umfassender Architektur und Innenarchitektur spezialisiert hat - alles mit einer ganz eigenen Note und ohne Kompromisse bei der Ästhetik.

Das Büro ist bestrebt, einzigartige Gebäude und nachhaltige Umgebungen zu schaffen, die qualitativ, atmosphärisch und architektonisch hochwertig sind und mit einem kostenbewussten und verantwortungsbewussten Service des Kunden durchgeführt werden. Die aufgeschlossene, unvoreingenommene Haltung sowie die mutige Hinterfragung etablierter Ideen und Lösungen ist der Kern für neue, bessere Designs.

Die Beziehung zwischen Gebäuden in ihrem Gesamtkontext, wie z.B. den örtlichen Gegebenheiten und der Umgebung, gibt jedem Projekt einen individuellen Ausgangspunkt. Mit PAVE Architects wird jedes Projekt einzigartig, da die Entwürfe aus einem sauberen Schiefer stammen. So hat das Büro nicht wirklich einen eigenen Stil, da jedes Design individuell auf die Bedürfnisse der Kunden zugeschnitten ist - von echten Profis der Branche.

PAVE Architects, dirigé par Pave Mikkonen, est un bureau d'études de haut niveau spécialisé dans la création d'une architecture et d'un design d'intérieur innovants et complets, tous avec une touche personnelle et sans compromis esthétique.

Le bureau aspire à créer des bâtiments uniques et des environnements durables, hauts en termes de qualité, d'ambiance et d'architecture, réalisés avec un service au client soucieux des coûts et responsable. L'ouverture d'esprit, l'absence de préjugés et la remise en question audacieuse d'idées et de solutions bien établies sont au cœur de la création de nouveaux designs de qualité. La relation entre les bâtiments dans leur contexte plus large, comme les conditions locales et l'environnement, donne à chaque projet un point de départ individuel. Avec PAVE Architects, chaque projet devient unique car les conceptions sont issues d'une ardoise vierge. Ainsi, le bureau n'a pas vraiment un style distinct, car chaque design est adapté individuellement pour répondre aux besoins des clients - par de vrais professionnels du domaine.

PAVE Architects, dirigida por Pave Mikkonen, es una oficina de diseño de alto perfil especializada en la creación de arquitectura y diseño de interiores innovadores e integrales, todo ello con un toque propio y sin compromisos estéticos.

La oficina aspira a crear edificios únicos y entornos sostenibles de alta calidad, ambiente y arquitectura, realizados con un servicio responsable y consciente de los costes del cliente. La actitud abierta y sin prejuicios, así como el cuestionamiento audaz de ideas y soluciones establecidas, es la base para crear nuevos y mejores diseños.

La relación entre los edificios en su contexto más amplio, como las condiciones locales y el medio ambiente, da a cada proyecto un punto de partida individual. Con PAVE Architects, cada proyecto se convierte en único. La oficina no tiene un estilo propio, ya que cada diseño está hecho a medida por verdaderos profesionales del sector para satisfacer las necesidades de los clientes.

CO-OP OULUN TERVAHOVIN SIILOT

Location: Oulu, Finland

Building area: 7,700 m²

Project completion date: 2014

Architecture team:
Pave Mikkonen, Kai Ruuhonen,
Marttiina Vierimaa,
Pekka Tuominen, Sami Kylli,
Susanna Ojala

Photo credits:
© Arno de la Chapelle

CO-OP OULUN TERVAHOVIN VANHAT SIILOT

Location: Oulu, Finland

Building area: 4,000 m²

Project completion date: 2014

Architecture team:
Pave Mikkonen, Kai Ruuhonen,
Sami Kylli, Susanna Ojala,
Pekka Tuominen, Marttiina
Vierimaa, Paula Kouri

Photo credits:
© Hannu Uusitalo,
© Heikki Salmi,
© Arno de la Chapelle

The transformation of historic cylindrical grain silos into a contemporary residential building gave new life to the Toppilansalmi area. The poor condition of most of the original buildings forced them to be dismantled, but much of their exterior image was recreated following the guidelines of municipal regulations. The round shapes of the silos are used as balcony areas of various sizes. The extension of the building, cubic and dark in composition, expands naturally in the plot. In keeping with the area's industrial environment, the in-situ cast concrete surfaces are a prominent element throughout the building's interior. The first two floors out of thirteen contain neo-lofts with galleries and wide open spaces five metres high. The rest of the units constitute a variety of loft-type apartments.

Die Umwandlung von historischen zylindrischen Getreidesilos in ein zeitgenössisches Wohnhaus gab dem Gebiet von Toppilansalmi neues Leben. Der schlechte Zustand der meisten Originalgebäude zwang sie zur Demontage, aber ein Großteil ihres Aussehens wurde nach den Richtlinien der Gemeinde wiederhergestellt. Die runden Formen der Silos werden als Balkonflächen unterschiedlicher Größe genutzt. Die Erweiterung des Gebäudes, kubisch und dunkel in der Zusammensetzung, dehnt sich im Grundstück natürlich aus. Im Einklang mit der industriellen Umgebung des Gebietes sind Ortbetonflächen ein herausragendes Element im gesamten Gebäudeinneren. In den ersten beiden Stockwerken der dreizehn Häuser befinden sich Neubauten mit Galerien und fünf Meter hohen Freiflächen. Die restlichen Einheiten bilden eine Vielzahl von Dachgeschosswohnungen.

CO-OP OULUN TERVAHOVIN SIILOT
OULU, FINLAND

La transformation des silos à grains cylindriques historiques en un bâtiment résidentiel contemporain a redonné vie au quartier Toppilansalmi. Le mauvais état de la plupart des bâtiments d'origine a forcé leur démantèlement, mais une grande partie de leur image extérieure a été recréée en suivant les directives des règlements municipaux. Les formes arrondies des silos servent de balcons de différentes tailles. L'extension du bâtiment, de composition cubique et sombre, s'étend naturellement dans la parcelle. Dans le respect de l'environnement industriel de la région, les surfaces en béton coulé sur place sont un élément exceptionnel à l'intérieur du bâtiment. Les deux premiers étages des treize maisons offrent des néo-lofts avec des galeries et de grands espaces ouverts de cinq mètres de haut. Les autres unités forment une variété d'appartements en loft.

La transformación de unos históricos silos cilíndricos de grano en un edificio residencial contemporáneo dió una nueva vida al área de Toppilansalmi. El mal estado de la mayoría de las construcciones originales obligó a desmantelarlas, pero gran parte de su imagen exterior fue recreada siguiendo las directrices de la normativa municipal. Las formas redondas de los silos se utilizan como zonas de balcón de tamaños variados. La extensión del edificio, de composición cúbica y oscura, se expande de forma natural en la parcela. En consonancia con el ambiente industrial de la zona, las superficies de hormigón *in situ* son un elemento destacable en todo el interior del edificio. Las dos primeras plantas de las trece alojan neo-*lofts* con galerías y amplios espacios abiertos de cinco metros de altura. El resto de unidades constituye una variedad de apartamentos tipo *loft*.

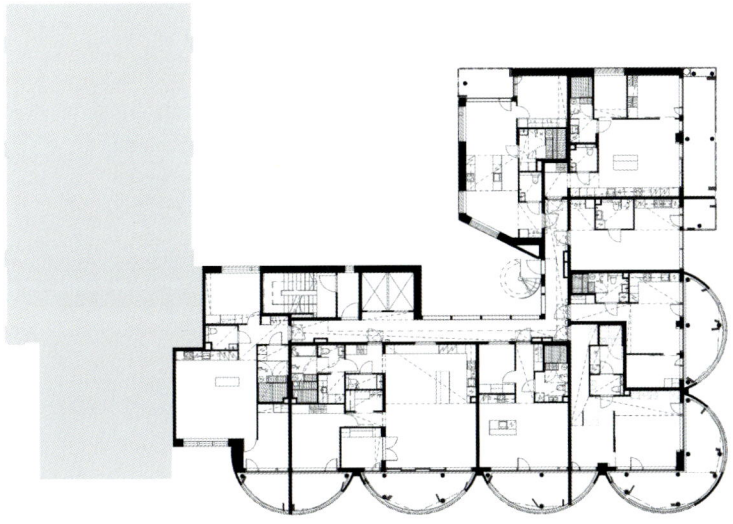

Regular floor plan

Loft gallery floor plan

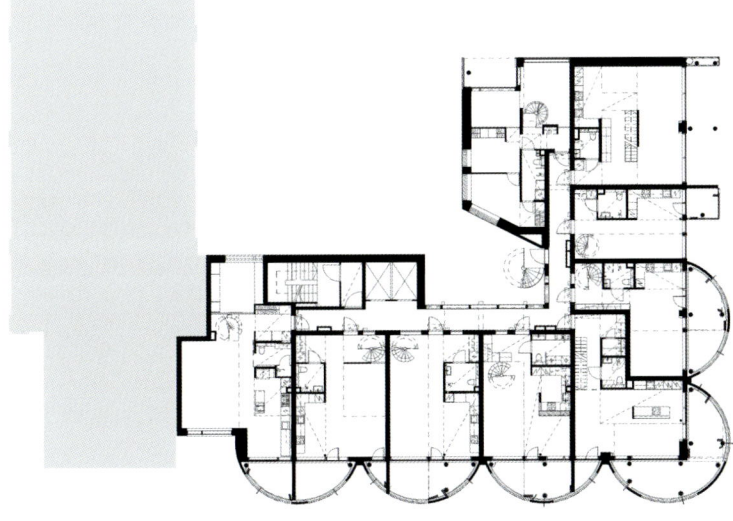

Loft floor plan

Longitudinal section 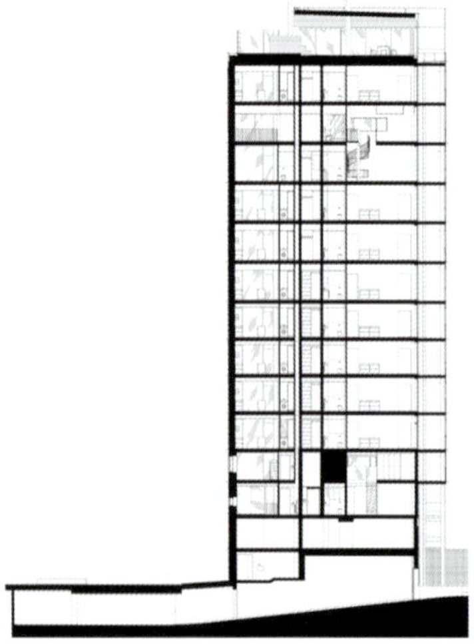   Cross section

The project transforms a 1928 grain silo representative of Nordic classicism for residential use. The building, located next to the largest round silos from 1960, retains its original façade and houses a wide variety of apartments in its narrow enclosure. The first two floors contain a series of townhouses that occupy the entire width of the building and have individual access from the street level, while the next three floors contain small rental apartments. The upper three floors house three-level loft penthouses with coloured glass greenhouses and medium-sized open floor spaces. The concrete structural elements were left in view along with the rest of the materials and tones chosen to respect the original concept of the building.

Das Projekt verwandelt ein Getreidesilo aus dem Jahr 1928, das für den nordischen Klassizismus repräsentativ ist, in ein Wohngebäude. Das Gebäude, das sich neben den größten Rundsilos von 1960 befindet, behält seine ursprüngliche Fassade und beherbergt in seiner engen Einfriedung eine Vielzahl von Wohnungen. In den ersten beiden Stockwerken befindet sich eine Reihe von Stadtwohnungen, die sich über die gesamte Breite des Gebäudes erstrecken und einen individuellen Zugang von der Straße aus haben, während die nächsten drei Stockwerke kleine Mietwohnungen beherbergen. In den oberen drei Stockwerken befinden sich dreistöckige Penthäuser im Loft-Stil mit farbigen Gewächshäuser und mittelgroßen Lofts in der dem Hafen zugewandten Zone. Die vor Ort befindlichen Betonelemente wurden ebenso wie die übrigen Materialien und Töne, die unter Berücksichtigung der ursprünglichen Lichtideologie des Gebäudes gewählt wurden, im Auge behalten.

CO-OP OULUN TERVAHOVIN VANHAT SIILOT
OULU, FINLAND

Le projet transforme un silo à grain de 1928 représentatif du classicisme nordique pour un usage résidentiel. Le bâtiment, situé à côté des plus grands silos ronds de 1960, conserve sa façade d'origine et abrite une grande variété d'appartements dans son enceinte étroite. Les deux premiers étages contiennent une série de maisons de ville qui occupent toute la largeur de l'immeuble et ont un accès individuel depuis la rue, tandis que les trois étages suivants contiennent de petits appartements locatifs. Les trois étages supérieurs abritent des penthouses de trois étages de style loft avec des serres en verre coloré et des lofts de taille moyenne dans la zone faisant face au port. Les éléments structuraux en béton in situ ont été laissés en vue avec le reste des matériaux et des tons choisis pour respecter l'idéologie lumineuse d'origine du bâtiment.

El proyecto transforma un silo de grano de 1928 representativo del clasicismo nórdico para darle un uso residencial. El edificio, situado junto a unos silos redondos y más grandes de 1960, conserva su fachada original y aloja en su estrecha envolvente una amplia variedad de apartamentos. Las dos primeras plantas contienen una serie de casas adosadas que ocupan todo el ancho del edificio y tienen acceso individual desde la calle, mientras que las tres plantas siguientes contienen pequeños apartamentos de alquiler. Las tres plantas superiores albergan penthouses tipo loft de tres niveles de altura con invernaderos de cristal coloreado y lofts de tamaño medio en la zona orientada hacia el puerto. Los elementos estructurales de hormigón in situ se dejaron a la vista junto al resto de materiales y tonos elegidos para respetar la ideología de luz original del edificio.

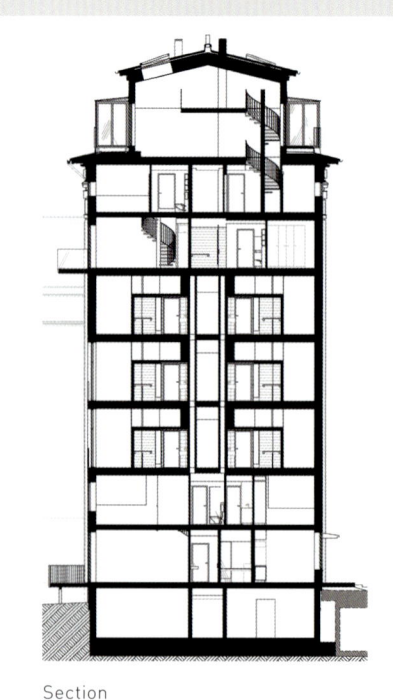

Section

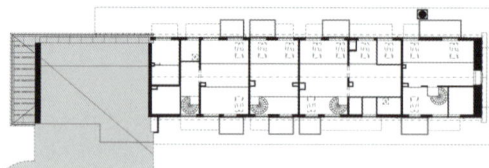

Penthouse balcony plan

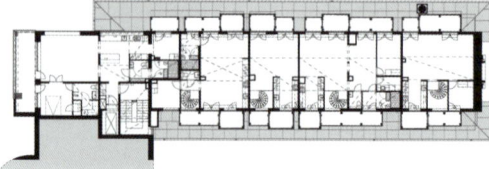

Seventh floor plan

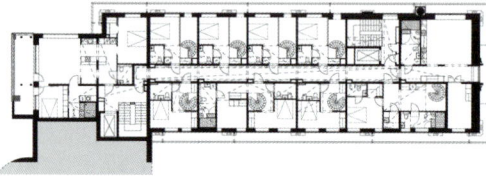

Sixth floor plan

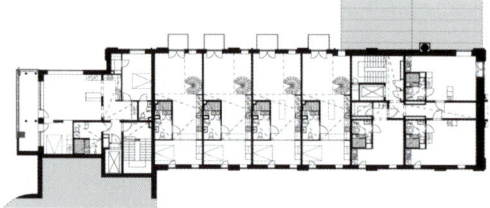

Fifth floor plan

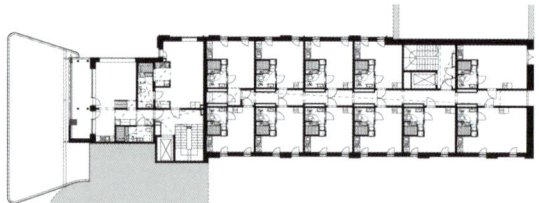

Second floor plan

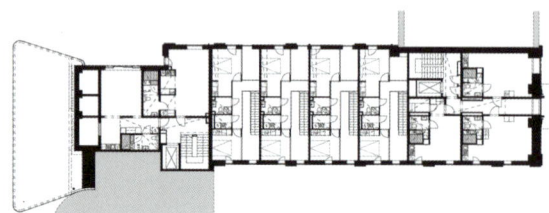

First floor plan

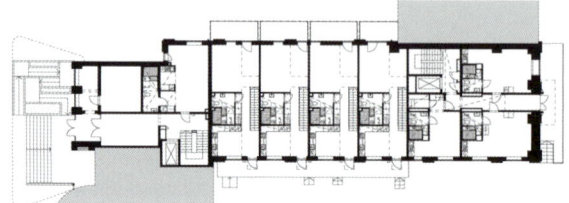

Ground floor plan

Section

PEDRO FERREIRA
ARCHITECTURE STUDIO

www.pfarchstudio.com

Between offices in Esposende and Porto, Pedro Ferreira Architecture Studio shares an extensive experience in the various sectors in the building market. The studio has designed buildings for both the public and private sectors, specializing in preexisting interventions, with a special focus on residential buildings from the 18th century to the beginning of the 20th century.
PF Architecture Studio has, over the years, seen its work published in various countries as diversified as South Korea, China, Germany, Chile, and Brazil.
Assembling a group of professionals who, directly and indirectly collaborate among themselves, setting-up a network of knowledge and experience which is placed at the service of the projects, the studio tries to develop a strong relationship with the client, anticipating and surpassing their expectations, offering a vertical service characterized by a full assistance during the whole process, from the design to the decoration.

Zwischen den Büros in Esposende und Porto verfügt Pedro Ferreira Architecture Studio über umfangreiche Erfahrungen in den verschiedenen Sektoren des Baumarktes. Das Studio hat Gebäude für den öffentlichen und privaten Sektor entworfen, die sich auf bereits bestehende Interventionen spezialisiert haben, mit einem besonderen Fokus auf Wohngebäude vom 18. bis Anfang des 20. Jahrhunderts.
PF Architecture Studio hat im Laufe der Jahre seine Arbeiten in verschiedenen Ländern wie Südkorea, China, Deutschland, Chile und Brasilien veröffentlicht.
Das Studio besteht aus einer Gruppe von Fachleuten, die direkt und indirekt zusammenarbeiten und ein Netzwerk von Wissen und Erfahrung aufbauen, das in den Dienst der Projekte gestellt wird. Es versucht, eine starke Beziehung zum Kunden aufzubauen, seine Erwartungen zu antizipieren und zu übertreffen und bietet einen vertikalen Service, der sich durch eine umfassende Unterstützung während des gesamten Prozesses vom Entwurf bis zur Dekoration auszeichnet.

Entre les bureaux d'Esposende et de Porto, Pedro Ferreira Architecture Studio partage une vaste expérience dans les différents secteurs du marché du bâtiment. Le studio a conçu des bâtiments pour les secteurs public et privé, se spécialisant dans les interventions préexistantes, avec un accent particulier sur les bâtiments résidentiels du 18e siècle au début du 20e siècle.
Au fil des ans, PF Architecture Studio a vu ses travaux publiés dans divers pays aussi diversifiés que la Corée du Sud, la Chine, l'Allemagne, le Chili et le Brésil.
Réunissant un groupe de professionnels qui, directement et indirectement, collaborent entre eux, mettant en place un réseau de connaissances et d'expériences au service des projets, l'atelier cherche à développer une relation forte avec le client, anticipant et dépassant ses attentes, offrant un service vertical caractérisé par une assistance complète pendant tout le processus, de la conception à la décoration.

Entre las oficinas de Esposende y Oporto, Pedro Ferreira Estudio de Arquitectura comparte una amplia experiencia en los diferentes sectores del mercado de la construcción. El estudio ha diseñado edificios tanto para el sector público como para el privado, especializándose en intervenciones preexistentes, con especial atención a los edificios residenciales del siglo XVIII hasta principios del siglo XX.
PF Architecture Studio ha visto su trabajo publicado en varios países tan diversos como Corea del Sur, China, Alemania, Chile o Brasil.
Conforman un grupo de profesionales que, directa e indirectamente colaboran entre sí, estableciendo una red de conocimientos y experiencia al servicio de los proyectos. El estudio trata de desarrollar una fuerte relación con el cliente, anticipándose y superando sus expectativas, ofreciendo un servicio vcaracterizado por una asistencia completa durante todo el proceso, desde el diseño hasta la decoración.

Architecture:
Pedro Ferreira Architecture Studio

Structural engineering:
ASL & Associados

Contractor: HomeReab

Styling/interior design:
Rute Moreda

Date: 2013 – 2015

Photo credits: © João Morgado

SANTA TERESA

The project deals with the renovation of a typical 19th century residential building in Oporto, with a ground floor and four storeys high and a deep rectangular floor with an asymmetrical central staircase. The proposal seeks to maximise space based on respect between the past and the present, the existing and the new. Ironically, the solution came from a song by Malvina Reynolds entitled Little Boxes. As a principle, the entire structure of the building, floors, walls, ceilings, doors and openings were preserved with their original formal and tectonic characteristics, integrating small discrete and abstract white boxes that house the new elements of the programme, such as kitchens and bathrooms, and that formally delimit the existing from the new. The result is nine apartments where light plays a key role.

Das Projekt betrifft die Renovierung eines typischen Wohngebäudes aus dem 19. Jahrhundert in Porto, mit einem Erdgeschoss und vier Stockwerken sowie einem tiefen rechteckigen Stockwerk mit einer asymmetrischen zentralen Treppe. Der Vorschlag zielt darauf ab, den Raum zu maximieren, der auf dem Respekt zwischen der Vergangenheit und der Gegenwart, dem Bestehenden und dem Neuen basiert. Ironischerweise kam die Lösung aus einem Lied von Malvina Reynolds mit dem Titel „Little Boxes". Grundsätzlich wurde die gesamte Struktur des Gebäudes, der Böden, Wände, Decken, Türen und Öffnungen mit ihren ursprünglichen formalen und tektonischen Merkmalen erhalten, indem kleine diskrete und abstrakte weiße Kästen integriert wurden, die die neuen Elemente des Programms, wie Küchen und Bäder, beherbergen und das Bestehende formal vom Neuen abgrenzen. Das Ergebnis sind neun gereinigte Wohnungen, in denen Licht eine Schlüsselrolle bei der Gestaltung des Raumes spielt.

SANTA TERESA
PORTO, PORTUGAL

Le projet porte sur la rénovation d'un immeuble d'habitation typique du XIXe siècle à Porto, comprenant un rez-de-chaussée et quatre étages de hauteur et un étage rectangulaire profond avec un escalier central asymétrique. La proposition vise à maximiser l'espace sur la base du respect entre le passé et le présent, l'existant et le nouveau. Ironiquement, la solution vient d'une chanson de Malvina Reynolds intitulée Little Boxes. En principe, toute la structure du bâtiment, les planchers, les murs, les plafonds, les portes et les ouvertures ont été conservés avec leurs caractéristiques formelles et tectoniques d'origine, intégrant de petites boîtes blanches discrètes et abstraites qui abritent les nouveaux éléments du programme, comme les cuisines et les salles de bains, et qui délimitent officiellement l'existant du nouveau. Il en résulte neuf appartements épurés, où la lumière joue un rôle clé dans la conception de l'espace.

El proyecto aborda la renovación de un típico edificio de viviendas del siglo XIX de Oporto, de planta baja y cuatro pisos de altura y una planta rectangular profunda con una escalera central asimétrica. La propuesta trata de maximizar el espacio basándose en el respeto entre el pasado y el presente, lo existente y lo nuevo. Irónicamente, la solución vino de una canción de Malvina Reynolds titulada Little Boxes. Como principio, toda la estructura del edificio, pisos, paredes, techos, puertas y aberturas se conservaron con sus características formales y tectónicas originales, integrando pequeñas cajas blancas discretas y abstractas que albergan los nuevos elementos del programa, como las cocinas y los baños, y que delimitan formalmente lo existente de lo nuevo. El resultado son nueve apartamentos depurados, donde la luz juega un papel clave en el diseño del espacio.

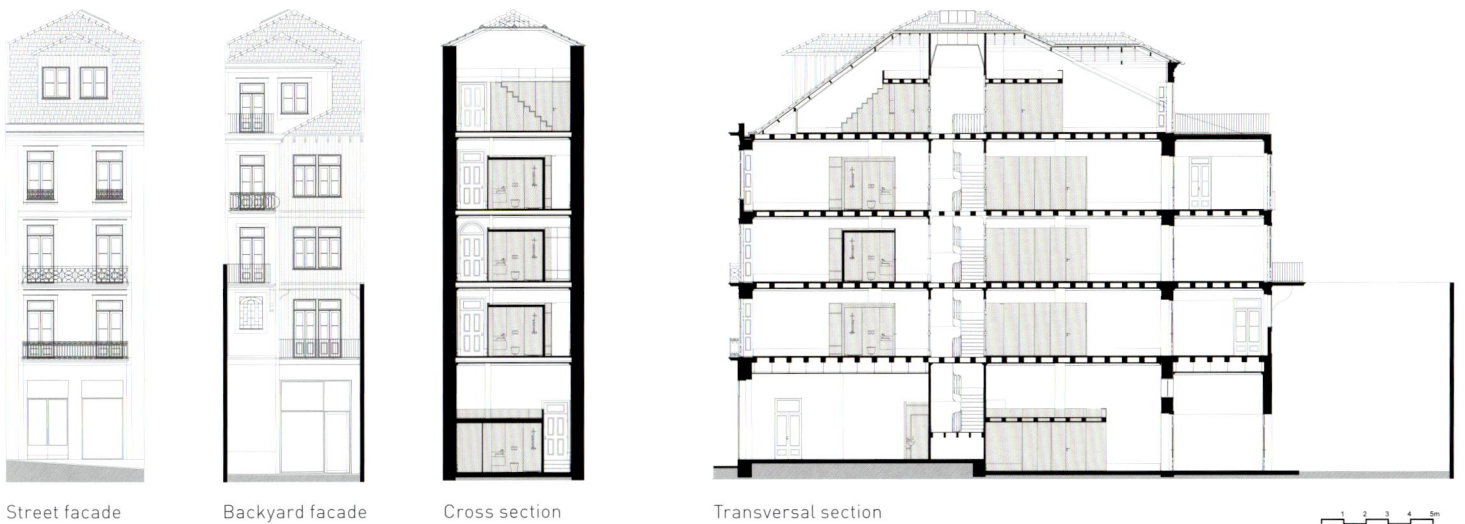

Street facade   Backyard facade   Cross section   Transversal section

1 2 3 4 5m

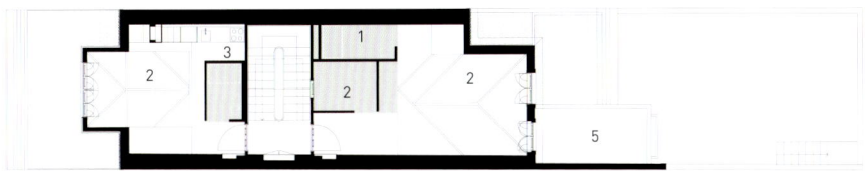

Second floor plan

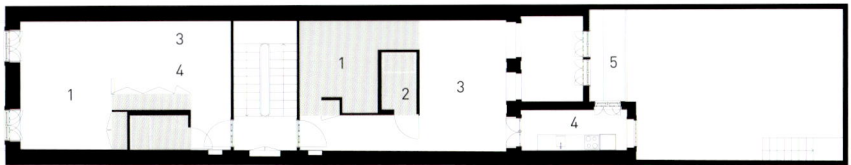

First floor plan

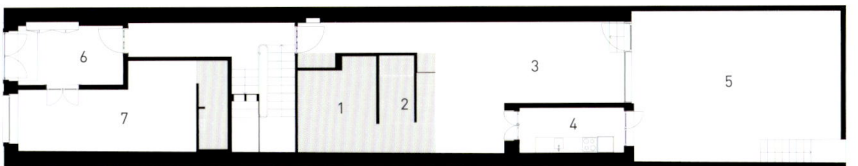

Ground floor plan

1. Bedroom
2. Bathroom
3. Living room
4. Kitchen
5. Balcony
6. Atrium
7. Store

PLASMA STUDIO

www.plasmastudio.com

Folding space into space, Plasma draws landscapes into buildings, streets into facades, from the inside out. Its transformative tectonics set spaces, planes and bodies into unforeseen relationships that challenge conventional spatial codes: an architecture of trajectory and momentum, which responds to the specificities of the local context and the possibilities of engagement.

From Beijing, Hong Kong, Singapore and Bolzano Plasma engages the local with the global whilst fostering synergies by working across scales, from furniture and installations to a wide range of buildings, urbanism and master planning. A critical design-led structure and comprehensive approach address the limits of discrete conditions, conventional topographies and spatial codes; whereby the need for conductivity and complexity give rise to transformative tectonics and new relationships that respond directly to the specificities of the local context.

Plasma studio faltet Raum in Raum, zieht Landschaften in Gebäude, Straßen auf Fassaden, innen nach außen. Seine transformative Tektonik setzt Räume, Ebenen und Körper in unvorhergesehene Beziehungen, die herkömmliche räumliche Codes herausfordern: eine Architektur aus Trajektorie und Impuls, die auf die Besonderheiten des lokalen Kontextes und die Möglichkeiten des Engagements reagiert.

Von Peking, Hongkong, Singapur und Bozen arbeitet Plasma studio stark vernetzt an lokalen und globalen Projekten in allen Maßstäben, von Möbeln und Installationen bis hin zu Gebäuden, Städtebau und Masterplänen.

Durch die Kalibrierung der dynamischen und fließenden Natur von Strömungen, Ereignissen und Ephemera einerseits und den rationalen, strukturellen und systemischen Parametern von Material, Organisation und Widerstand andererseits entwickelt Plasma einzigartige, evokative und elegante Projekte.

Der Bedarf an Konnektivität und Komplexität führt zu transformativen Tektoniken und neuen Beziehungen, die direkt auf die Besonderheiten des lokalen Kontexts reagieren.

Pliant l'espace dans l'espace, Plasma dessine des paysages dans les bâtiments, des rues dans les façades, de l'intérieur vers l'extérieur. Sa tectonique transformatrice transforme les espaces, les plans et les corps en relations imprévues qui remettent en question les codes spatiaux conventionnels : une architecture de trajectoire et d'élan, qui répond aux spécificités du contexte local et aux possibilités d'engagement.

De Pékin, Hong Kong, Singapour et Bolzano Plasma engage le local avec le global tout en favorisant les synergies en travaillant à travers les échelles, du mobilier et des installations à une large gamme de bâtiments, l'urbanisme et la planification d'ensemble. Une structure critique axée sur la conception et une approche globale abordent les limites des conditions discrètes, des topographies conventionnelles et des codes spatiaux, le besoin de conductivité et de complexité donnant lieu à une tectonique transformatrice et à de nouvelles relations qui répondent directement aux spécificités du contexte local.

Convirtiendo espacios dentro de espacios, Plasma dibuja paisajes en edificios, calles en fachadas, de adentro hacia afuera. Su técnica transformadora transforma espacios, planos y cuerpos en relaciones imprevistas que desafían los códigos espaciales convencionales: una arquitectura de trayectoria e impulso que responde a los requisitos del contexto local y al compromiso ambiental.

Desde Pekín, Hong Kong, Singapur y Bolzano, Plasma involucra lo local con lo global a la vez que fomenta las sinergias a través de escalas, desde mobiliario e instalaciones hasta una amplia gama de edificios, urbanismo y planificación. Una estructura crítica basada en el diseño y un enfoque integral abordan los límites de las condiciones discretas, las topografías convencionales y los códigos espaciales. La necesidad de conductividad y complejidad da lugar a técnicas transformadoras y a nuevas relaciones que responden a las especificidades del contexto local.

SCHÄFER ROOFSCAPE

Location: San Candido (BZ), Italy

Year: 2014

Team: Ulla Hell, Eva Castro,
Holger Kehne, Peter Pichler

Photo credits: © Michael Pezzei,
© Holger Kehne (p. 209 bottom
left, p. 210)

DOLOMITENBLICK

Location: Sesto (BZ), Italy

Year: 2012

Team: Ulla Hell, Eva Castro,
Holger Kehne, David Preindl,
Nicoletta Gerevini, Peter Pichler,
Daniela Walder, Maya Shopova

Awards: European Copper in
Architecture Awards: Shortlisted,
Commended, Public Choice
Winner Architizer A+ Award

Photo credits: © Hertha Hurnaus

Located in the medieval centre of San Candido, Schäfer Roofscape is a newly-completed restoration and conversion of a historical building. The first 3 storeys house a department store while the upper three storeys serve as four large, independent apartments within the formerly underused attic space. The building faces a public plaza protected by local regulations, thus, efforts were directed towards its rear facade. This west-facing elevation explores how slicing and folding can be employed to expand the limits of the ubiquitous pitched roof typology: large balcony slots produce bright living conditions and generous exterior expansion space within this dense urban situation.

Das Gebäude befindet sich im historischen Zentrum der Fußgängerzone von Innichen. In den drei unteren Stockwerken (inklusiv Keller) befindet sich ein Kaufhaus, welches nicht verändert wurde. Die oberen, zum Teil ungenutzten Stockwerke und der Dachraum wurden in vier großzügige Wohnungen für den Bauherrn und seine drei Töchter umstrukturiert. Die Hauptfassade Richtung Michaelsplatz und Fußgängerzone unterliegt dem Ensembleschutz und wurde über den Umbau beinahe nicht verändert. Der Entwurf konzentriert sich größtenteils auf die dem Platz abgewandte Seite Richtung Westen: Durch Einschnitte im Satteldach dringt Tageslicht in das Innere der neu geschaffenen Wohneinheiten, gleichzeitig werden großzügige Außenterrassen gebildet. Das Satteldach bleibt in seiner Großform erhalten.

SCHÄFER ROOFSCAPE

SAN CANDIDO (BZ), ITALY

Situé dans le centre médiéval de San Candido, Schäfer Roofscape est un bâtiment historique récemment restauré et transformé. Les trois premiers étages abritent un grand magasin, tandis que les trois étages supérieurs servent de quatre grands appartements indépendants dans l'ancien grenier sous-utilisé. Le bâtiment fait face à une place publique protégée par la réglementation locale, les efforts ont donc été orientés vers sa façade arrière. Cette élévation orientée à l'ouest explore comment le découpage et le pliage peuvent être utilisés pour repousser les limites de la typologie omniprésente du toit en pente : les grandes fentes de balcon produisent des conditions de vie lumineuses et un espace extérieur généreux dans cette situation urbaine dense.

Situado en el centro medieval de San Cándido, Schäfer Roofscape es un edificio histórico recientemente restaurado y reconvertido. Los primeros tres pisos albergan un centro comercial, mientras que los tres pisos superiores albergan cuatro grandes apartamentos e independientes dentro del espacio del ático, que antes estaba infrautilizado. El edificio da a una plaza pública protegida por la normativa local, por lo que los esfuerzos se dirigieron al diseño de la fachada posterior. Este alzado orientado hacia el oeste explora cómo se pueden utilizar el corte y el plegado para expandir los límites de la omnipresente tipología de techos inclinados: grandes ranuras para la construcción de balcones mejoran las condiciones de vida y aportan un generoso espacio exterior dentro de una densa situación urbana.

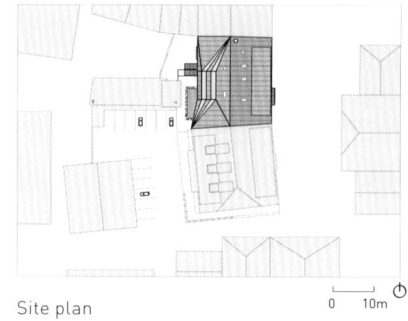

Site plan

0   10m

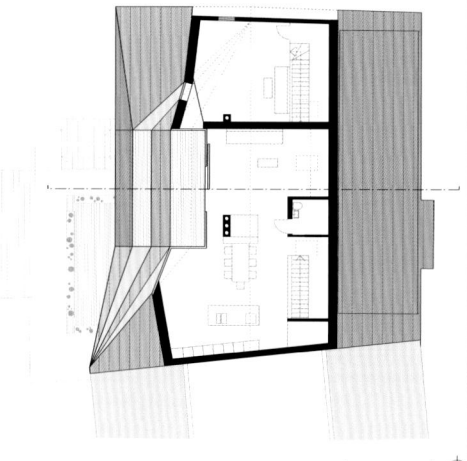

Fourth floor plan

0   5m

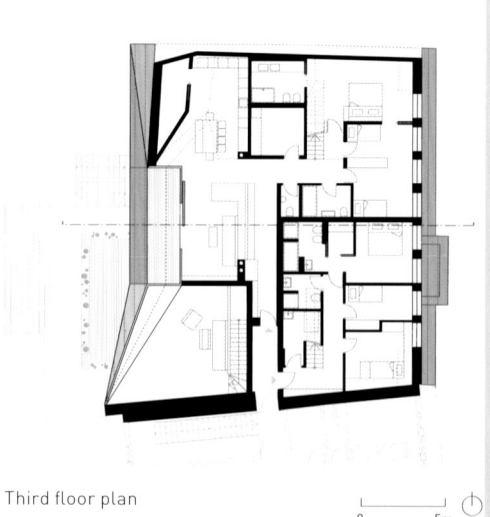

Third floor plan

0   5m

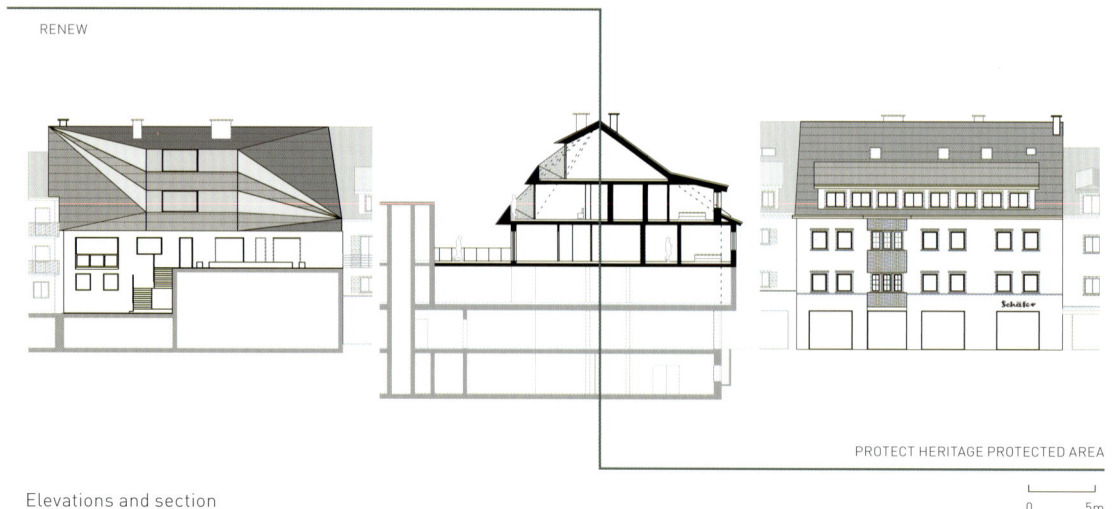

PROTECT HERITAGE PROTECTED AREA

Elevations and section

0   5m

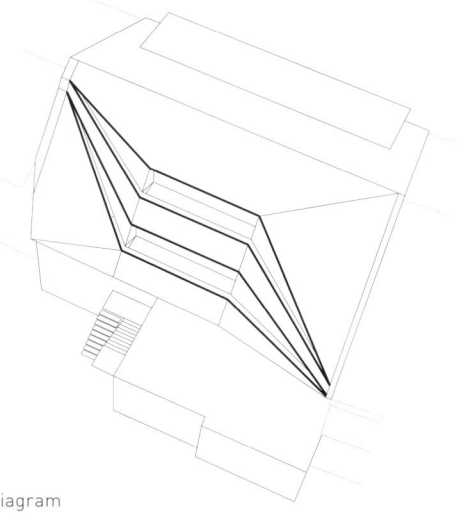

Diagram

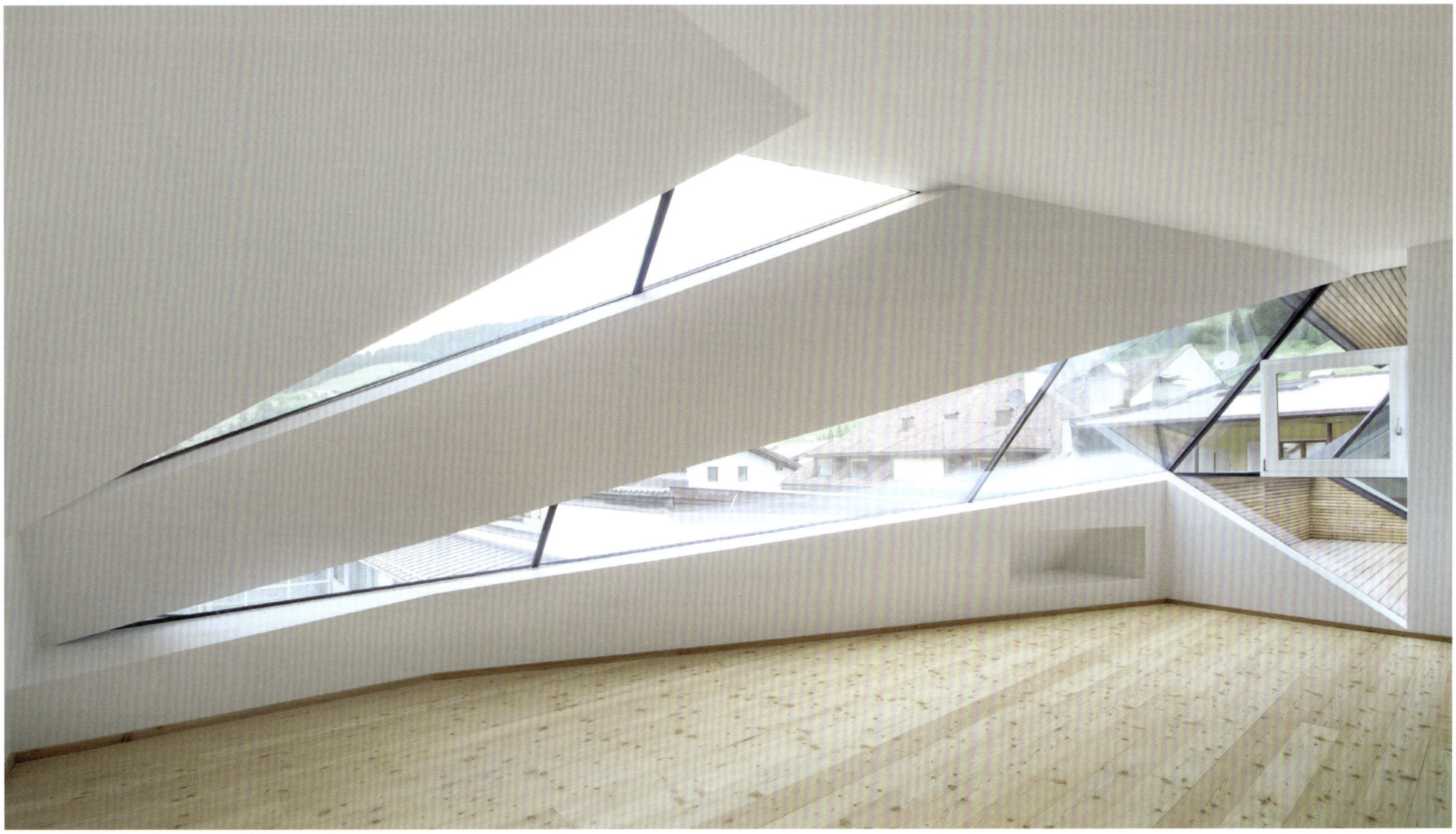

Located on a hillside in the Dolomites, the building was designed to satisfy the functional requests of 6 units with one circulation core. This is rendered legible in the project's massing through 2 defining gestures: a vertical incision splitting the volume and the unfolding of horizontal strips that form the balustrades of terrace spaces blending into the natural hillside, stepping back to maximize privacy, southern exposure and views of the mountain range.
The volume that merges with the natural topography and reduces the material palette to a very local, almost vernacular code: larch wood and pre oxidized copper. The copper defines the roof as a continuation of the overall facade, its form draws on the local planning regulation which allows only a pitched roof. Slightly deformed, it merges with the design concept as well as with the traditional pitched roof typology.

Das Gebäude befindet sich in einer Hanglage am Rande eines Wohngebietes. Die Volumen wurde hauptsächlich aus der pragmatischen funktionalen Anforderung entwickelt, 6 voneinander unabhängige Wohnungen mit einem gemeinsam genutzten Treppenhaus unterzubringen: durch eine Einkerbung in der Fassade, welche auch den Hauptzugang markiert, sowie durch ein visuelles Trennen der Einheiten ist das Gebäude in zwei Hälften geteilt. Neben seiner funktionalen Bedeutung bildet dieser Einschnitt das prägende Element des Gebäudes: von der Einbuchtung ausgehend, verläuft je ein Band zu beiden Seiten. Dieses Band bildet die Brüstung von großzügig überdachten Balkonen und endet im Gelände der umgebenden Topografie. Materialität und Farbgebung beschränken sich auf regionale, fast ortsbezogene Kodes, verwendet werden neben Glas lediglich Lärchenholz und voroxidiertes Kupfer.
Das dunkle Kupfer umgibt das Objekt von allen Seiten. Die Typologie des Satteldachs wird in die volumetrische Gestaltung des Gebäudes als Fortsetzung der Fassadenausbildung aufgenommen.

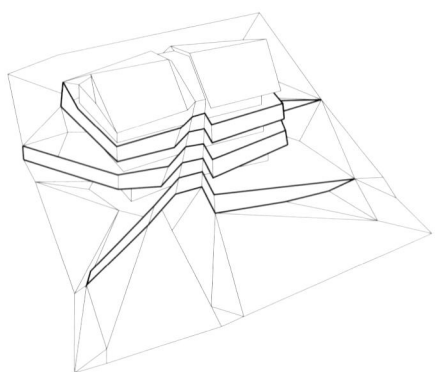

Horizontal diagram

DOLOMITENBLICK
SESTO (BZ), ITALY

Situé à flanc de colline dans les Dolomites, le bâtiment a été conçu pour répondre aux demandes fonctionnelles de 6 unités avec un noyau de circulation. Ceci est rendu lisible dans la volumétrie du projet à travers deux gestes déterminants : une incision verticale séparant le volume et le déploiement de bandes horizontales qui forment les balustrades d'espaces terrasses se fondant dans le versant naturel de la colline, en reculant pour maximiser l'intimité, l'exposition sud et les vues sur la chaîne de montagnes.
Le volume qui se confond avec la topographie naturelle et réduit la palette de matériaux à un code très local, presque vernaculaire : le bois de mélèze et le cuivre pré oxydé. Le cuivre définit le toit comme un prolongement de la façade globale, sa forme s'inspire de la réglementation d'urbanisme locale qui ne permet qu'un toit en pente. Légèrement déformée, elle se confond aussi bien avec le concept de conception qu'avec la typologie traditionnelle du toit en pente.

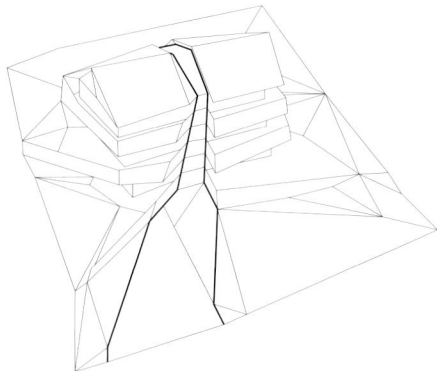

Vertical diagram

Situado en una ladera de las Dolomitas, el edificio fue diseñado para satisfacer las necesidades funcionales de seis espacios con un núcleo de circulación. Esto se hace legible en el conjunto del proyecto a través de dos gestos definitorios: una incisión vertical que divide el volumen y el despliegue de franjas horizontales que forman las balaustradas de las terrazas que se mezclan con la ladera natural, retrocediendo para maximizar la privacidad, la exposición al sur y las vistas de la cordillera.
El volumen se funde con la topografía natural y reduce la paleta de materiales a un código muy local, casi vernáculo: madera de alerce y cobre preoxidado. El cobre define el techo como una continuación de la fachada general, su forma se basa en la normativa de planificación local que sólo permite un techo inclinado. Ligeramente deformado, se funde con el concepto de diseño y con la tipología tradicional del tejado a dos aguas.

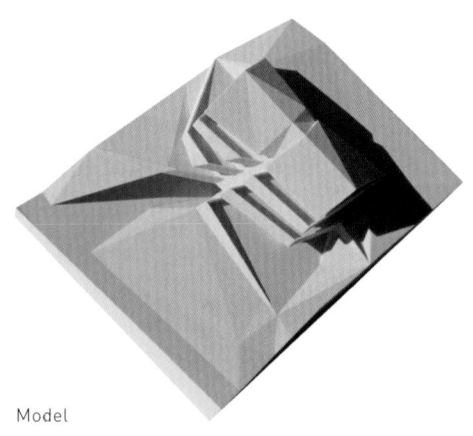

Model

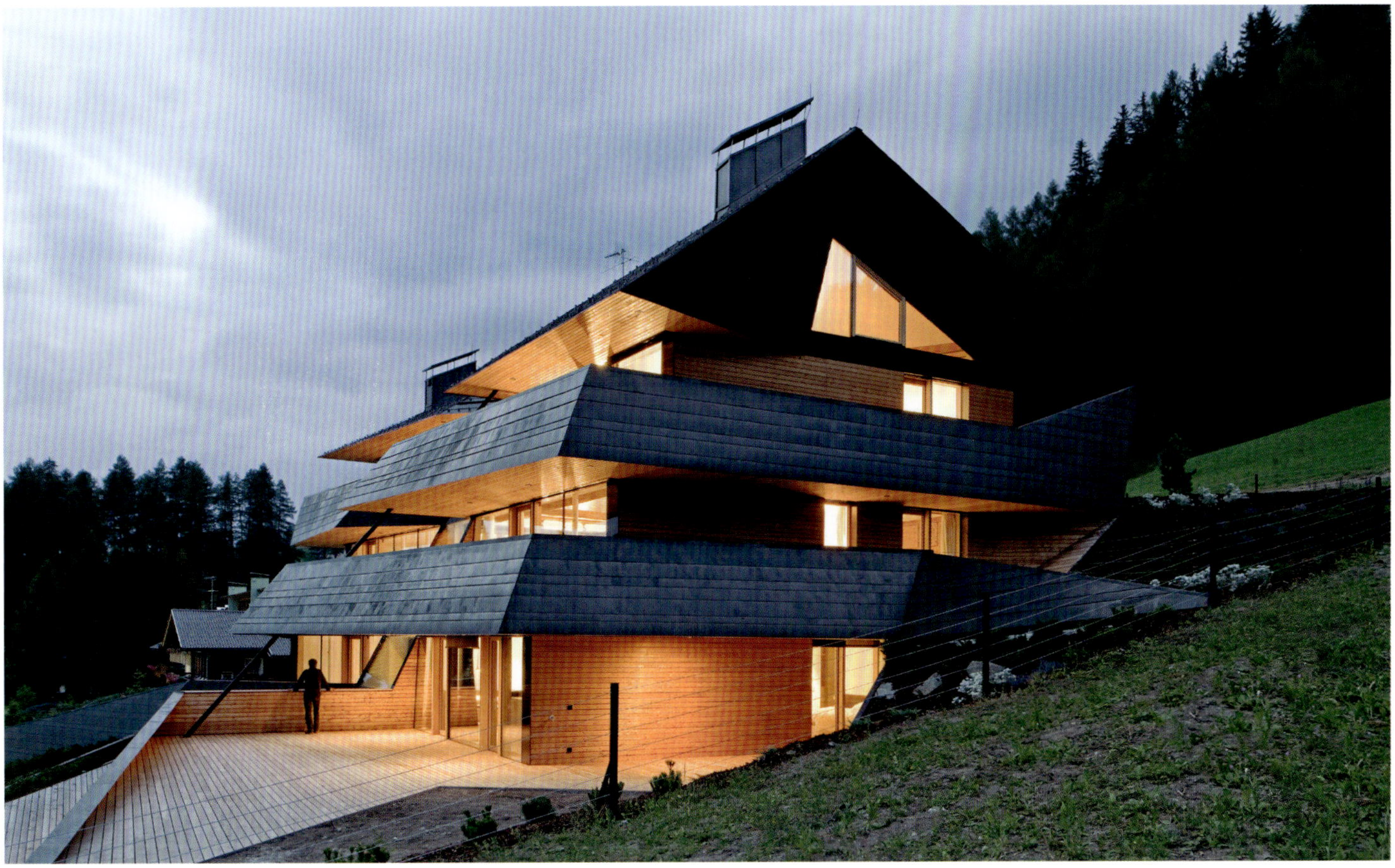

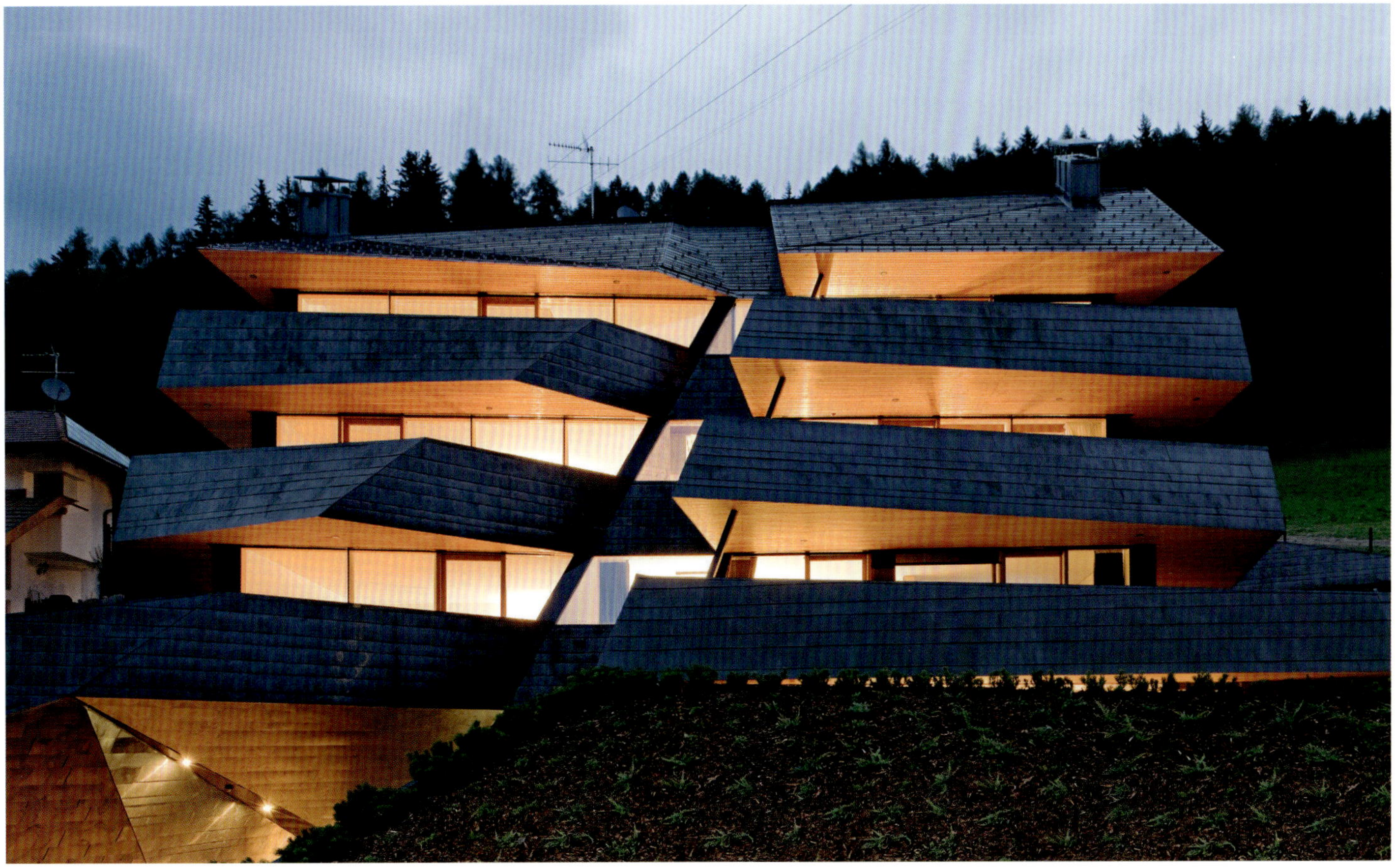

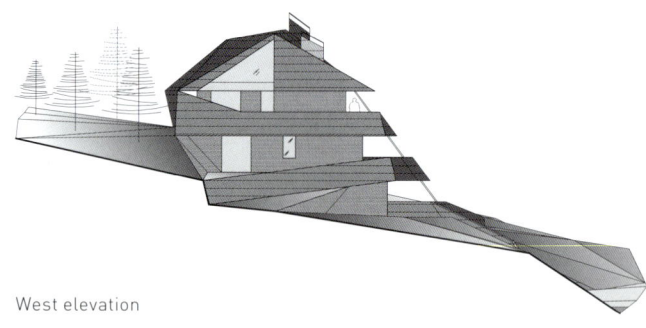

West elevation

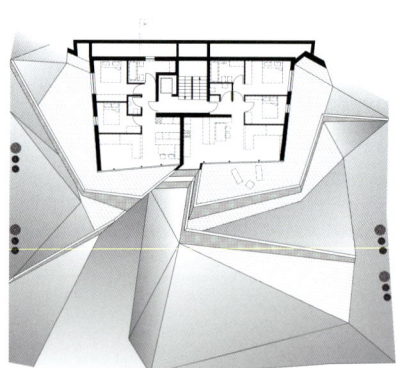

Third floor plan

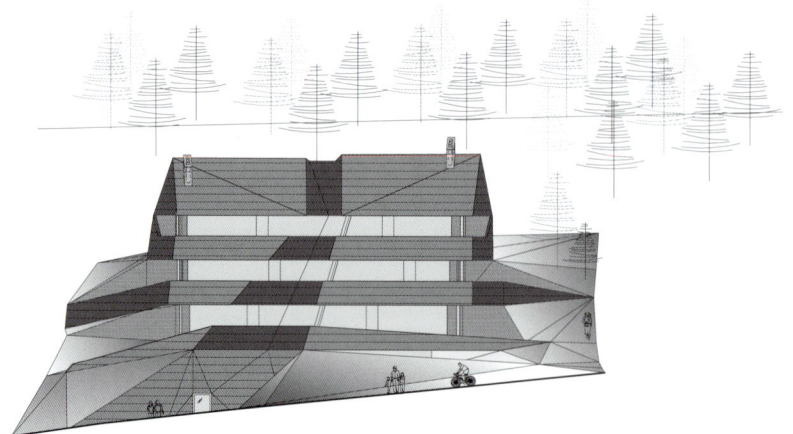

South elevation

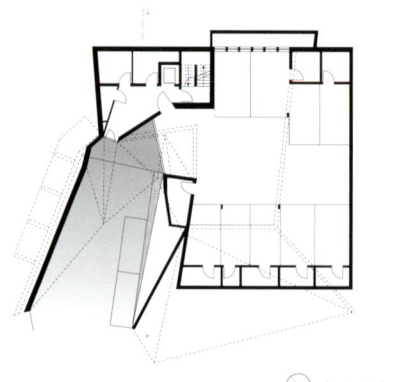

Ground floor plan

0 m   5 m

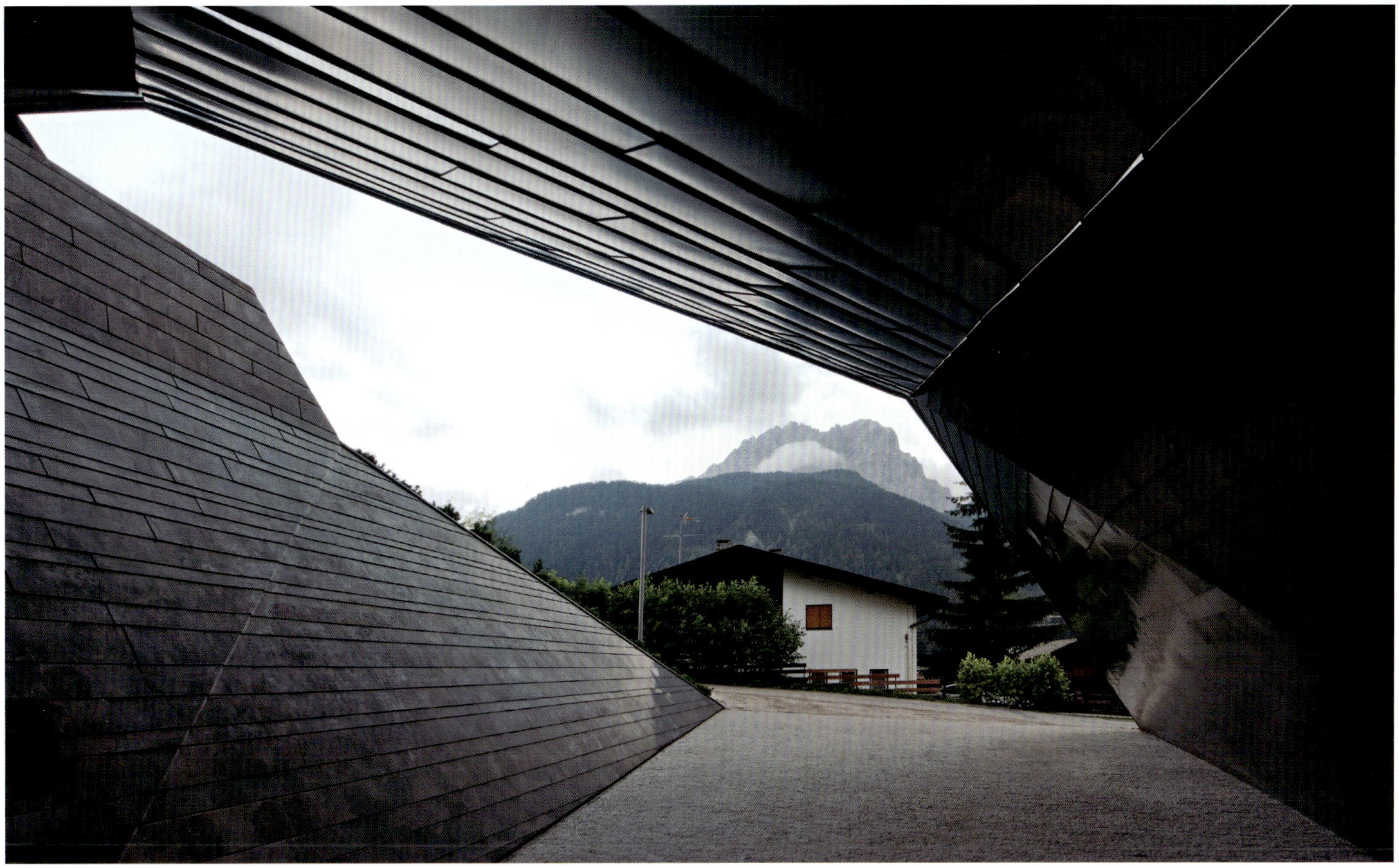

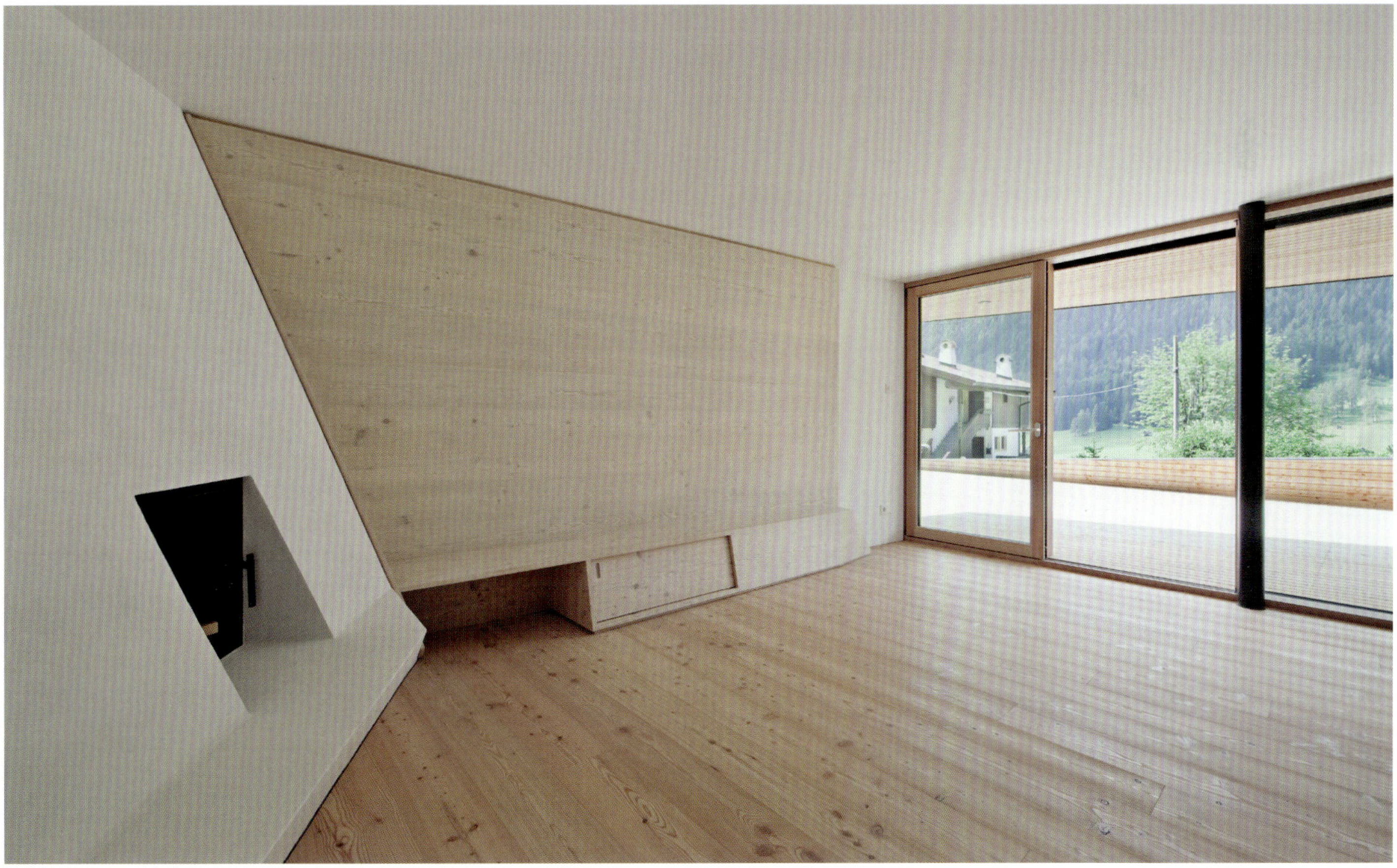

RH + ARCHITECTURE
www.rhplus-architecture.com

The studio was created in 2000 by Alix Héaume and Adrien Robain, both architects and associate managers. In parallel with the studio's activities, the two partners are involved in several associations and institutions dedicated to the promotion of architecture: Adrien Robain was Vice-President of the Maison de l'Architecture in Ile-de-France for 8 years; Alix and Adrien were part of the association "French Touch".
Both took part in numerous architectural juries and were at the initiative of the "Festival of Vivid Architectures" in 2004 and 2006 with the a-Pack association. In 1999, Alix and Adrien were laureates of the Europan Dom. In 2006, the studio won the Nouveaux Albums des Jeunes Architectes. The two partners received a HEQ training and in 2010 the agency received "L'appel à Projets BBC" launched by ADEME and the Ile-de-France region. In 2014, the TEAM won the 2nd prize of "Grand Public Archicontemporaine" for the dwellings and the nursery on Riquet Street.

Das Studio wurde im Jahr 2000 von Alix Héaume und Adrien Robain, Architekten und Associate Manager, gegründet. Parallel zu den Aktivitäten des Studios beteiligen sich die beiden Partner an mehreren Verbänden und Institutionen, die sich der Förderung der Architektur widmen: Adrien Robain war 8 Jahre lang Vizepräsident des Maison de l'Architecture de Île-de-France; Alix und Adrien waren Teil des Vereins „French Touch".
Beide haben in zahlreichen Architekturjurys mitgewirkt und wurden 2004 und 2006 auf Initiative des „Festival of Living Architectures" in den Verein a-Pack eingeladen. 1999 erhielten Alix und Adrien den Europan Dom. Im Jahr 2006 gewann das Studio die Nouveaux Albums des Jeunes Architectes; beide Partner erhielten HEQ-Schulungen und im Jahr 2010 erhielt die Agentur „L'Appel à Projets BBC", das von ADEME und der Region Ile-de-France ins Leben gerufen wurde. Im Jahr 2014 gewann das TEAM den 2. Preis des „Grand Public Archicontemporaine" für die Häuser und die Kindertagesstätte in der Riquet Street.

L'agence a été créée en 2000 par Alix Héaume et Adrien Robain, tous deux architectes et directeurs associés. Parallèlement aux activités du studio, les deux partenaires participent à plusieurs associations et institutions dédiées à la promotion de l'architecture : Adrien Robain a été vice-président de la Maison de l'Architecture en l'Île-de-France pendant 8 ans ; Alix et Adrien faisaient partie de l'association « French Touch ».
Tous deux ont participé à de nombreux jurys d'architecture et ont été à l'initiative du « Festival des Architectures Vives » en 2004 et 2006 avec l'association a-Pack. En 1999, Alix et Adrien ont reçu le prix de l'Europan Dom. En 2006, le studio a remporté les Nouveaux Albums des Jeunes Architectes ; les deux partenaires ont reçu une formation HQE et l'agence a reçu en 2010 le prix de l'Appel à Projets BBC lancé par l'ADEME et la région Ile-de-France. En 2014, l'équipe a remporté le 2e prix du Grand Public Archicontemporaine pour les logements et la crèche de la rue Riquet.

El estudio fue creado en el año 2000 por Alix Héaume y Adrien Robain, ambos arquitectos y gerentes asociados. Paralelamente a las actividades del estudio, los dos socios participan en varias asociaciones e instituciones dedicadas a la promoción de la arquitectura: Adrien Robain fue vicepresidente de la Maison de l'Architecture de Île-de-France durante 8 años; Alix y Adrien formaron parte de la asociación «French Touch».
Ambos han participado en numerosos jurados de arquitectura y han sido invitados a la iniciativa del «Festival de Arquitecturas Vivas» en 2004 y 2006 con la asociación a-Pack. En 1999, Alix y Adrien fueron galardonados con el Europan Dom. En 2006, el estudio ganó los Nouveaux Albums des Jeunes Architectes; ambos socios recibieron una formación HEQ y en 2010 la agencia recibió «L'Appel à Projets BBC» lanzada por ADEME y la región de Île-de-France. En 2014, el EQUIPO ganó el 2º premio de «Grand Public Archicontemporaine» por las viviendas y el vivero de la calle Riquet.

Location: Paris, France

Building area:
2.560 m² / 27,555 sq ft

Project completion date: 2012

Architecture team:
rh + architecture

Sustainability: RFR elements

General contractor:
Capaldi Construction

Photo credits: © Luc Boegly

Awards:
- 2010 for BBC projects
  organised by ADEME
  and Region Ile-de-France

- 2014 for « *Prix grand public
  archicontemporaine des Maisons
  de l'architecture en France* »

Located in a block near the bassin de la Villette, the building integrates 28 apartments and a nursery located on the ground floor. Its long main façade takes advantage of the southern orientation through a design based on galleries that regulate the temperature in the summer and winter months. These external damping spaces are closed with sliding glass panels that allow the sun's heat to be absorbed during the day and released at night. In colder climates, air from mechanical ventilation is preheated.

The apartments consist of a north-facing entrance, kitchen and bathroom, and south-facing bedrooms and living rooms with galleries. Some floors contain double-height living rooms. The western part of the building is developed in a staggered shape that generates private terraces and green roofs with views.

Das Gebäude befindet sich in einem Block in der Nähe des Bassins de la Villette und umfasst 28 Wohnungen und eine Kindertagesstätte im Erdgeschoss. Die lange Hauptfassade nutzt die Südorientierung durch eine Gestaltung auf der Basis von Galerien, die die Temperatur in den Sommer- und Wintermonaten regeln. Diese äußeren Polsterräume sind mit verschiebbaren Glasscheiben verschlossen, die es ermöglichen, dass tagsüber Sonnenwärme aufgenommen und nachts abgegeben werden kann. In kälteren Klimazonen wird die Luft aus der mechanischen Lüftung vorgewärmt.

Die Appartements bestehen aus einem Eingangsbereich, einer Küche und einem Badezimmer mit Blick nach Norden und Schlaf- und Wohnzimmer mit Galerien mit Blick nach Süden. In einigen Stockwerken befinden sich doppelt hohe Wohnräume. Der westliche Teil des Gebäudes ist versetzt angelegt, sodass private Terrassen und Gründächer mit Aussicht entstehen können.

PLEIN SOLEIL
FRANCE, PARIS

Situé proche du bassin de la Villette, l'immeuble comprend 28 appartements et une crèche située au rez-de-chaussée. Sa longue façade principale profite de l'orientation sud grâce a une conception basée sur une double peau qui régule la température en été et en hiver. Ces espaces «tampon» extérieurs sont fermés par des panneaux de verre coulissants qui permettent à la chaleur du soleil d'être absorbée pendant la journée et libérée la nuit. Dans les climats plus froids, l'air provenant de la ventilation mécanique est préchauffé.

Les appartements se composent d'une entrée, d'une cuisine et d'une salle de bains, orientées au nord, et de chambres et de salons avec loggias, orientées au sud. Certains étages contiennent des salons à double hauteur. La partie ouest du bâtiment est aménagée en quinconce, ce qui génère des terrasses privées et des toits vegetalisés avec vue.

Situado en una manzana cercana al bassin de la Villette, el edificio integra 28 apartamentos y una guardería situada en planta baja. Su larga fachada principal aprovecha la orientación sur mediante un diseño basado en galerías que regulan la temperatura en los meses de verano e invierno. Estos espacios de amortiguación exterior se cierran con paneles correderos de vidrio que permiten que el calor del sol sea absorbido durante el día y liberado por la noche. Con clima más frío, el aire procedente de la ventilación mecánica es precalentado.

Los apartamentos constan de entrada, cocina y baño, orientados hacia el norte, y habitaciones y salas de estar con galerías, orientadas hacia el sur. Algunos pisos contienen salas de estar de doble altura. La parte oeste del edificio se desarrolla con una forma escalonada que genera terrazas privadas y cubiertas verdes con vistas.

South facade

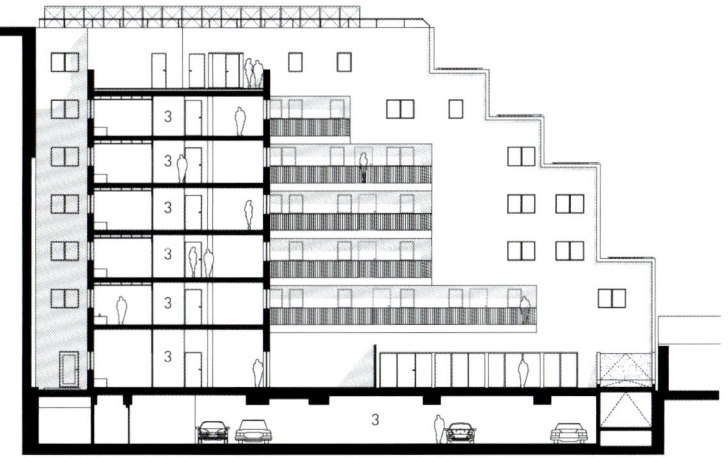

North facade

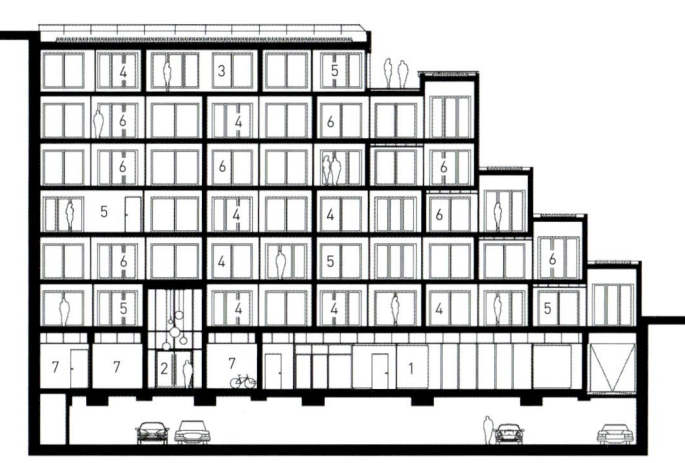

Longitudinal section

1. Nursery
2. Entry hall
3. Study
4. 2 rooms
5. 3 rooms
6. 4 rooms
7. Technical local
8. Parking
9. Courtyard

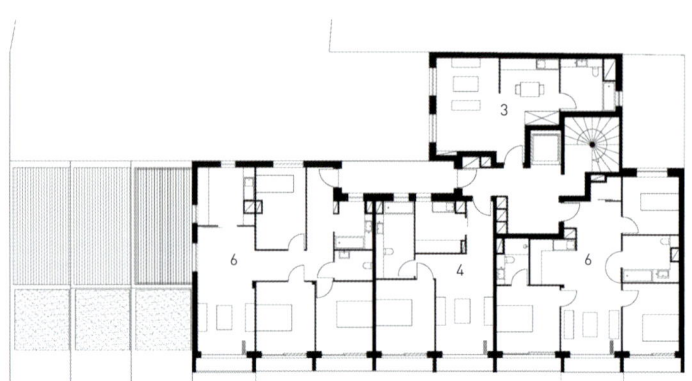

Fifth floor plan

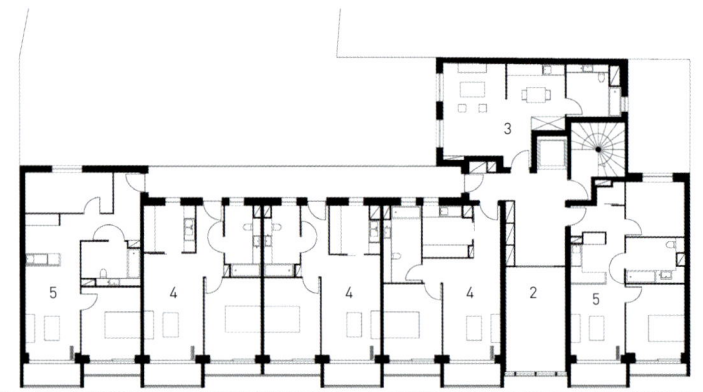

First floor plan

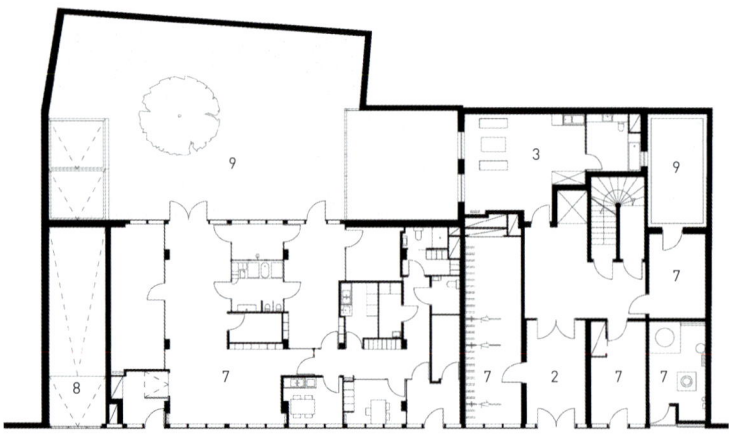

Ground floor plan

1. Nursery
2. Entry hall
3. Study
4. 2 rooms
5. 3 rooms
6. 4 rooms
7. Technical local
8. Parking
9. Courtyard

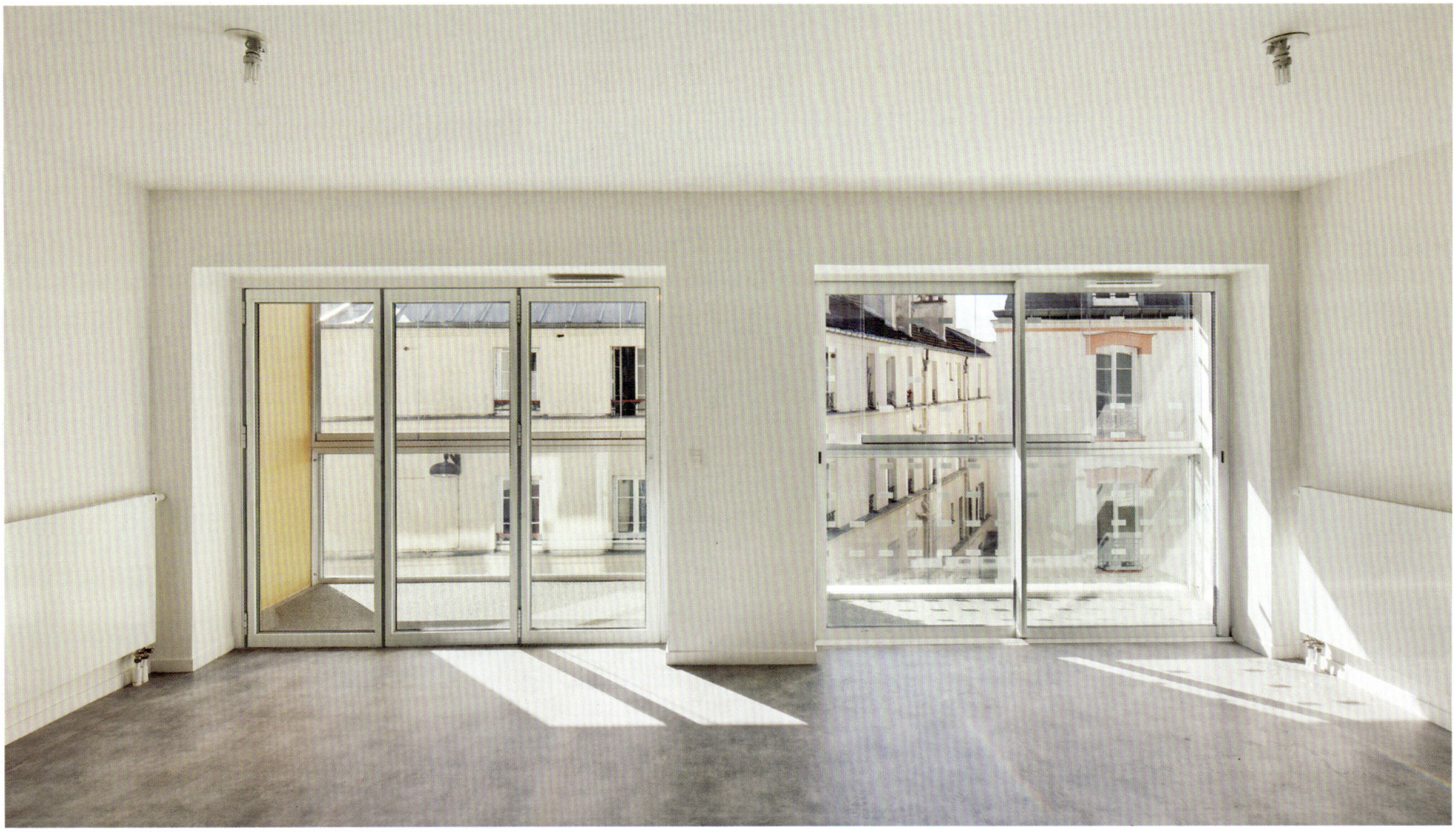

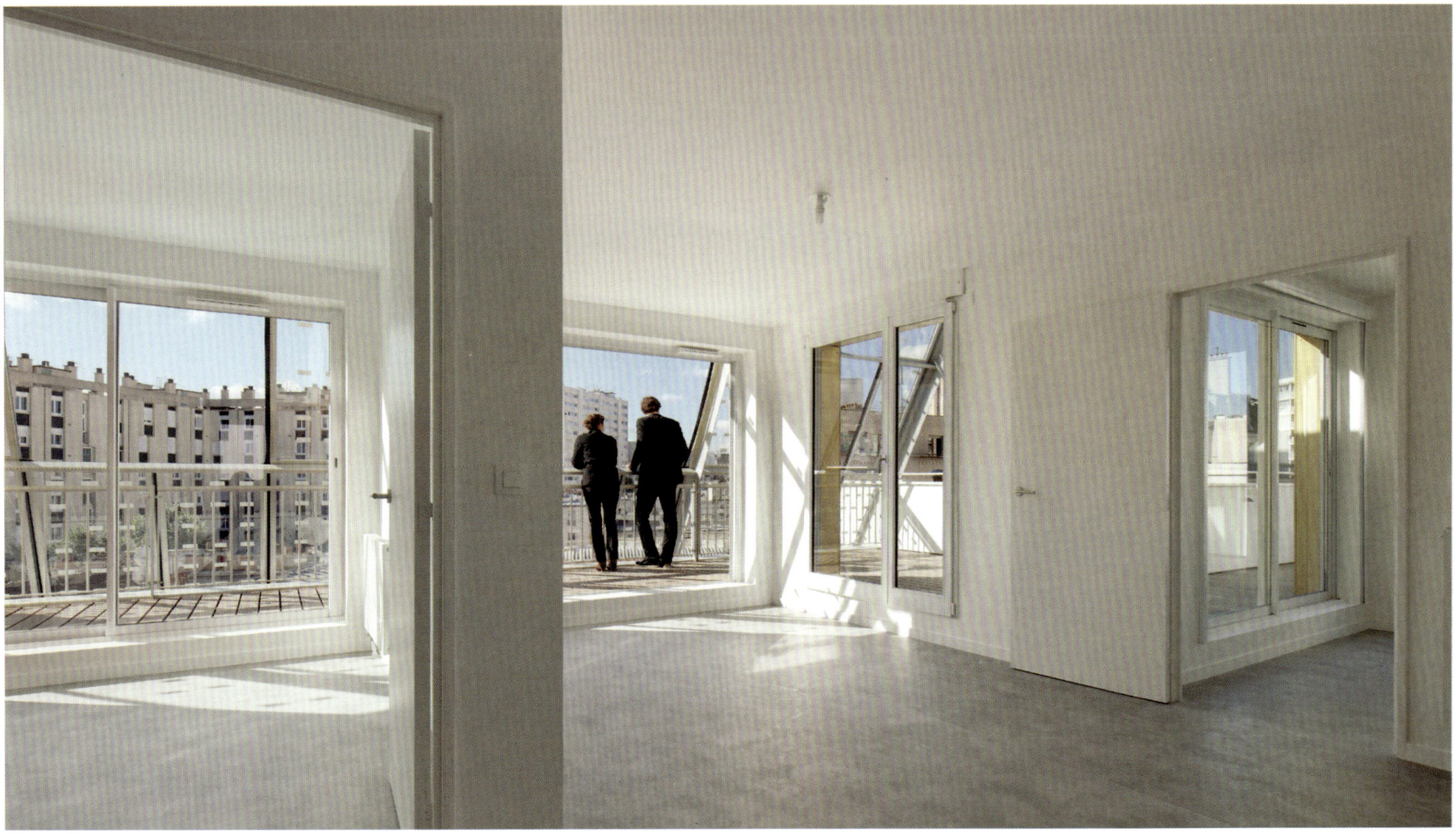

SOMDOON ARCHITECTS

www.somdoonarchitects.com

Founded in 2010, Somdoon Architects has gained recognition for its design, most notably known for residential projects, including entry-level housing, mid-rise and high-rise developments.
The name, 'Somdoon' deriving from the Thai word, means 'balance'. Our team believe that each project has different conditions and challenges. It is crucial to look around, research in depth and collaborate with others to find the balance for each project, and the unique design is the result of the process.
Our works has won several internationally-acclaimed awards, including: the WAF World Architecture Festival for 'Best Future Project'; The Asia Pacific Property Awards for 'Best High-Rise Thailand' and 'Best Architecture Multiple Residence Asia Pacific'; and 'Silver Winner' at the MIPIM (Asia) Awards for 'Best Residential Development'.
Today, our practice consists of architects, interior architects and designers positioned in a combined workspace in the heart of Bangkok, Thailand.

Somdoon Architects wurde 2010 gegründet und hat sich durch sein Design einen Namen gemacht, vor allem durch Wohnprojekte, darunter Einstiegswohnungen, Mittel- und Hochhäuser.
Der Name „Somdoon" leitet sich vom thailändischen Wort ab und bedeutet „Gleichgewicht". Unser Team ist davon überzeugt, dass jedes Projekt unterschiedliche Bedingungen und Herausforderungen hat. Es ist entscheidend, sich umzusehen, gründlich zu recherchieren und mit anderen zusammenzuarbeiten, um das Gleichgewicht für jedes Projekt zu finden, und das einzigartige Design ist das Ergebnis des Prozesses.
Unsere Arbeiten wurden mehrfach international ausgezeichnet, darunter: das WAF World Architecture Festival für das „Best Future Project", die Asia Pacific Property Awards für „Best High-Rise Thailand" und „Best Architecture Multiple Residence Asia Pacific" sowie der „Silver Winner" bei den MIPIM (Asia) Awards für „Best Residential Development".
Heute besteht unser Büro aus Architekten, Innenarchitekten und Designern, die sich in einem gemeinsamen Arbeitsbereich im Herzen von Bangkok, Thailand, befinden.

Fondé en 2010, Somdoon Architects s'est fait connaître par son design, notamment pour ses projets résidentiels, notamment pour ses résidences d'entrée de gamme, ses immeubles de moyenne et de grande hauteur.
Le nom, 'Somdoon' dérivant du mot thaïlandais, signifie 'équilibre'. Notre équipe croit que chaque projet a des conditions et des défis différents. Il est crucial de regarder autour de soi, de faire des recherches approfondies et de collaborer avec les autres pour trouver l'équilibre pour chaque projet, et la conception unique est le résultat du processus.
Nos travaux ont remporté plusieurs prix de renommée internationale, notamment : le WAF World Architecture Festival for 'Best Future Project' ; The Asia Pacific Property Awards for 'Best High-Rise Thailand' et 'Best Architecture Multiple Residence Asia Pacific' ; et 'Silver Winner' aux MIPIM (Asia) Awards for 'Best Residential Development'.
Aujourd'hui, notre cabinet est composé d'architectes, d'architectes d'intérieur et de designers positionnés dans un espace de travail combiné au cœur de Bangkok, en Thaïlande.

Fundada en 2010, Somdoon Architects ha ganado reconocimiento por su diseño, conocido sobre todo por sus proyectos residenciales, incluyendo viviendas de nivel básico, edificios de mediana y alta altura.
El nombre «Somdoon» significa «equilibrio» en tailandés. Nuestro equipo cree que cada proyecto tiene diferentes condiciones y desafíos. Es crucial mirar alrededor, investigar en profundidad y colaborar con otros profesionales para encontrar el equilibrio adecuado y un diseño único como resultado del proceso.
Nuestros trabajos han sido galardonados con varios premios de renombre internacional, entre los que se incluyen: el Festival Mundial de Arquitectura WAF («Mejor Proyecto del Futuro»); los premios inmobiliarios de Asia Pacífico («Mejor Tailandia de Gran Altura») y «Mejor Residencia Múltiple de Arquitectura de Asia Pacífico». El estudio has sido además, «Ganador de Plata» en los premios MIPIM Asia («Mejor Desarrollo Residencial»).
Hoy en día, nuestro estudio está formado por arquitectos, arquitectos de interiores y diseñadores ubicados en un espacio de trabajo común en el corazón de Bangkok, Tailandia.

Project location:
Patong, Phuket

Design inception: April 2013

Start of construction:
December 2013

Completed: August 2015

Size plot area: 8,639 m²

Tower A
Gross floor area: 9,889 m²
Unit size: 42.11-67.38 m²
Number of units: 139, 7 Floors
Tower B
Gross floor area: 7,865 m²
Unit size: 42.11-71.62 m²
Number of units: 131, 7 Floors

Design architect:
Somdoon Architects

Collaboration with Creative Crews

Project architect:
Punpong Wiwatkul

Landscape architect:
Shma Company Limited

Interior design:
Somdoon Architects Co., Ltd.

Photo credits: W Workspace

THE DECK

This set of two 7-storey buildings is located near Patong Beach, known for its natural beauty and nightlife. Each of the buildings is oriented to offer a unique view of the natural environment and its large façades allow abundant sunlight and ventilation in all rooms. The unique composition is based on a pattern formed by the large balconies in flight of each residential unit, whose length varies between 2.2 and 3.3 m. The design of the handrails, made up of vertical aluminium plates arranged at different angles, guarantees the privacy of each unit and makes it possible to conceal elements from the installations. The bright navy blue colour of the lower part of the balconies mixes with the colour of the Andaman Sea and symbolises the nightlife of the area.

Dieses Set von zwei 7-stöckigen Gebäuden befindet sich in der Nähe von Patong Beach, bekannt für seine natürliche Schönheit und sein Nachtleben. Jedes der Gebäude ist so ausgerichtet, dass es einen einzigartigen Blick auf die natürliche Umgebung bietet, und seine großen Fassaden ermöglichen viel Sonnenlicht und Belüftung in allen Räumen. Die einzigartige Zusammensetzung der Fassaden basiert auf einem Muster, das aus den großen Balkonen jeder Wohneinheit besteht, deren Länge zwischen 2,2 und 3,3 Metern variiert. Das Design der Geländer, die aus vertikalen Aluminiumplatten bestehen, die in verschiedenen Winkeln angeordnet sind, garantiert die Privatsphäre jeder Einheit und ermöglicht es, Elemente der Installationen zu verdecken. Das auffällige leuchtende Marineblau am Boden der Balkone vermischt sich mit der Farbe der Andamanensee und symbolisiert das Nachtleben der Gegend.

THE DECK
PATONG, KATHU DISTRICT, PHUKET, THAILAND

Cet ensemble de deux bâtiments de 7 étages est situé près de Patong Beach, connu pour sa beauté naturelle et sa vie nocturne. Chacun des bâtiments est orienté pour offrir une vue unique sur l'environnement naturel, et ses grandes façades permettent un ensoleillement et une ventilation abondants dans toutes les pièces. La composition unique des façades est basée sur un motif formé par les grands balcons en vol de chaque unité résidentielle, dont la longueur varie entre 2,2 et 3,3 mètres. La conception des garde-corps, composés de plaques verticales en aluminium disposées à différents angles, garantit l'intimité de chaque unité et permet de dissimuler des éléments des installations. L'éclatant bleu marine du fond des balcons se mêle à la couleur de la mer d'Andaman et symbolise la vie nocturne de la région.

Este conjunto de dos edificios de 7 plantas se encuentra cerca de la playa de Patong, conocida por su belleza natural y su vida nocturna. Cada uno de los edificios se orienta para ofrecer una vista única del entorno natural y sus amplias fachadas permiten la entrada abundante de luz solar y la ventilación en todas las estancias. La singular composición de las fachadas se basa en un patrón formado por los grandes balcones en vuelo de cada unidad residencial, cuya longitud varía entre los 2,2 y 3,3 m. El diseño de sus barandillas, compuestas por pletinas de aluminio verticales dispuestas en diferentes ángulos, garantiza la privacidad de cada unidad y permite ocultar elementos de las instalaciones. El llamativo color azul marino brillante de la parte inferior de los balcones se mezcla con el color del mar de Andaman y simboliza la vida nocturna de la zona.

SITE

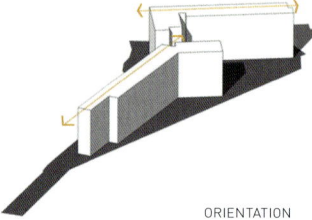
ORIENTATION

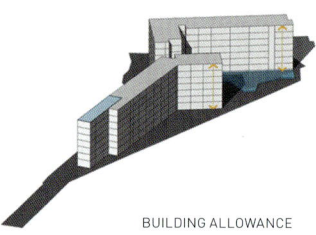
BUILDING ALLOWANCE

CANTILEVERED BALCONY

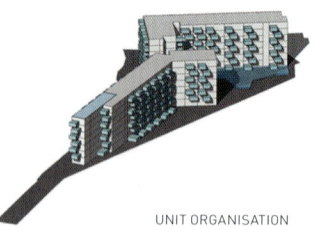
UNIT ORGANISATION

GREEN

Construction diagram

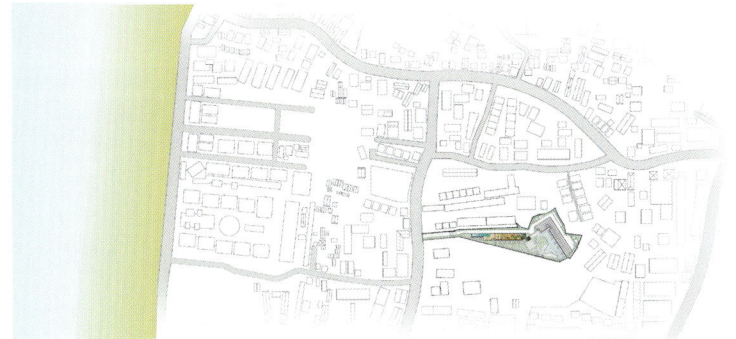

Surroundings

Site plan

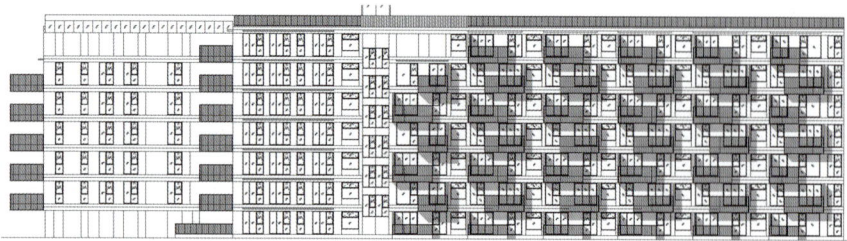

South elevation tower A

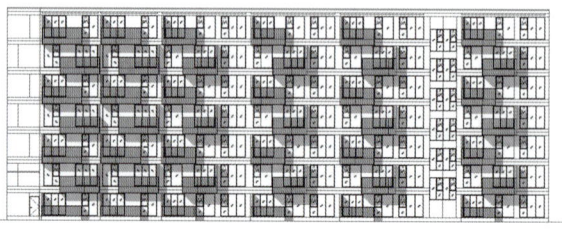

West elevation tower B

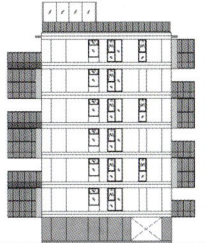

Southeast elevation tower A

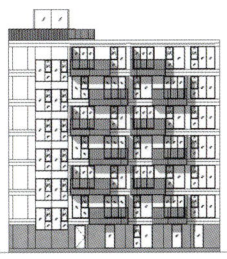

Southwest elevation tower A

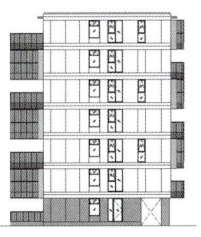

South elevation tower B

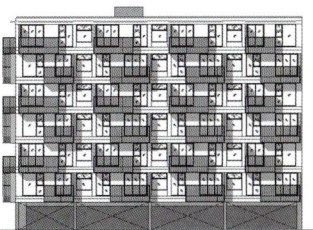

North elevation tower B

1. Lobby
2. Service
3. Unit
4. Parking
5. Pool
6. Pond

TOWER A

TOWER B

Section

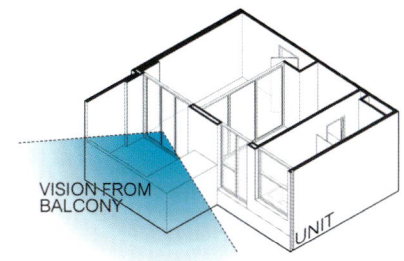

VISION FROM BALCONY

UNIT

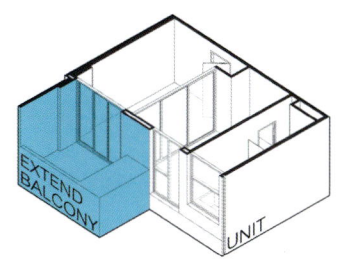

EXTEND BALCONY

UNIT

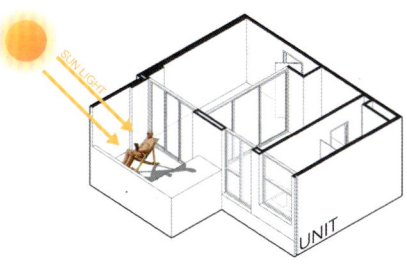

SUNLIGHT

UNIT

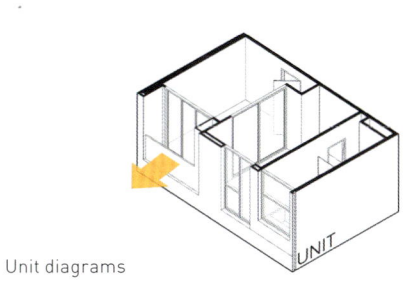

UNIT

Unit diagrams

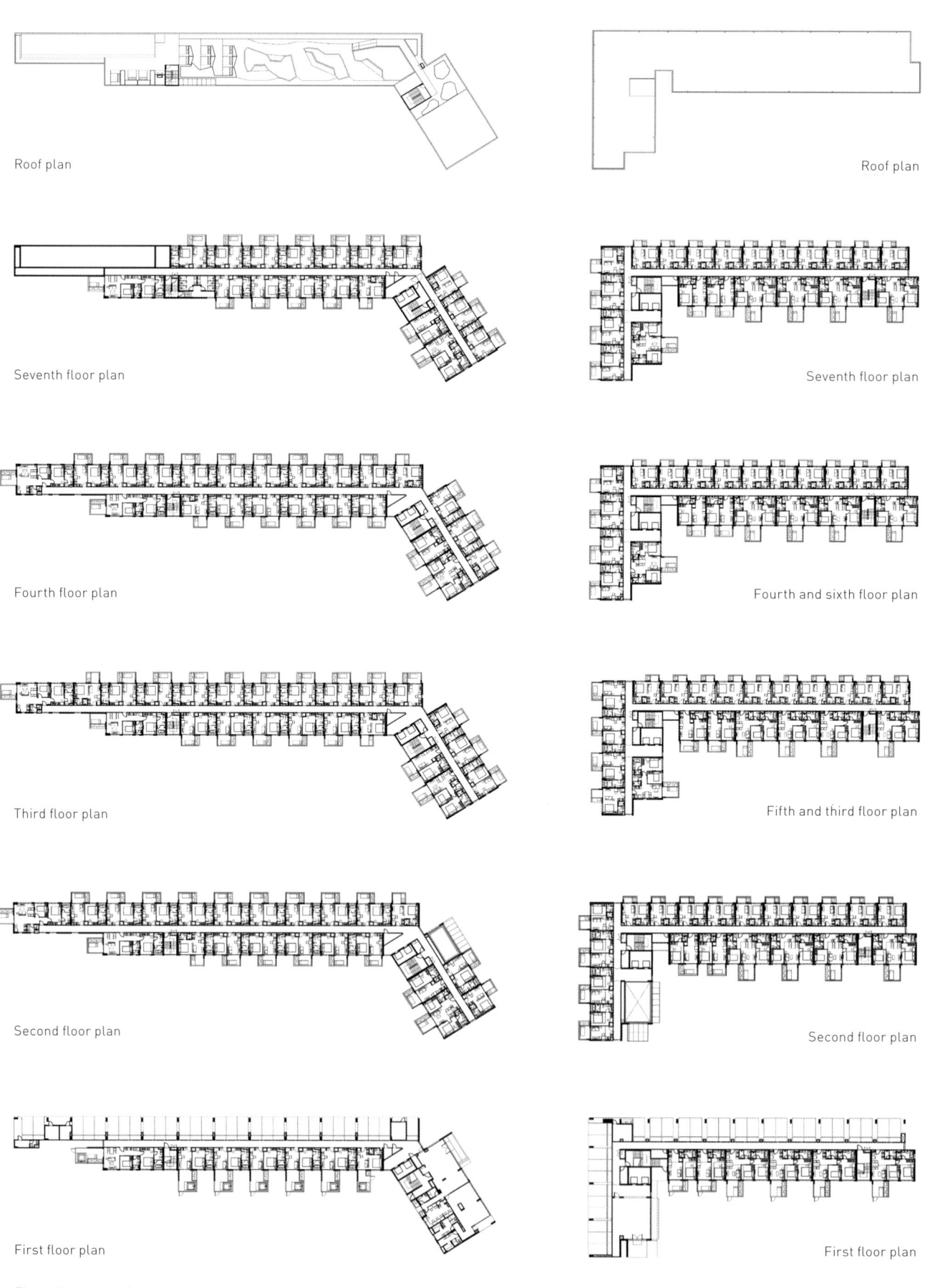

Roof plan

Roof plan

Seventh floor plan

Seventh floor plan

Fourth floor plan

Fourth and sixth floor plan

Third floor plan

Fifth and third floor plan

Second floor plan

Second floor plan

First floor plan

First floor plan

Floor plans tower A

Floor plans tower B

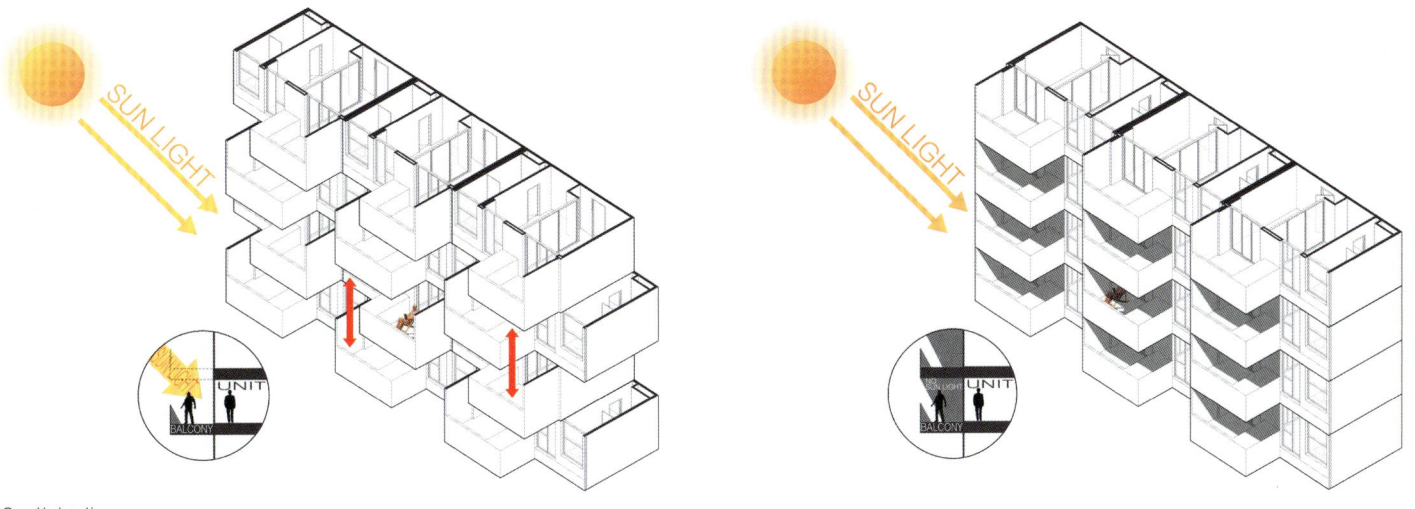

Sunlight diagram

STARH was created with a devotion to a cause, which benefits the society and brings the architects' inner satisfaction.
The studio has taken the mission to break through stereotypes with a fresh, different and bold approach, expressed in strong and determined forms.
The architects at STARH believe that the limits could be overcome with a spirit of creativity, innovation and a sense of aesthetics. Their work covers the spectrum of major architectural challenges —from small, fine architectural edifices for private clients to large public projects. By welcoming them in new ways, putting feeling and enjoying every step of the process, they believe that they change and create new dimensions in the environment we inhabit.

STARH wurde mit der Hingabe an eine Sache geschaffen, die der Gesellschaft zugute kommt und die innere Zufriedenheit der Architekten bringt.
Das Studio hat es sich zur Aufgabe gemacht, Stereotypen mit einem frischen, anderen und mutigen Ansatz zu durchbrechen, der sich in starken und entschlossenen Formen ausdrückt.
Die Architekten von STARH glauben, dass die Grenzen mit einem Geist der Kreativität, Innovation und Ästhetik überwunden werden können. Ihre Arbeit deckt das Spektrum der großen architektonischen Herausforderungen ab - von kleinen, feinen architektonischen Gebäuden für Privatkunden bis hin zu großen öffentlichen Projekten. Indem sie sie auf neue Weise willkommen heißen, Gefühle vermitteln und jeden Schritt des Prozesses genießen, glauben sie, dass sie sich verändern und neue Dimensionen in der Umgebung, in der wir leben, schaffen.

STARH a été créé avec un dévouement à une cause qui profite à la société et apporte la satisfaction intérieure des architectes.
Le studio s'est donné pour mission de briser les stéréotypes avec une approche fraîche, différente et audacieuse, exprimée sous des formes fortes et déterminées.
Les architectes de STARH croient que les limites peuvent être surmontées avec un esprit de créativité, d'innovation et un sens de l'esthétique. Leur travail couvre tout l'éventail des grands défis architecturaux – des petits et beaux édifices architecturaux pour des clients privés aux grands projets publics. En les accueillant d'une nouvelle façon, en leur donnant un sentiment et en appréciant chaque étape du processus, ils croient qu'ils changent et créent de nouvelles dimensions dans l'environnement que nous habitons.

STARH fue creado con una devoción por una causa que beneficiara a la sociedad y aportara satisfacción personal a los arquitectos.
El estudio ha asumido la misión de romper con los estereotipos con un enfoque fresco, diferente y audaz, expresado en formas fuertes y decididas.
Los arquitectos de STARH creen que los límites se pueden superar con un espíritu de creatividad, innovación y sentido de la estética. Su trabajo cubre el espectro de los principales desafíos arquitectónicos –desde pequeños y finos edificios para clientes privados hasta grandes proyectos públicos. Al darles la bienvenida de nuevas maneras, poniendo sentimiento y disfrutando cada paso del proceso, creen que cambian y crean nuevas dimensiones en el ambiente que habitamos.

VARNA WAVE

Design year: 2015

Completion date: August 2018

Built-up area: 10,668 m²

Site area: 1,295 m²

Program: Residential

Lead architect:
Svetoslav Stanislavov

Design team: Dimitar Katsarov, Radostina Petkova, Iva Kostova, Hristo Dushev, Georgi Pasev

Structural engineer:
Ilia Alashki, AEC

Client: Eco Furaj

Main contractor: Comfort

Main structure: Reinforced Concrete

Façade structure: Acrylic Stone by Corian, Fibre Cement by Swisspearl

Manufacturers:
Corian, Swisspearl, Schuco, Guardian Glass, Kone

Photo credits: © Assen Emilov

Design year: 2014

Completion date: November 2017

Built-up area: 31,218 m²

Site area: 6,684 m²

Program: Residential

Lead architect:
Svetoslav Stanislavov

Design team: Dimitar Katsarov, Radostina Petkova, Iva Kostova, Hristo Dushev, Georgi Pasev

Structural engineer:
Ilia Alashki, AEC

Client: Sofbuild

Main contractor: Argogrup Exact

Main structure:
Reinforced Concrete

Façade frames structure:
Glassfibre Reinforced Concrete – fibreC by Rieder

Manufacturers: fibreC by Rieder, Swisspearl, Reynaers Aluminium, Guardian Glass, Otis

Photo credits: © Assen Emilov

Awards:
-ArchDaily Building of the year 2018 – Nomination
-National contest Building of the year 2017 – Winner | Residential building over 10 000 sq.m total build-up area National contest Building of the year 2017 – Winner | Audience award
-American Architecture Prize 2016 - Honorable mention for residential building

A3 - ADVANCED ARCHITECTURE APARTMENTS

The design of this building is inspired by the movement of the waves of the sea. The "wave" effect of the façade is achieved by using two different materials: Corian and glass. The dark graphite colour of the lodges highlights the elegance of the white horizontal elements. The oval shape of the corners softens the general perception of the building and gives it an elegant and subtle appearance. Varna Wave's contemporary image is further enhanced by the materials used in the façade: Corian, Swisspearl cement reinforced with fibre, glass and aluminium. Corian is an innovative material with an extraordinary ability to adopt forms when subjected to heat, which gives the opportunity to create free composite forms. Used as a ventilated façade, Corian increases the energy efficiency of the building and offers a high resistance to humidity.

Das Design dieses Gebäudes ist von der Bewegung der Meereswellen inspiriert. Der „Wellen"-Effekt der Fassade wird durch den Einsatz von zwei verschiedenen Materialien erreicht: Corian und Glas. Die dunkle Graphitfarbe der Hütten unterstreicht die Eleganz der weißen horizontalen Elemente. Die ovale Form der Ecken mildert die Gesamtwahrnehmung des Gebäudes und verleiht ihm eine elegante und subtile Optik. Das zeitgenössische Bild von Varna Wave wird durch die in der Fassade verwendeten Materialien noch verstärkt: Corian, Swisspearl Zement, verstärkt mit Fasern, Glas und Aluminium. Corian ist ein innovatives Material mit einer außergewöhnlichen Fähigkeit, unter Hitzeeinwirkung Formen anzunehmen und bietet die Möglichkeit, zusammengesetzte freie Formen zu schaffen. Als hinterlüftete Fassade erhöht der Corian die Energieeffizienz des Gebäudes und bietet eine hohe Beständigkeit gegen Feuchtigkeit.

VARNA WAVE
VARNA, BULGARIA

La conception de ce bâtiment s'inspire du mouvement des vagues de la mer. L'effet « vague » de la façade est obtenu en utilisant deux matériaux différents : Corian et verre. La couleur graphite foncé des lodges souligne l'élégance des éléments horizontaux blancs. La forme ovale des coins adoucit la perception globale du bâtiment et lui donne un aspect élégant et subtil. L'image contemporaine de Varna Wave est encore rehaussée par les matériaux utilisés pour la façade : Corian, ciment Swisspearl renforcé de fibre, verre et aluminium. Le Corian est un matériau innovant avec une extraordinaire capacité à prendre des formes lorsqu'il est soumis à la chaleur, ce qui permet de créer des formes composites libres. Utilisé comme façade ventilée, le Corian augmente l'efficacité énergétique du bâtiment et offre une grande résistance à l'humidité.

El diseño de este edificio se inspira en el movimiento de las olas del mar. El efecto de «ola» de la fachada se consigue utilizando dos materiales diferentes: Corian y vidrio. El color grafito oscuro de las logias resalta la elegancia de los elementos horizontales blancos. La forma ovalada de las esquinas suaviza la percepción general del edificio y le ada un aspecto elegante y sutil. La imagen contemporánea de Varna Wave se realza aún más por los materiales utilizados en la fachada: Corian, cemento Swisspearl reforzado con fibra, vidrio y aluminio. El Corian es un innovador material con una extraordinaria capacidad para adoptar formas cuando está sometido a calor, lo cual brinda la oportunidad de crear formas libres compuestas. Utilizado como fachada ventilada, el Corian aumenta la eficiencia energética del edificio y ofrece una alta resistencia a la humedad.

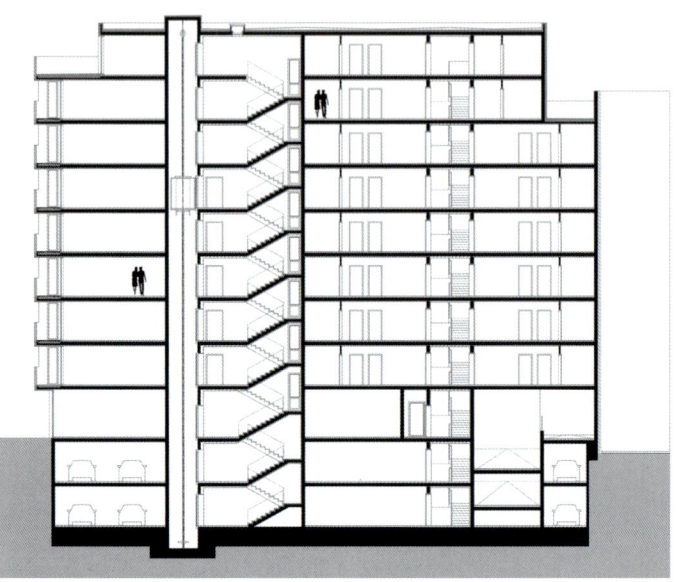

Section

Fifth floor plan

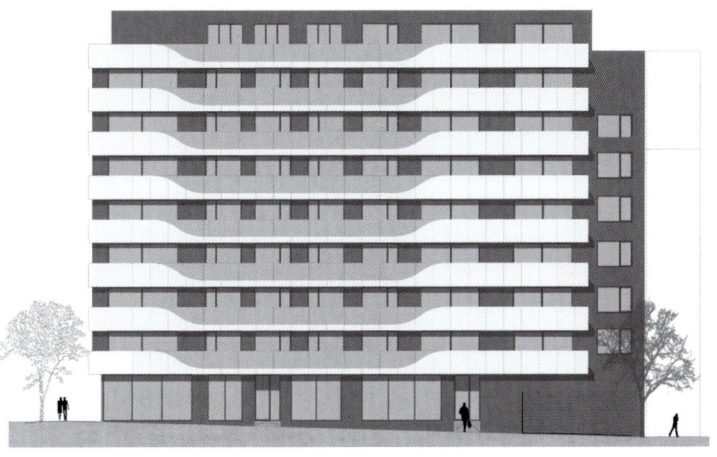

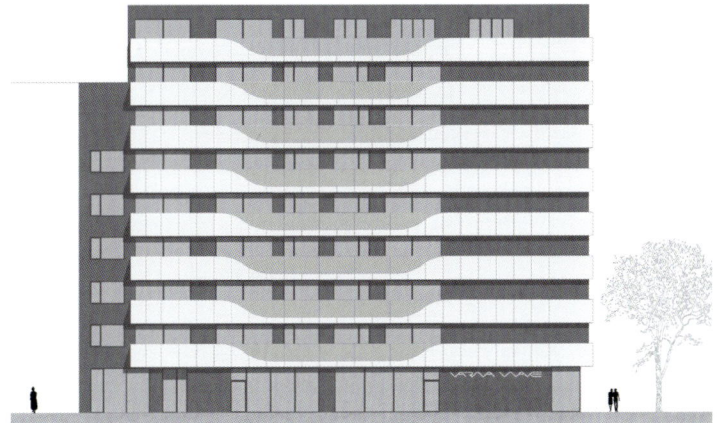

North west elevation

South west elevation

A3 is an exciting building, harmoniously incorporated into the context of the environment. Two starting points, the mountain and the city, set the overall architectural concept. The plot is in the border area, where the city and the mountain overflow into one. Combining these two elements we've created a dynamic and modern shape of the building. Lines and clear borders are blurred in smooth and soft forms, allowing everyone to determine exactly where and how to perceive shape and space. The design of A3 contains strict elegance and soft organic forms. The building is perceived equally well in the overall silhouette and from different angles. The feeling of elegance is emphasized by the facade materials: glass and fibreC, an innovative material made of glass-fiber concrete. Besides aesthetics and functionality the materials provide durability and easy maintenance of the building.

Der A3 ist ein spannendes Gebäude, das sich harmonisch in den Kontext der Umgebung einfügt. Zwei Ausgangspunkte, der Berg und die Stadt, bestimmen das architektonische Gesamtkonzept. Das Grundstück liegt im Grenzgebiet, wo die Stadt und der Berg ineinander übergehen. Durch die Kombination dieser beiden Elemente haben wir eine dynamische und moderne Form des Gebäudes geschaffen. Linien und klare Grenzen verschwimmen in glatten und weichen Formen, so dass jeder genau bestimmen kann, wo und wie er Form und Raum wahrnimmt. Das Design des A3 enthält strenge Eleganz und weiche organische Formen. Das Gebäude wird in der gesamten Silhouette und aus verschiedenen Blickwinkeln gleichermaßen gut wahrgenommen. Das Gefühl von Eleganz wird durch die Fassadenmaterialien unterstrichen: Glas und fibreC, ein innovatives Material aus Glasfaserbeton. Neben Ästhetik und Funktionalität bieten die Materialien eine lange Lebensdauer und eine einfache Wartung des Gebäudes.

A3 – ADVANCED ARCHITECTURE APARTMENTS
SOFIA, BULGARIA

A3 est un bâtiment passionnant, harmonieusement intégré dans le contexte de l'environnement. Deux points de départ, la montagne et la ville, définissent le concept architectural global. La parcelle se trouve dans la zone frontalière, où la ville et la montagne ne font plus qu'un. En combinant ces deux éléments, nous avons créé une forme dynamique et moderne du bâtiment. Les lignes et les bordures claires sont floues dans des formes lisses et douces, permettant à chacun de déterminer exactement où et comment percevoir la forme et l'espace. Le design de l'A3 contient une élégance stricte et des formes organiques douces. Le bâtiment est perçu tout aussi bien dans sa silhouette globale que sous différents angles. La sensation d'élégance est soulignée par les matériaux de façade : verre et fibreC, un matériau innovant en béton de fibre de verre. En plus de l'esthétique et de la fonctionnalité, les matériaux assurent la durabilité et la facilité d'entretien du bâtiment.

A3 es un edificio apasionante, que se integra armoniosamente en entorno. Dos puntos de partida, la montaña y la ciudad, marcan el concepto arquitectónico global. La parcela se encuentra en la zona fronteriza, entre la ciudad y la montaña. Combinando estos dos elementos hemos creado un edificio de forma dinámica y moderna. Las líneas y los bordes claros se difuminan en formas suaves, permitiendo que cada una determine exactamente dónde y cómo percibir la forma y el espacio. El diseño de A3 es de una elegancia estricta y formas orgánicas suaves. El edificio se percibe bien desde diferentes ángulos. La sensación de elegancia se acentúa con los materiales utilizados en la construcción de la fachada: vidrio y fibra C, un material innovador resultado de la mezcla de hormigón con fibra de vidrio. Además estética y la funcionalidad, los materiales proporcionan durabilidad y facilidad en el mantenimiento del edificio.

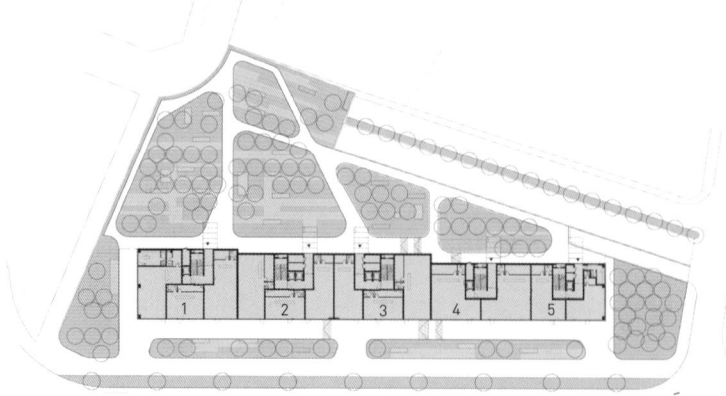

Site plan

1. Entrance D
2. Entrance G
3. Entrance V
4. Entrance B
5. Entrance A

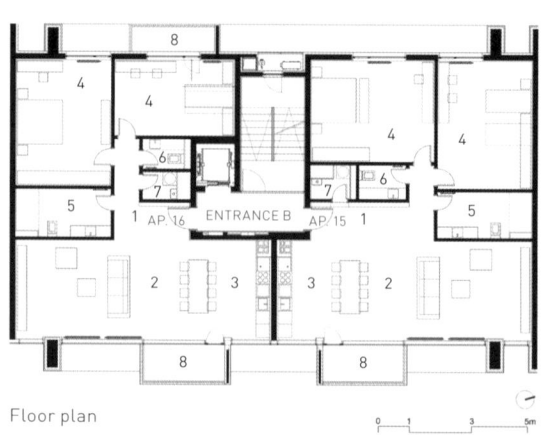

Floor plan

1. Entry hall
2. Living room
3. Kitchen
4. Bedroom
5. Bathroom
6. Toilet
7. Storage
8. Balcony

Floor plan

STUDIO_SUSPICION

www.suspicion.co.kr

Principal/Architect: Taesang Park
Principal/Architect: Sooyoung Cho
studio_suspicion is an architectural design office.
Our project usually begins by observing and exploring existing systems.
But we hope that the conditions of the reality, which refuse the conventional use of the system, are integrated into a single architectural concept.
Not the realization of ideas, but the conceptualization of reality.
That is our goal.

Direktor / Architekt: Taesang Park
Direktor / Architekt: Sooyoung Cho
studio_suspicion ist ein Architekturstudio.
Unsere Projekte beginnen in der Regel mit der Beobachtung und Erforschung bestehender Systeme.
Wir hoffen jedoch, dass die Realitätsbedingungen, die die konventionelle Nutzung des Systems ablehnen, in ein einziges architektonisches Konzept integriert werden.
Nicht die Verwirklichung von Ideen, sondern die Konzeptualisierung der Realität. Das ist unser Ziel.

Directeur/Architecte : Taesang Park
Réalisateur/Architecte : Sooyoung Cho
studio_suspicion est un studio d'architecture.
Nos projets commencent généralement par l'observation et l'exploration des systèmes existants.
Mais nous espérons que les conditions de la réalité, qui rejettent l'utilisation conventionnelle du système, seront intégrées dans un concept architectural unique.
Pas la réalisation d'idées, mais la conceptualisation de la réalité. C'est notre objectif.

Director/Arquitecto: Taesang Park
Director/Arquitecto: Sooyoung Cho
studio_suspicion es un estudio de arquitectura.
Nuestros proyectos suelen comenzar con la observación y exploración de los sistemas existentes.
Pero esperamos que las condiciones de la realidad, que rechazan el uso convencional del sistema, se integren en un único concepto arquitectónico.
No la realización de ideas, sino la conceptualización de la realidad. Ese es nuestro objetivo.

Architects: studio_suspicion

Architect in charge:
Park, Taesang & Cho, Sooyoung

Location: Sageun-dong 8ga-gil 11, Seongdong-gu, Seoul, Korea

Building use: Residential (Multiplex housing unit)

Site area: 137.80 m²

Built area: 82.24 m²

Total floor area: 274.78 m²

Building scope: 5 above ground

Building to land ratio: 59.68 %

Floor area ratio: 199.40 %

Construction: Hyunkang construction

Year completed: 2017

Photo credits: © Ryoo, In Keun & © Narsilion Photography

FIGHTING HOUSE

The aim of the project, located in the Sageun-Dong neighbourhood, was to build a block of rented apartments that would provide a welcoming environment for students from neighbouring universities. The approach to achieving this was based on diversity: although the shape and size of the units is similar, each of them includes variations in their composition and design that present them as unique. This diversity, together with the division of the apartments into functional areas, fosters a sense of home among the users.

The shape of the building sought to maximise useful space within a small plot. The sloping shape of the main façade emerged as a "discovery" derived from the enveloping line established by the regulations. Its slopes, covered with zinc sheets, contrast softly with the white stucco of the vertical facades.

Ziel des Projekts, das sich im Stadtteil Sageun-Dong befindet, war es, einen Mietwohnungsbau zu errichten, der eine einladende Umgebung für Studenten von benachbarten Universitäten bietet. Der Ansatz, dies zu erreichen, basierte auf Vielfalt: Obwohl die Form und Größe der Einheiten ähnlich ist, beinhaltet jede von ihnen Variationen in ihrer Zusammensetzung und Gestaltung, die sie als einzigartig darstellen. Diese Vielfalt sowie die Aufteilung der Wohnungen in Funktionsbereiche fördern das Wohngefühl der Nutzer.

Die Form des Gebäudes versuchte, die Nutzfläche innerhalb eines kleinen Grundstücks zu maximieren. Die schräge Form der Hauptfassade entpuppte sich als „Entdeckung", die sich aus der durch die Anordnungen festgelegten Einsätze ableitet. Ihre Neigungen, die mit Zinkplatten bedeckt sind, kontrastieren sanft mit dem weißen Stuck der vertikalen Fassaden.

FIGHTING HOUSE
SEOUL, KOREA

L'objectif du projet, situé dans le quartier de Sageun-Dong, était de construire un immeuble d'appartements loués qui offrirait un environnement accueillant aux étudiants des universités voisines. L'approche pour y parvenir était basée sur la diversité : bien que la forme et la taille des unités soient similaires, chacune d'entre elles comprend des variations dans leur composition et leur conception qui les présentent comme uniques. Cette diversité, associée à la division des appartements en zones fonctionnelles, favorise le sentiment d'appartenance des utilisateurs.

La forme du bâtiment a essayé de maximiser l'espace utile à l'intérieur d'une petite parcelle. La forme inclinée de la façade principale est apparue comme une « découverte » dérivée de la ligne enveloppante établie par la réglementation. Leurs boucles, recouvertes de plaques de zinc, contrastent doucement avec le stuc blanc des façades verticales.

El objetivo del proyecto, situado en el barrio de Sageun-Dong, fue construir un bloque de apartamentos de alquiler que ofreciese un entorno acogedor a los estudiantes de las universidades vecinas. El enfoque para conseguirlo se basó en la diversidad: si bien la forma y tamaño de las unidades es parecido, cada una de ellas incluye variaciones en su composición y diseño que las presentan como únicas. Esta diversidad, unida a la división de los apartamentos en áreas funcionales, fomenta una sensación de hogar entre los usuarios.

La forma del edificio trató de maximizar el espacio útil dentro de una parcela pequeña. La forma inclinada de la fachada principal surgió como un «descubrimiento» derivado de la línea envolvente establecida por la normativa. Sus pendientes, recubiertas de planchas de zinc, contrastan suavemente con el estuco blanco de las fachadas verticales.

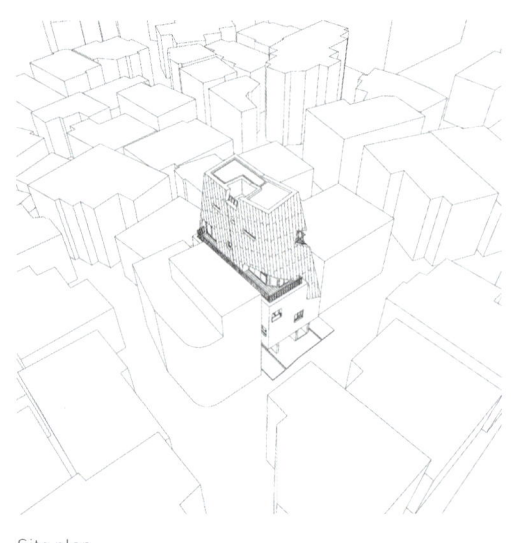

Site plan

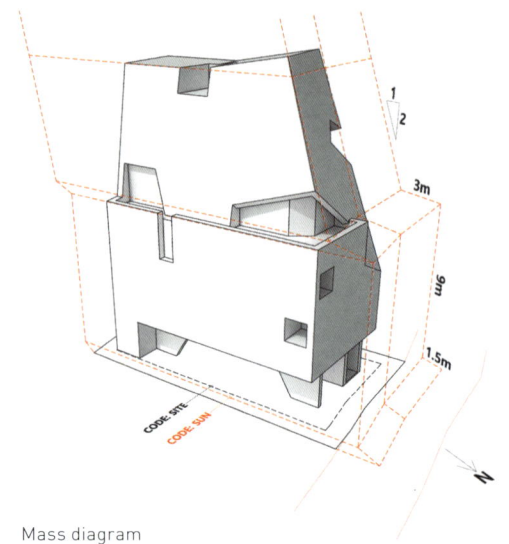

Mass diagram

Axonometric section

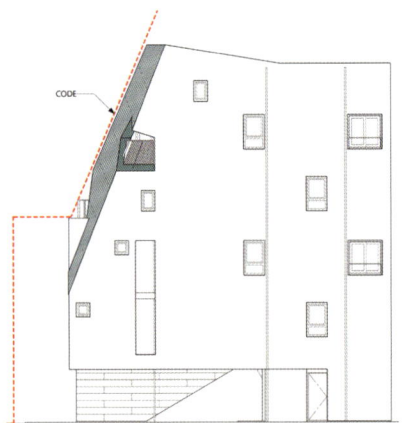

Right elevation

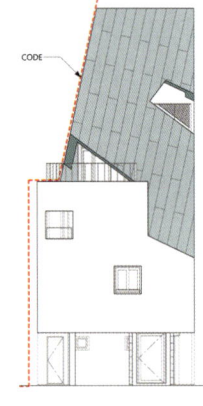

Front elevation

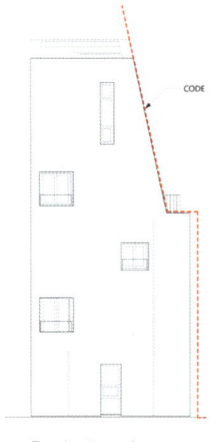

Back elevation

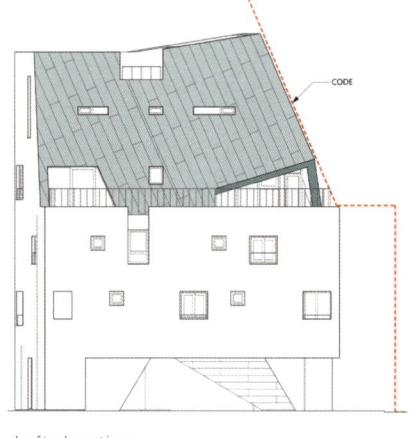

Left elevation

Axonometric section

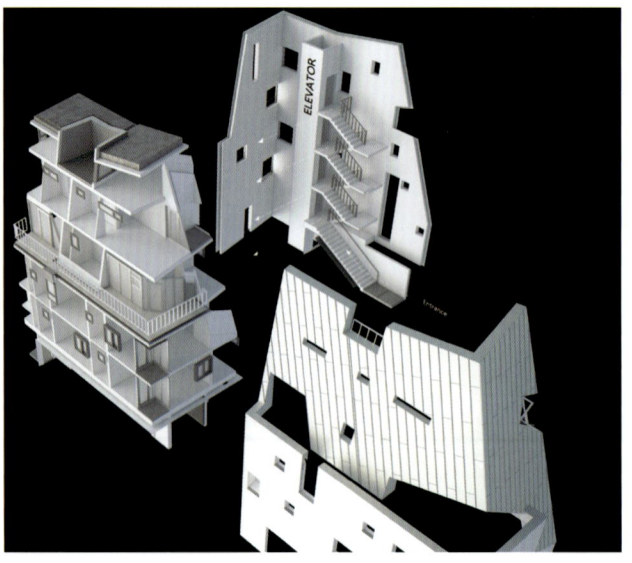

Exploded axonometric

Third floor plan

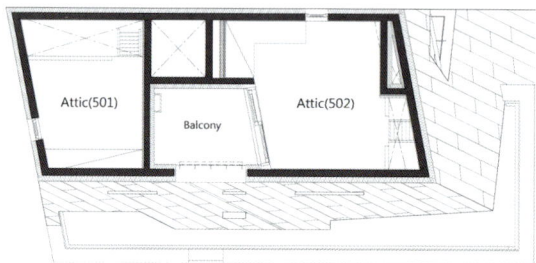

Attic floor plan

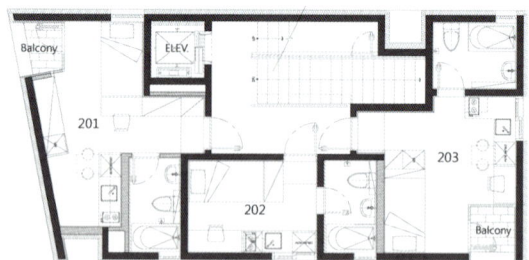

Second floor plan

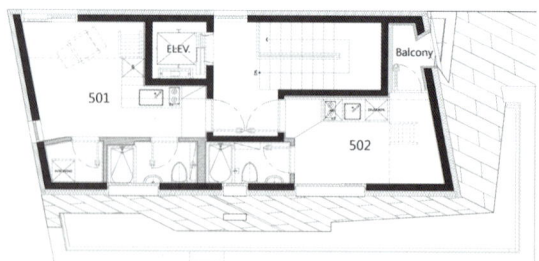

Fifth floor plan

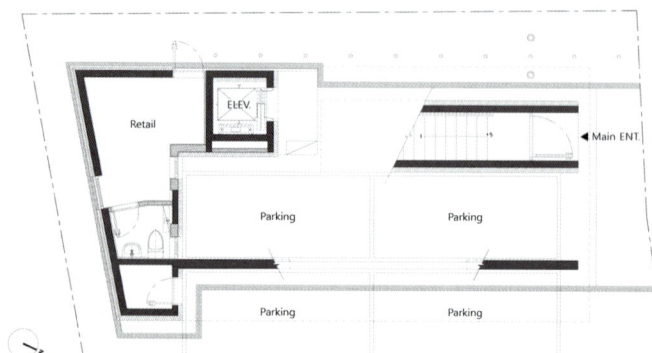

Ground floor plan

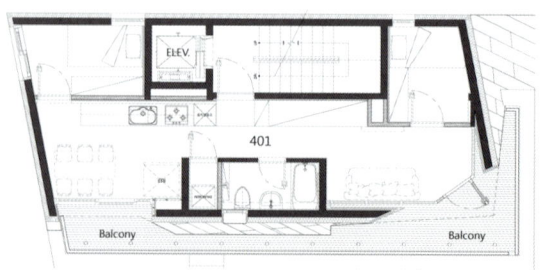

Fourth floor plan

TONY OWEN PARTNERS

www.tonyowen.com.au

Tony Owen Partners was founded in 2004 and is headquartered in Sydney with offices in Brisbane, Vietnam and Abu Dhabi. Conceived as a company halfway between theoretical research and commercial practice, the company advocates a sustainable and efficient architecture that adapts to the new imperatives of today's world, using the new tools and digital capabilities offered by technology. TOP represents a fully digital company that applies the principles of parametric design in the commercial practice of architecture. Over the past 15 years, TOP has designed and built more than 50 projects, most of which have been medium and high density residential buildings. These projects have served to explore the application of reactive digital modeling, which analyzes the environmental, constructive and commercial parameters of each of them. The result is a flexible architecture that is sensitive to the environment and the changing urban planning.

Tony Owen Partners wurde 2004 gegründet und hat seinen Hauptsitz in Sydney sowie Niederlassungen in Brisbane, Vietnam und Abu Dhabi. Konzipiert als Unternehmen auf halbem Weg zwischen theoretischer Forschung und kommerzieller Praxis, setzt sich das Unternehmen für eine nachhaltige und effiziente Architektur ein, die sich an die neuen Erfordernisse der heutigen Welt anpasst und dabei die neuen Werkzeuge und digitalen Möglichkeiten der Technologie nutzt. TOP repräsentiert ein volldigitales Unternehmen, das die Prinzipien des parametrischen Designs in der kommerziellen Praxis der Architektur anwendet. In den letzten 15 Jahren hat TOP mehr als 50 Projekte geplant und gebaut, von denen die meisten mit mittlerer und hoher Wohnungsdichte waren. Diese Projekte haben dazu gedient, die Anwendung der reaktiven digitalen Modellierung zu erforschen, die die ökologischen, konstruktiven und kommerziellen Parameter jedes einzelnen von ihnen analysiert. Das Ergebnis ist eine Architektur, die flexibel und sensibel auf die Umwelt und das sich verändernde Stadtgefüge reagiert.

Tony Owen Partners a été fondé en 2004 et a son siège social à Sydney avec des bureaux à Brisbane, au Vietnam et à Abu Dhabi. Conçue comme une entreprise à mi-chemin entre la recherche théorique et la pratique commerciale, l'entreprise préconise une architecture durable et efficace qui s'adapte aux nouveaux impératifs du monde d'aujourd'hui, en utilisant les nouveaux outils et capacités numériques offerts par la technologie. TOP représente une entreprise entièrement numérique qui applique les principes de la conception paramétrique dans la pratique commerciale de l'architecture. Au cours des 15 dernières années, TOP a conçu et construit plus de 50 projets, dont la plupart étaient des bâtiments résidentiels de densité moyenne et élevée. Ces projets ont permis d'explorer l'application de la modélisation numérique réactive, qui analyse les paramètres environnementaux, constructifs et commerciaux de chacun d'entre eux. Il en résulte une architecture flexible et sensible à l'environnement et à l'évolution du tissu urbain.

Tony Owen Partners fue fundada en 2004 y tiene sede en Sidney y oficinas en Brisbane, Vietnam y Abu Dhabi. Concebida como una empresa a medio camino entre la investigación teórica y la práctica comercial, la empresa aboga por una arquitectura sostenible y eficiente que se adapte a los nuevos imperativos del mundo actual, para lo cual utiliza las nuevas herramientas y capacidades digitales que ofrece la tecnología. TOP representa una empresa totalmente digital que aplica los principios del diseño paramétrico en la práctica comercial de la arquitectura. Durante los últimos 15 años, TOP ha diseñado y construido más de 50 proyectos, la mayoría de los cuales han sido edificios residenciales de media y alta densidad. Estos proyectos han servido para explorar la aplicación del modelado digital reactivo, que analiza los parámetros ambientales, constructivos y comerciales de cada uno de ellos. El resultado es una arquitectura flexible y sensible al entorno y al tejido urbano cambiante.

ELIZA APARTMENTS

Location: Sydney, Australia

Building area: 3,160 m²

Date of completion: 2012

Project team: Tony Owen, Esan Rahmani, Gerardo Oiz, Claudio Porley, Michael Civovic, Byan Li

Developer: Cerrose Pty Ltd

Structural engineer: M&G Consulting

Services engineer: Cardno ITC

Landscape consultant: Formed Gardens

Photo credits: © John Gollings

ALPHA APARTMENTS

Location: Sydney, Australia

Building area: 3,160 m²

Date of completion: 2015

Project team: Tony Owen, Sumir Diwan, Esan Rahmani, Marianna Mioduszewski, Eugene Burda, Chong Loh

Developer: Mars Property

Builder: Deicorp Pty Ltd

Structural engineer: Australian Consulting Engineers

Services engineer: Engineering Partners

Façade contractor: Colt International

Landscape consultant: Formed Gardens

Photo credits: © Steve Back

SOVEREIGN

Location: Sydney Australia

Building area: 3,450m²

Completion date: 2018

Project team: Tony Owen, Wendy Tong, Terry Leung, Byan Li.

Developer: QY Hansen

Structural engineer: Meinhardt

Services engineer: Erbas Consulting

Landscape consultant: John Locke Associates

Photo credits: © John Gollings

This exclusive apartment building is located on the historical Elizabeth Street in Sydney's financial district. Its design is based on the traditional lookout window, common in Elizabeth and Macquarie Streets, and combines classic 20th century style with parametric design tools to create an iconic and sustainable building. The use of digital technology allowed a façade to be shaped with a changing profile that adapts to the different distributions, views and direction of the sun at each level. The façade was constructed with hundreds of metal panels of different shapes which, like sandstone panels, were laser-cut. The 17 floors of the building house 19 dwellings, most of which have 4 bedrooms and a 3-storey attic on the top, whose main rooms have views over the harbour and Hyde Park.

Dieses exklusive Apartmenthaus befindet sich in der historischen Elizabeth Street im Finanzviertel von Sydney. Das Design basiert auf dem traditionellen Aussichtsfenster, das in den Straßen Elizabeth und Macquarie üblich ist, und kombiniert klassischen Stil des 20. Jahrhunderts mit parametrischen Entwurfswerkzeugen, um ein ikonisches und nachhaltiges Gebäude zu schaffen. Durch den Einsatz der Digitaltechnik ist es gelungen, eine Fassade mit einem sich verändernden Profil zu gestalten, das sich den unterschiedlichen Verteilungen, Ansichten und Sonnenrichtungen auf jeder Ebene anpasst. Die Fassade wurde mit Hunderten von Metallplatten unterschiedlicher Form gebaut, die wie Sandsteinplatten, per Laser geschnitten wurden. Auf 17 Stockwerken befinden sich 19 Wohnungen, die meisten davon mit 4 Schlafzimmern und einem 3-geschossigen Penthouse im Obergeschoss, dessen Haupträume den Hafen und den Hyde Park überblicken.

ELIZA APARTMENTS
SYDNEY, AUSTRALIA

Cet immeuble d'appartements exclusif est situé sur l'historique Elizabeth Street, dans le quartier financier de Sydney. Son design s'inspire de la fenêtre d'observation traditionnelle, courante dans les rues Elizabeth et Macquarie, et combine le style classique du 20e siècle avec des outils de conception paramétrique pour créer un bâtiment iconique et durable. L'utilisation de la technologie numérique a permis de mouler une façade avec un profil changeant qui s'adapte aux différentes distributions, vues et directions du soleil à chaque niveau. La façade a été construite avec des centaines de panneaux métalliques de différentes formes qui, comme les panneaux en grès, ont été découpés au laser par robot. Les 17 étages de l'immeuble abritent 19 logements, la plupart comprenant 4 chambres à coucher et un penthouse de 3 étages dont les pièces principales donnent sur le port et Hyde Park.

Este exclusivo edificio de apartamentos se sitúa en la histórica calle Elizabeth, en del distrito financiero de Sidney. Su diseño se basa en la tradicional ventana mirador, habitual en las calles Elizabeth y Macquarie, y combina el estilo clásico el siglo XX con herramientas de diseño paramétrico para crear un edificio icónico y sostenible. El uso de tecnología digital permitió moldear una fachada con un perfil cambiante que se adapta a las diferentes distribuciones, vistas y dirección del sol de cada nivel. La fachada se construyó con cientos de paneles metálicos de diferentes formas que, al igual que los paneles de piedra arenisca, fueron cortados con láser por robot. Las 17 plantas del edificio albergan 19 viviendas, la mayoría de 4 habitaciones y un ático de 3 pisos en la parte superior, cuyas estancias principales gozan de vistas sobre el puerto y el Hyde Park.

Penthouse ground floor plan

10th floor plan

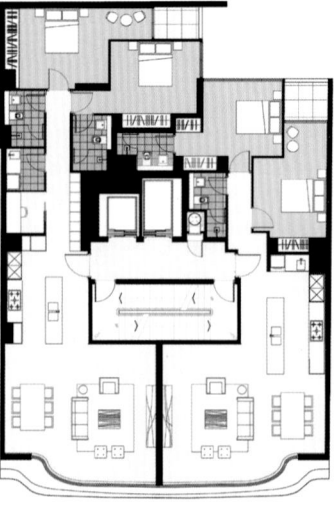

Second floor plan

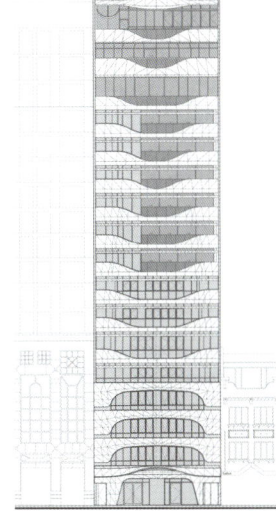

Front elevation

The design of this building explores the relationship between public and private space and between interior and exterior within the context of Sydney's periphery and temperate climate. Its hexagonal capsule-shaped façade creates an ambient screen that controls light and frames views, allowing for maximum exposure and privacy. The construction of this façade employed digital software techniques that optimised its cost, demonstrating that progressive design elements may not be more expensive than standard designs. The building houses commercial spaces, 1 and 2 bedroom flats and 2 and 3 bedroom penthouses with large terraces overlooking the city and surrounding parks. The project encourages interaction between residents through childcare facilities on the ground floor or common living areas on each level.

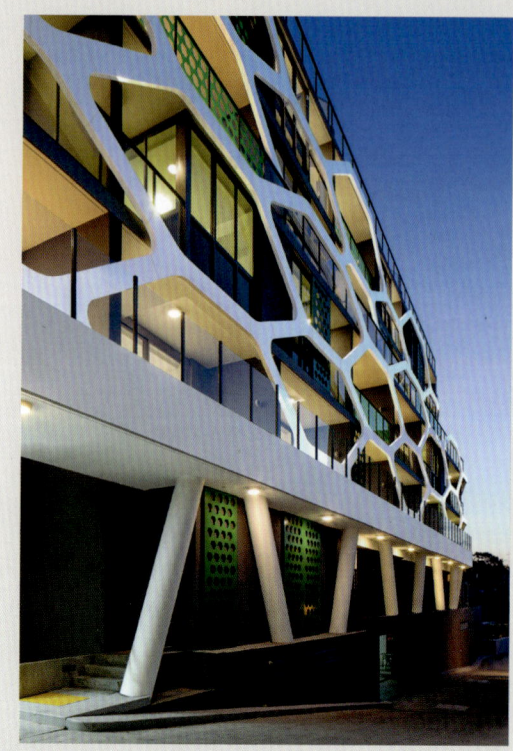

Der Entwurf dieses Gebäudes untersucht die Beziehung zwischen öffentlichem und privatem Raum und zwischen Innen und Außen im Kontext der Peripherie und des gemäßigten Klimas von Sydney. Die sechseckige kapselförmige Fassade schafft einen Raumschirm, der Licht steuert und die Sicht umrahmt, was eine maximale Sichtbarkeit und Privatsphäre ermöglicht. Bei der Konstruktion dieser Fassade wurden digitale Softwaretechniken eingesetzt, die die Kosten optimierten und zeigten, dass fortschrittliche Gestaltungselemente nicht teurer sein müssen als Standarddesigns. Das Gebäude beherbergt Geschäftsräume, 1- und 2-Zimmer-Wohnungen sowie 2- und 3-Zimmer-Penthäuser mit geräumigen Terrassen sowie Blick auf die Stadt und die umliegenden Parks. Das Projekt fördert die Interaktion zwischen den Bewohnern durch Kinderbetreuungseinrichtungen im Erdgeschoss oder gemeinsame Wohnräume auf jeder Ebene.

ALPHA APARTMENTS
LEWISHAM, SYDNEY, AUSTRALIA

La conception de ce bâtiment explore la relation entre l'espace public et privé et entre l'intérieur et l'extérieur dans le contexte de la périphérie de Sydney et du climat tempéré. Sa façade hexagonale en forme de capsule crée un écran ambiant qui contrôle la lumière et encadre les vues, permettant une exposition et une intimité maximales. La construction de cette façade a fait appel à des techniques logicielles numériques qui en ont optimisé le coût, démontrant que les éléments de conception progressive ne doivent pas nécessairement être plus coûteux que ceux des conceptions standard. L'immeuble abrite des espaces commerciaux, des appartements de 1 et 2 chambres à coucher et des penthouses de 2 et 3 chambres à coucher avec de vastes terrasses donnant sur la ville et les parcs environnants. Le projet encourage l'interaction entre les résidents par le biais de garderies au rez-de-chaussée ou d'espaces de vie communs à chaque niveau.

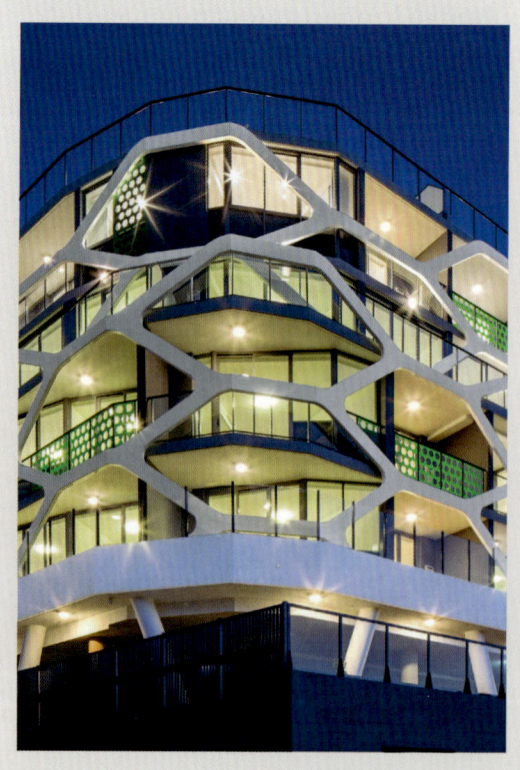

El diseño de este edificio explora la relación entre espacio público y privado y entre interior y exterior dentro del contexto de la periferia y el clima templado de Sidney. Su fachada hexagonal en forma de cápsula crea una pantalla ambiental que controla la luz y enmarca las vistas, lo que permite la máxima exposición y privacidad. En la construcción de esta fachada se emplearon técnicas de software digital que optimizaron su coste, demostrando que los elementos de diseño progresivo no tienen por qué ser más caros que los diseños estándar. El edificio alberga espacios comerciales, pisos de 1 y 2 dormitorios y áticos de 2 y 3 dormitorios con amplias terrazas sobre la ciudad y los parques circundantes. El proyecto fomenta la interacción entre los residentes mediante instalaciones para el cuidado de los niños en la planta baja o zonas de estar comunes en cada nivel.

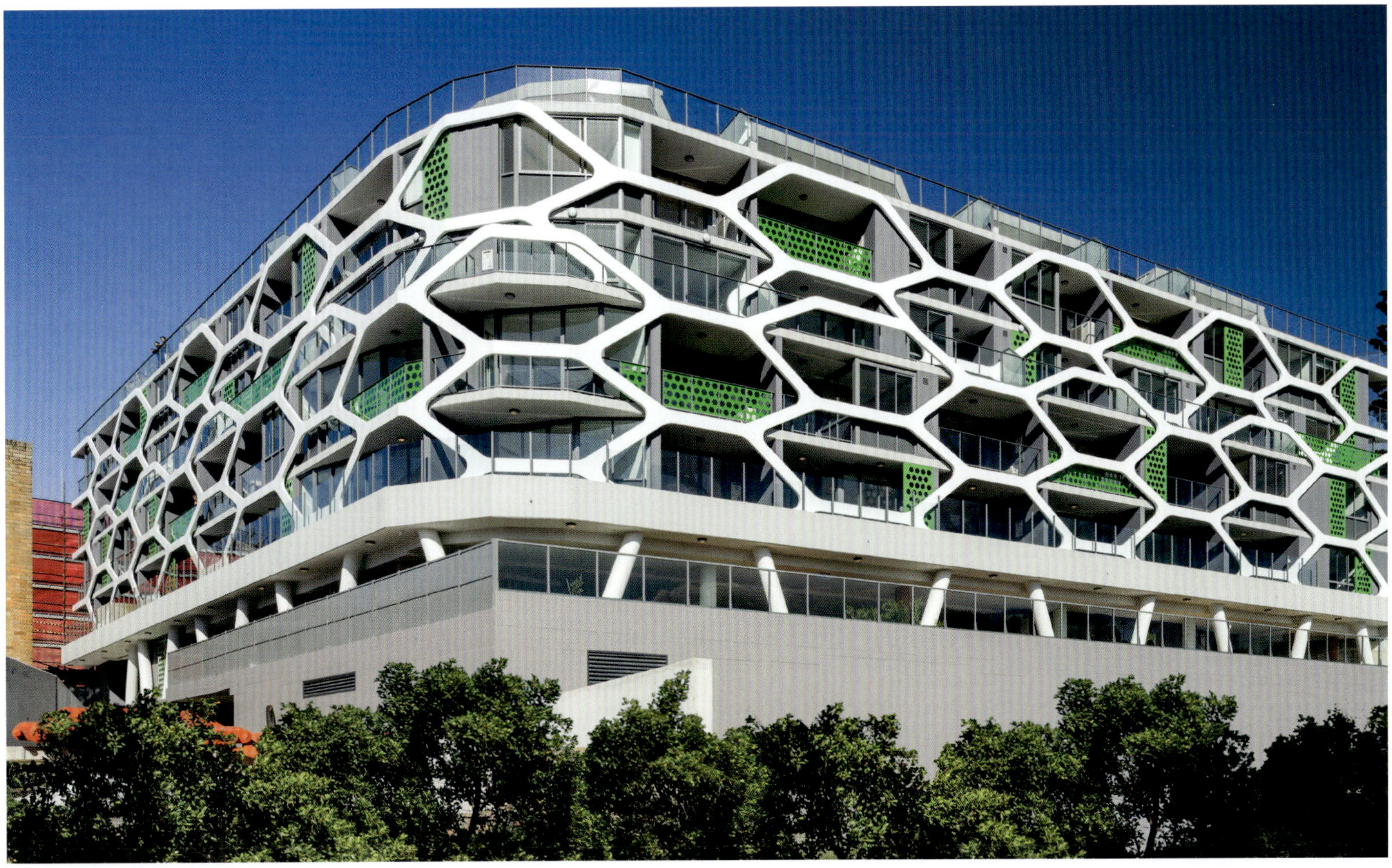

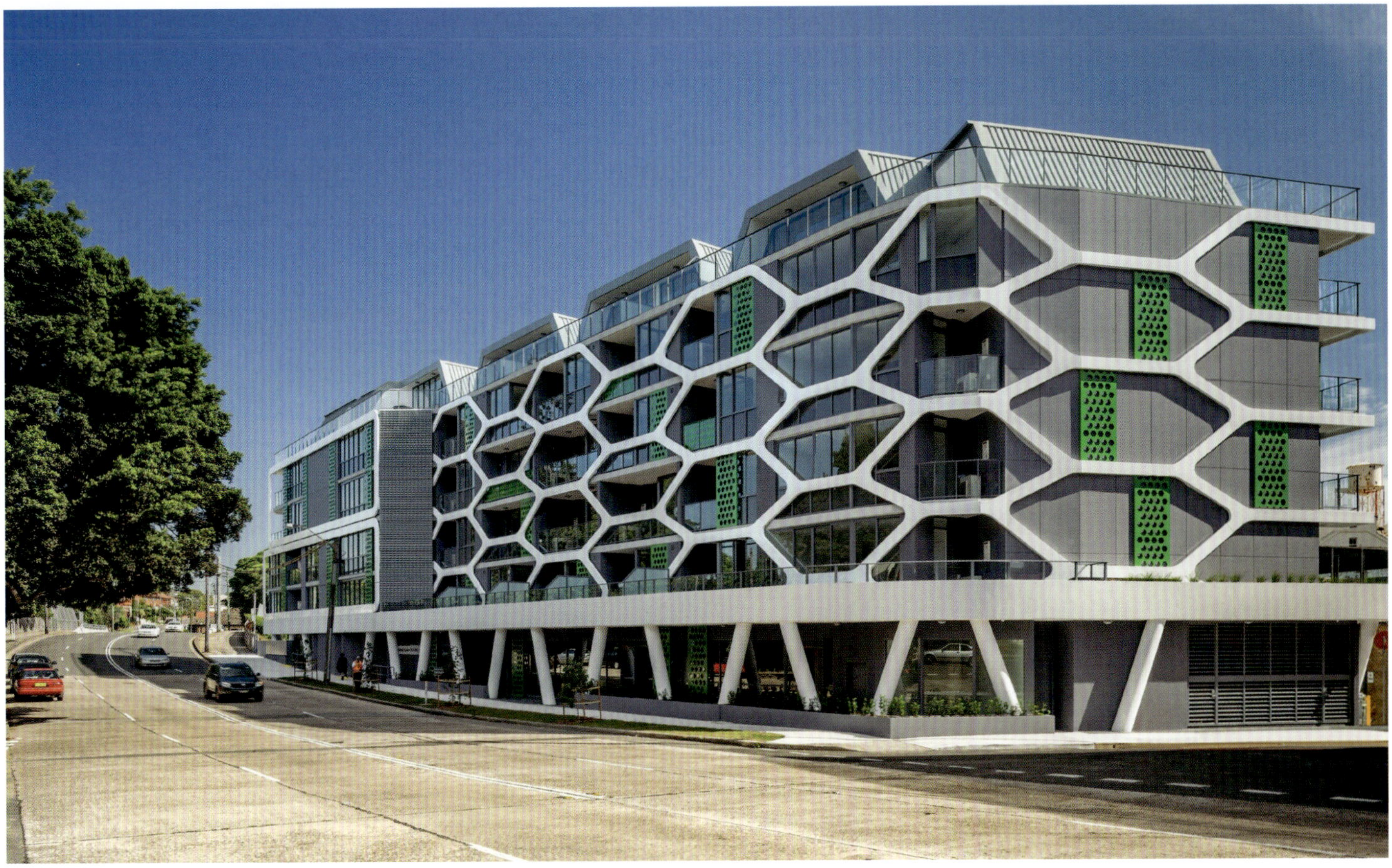

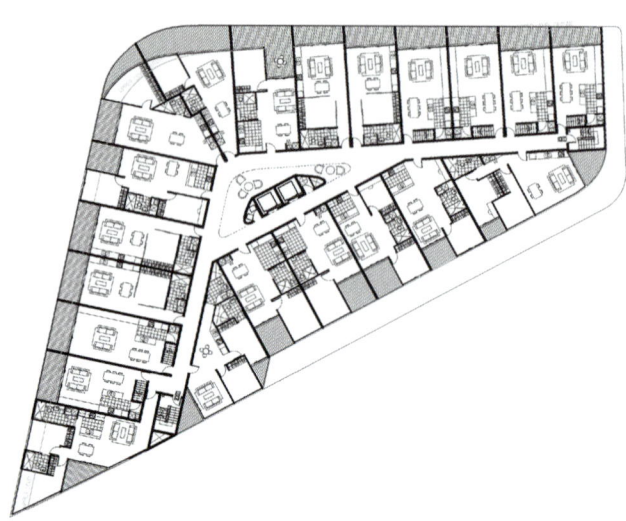

Floor plan level 1

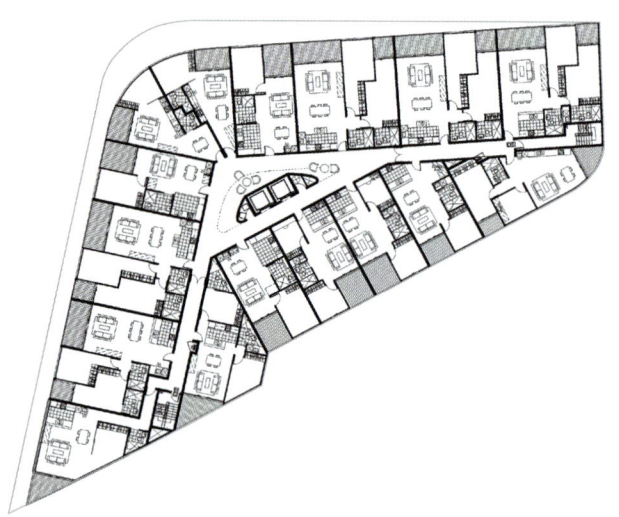

Floor plan level 3

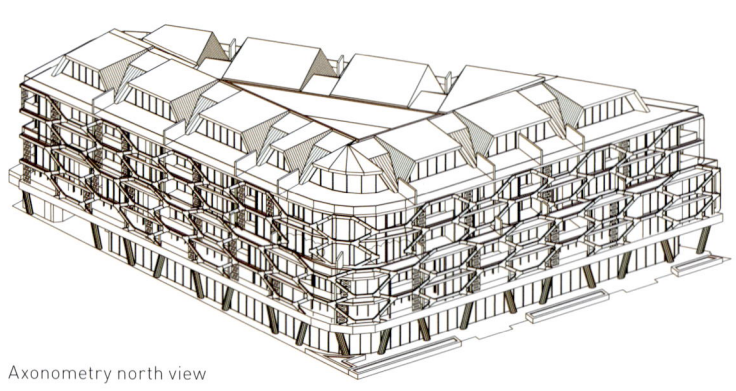

Axonometry north view

This set of 23 houses is situated on a sloping plot facing the river Georges. In order to provide privacy and optimise views and solar installations, a network of two-storey "L" shaped houses was designed on three levels leading down to the river. This L-shaped form generates central courtyards that create internal perspectives and maximise the sun in the bedrooms. The homes are stacked in such a way that the living rooms face a terrace on the roof of the lower unit. The interaction of the communal access roads, together with the use of topography and the definition of private spaces make the result resemble a small village. This sensation is reinforced by the use of a limited palette of materials that give homogeneity to the whole and add strength to the overall composition.

Dieses Set von 23 Häusern befindet sich auf einem Hanggrundstück mit Blick auf den Fluss Georges. Um Privatsphäre zu gewährleisten und die Aussicht und Solaranlagen zu optimieren, wurde ein Netz von zweigeschossigen L-Häusern auf drei Ebenen bis zum Fluss angelegt. Diese L-Form erzeugt zentrale Terrassen, die Innenperspektiven schaffen und die Sonne in den Schlafzimmern maximieren. Die Häuser sind so konzipiert, dass die Wohnräume auf eine Terrasse auf dem Dach der unteren Einheit ausgerichtet sind. Das Zusammenspiel der kommunalen Zufahrtsstraßen, die Verwendung von Topographie und die Definition von Privaträumen lassen das Ergebnis wie ein kleines Dorf erscheinen. Dieses Gefühl wird durch die Verwendung einer begrenzten Palette von Materialien verstärkt, die dem Ganzen Homogenität und der Gesamtkomposition Festigkeit verleihen.

SOVEREIGN
SYLVANIA, SYDNEY, AUSTRALIA

Cet ensemble de 23 maisons est situé sur un terrain en pente face à la rivière Georges. Pour assurer l'intimité et optimiser les vues et les installations solaires, un réseau de maisons en «L» à deux étages a été conçu sur trois niveaux jusqu'à la rivière. Cette forme en «L» génère des patios centraux qui créent des perspectives intérieures et maximisent le soleil dans les chambres. Les maisons sont empilées de telle sorte que les salons sont orientés vers une terrasse située sur le toit de l'unité inférieure. L'interaction des voies d'accès communales, l'utilisation de la topographie et la définition des espaces privés font que le résultat ressemble à un petit village. Cette sensation est renforcée par l'utilisation d'une palette limitée de matériaux qui donnent de l'homogénéité à l'ensemble et renforcent la composition globale.

Este conjunto de 23 casas se sitúa en una parcela en pendiente orientada hacia el río Georges. Para proporcionar privacidad y optimizar las vistas y las instalaciones solares, se proyectó un entramado de casas de dos plantas en forma de "L" dispuestas en tres niveles que bajan hacia el río. Esta forma en "L" genera patios centrales que crean perspectivas internas y maximizan el sol en los dormitorios. Las viviendas se apilan de tal manera que las salas de estar se orientan hacia una terraza situada en el techo de la unidad inferior. La interacción de los caminos comunales de acceso, junto al uso de la topografía y la definición de los espacios privados hacen que el resultado se asemeje a un pequeño pueblo. Esta sensación se refuerza mediante el uso de una limitada paleta de materiales que dan homogeneidad al conjunto y agregan fuerza a la composición global.

Site plan

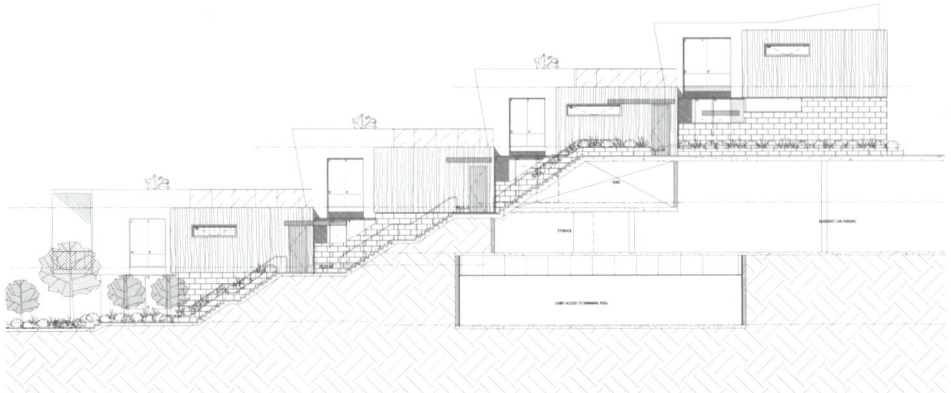

West elevation

TRAMA ARQUITECTOS

www.trama.com.mx

MISSION: The fusion of ideas that promotes full human activity through architectural space

VISION: The human values are pillars that sustain our ideology to be an architecture workshop worthy to serve, enrich and achieve an effective result to meet the spiritual, aesthetic and functional requirements of the client, generating a relationship of intimacy and trust towards the future.

At Trama Arquitectos we believe in the roots that architecure must have. Our language of expression is the space, which must speak with honesty of our identity as Mexicans and as architects of the XXI Century. Honesty in architecture makes us treating all aspects of the work with the utmost respect. An efficient and logical structure, an envelope that takes care of function and beauty, an assertive and safe construction system. An exciting space that is co-responsible for the perfect execution of the human activities that take place there.

MISSION: Die Fusion von Ideen, die durch den architektonischen Raum die volle menschliche Aktivität fördern.

VISION: Die menschlichen Werte sind Säulen, die unsere Ideologie stützen, eine Architekturwerkstatt zu sein, die es wert ist, den spirituellen, ästhetischen und funktionalen Anforderungen des Kunden zu dienen, sie zu bereichern und ein effektives Ergebnis zu erzielen, um so ein Verhältnis von Intimität und Vertrauen in die Zukunft zu schaffen.

Bei Trama Arquitectos glauben wir an die Wurzeln, die die Architekturarbeit haben muss. Unsere Ausdruckssprache ist der Raum, der ehrlich über unsere Identität als Mexikaner und als Architekten des 21. Jahrhunderts sprechen muss. Ehrlichkeit in der Architektur verpflichtet uns, alle Aspekte der Arbeit mit höchstem Respekt zu behandeln. Eine effiziente und logische Struktur, ein Gehäuse, das für Funktion und Schönheit sorgt, ein selbstbewusstes und sicheres Bausystem. Ein spannender Raum, der mitverantwortlich ist für die perfekte Umsetzung der menschlichen Aktivitäten, die dort stattfinden.

MISSION : La fusion d'idées qui, à travers l'espace architectural, favorise la pleine activité humaine.

VISION : Les valeurs humaines sont les piliers qui soutiennent notre idéologie d'être un atelier d'architecture digne de servir, d'enrichir et d'atteindre un résultat efficace pour répondre aux exigences spirituelles, esthétiques et fonctionnelles du client, générant ainsi une relation d'intimité et de confiance envers l'avenir.

Chez Trama Arquitectos, nous croyons aux racines que l'œuvre architecturale doit avoir. Notre langage d'expression est l'espace, qui doit parler honnêtement de notre identité en tant que Mexicains et architectes du XXIe siècle. L'honnêteté en architecture nous oblige à traiter tous les aspects du travail avec le plus grand respect. Une structure efficace et logique, une enceinte qui prend soin de la fonction et de la beauté, un système de construction affirmé et sûr. Un espace passionnant et coresponsable dans la parfaite réalisation des activités humaines qui s'y déroulent.

MISIÓN: La fusión de ideas que mediante el espacio arquitectónico promueva la actividad humana plena.

VISIÓN: Los valores humanos son pilares que sustentan nuestra ideología para ser un taller de arquitectura digno de servir, enriquecer y lograr un resultado eficaz para satisfacer los requerimientos espirituales, estéticos y funcionales del cliente, generando así una relación de intimidad y confianza hacia el futuro

En Trama Arquitectos creemos en las raices que debe tener la obra arquitectónica. Nuestro lenguaje de expresión es el espacio, que debe hablar con honestidad de nuestra identidad como mexicanos y como arquitectos del siglo XXI. La honestidad en arquitectura nos obliga a tratar todos los aspectos de la obra con el mayor respeto. Una estructura eficiente y lógica, una envolvente que cuide función y belleza, un sistema constructivo asertivo y seguro. Un espacio ilusionante que sea corresponsable en la perfecta realización de las actividades humanas que ahí se desarrollen.

CÍRCULO FRANCÉS

Name of the project: Círculo Francés

Location: López Cotilla #1223 corner with Atenas street, American colony, Guadalajara, Jalisco, Mexico

Year of construction: 2017

Built area: 16,800 m²

Architects authors of the work: Jaime Castiello Chávez, Héctor Santana, Edgardo Sandoval

Leading architects: Jorge I. Gutiérrez, Héctor Lozano Gray

Design team: Juan Carlos Barriga, Susana Cortés, Ana Castellanos, Salvador Hernández, Hugo Yáñez, Miguel A. Martínez

Project management: Emmanuel Calles and Gabriela González Lavalle

Structural calculation: Jorge Suárez M.

Electrical engineering: FMS Ingeniería

Hydrosanitary engineering: Hydrotechnics

Urban gardens: Nucleus Study, urban_cultivation deraiz

Landscaping: Between Plants

Photo credits / website: © Lorena Darquea

EDIFICIO CASA CORONADO

Construction year: 2016

Built area: 2,800 m²

Architects authors of the work: Jaime Castiello Chávez, Héctor Santana, Edgardo Sandoval

Lead architect of the project: Jorge I. Gutiérrez

Design team: Héctor Lozano Gray, Juan Carlos Barriga, Susana Cortés, Ana Castellanos, Salvador Hernández, Hugo Yáñez, Miguel A. Martínez

Construction: Orozco y Soto Construcciones / Ing. Ignacio A. Orozco

Structural calculations: Álvaro Vallejo

Hydrosanitary engineering: Hydrotechnics

Electrical engineering: José Luis Orozco

Urban gardens: Nucleus Study, urban_cultivation deraiz

Photo credits / website: © Lorena Darquea

The building is located in the Colonia Americana, one of the former neighborhoods that are reborn in the city, originally inhabited by the upper classes and later occupied by shops and offices. The project proposes the return of settlers to the area, trying not to promote an uncontrolled gentrification.

The building is divided into two blocks parallel to the streets that define the site and are opening from east to west. This layout, which enhances the trapezoidal shape of the site, creates an interior void that houses the nucleus of vertical communication and a communal space on the ground floor that contains the access to the dwellings and an urban garden.

The complex consists of a commercial ground floor, in front of which pleasant living spaces are developed. 60 dwellings of different types spread over the 6 upper floors.

Das Gebäude befindet sich in der American Colony, einer der ehemaligen Kolonien, die in der Stadt wiedergeboren werden. Ursprünglich von der Oberschicht bewohnt, haben sich später Geschäfte und Büros angesiedelt. Das Projekt schlägt die Rückkehr von Siedlern in das Gebiet vor und versucht, eine unkontrollierte Gentrifizierung nicht zu fördern.

Zusammenfassend ist das Gebäude in zwei Blöcke unterteilt, die parallel zu den Straßen verlaufen, die den Standort definieren und sich von Ost nach West öffnen. Dieses Layout, das die trapezförmige Form des Grundstücks unterstreicht, schafft eine innere Lücke, die den Kern der vertikalen Kommunikation beherbergt, und einen Gemeinschaftsraum im Erdgeschoss, der den Zugang zu den Wohnungen und einen städtischen Garten beinhaltet.

Der Komplex besteht aus einem gewerblichen Erdgeschoss, vor dem angenehme Wohnräume entstehen, und 60 Wohnungen unterschiedlicher Art, die sich auf die 6 Obergeschosse verteilen.

CÍRCULO FRANCÉS
GUADALAJARA, JALISCO, MÉXICO

Le bâtiment est situé dans la Colonia Americana, l'une des anciennes colonies qui renaissent dans la ville, à l'origine habitée par les classes supérieures et ensuite occupée par des magasins et des bureaux. Le projet propose le retour des colons dans la région, en essayant de ne pas promouvoir une gentrification incontrôlée.

D'un point de vue positif, le bâtiment est divisé en deux blocs parallèles aux rues qui définissent le site et qui s'ouvrent d'est en ouest. Ce tracé, qui met en valeur la forme trapézoïdale de la parcelle, crée un vide intérieur qui abrite le noyau de communication verticale ainsi qu'un espace commun au rez-de-chaussée, qui contient l'accès aux logements et un jardin urbain.

Le complexe se compose d'un rez-de-chaussée commercial, devant lequel sont aménagés des espaces de vie agréables, et de 60 logements de différents types répartis sur les 6 étages supérieurs.

El edificio se ubica en la Colonia Americana, una de las antiguas colonias que renacen en la ciudad, habitada en su origen por clases altas y posteriormente ocupada por comercios y oficinas. El proyecto plantea el retorno de pobladores a la zona, intentando no promover una gentrificación descontrolada.

Compositivamente, el edificio se desdobla en dos bloques paralelos a las calles que definen el solar y que se van abriendo de oriente a poniente. Esta disposición, que potencia la forma trapezoidal del solar, crea un vacío interior que aloja el núcleo de comunicación vertical y un espacio comunitario en planta baja que contiene el acceso a las viviendas y un huerto urbano.

El conjunto consta de unn planta baja comercial, frente a la que se desarrollan agradables espacios de convivencia, y 60 viviendas de diversas tipologías repartidas entre las 6 plantas superiores.

Sketch

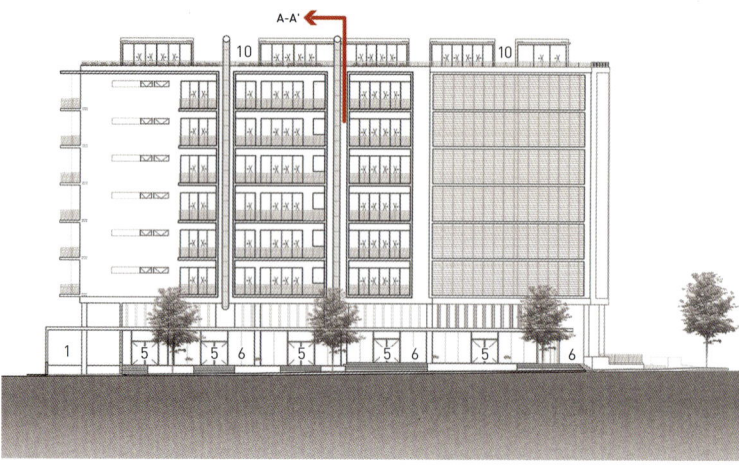

Elevation López Cotilla Street

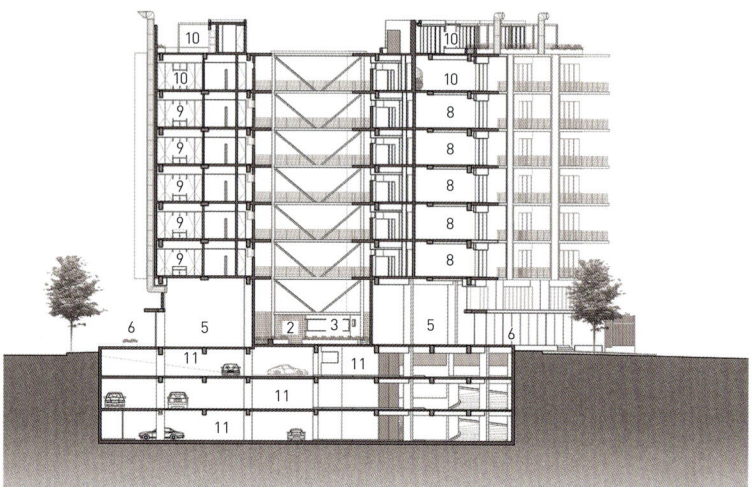

Section A-A'

1. Parking entrance
2. Departments entrance
3. Surveillance booth
4. Urban orchard
5. Commercial
6. Commercial terrace
7. Services
8. Studio Department
9. 2 bedroom apartment
10. Penthouse
11. Underground parking

Sketch

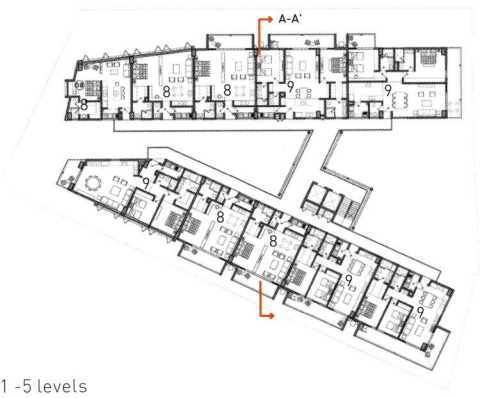

1 -5 levels

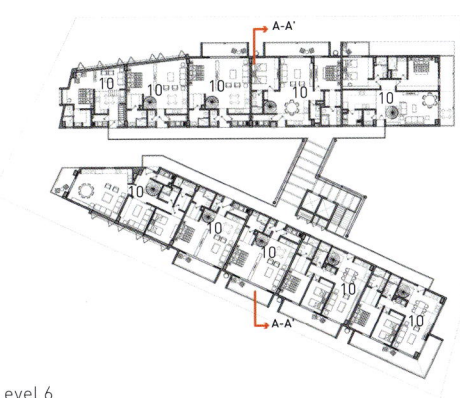

Level 6

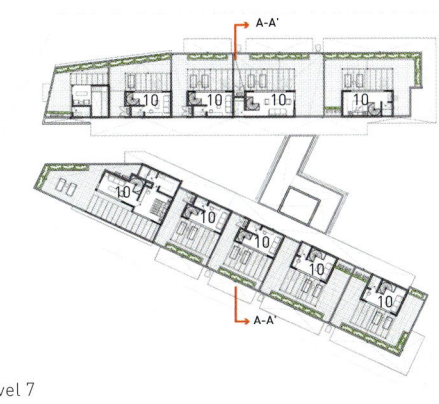

Level 7

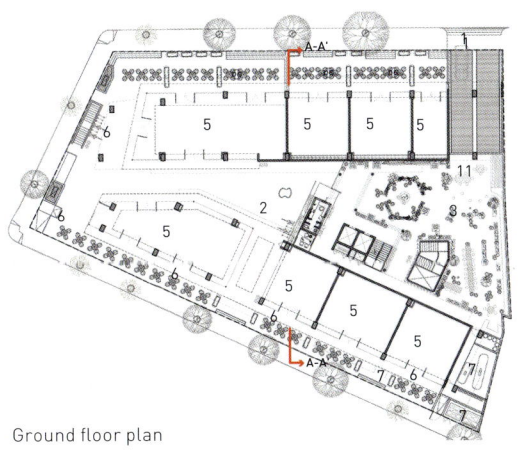

Ground floor plan

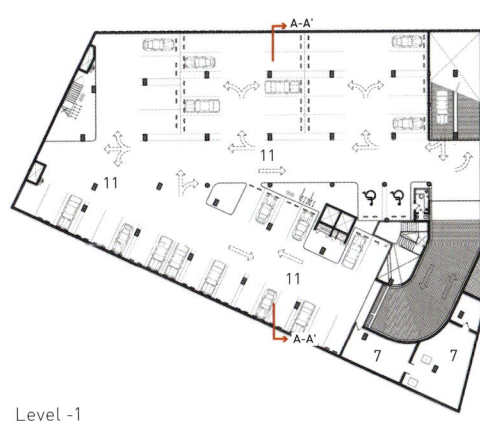

Level -1

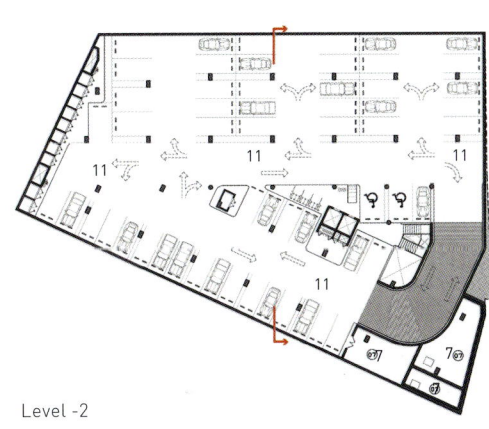

Level -2

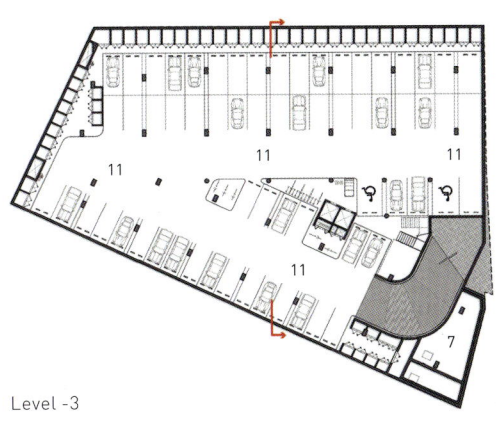

Level -3

1. Parking entrance
2. Departments entrance
3. Surveillance booth
4. Urban orchard
5. Commercial
6. Commercial terrace
7. Services
8. Studio Department
9. 2 bedroom apartment
10. Penthouse
11. Underground parking

Sketch

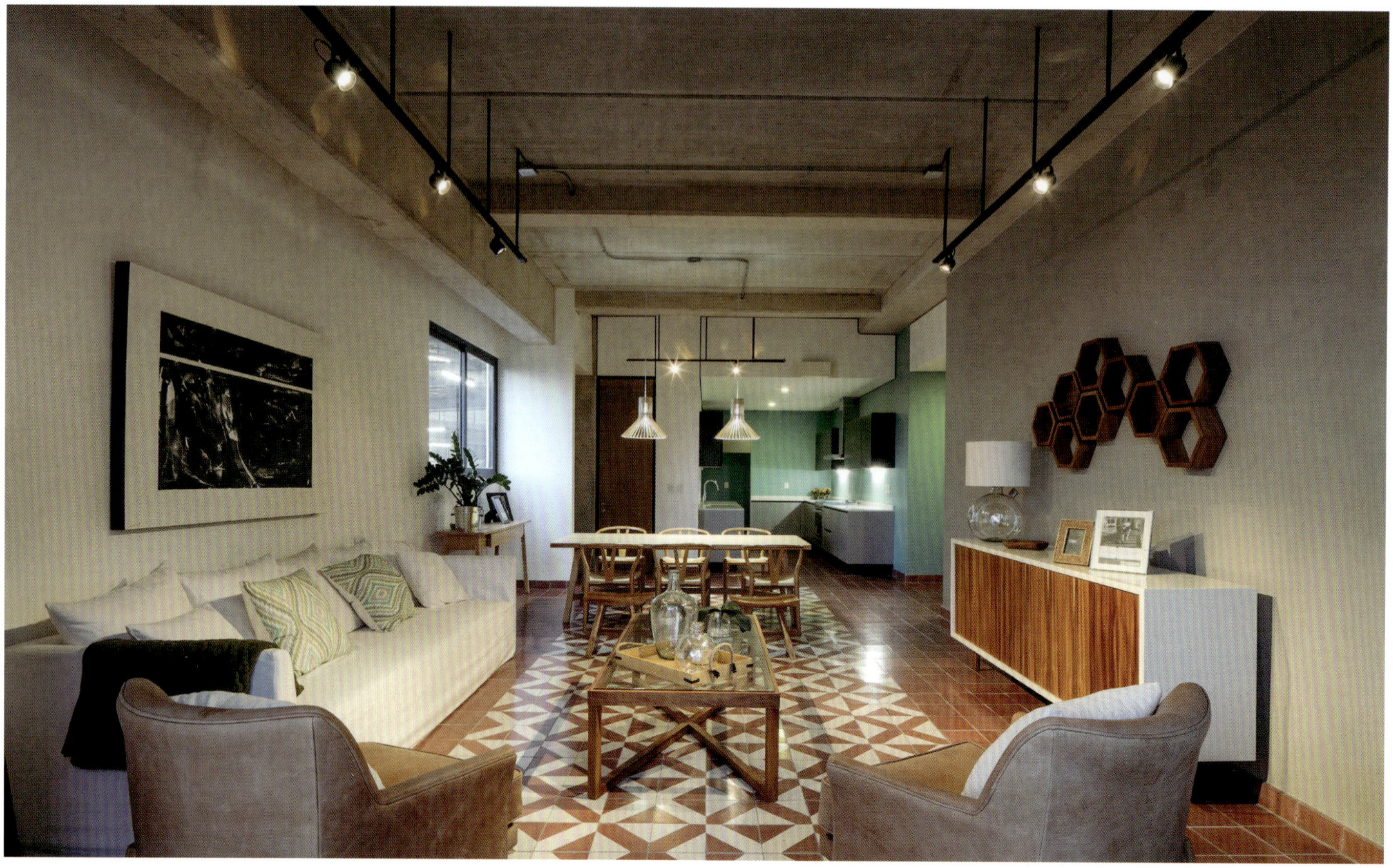

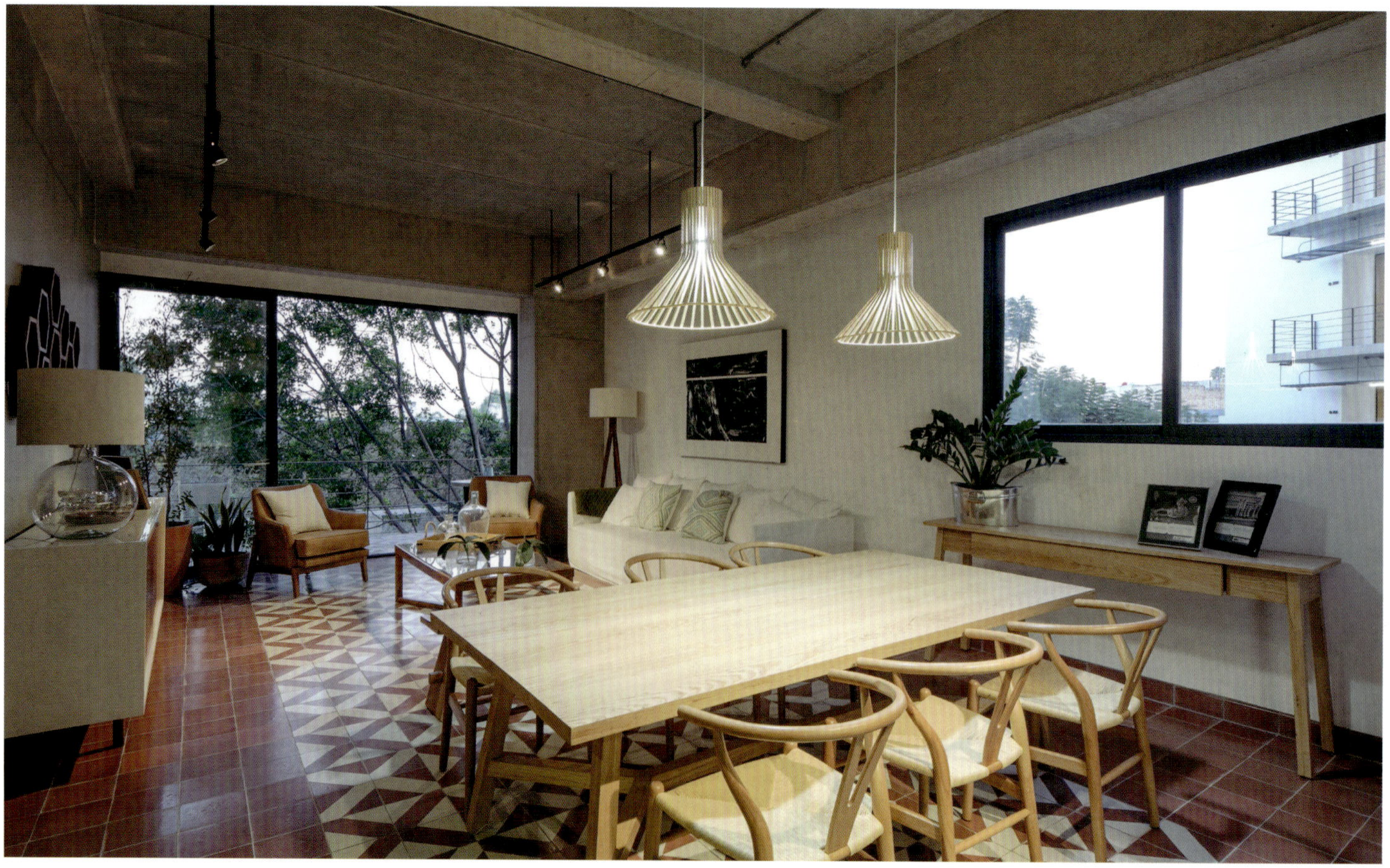

Within a plot of land located in the Colonia Americana, the project tries to find the dialogue between an abandoned property, catalogued as architectural heritage, and a proposal for a vertical building located in the area of a former orchard.

The new 8-storey building faces mainly to the south, with views over the existing construction, and to the east, with views over the city historic centre. The new building locates 16 studio-type dwellings that are dynamically organised to reduce the weight of the building's volume as it grows in height, achieving a slender formal proposal. Important elements of the project are the outdoor spaces generated on the different floors, such as the terraces that offer relief to the dwellings or the roofs of the two buildings, converted into meeting places around urban gardens.

Innerhalb eines Grundstücks in der amerikanischen Kolonie versucht das Projekt, den Dialog zwischen einem verlassenen, als architektonisches Erbe katalogisierten, Anwesen und einem Vorschlag für ein vertikales Gebäude auf dem Gelände des ehemaligen Obstgartens des Anwesens zu finden.

Das neue 8-geschossige Gebäude ist hauptsächlich nach Süden ausgerichtet, mit Blick auf das bestehende Gebäude, und nach Osten, mit Blick auf das historische Stadtzentrum. Es beherbergt 16 Atelierwohnungen, die dynamisch organisiert sind, um das Gewicht vom Volumen des Gebäudes abzuziehen, wenn es in der Höhe wächst, und so einen schlanken formalen Vorschlag zu erhalten. Wichtige Elemente des Projekts sind die auf den verschiedenen Stockwerken entstehenden Außenflächen, wie z. B. die Terrassen, die den Wohnungen Entlastung bieten, oder die Dächer der beiden Gebäude, die zu Treffpunkten rund um städtische Orkengärten umgebaut wurden.

CORONADO HOUSE BUILDING
GUADALAJARA, JALISCO, MÉXICO.

Dans un terrain situé dans la Colonia Americana, le projet tente de trouver le dialogue entre un domaine abandonné, catalogué comme patrimoine architectural, et une proposition de bâtiment vertical situé dans la zone de l'ancien verger du domaine.

Le nouvel immeuble de huit étages est orienté principalement vers le sud, avec vue sur le bâtiment existant, et vers l'est, avec vue sur le centre historique de la ville. Il abrite 16 logements de type studio qui sont organisés dynamiquement pour soustraire le poids du volume du bâtiment au fur et à mesure qu'il prend de la hauteur et ainsi obtenir une proposition formelle mince. Les éléments importants du projet sont les espaces extérieurs générés sur les différents étages, tels que les terrasses qui offrent du relief aux habitations ou les toits des deux bâtiments, transformés en lieux de rencontre autour des vergers et des jardins urbains.

Dentro de un solar ubicado en la Colonia Americana, el proyecto trata de encontrar el diálogo entre una finca abandonada, catalogada como patrimonio arquitectónico, y una propuesta de edificio vertical situado en el ámbito del antiguo huerto de la finca.

El nuevo edificio de 8 plantas se orienta principalmente hacia el sur, con vistas sobre el edificio existente, y hacia el este, con vistas sobre el centro histórico de la ciudad. En el se ubican 16 viviendas tipo estudio que se organizadan de forma dinámica para restar peso al volumen del edificio conforme crece en altura y lograr así una propuesta formal esbelta. Elementos importantes del proyecto son los espacios exteriores generados en las diferentes plantas, como las terrazas que ofrecen desahogo a las viviendas o las azoteas de los dos edificios, convertidas en lugares de encuentro alrededor de huertos urbanos.

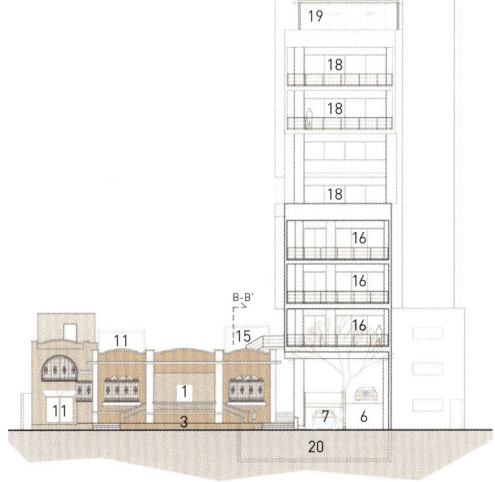

Section A-A'

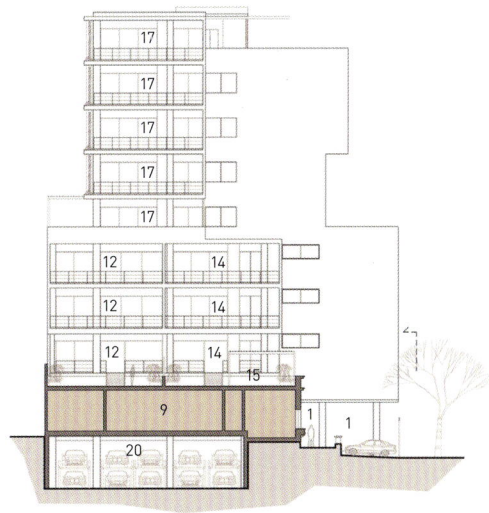

Section B-B'

1. Entrance portico
2. Entrance courtyard
3. Visitor parking
4. Parking departments
5. Elevator
6. Ground floor parking entrance
7. Basement parking entrance
8. Coronado General Street
9. House 1
10. House 2
11. Terrace house 2
12. Apartments type A
13. Terrace apartment type A
14. Apartment type B
15. Terrace apartment type B
16. Apartment type C
17. Apartment type D
18. Apartment type E
19. Urban orchard-gardens
20. Basement parking

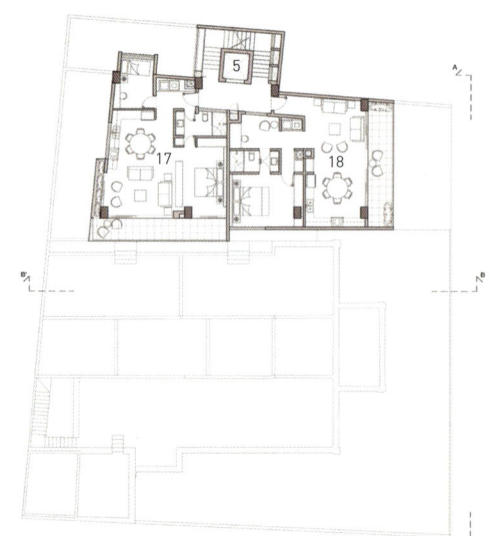

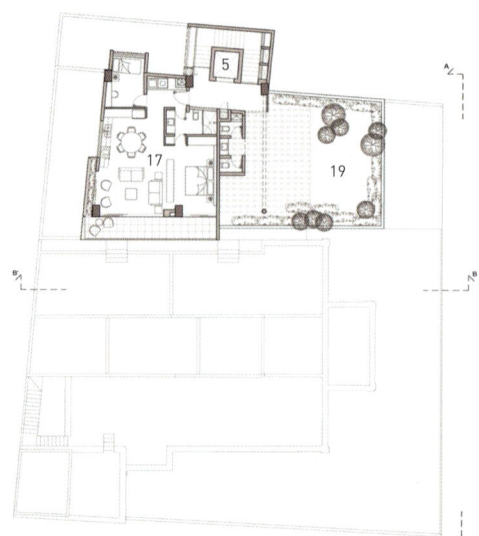

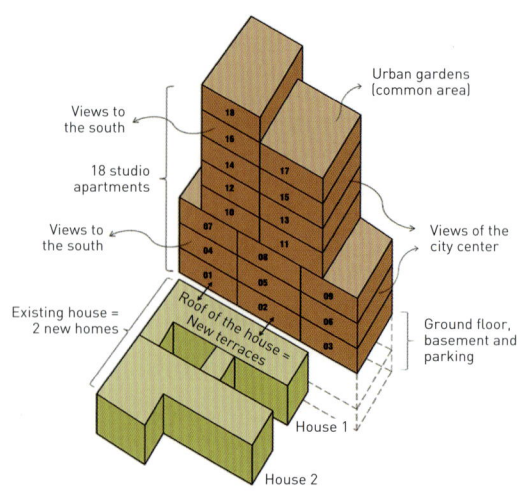

Axonometric diagram

Urban gardens (common area)

Views to the south

18 studio apartments

Views to the south

Views of the city center

Existing house = 2 new homes

Roof of the house = New terraces

Ground floor, basement and parking

House 1

House 2

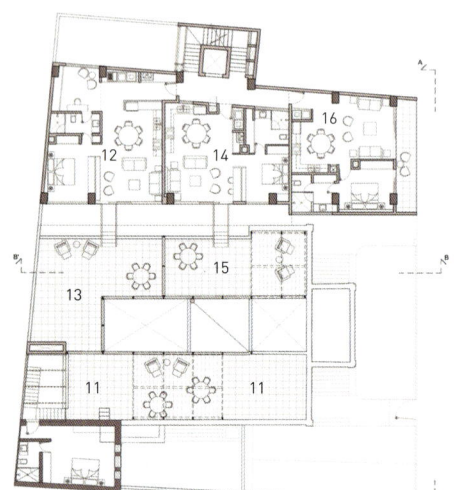

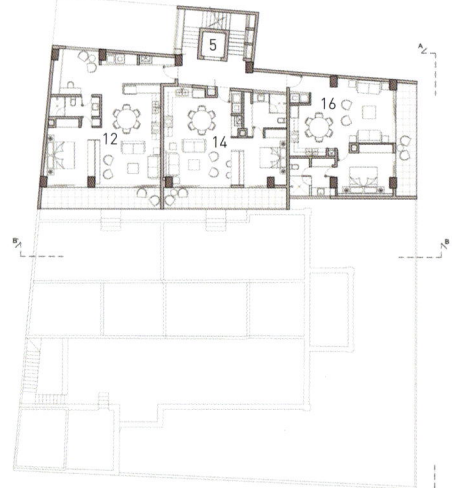

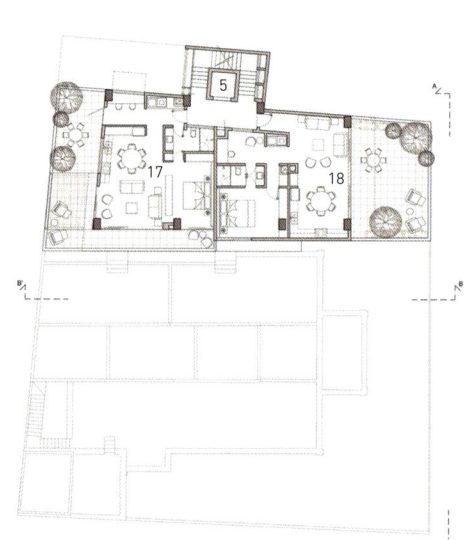

Floor plans

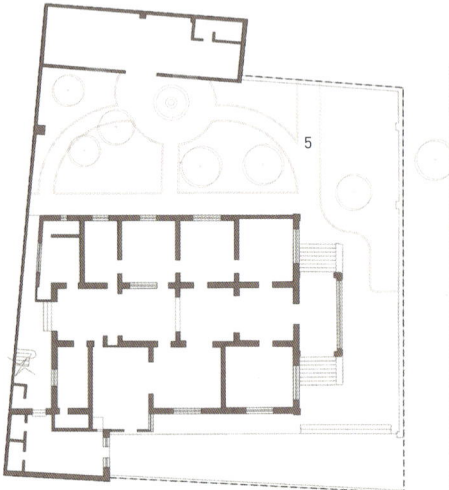

Existing ground floor plan

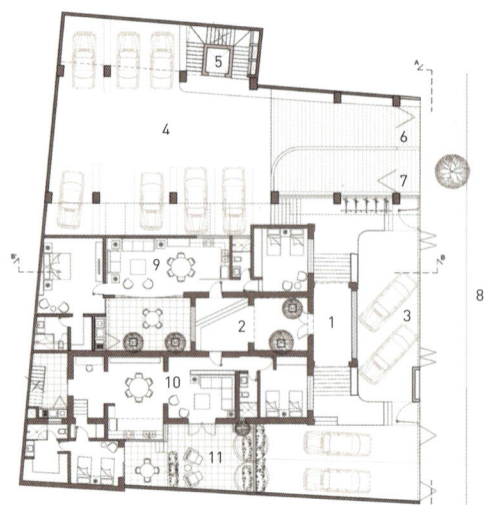

New ground floor plan

1. Entrance portico
2. Entrance courtyard
3. Visitor parking
4. Parking departments
5. Elevator
6. Ground floor parking entrance
7. Basement parking entrance
8. Coronado General Street
9. House 1
10. House 2
11. Terrace house 2
12. Apartments type A
13. Terrace apartment type A
14. Apartment type B
15. Terrace apartment type B
16. Apartment type C
17. Apartment type D
18. Apartment type E
19. Urban orchard-gardens
20. Basement parking

VALERIE SCHWEITZER ARCHITECTS

http://schweitzerarchitecture.com/

Valerie Schweitzer Architects aims to create inventive spaces that deepen a sense of place. With an emphasis on the overlap of art and architecture, Schweitzer's designs communicate a central purpose. That purpose might be the transporting dimensions of an artist's studio, or the playfulness of a Los Angeles multi-family mid-rise. Schweitzer specializes in place-making that aims to uplift individuals and entire neighborhoods.

Schweitzer established her own practice in 2008 after working at various New York firms including Skidmore Owings and Merrill. In 2008 she was a winner of the Open Auditions competition sponsored by Architectural Digest. In 2017 she won an American Architecture Prize. Her entrant of a shade structure, Bubble Shade, into Architizer's Future of Shade contest (2017), received a citation and is currently being considered by the NYC Parks commission for one its parks. Most recently her entry for a wildlife pavilion competition in Kenya, Pangolin Pavilion, received a citation by Archasm, 2018.

Valerie Schweitzer Architekten zielt darauf ab, erfinderische Räume zu schaffen, die das Gefühl des Ortes vertiefen. Mit dem Schwerpunkt auf kontextueller Integration und nachhaltiger Praxis kommunizieren Schweitzers Designs einen zentralen Zweck. Dieser Zweck kann die transportablen Dimensionen eines Künstlerstudios, oder die Verspieltheit einer Los Angeles Mehrfamilien-Mittelklasse sein. Schweitzer ist spezialisiert auf die Herstellung von Räumlichkeiten, die darauf abzielen, Einzelpersonen und ganze Stadtviertel zu verbessern.

Schweitzer gründete ihre eigene Praxis im Jahr 2008, nachdem sie für verschiedene New Yorker Unternehmen wie Skidmore Owings und Merrill gearbeitet hatte. Im Jahr 2008 gewann sie den Wettbewerb Open Auditions, gesponsert von Architectural Digest. Im Jahr 2017 erhielt sie einen amerikanischen Architekturpreis. Ihr Teilnehmer einer Schattenstruktur, Bubble Shade, am Architizer's Future of Shade Wettbewerb (2017), erhielt ein Zitat und wird derzeit von der NYC Parks Commission für einen seiner Parks berücksichtigt. Zuletzt erhielt ihr Beitrag für einen Wildpavillon-Wettbewerb in Kenia, den Pangolin Pavilion, eine Zitierung von Archasm, 2018.

Valerie Schweitzer Architects vise à créer des espaces inventifs qui approfondissent le sentiment d'appartenance. En mettant l'accent sur l'intégration contextuelle et la pratique durable, les conceptions de Schweitzer communiquent un objectif central. Il peut s'agir des dimensions de transport d'un atelier d'artiste ou de l'aspect ludique d'un immeuble de Los Angeles multifamilial. Schweitzer se spécialise dans l'aménagement de lieux qui vise à élever les individus et des quartiers entiers.

Mme Schweitzer a fondé son propre cabinet en 2008 après avoir travaillé dans divers cabinets new-yorkais, notamment Skidmore Owings et Merrill. En 2008, elle a été la lauréate du concours d'auditions publiques parrainé par Architectural Digest. En 2017, elle a remporté un prix d'architecture américain. Sa participation au concours Architizer's Future of Shade (2017) pour une structure d'ombrage, Bubble Shade, a reçu une citation et est actuellement à l'étude par la commission des parcs de NYC pour un de ses parcs. Plus récemment, sa participation à un concours pour un pavillon de la faune sauvage au Kenya, le Pavillon Pangolin, a reçu une citation d'Archasm, 2018.

Valerie Schweitzer Architects tiene como objetivo crear espacios creativos que profundicen el sentido del lugar. Con un énfasis en la integración contextual y la práctica sostenible, los diseños de Schweitzer comunican un propósito claramente definido: las dimensiones del estudio de un artista o la juguetonería de un edificio multifamiliar en Los Ángeles. Schweitzer se especializa en la creación de lugares con el objetivo de mejorar a individuos y vecindarios enteros.

Schweitzer estableció su propio estudio en 2008 después de trabajar en varias firmas de Nueva York, incluyendo Skidmore Owings y Merrill. En 2008 fue ganadora del concurso Open Auditions patrocinado por Architectural Digest. En 2017 ganó el Premio de Arquitectura Americana. Su proyecto Bubble Shade, en el concurso de Architizer's Future of Shade (2017), recibió una mención especial y actualmente, Schweitzer está siendo considerada por la comisión de Parques de la ciudad de Nueva York para uno de sus próximos proyectos. Más recientemente, su entrada para un concurso de un pabellón de vida silvestre en Kenia, Pangolin Pavilion, recibió una mención de Archasm, 2018.

THE TIDES BRENTWOOD

Location: 1157 South Bundy Drive, Los Angeles, CA

Completion: April 2017

Design architect:
Valerie Schweitzer AIA
of Valerie Schweitzer Architects—
NYC, New York

Architect of record:
Plus Architects, Los Angeles, CA

GC and construction manager:
Kennedy Construction (Seamus
Kennedy and Bob Van Dyke)

Photo credits:
© Dan Arnold Photography, LA, CA
JWP Studio, LA, CA

HIDE AND SEEK HOUSE

Location: 1946 Overland Avenue, Los Angeles, CA

Start of works: March 2019

Design architect:
Valerie Schweitzer AIA of
Valerie Schweitzer Architects—
NYC, New York

Architect of record:
Andrew Ratzsch, Los Angeles, CA

The main objective in designing this five-story building was to enhance the neighborhood and celebrate the iconoclastic spirit of Los Angeles. Located in an interstitial area, the project promotes through the design of its façades a sense of place that pools ecological elements of the area, such as the Pacific Ocean, the predominant sun and the high palms that surround the site. Its exterior facade builds a dynamic connection with street life through elements such as large balconies that expand the interior through large windows. The façades include a pictorial component reflected in the Mondrian-inspired cavities that scale the vertical transportation cores, clad in grey stucco. Colour is used throughout the building not only as a cladding, but also as an architectural element that helps to sculpt the space.

Das Hauptziel bei der Planung dieses fünfstöckigen Gebäudes war es, die Nachbarschaft anzuziehen und den ikonoklastischen Geist von Los Angeles zu feiern. Das Projekt liegt in einem Zwischenraum und fördert durch die Gestaltung seiner Fassaden ein Gefühl des Ortes, das ökologische Elemente des Gebietes, wie den Pazifischen Ozean, die vorherrschende Sonne und die hohen Palmen, die den Ort umgeben, verbindet. Sein Außenbild stellt eine dynamische Verbindung zum Straßenleben her, durch Elemente wie große Balkone, die den Innenraum durch große Fenster erweitern. Die Fassaden beinhalten eine Bildkomponente, die sich in den von Mondrian inspirierten Hohlräumen spiegelt, die die mit grauem Stuck verkleideten vertikalen Kommunikationskerne skalieren. Farbe wird im gesamten Gebäude nicht nur als Verkleidung, sondern auch als architektonisches Element eingesetzt, das den Raum mitgestaltet.

THE TIDES BRENTWOOD
LOS ANGELES, CALIFORNIA, USA

L'objectif principal de la conception de ce bâtiment de cinq étages était d'attirer le quartier et de célébrer l'esprit iconoclaste de Los Angeles. Situé dans une zone interstitielle, le projet favorise par la conception de ses façades un sentiment d'appartenance qui agglutine les éléments écologiques de la région, tels que l'océan Pacifique, le soleil prédominant et les hautes palmes qui entourent le lieu. Son image extérieure crée un lien dynamique avec la vie dans la rue grâce à des éléments tels que de grands balcons qui agrandissent l'intérieur par de grandes fenêtres. Les façades comportent un élément pictural se reflétant dans les cavités d'inspiration Mondrian qui donnent une échelle aux noyaux de communication verticaux revêtus de stuc gris. La couleur est utilisée dans tout le bâtiment non seulement comme revêtement, mais aussi comme élément architectural qui aide à sculpter l'espace.

El objetivo principal al diseñar este edificio de cinco plantas fue atraer al vecindario y celebrar el espíritu iconoclasta de Los Ángeles. Situado en un área intersticial, el proyecto promueve a través del diseño de sus fachadas una sensación de lugar que aglutina elementos ecológicos de la zona, como el Océano Pacífico, el sol predominante y las elevadas palmeras que rodean el lugar. Su imagen exterior construye una conexión dinámica con la vida de la calle mediante elementos como los amplios balcones que expanden el interior a través de grandes ventanales. Las fachadas incluyen un componente pictórico reflejado en las cavidades de inspiración Mondrian que escalan los núcleos de comunicación vertical revestidos de estuco gris. El color es utilizado en todo el edificio no sólo como revestimiento, sino como un elemento arquitectónico que ayuda a esculpir el espacio.

East elevation

North elevation

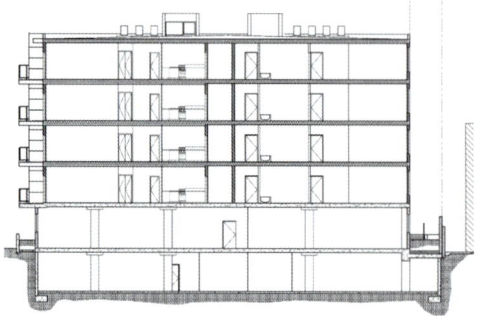

Cross section

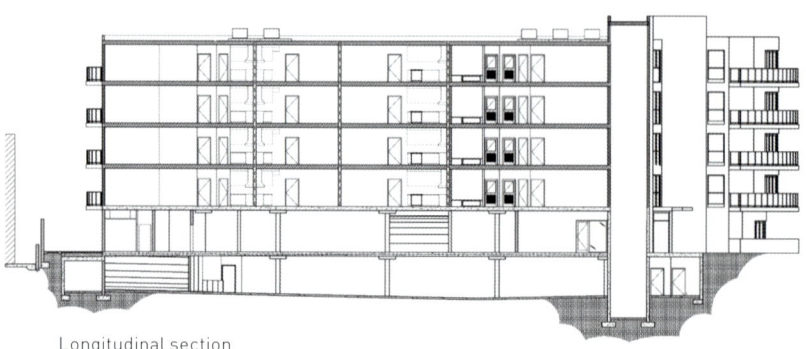

Longitudinal section

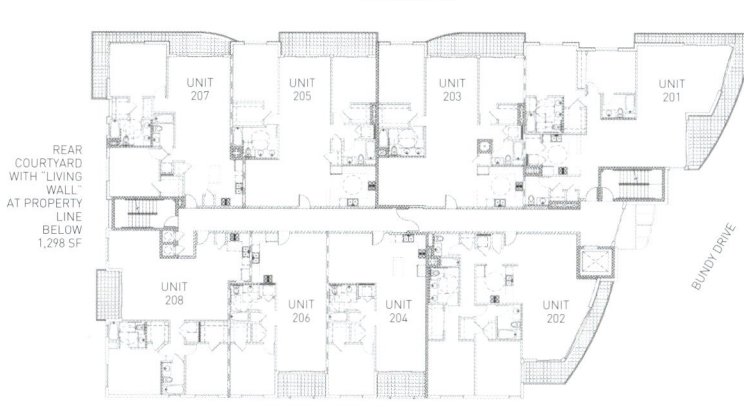

REAR
COURTYARD
WITH "LIVING
WALL"
AT PROPERTY
LINE
BELOW
1,298 SF

UNIT 207
UNIT 205
UNIT 203
UNIT 201

UNIT 208
UNIT 206
UNIT 204
UNIT 202

BUNDY DRIVE

Second floor plan

This 15-unit apartment building, a candidate for LEED Gold, will begin construction in March 2019. It consists of a concrete base, wooden superstructure, and façades combining concrete panels, glass, and weathered steel sheets that shade and partially conceal the apartment units. For architectural purposes, the project uses these rusty-tone industrial steel elements also in shade devices located in the lobby and on the communal landscaped roof, introducing the earthy tones of a forest throughout the building. The Euclidean geometry of the glazing modules located in front of Overland Avenue is interrupted by dinosaur-like curves, transmitting towards the street an aspect of scenery and fantasy. It is as if the pedestrian had stumbled upon a jungle scene from the game of hide-and-seek.

Dieser 15 Wohnungen umfassende LEED Gold zertifizierte Block, der im März 2019 mit dem Bau beginnen wird, besteht aus einem Betonsockel, einem Holzüberbau und Fassaden, die Betonplatten, Glas und gealterte Stahlbleche kombinieren, die die Häuser verschatten und teilweise verdecken. Das Projekt verwendet diese rostigen industriellen Stahlelemente auch in Schattenvorrichtungen in der Lobby und auf dem kommunal begrünten Dach für architektonische Zwecke und bringt die erdigen Farbtöne eines Waldes in das Gebäude ein. Die euklidische Geometrie der Verglasungsmodule vor der Overland Avenue wird durch dinosaurierähnliche Kurven von Dornen unterbrochen, die Aspekte von Bühne und Fantasie auf die Straße übertragen. Es ist, als wäre der Fußgänger über eine Dschungelszene aus dem Versteck gestolpert.

Roof plan

HIDE AND SEEK HOUSE
LOS ANGELES, CALIFORNIA, USA

Fourth floor reflected ceiling plan

Cet immeuble de 15 appartements certifié LEED Or, dont la construction débutera en mars 2019, se compose d'une base en béton, d'une superstructure en bois et de façades combinant des panneaux de béton, du verre et des tôles d'acier vieilli qui ombragent et masquent partiellement les maisons. Le projet utilise à des fins architecturales ces éléments en acier industriel de couleur rouille également dans les dispositifs d'ombrage situés dans le hall d'entrée et sur le toit paysager communal, introduisant les tons terreux d'une forêt dans le bâtiment. La géométrie euclidienne des modules de vitrage situés en face d'Overland Avenue est interrompue par des courbes d'épines semblables à des dinosaures, transmettant vers la rue un aspect de scène et de fantaisie. C'est comme si le piéton était tombé sur une scène de jungle à partir du jeu de *cache-cache*.

Este bloque de 15 apartamentos y certificación LEED Gold, cuya construcción comenzará en marzo de 2019, se compone de una base de hormigón, superestructura de madera y fachadas que combinan paneles de hormigón, vidrio y planchas envejecidas de acero que dan sombra y ocultan parcialmente las viviendas. El proyecto utiliza con fines arquitectónicos estos elementos de acero industrial de tonos oxidados también en dispositivos de sombra situados en el vestíbulo y en la cubierta ajardinada comunitaria, introduciendo los tonos terrosos de un bosque en el edificio. La geometría euclidiana de los módulos de acristalamiento situados frente a la avenida Overland se ve interrumpida por curvas de espinas similares a dinosaurios, transmitiendo hacia la calle un aspecto de escenario y fantasía. Es como si el peatón se hubiera topado con una escena selvática del juego del escondite.

Second floor plan

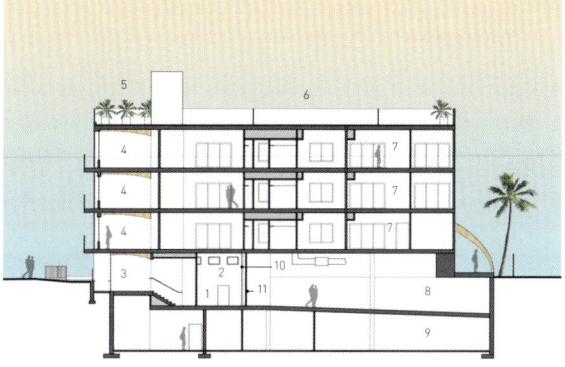

Section

1. Lobby
2. Mailbox
3. Entrance
4. Hall
5. Small palms
6. Roof garden
7. Unit
8. Garage
9. Basement
10. 3/8" steel plate
    with bracing tube
11. Astro-turf

WENINK HOLTKAMP
ARCHITECTEN

www.weninkholtkamp.nl

Since the founding of our office in 2012 a large part of our work has been focused on the repurposing of (industrial) heritage.

Our design philosophy when dealing with (industrial) heritage is about adding a new layer to the building. A layer which is evidently contemporary and clearly readable in both exterior and interior. The inspiration of our philosophy comes from the ancient Italian inner cities, in which almost all the facades show new and old alterations and thus showing the history of the building. Therefore we named our philosophy A New History. The alterations these Italian buildings underwent did not affect their monumentality and add a layer of intrigue as one wonders about the story behind the changes that have been made through time.

It is our vision that all the changes that are being made when repurposing a building are deliberate and precise. The existing architectonic strength and atmosphere are leading in the design and must be maintained as much as possible.

Seit der Gründung unseres Büros im Jahr 2012 konzentriert sich ein Großteil unserer Arbeit auf die Wiederverwendung von (industriellem) Erbe.

Unsere Designphilosophie ist es in diesen Fällen, dem Gebäude eine neue Schicht hinzuzufügen. Eine Schicht, die offensichtlich zeitgemäß und sowohl von außen als auch von innen gut lesbar ist. Die Inspiration kommt aus den alten italienischen Städten, in denen fast alle Fassaden neue und alte Reformen zeigen und so die Geschichte des Gebäudes zeigen. Deshalb nennen wir unsere Philosophie „A New History". Die Umbauten an diesen italienischen Gebäuden haben ihre Monumentalität nicht beeinträchtigt und eine gewisse Intrigenschicht hinzugefügt. Man fragt nach der Geschichte hinter den Veränderungen, die sich im Laufe der Zeit vollzogen haben.

Es ist unsere Absicht, dass alle Änderungen bei der Neuausrichtung eines Gebäudes bewusst und korrekt erfolgen. Architektonische Stärke und die vorhandene Umgebung bestimmen das Design und sollten immer so weit wie möglich erhalten bleiben.

Depuis la création de notre bureau en 2012, une grande partie de notre travail s'est concentrée sur la réutilisation du patrimoine (industriel).

Notre philosophie de conception dans ces cas est d'ajouter une nouvelle couche au bâtiment. Une couche qui est évidemment contemporaine et clairement lisible aussi bien à l'extérieur qu'à l'intérieur. L'inspiration vient des vieux centres urbains italiens, dont presque toutes les façades montrent des réformes nouvelles et anciennes, montrant ainsi l'histoire du bâtiment. C'est pourquoi nous appelons notre philosophie « Une nouvelle histoire ». Les modifications apportées à ces bâtiments italiens n'ont pas affecté leur monumentalité et ont ajouté une couche d'intrigue. On peut s'interroger sur l'histoire des changements qui se sont produits au fil du temps.

Notre intention est que tous les changements de réorientation d'un bâtiment soient délibérés et précis. La solidité architecturale et l'environnement existant sont à la base de la conception et doivent toujours être maintenus dans la mesure du possible.

Desde el origen de nuestra oficina en 2012, gran parte de nuestro trabajo se ha centrado en la reutilización del patrimonio (industrial).

Nuestra filosofía de diseño en estos casos consiste en añadir una nueva capa al edificio. Una capa que es evidentemente contemporánea y claramente legible tanto en el exterior como en el interior. La inspiración proviene de los antiguos cascos urbanos italianos, en los que casi todas las fachadas muestran nuevas y viejas reformas, mostrando así la historia del edificio. Por eso llamamos a nuestra filosofía «Una Nueva Historia». Las alteraciones que sufrieron estos edificios italianos no afectaron su monumentalidad y añadieron una capa de intriga. Uno se pregunta sobre la historia que existe detrás de los cambios llevados a cabo a través del tiempo.

Nuestra intención es que todos los cambios de reorientación de un edificio sean deliberados y precisos. La fuerza arquitectónica y el ambiente existente lideran el diseño y deben ser mantenidos siempre en la medida de lo posible.

Location: Oisterwijk,
The Netherlands

Building area:
1,200 m² / 13,000 sq ft

Project completion date:
beginning 2018

Lead architects: :
Wenink Holtkamp Architecten

Other participants :
BOEi

Contractor / developer:
Nico de Bont TBI

Constructor:
Vianen Bouwadvies

Photo credits:
© Tim van de Velde

DE LAKFABRIEK

This old lacquer factory was reconverted into 25 dwellings of different types, designed by the architects in collaboration with the users themselves. One of the premises of the project was to preserve the industrial character of the building. This intention is expressed in the visible structure of rough concrete inside the dwellings, or in the classic profile of the carpentry of the windows that evokes the original steel frames, which could not be conserved. On the roof, a new volume of glass is added to the original building. Its modern, minimalist structure clearly differs from the existing architecture through language and materialisation, but is naturally integrated into the whole. The façades of the new volume are removed from the perimeter of the building to create large terraces in the dwellings on the top floor.

Diese alte Lackfabrik wurde in 25 Wohnungen unterschiedlicher Art umgebaut, die von den Architekten in Zusammenarbeit mit den Nutzern selbst entworfen wurden. Eines der Ziele des Projekts war es, den industriellen Charakter des Gebäudes zu erhalten. Diese Absicht spiegelt sich in der sichtbaren rauen Betonstruktur des Innenraums der Wohnungen wider oder im klassischen Profil der Fensterschreinerei, das an die ursprünglichen Stahlrahmen erinnert, die nicht erhalten werden konnten. Auf dem Dach wird dem ursprünglichen Gebäude ein neues Glasvolumen hinzugefügt. Seine moderne und minimalistische Struktur unterscheidet sich deutlich von der bestehenden Architektur durch Ausdruck und Materialisierung, ist aber natürlich in das Ganze integriert. Die Fassaden des neuen Volumens sind weiter vom Gebäude entfernt, um große Terrassen in den Wohnungen im Dachgeschoss zu schaffen.

DE LAKFABRIEK
THE NETHERLANDS, OISTERWIJK

Cette ancienne usine de laques a été reconvertie en 25 logements de différents types, conçus par les architectes en collaboration avec les utilisateurs eux-mêmes. L'une des prémisses du projet était de préserver le caractère industriel du bâtiment. Cette intention s'incarne dans la structure apparente en béton brut de l'intérieur des habitations, ou dans le profil classique de la menuiserie des fenêtres qui évoque les charpentes métalliques d'origine, qui n'ont pu être conservées. Sur le toit, un nouveau volume de verre est ajouté au bâtiment d'origine. Sa structure moderne et minimaliste se distingue nettement de l'architecture existante par son langage et sa matérialisation, mais s'intègre naturellement dans l'ensemble. Les façades du nouveau volume sont retirées du périmètre du bâtiment pour créer de grandes terrasses dans les logements du dernier étage.

Esta antigua fábrica de lacas fue reconvertida en 25 viviendas de diferentes tipologías, diseñadas por los arquitectos en colaboración con los propios usuarios. Una de las premisas del proyecto fue preservar el carácter industrial del edificio. Esta intención se plasma en la estructura vista de hormigón en bruto del interior de las viviendas, o en el perfil clásico de la carpintería de las ventanas que evoca los marcos de acero originales, que no pudieron ser conservados. En la cubierta, un nuevo volumen de vidrio se agrega al edificio original. Su estructura moderna y minimalista se diferencia claramente de la arquitectura existente a través del lenguaje y la materialización, pero se integra de forma natural al conjunto. Las fachadas del nuevo volumen se retiran respecto del perímetro del edificio para crear amplias terrazas en las viviendas de la última planta.

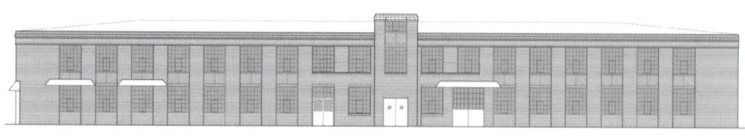

Existing elevations

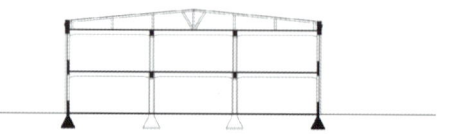

Existing sections

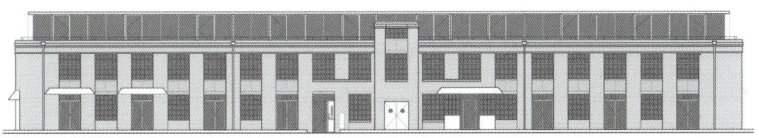

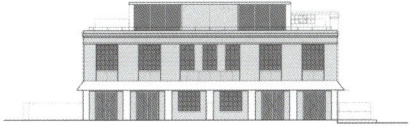

Elevations

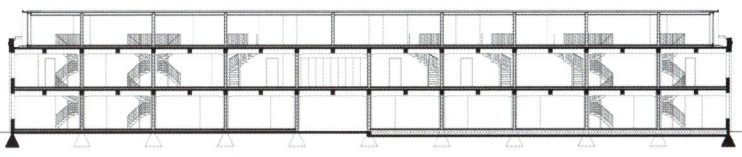

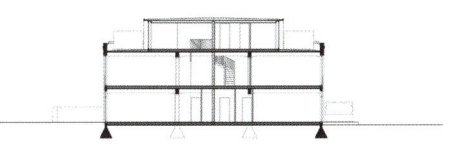

Sections

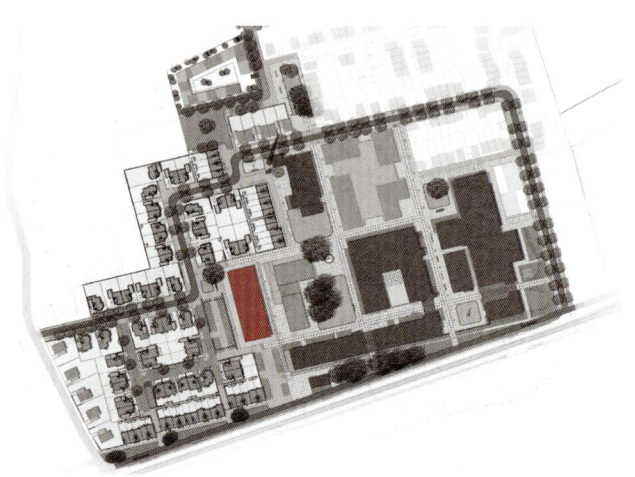

Site plan

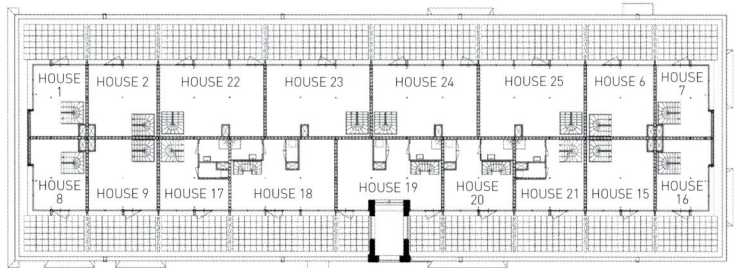

Roof extension plan

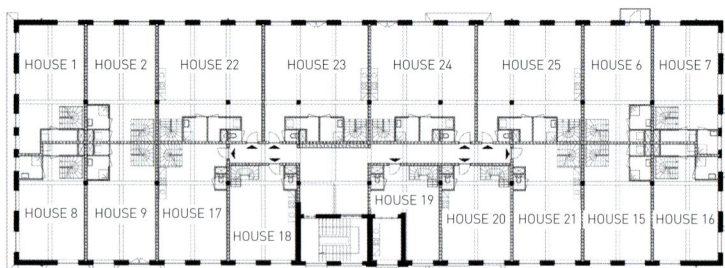

First floor plan

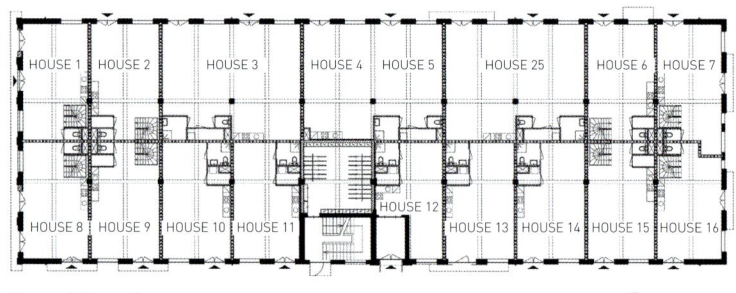

Ground floor plan

Ground floor plan

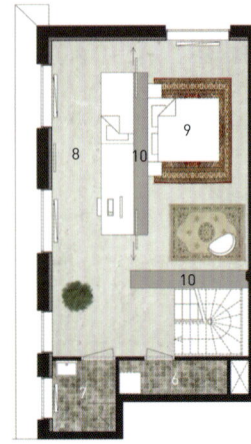

First floor plan

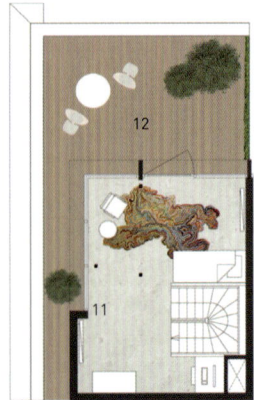

Roof extension

Ground floor plan

Ground floor plan

First floor plan

Roof extension plan

Example ground based housing plan

1. Terrace	8. Bedroom / study
2. Dining room	
3. Kitchen	9. Bedroom
4. Living room	10. Cupboard
5. Toilet	11. Bedroom / hobby room
6. Storage	
7. Bathroom	12. Roof terrace

Examples studio plans

1. Terrace	6. Storage
2. Dining room	7. Bathroom
3. Kitchen	8. Cupboard
4. Living room	9. Curtain
5. Bedroom	

Examples studio plans

1. Terrace	8. Movable wall / cupboard
2. Dining room	
3. Kitchen	9. Hall
4. Living room	10. Toilet
5. Bedroom	11. Storage
6. Study	12. Bathroom
7. Bedroom	

Example apartment plan

1. Toilet	7. Living room
2. Storage	8. Hobby room
3. Bathroom	9. Cupboard
4. Study	10. Bedroom
5. Kitchen	11. Roof terrace
6. Dining room	

0 1 2   6m

WHAT! ARKITEKTUR

www.whats.se

Our projects tell a story, in context and in form. We aim to be innovative and receptive in our designs and let the architecture interact with, and relate to location, history and circumstance. We want our buildings to have their own site-specific narrative, and to be honest and self-explanatory through their presence. Our designs may be uncommon and unexpected, though always with a contextual connection. This applies to our buildings, as well as to the spaces created within and around the structures.

We believe that the creation of architecture with a high level of accomplishment demands a synergetic and fun work environment. Our creative process is non-hierarchal, and we use group dynamics as an engine to enhance solutions, execution and results.

Unsere Projekte erzählen eine Geschichte, im Kontext und in der Form. Unser Ziel ist es, innovativ und reaktionsschnell zu sein und Architektur interagieren zu lassen und sich auf Ort, Geschichte und Umstände zu beziehen. Wir wollen, dass unsere Gebäude ihre eigene ortsspezifische Erzählung haben und durch ihre Präsenz ehrlich und selbsterklärend sind. Unsere Entwürfe sind vielleicht ungewöhnlich und unerwartet, aber immer mit einem kontextuellen Zusammenhang. Dies gilt sowohl für unsere Gebäude als auch für die in und um die Gebäude herum geschaffenen Räume.

Wir glauben, dass die Schaffung einer Architektur mit hohem Leistungsniveau ein synergistisches und angenehmes Arbeitsumfeld erfordert. Unser kreativer Prozess ist nicht hierarchisch und wir verwenden Gruppendynamik als Motor, um Lösungen, Ausführung und Ergebnisse zu verbessern.

Nos projets racontent une histoire, en contexte et en forme. Notre objectif est d'être innovant et réactif et de laisser l'architecture interagir et se relier au lieu, à l'histoire et aux circonstances. Nous voulons que nos bâtiments aient leur propre narration propre à chaque lieu et qu'ils soient honnêtes et explicites par leur présence. Nos conceptions peuvent être inhabituelles et inattendues, mais toujours avec une connexion contextuelle. Ceci s'applique aussi bien à nos bâtiments qu'aux espaces créés à l'intérieur et autour des structures.

Nous croyons que la création d'une architecture avec un haut niveau d'accomplissement exige un environnement de travail synergique et amusant. Notre processus créatif n'est pas hiérarchique et nous utilisons la dynamique de groupe comme moteur pour améliorer les solutions, l'exécution et les résultats.

Nuestros proyectos cuentan una historia, en contexto y en forma. Nuestro objetivo es ser innovadores y receptivos y dejar que la arquitectura interactúe y se relacione con la ubicación, la historia y las circunstancias. Queremos que nuestros edificios tengan su propia narrativa específica del lugar, y que sean honestos y auto explicativos a través de su presencia. Nuestros diseños pueden ser poco comunes e inesperados, aunque siempre en conexión con el contexto. Esto se aplica a nuestros edificios, así como a los espacios creados dentro y alrededor de las estructuras.

Creemos que la creación de una arquitectura con un alto nivel de realización exige un ambiente de trabajo sinérgico y divertido. Nuestro proceso creativo no es jerárquico y utilizamos la dinámica de grupo como motor para mejorar las soluciones, la ejecución y los resultados.

PUTSEGÅRDEN

Address: Inägogatan 14, Gothenburg, Sweden

New development of 44 housing units and the rebuilding of an old farm including a house for living and a barn from the 18th century

Architect: what! arkitektur

Client detail development plan: Alternus AB

Client building permit: Etikhus AB

Date completed: December 2016

Total area of building: 4,300 m²

Photo credits: © Ulf Celander

BOHEM

Address: Berzeliigatan 6, Gothenburg, Sweden

New development of 209 co-living housing units

Status: Conceptual project

Architect: what! arkitektur

Client: Familjebostäder AB

Total area of building above ground: 16.635 m²

Visualisations: © Adore Adore

Based on the conjunction of two different periods, the project combines a new structure with two existing buildings from the 18th century. The new building connects to the gable of a single-storey granary and progressively grows into a 10-storey tower. Its striking shape, reinforced by the consistency of its colour and material, is the heart of the project. By playing with the topography and the surrounding buildings, the shape creates articulated outdoor spaces. The cladding of roof and façades are made of aluminium sheets. Both the cladding technique and the colour scheme "Falu Röd", a traditional Swedish colour originating from the Falun copper mines, connect with ancient Swedish traditions and craftsmanship.

Basierend auf der Verbindung von zwei verschiedenen Perioden kombiniert das Projekt einen neuen Baukörper mit zwei bestehenden Gebäuden aus dem 18. Jahrhundert. Das neue Gebäude schließt an das Fronton einer eingeschossigen Scheune an und wird nach und nach zu einem 10-geschossigen Turm. Seine markante Form, verstärkt durch die Konsistenz von Farbe und Material, ist das Herzstück des Projekts. Im Spiel mit der Topographie und den umliegenden Gebäuden erreicht die Form gegliederte Außenräume. Die Abdeckungen von Dächern und Fassaden sind aus Aluminiumblech gefertigt. Sowohl die Bekleidungstechnik als auch die Farbgebung „Falu Röd", eine traditionelle schwedische Farbe aus den Falun-Kupferminen, sind mit den alten schwedischen Traditionen und Handwerken verbunden.

PUTSEGÅRDEN
GOTHENBURG, SWEDEN

Basé sur la conjonction de deux périodes différentes, le projet combine une nouvelle structure avec deux bâtiments existants du 18ème siècle. Le nouveau bâtiment est relié à l'avant d'une grange d'un étage et devient progressivement une tour de 10 étages. Sa forme frappante, renforcée par la consistance de sa couleur et de sa matière, est au cœur du projet. Jouant avec la topographie et les bâtiments environnants, la forme permet d'obtenir des espaces extérieurs articulés. Les revêtements des toitures et des façades sont en tôle d'aluminium. La technique de revêtement et la palette de couleurs « Falu Röd », une couleur suédoise traditionnelle des mines de cuivre de Falun, sont toutes deux liées aux traditions et à l'artisanat suédois anciens.

Basado en la conjunción de dos períodos diferentes, el proyecto combina una nueva estructura con dos edificios existentes del siglo XVIII. El nuevo edificio se conecta al frontón de un granero de una sola planta y se convierte progresivamente en una torre de 10 plantas. Su forma llamativa, reforzada por la consistencia de su color y material, es el corazón del proyecto. Jugando con la topografía y los edificios circundantes, la forma consigue espacios exteriores articulados. Los revestimientos de cubiertas y fachadas son de chapa de aluminio. Tanto la técnica de revestimiento como el esquema de colores «Falu Röd», un color tradicional sueco procedente de las minas de cobre de Falun, están relacionados con las antiguas tradiciones y artesanías suecas.

Section

4m   0   4   8   12   16   20m

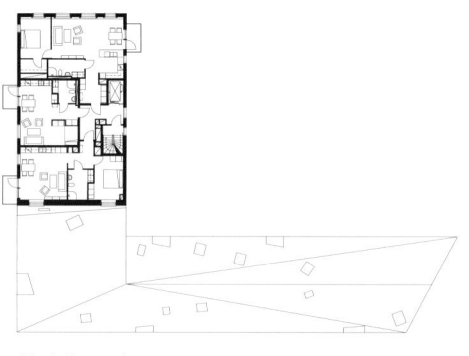

Sixth floor plan

Seventh floor
plan

Seventh floor
plan

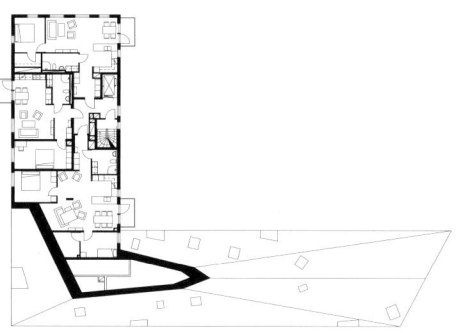

Fourth floor plan

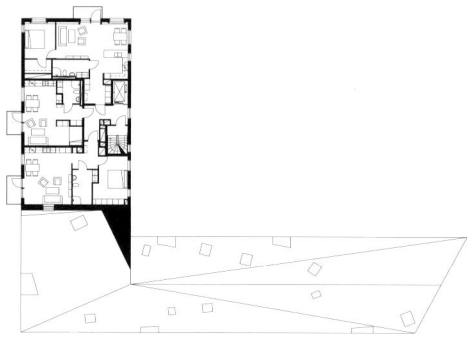

Fifth floor plan

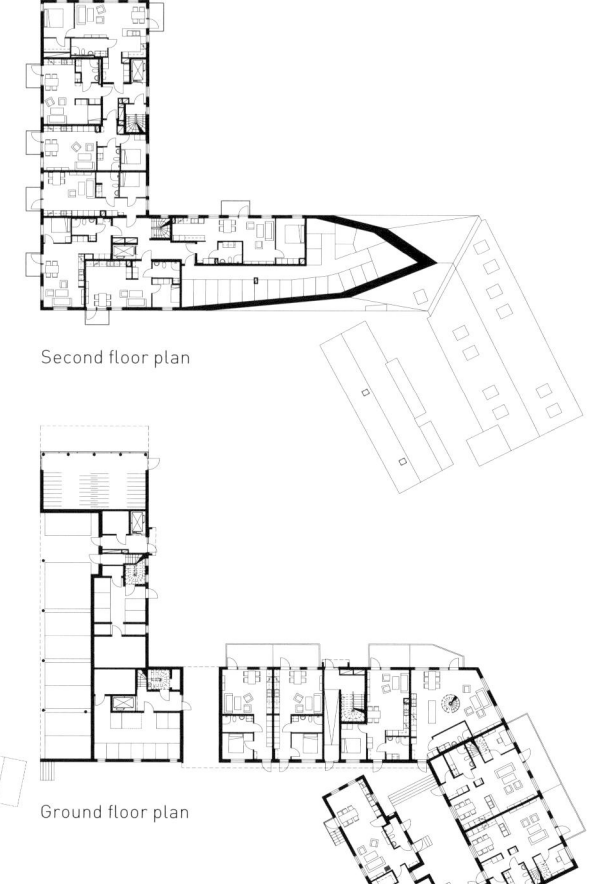

Second floor plan

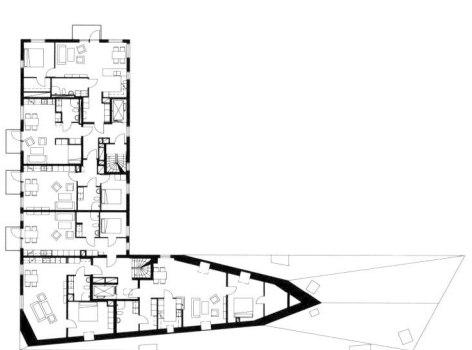

Third floor plan

Ground floor plan

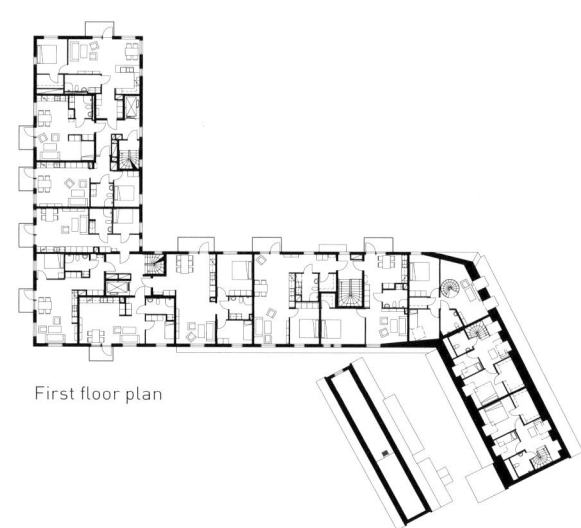

First floor plan

Bohem is a conceptual project developed together with the public housing company Familje-bostäder. It encourages social integration and development of affordable housing in an affluent urban context. Located at the confluence of several important pedestrian axes, the building has the potential to become a natural meeting point. Its curved façade emphasizes the movement and flow of people passing by. The ground floor contains flexible public spaces, adaptable to the varying needs of the neighbourhood. Its design allows pedestrians to cross the central courtyard, which encourages interaction between residents and visitors, and opens the building to the surroundings. The oval shape of the plan generates public spaces in the corners of the site and evokes the history of the place, which for many years was home to a circus.

Bohem ist ein konzeptionelles Projekt, das gemeinsam mit der öffentlichen Wohnungsbau-gesellschaft Familjebostäder entwickelt wurde. Sie fördert die soziale Integration und die Entwicklung erschwinglicher Wohnungen in einem prosperierenden städtischen Umfeld. Am Zusammenfluss mehrerer Fußgängerachsen gelegen, wird das Gebäude zu einem natürlichen Treffpunkt. Seine geschwungene Fassade betont die Bewegung und den Fluss der Fußgänger. Im Erdgeschoss befinden sich flexible öffentliche Räume, die sich an die unterschiedlichen Bedürfnisse des Quartiers anpassen lassen. Sein Design ermöglicht es Spaziergängern, den zentralen Innenhof zu überqueren, der die Interaktion zwischen Bewohnern und Besuchern fördert und das Gebäude für die Umgebung öffnet. Die ovale Form des Bodens erzeugt öffent-liche Räume in den Ecken des Geländes und erinnert an die Geschichte des Ortes, an dem viele Jahre lang ein Zirkus lebte.

BOHEM
GOTHENBURG, SWEDEN

Bohem est un projet conceptuel développé en collaboration avec la société de logement public Familjebostäder. Il favorise l'intégration sociale et le développement de logements abor-dables dans un contexte urbain prospère. Situé au confluent de plusieurs axes piétonniers, le bâtiment devient un point de rencontre naturel. Sa façade courbe souligne le mouvement et le flux des piétons. Le rez-de-chaussée contient des espaces publics flexibles, adaptables aux différents besoins du quartier. Sa conception permet aux promeneurs de traverser la cour centrale, ce qui favorise l'interaction entre les résidents et les visiteurs, et ouvre le bâtiment sur l'environnement. La forme ovale du sol génère des espaces publics dans les coins de l'enceinte et évoque l'histoire du lieu, qui a longtemps abrité un cirque.

Bohem es un proyecto conceptual desarrollado junto con la empresa pública de vivienda Fa-miljebostäder. Fomenta la integración social y el desarrollo de viviendas asequibles en un contexto urbano próspero. Situado en la confluencia de varios ejes peatonales, el edificio se convierte en un punto de encuentro natural. Su fachada curva enfatiza el movimiento y el flujo de los peatones. La planta baja contiene espacios públicos flexibles, adaptables a las diferen-tes necesidades del barrio. Su diseño permite a los paseantes atravesar el patio central, lo que favorece la interacción entre residentes y visitantes, y abre el edificio al entorno. La forma ovalada de la planta genera espacios públicos en los rincones del recinto y evoca la historia del lugar, que durante muchos años fue sede de un circo.

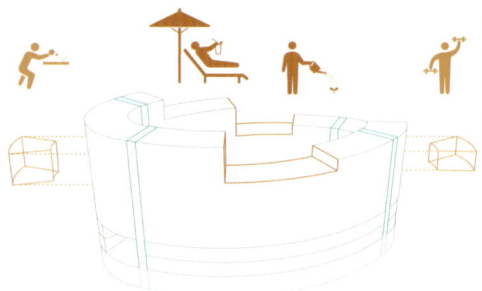

Terrasse

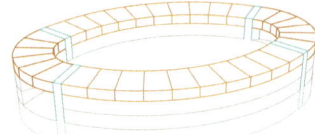

Apartments

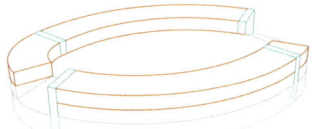

Common areas

Premises

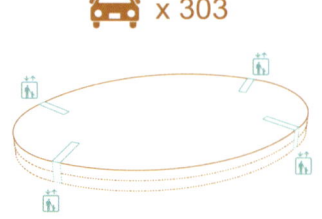

Garage

Concept diagram

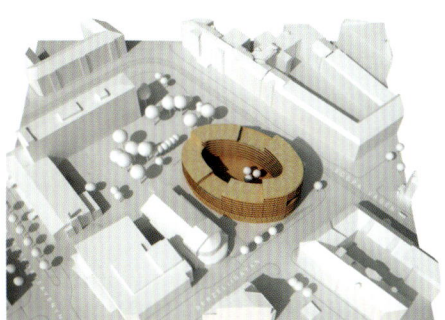

Site model

Section

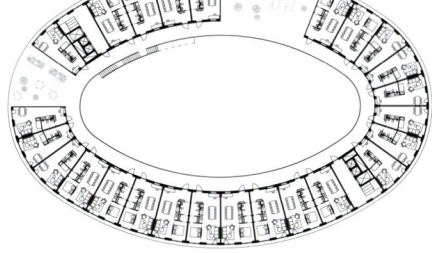

Sixth floor plan

Elevation Berzeliigatan Street

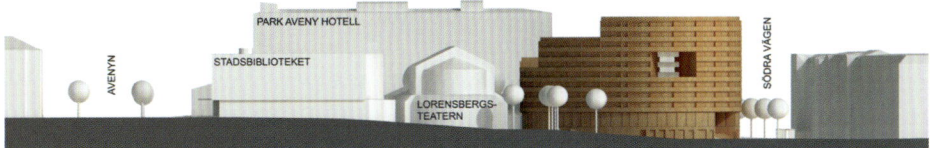

Elevation Södra Vägen Street

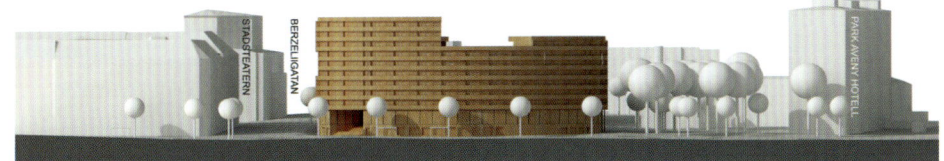

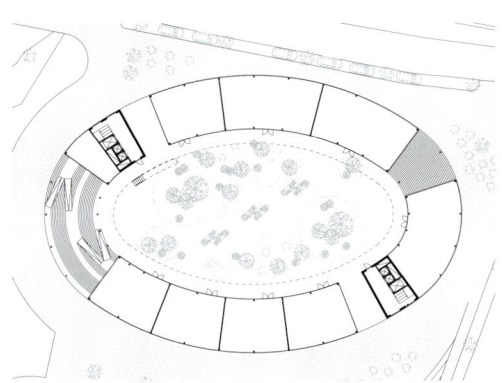

First floor plan

YDS ARCHITECTS

http://www.ydsaa.net/

YDS Architects is a group of architects who strive for innovation in design with the vision 'Architects should be visionaries of Art and Science with Philosophy'. The practice aims to create beautiful spaces with nature where people feel transitions of light and shadow, and has been awarded numerous prizes including LEAF Awards, German Design Awards and SIA-GETZ Architecture Prize. The aim is to realize compatibility of beauty and science concerning ecosystem and unify architectures and nature by breaking down boundaries between them.
Driven by its original visions, they design 'Wavering Architectures' which stimulate human minds and invoke communications between human and nature. By employing simple geometry including circles, squares, and uniform grids as a methodology, and based upon five principles (Wavering Nature, Organic Voids, Urban Agora, Flowing Promenade, Forests of Symbiosis), the practice pursues to integrate architectures and nature, East and West, past and present.

YDS Architects ist eine Gruppe von Architekten, die nach Innovationen im Design mit der Vision „Architekten sollten Visionäre von Kunst und Wissenschaft mit Philosophie sein" streben. Das Büro hat sich zum Ziel gesetzt, schöne Räume mit der Natur zu schaffen, in denen Menschen den Übergang von Licht und Schatten spüren, und wurde mit zahlreichen Preisen ausgezeichnet, darunter LEAF Awards, German Design Awards und SIA-GETZ Architecture Prize. Ziel ist es, die Kompatibilität von Schönheit und Wissenschaft im Hinblick auf das Ökosystem zu realisieren und Architektur und Natur zu vereinen, indem die Grenzen zwischen ihnen aufgehoben werden.
Angetrieben von ihren ursprünglichen Visionen entwerfen sie „Wavering Architectures", die den menschlichen Geist stimulieren und die Kommunikation zwischen Mensch und Natur herstellen. Durch die Verwendung einfacher Geometrie, einschließlich Kreise, Quadrate und einheitlicher Gitter, als Methodik und basierend auf fünf Prinzipien (Schwankende Natur, organische Hohlräume, urbane Agora, fließende Promenade, Symbiosewälder), verfolgt die Praxis die Integration von Architekturen und Natur, Ost und West, Vergangenheit und Gegenwart.

YDS Architects est un groupe d'architectes qui s'efforcent d'innover en matière de design avec la vision « Les architectes doivent être des visionnaires de l'art et de la science avec philosophie ». Le cabinet a pour objectif de créer de beaux espaces avec la nature où les gens ressentent des transitions de lumière et d'ombre, et a reçu de nombreux prix dont les prix LEAF, German Design Awards et SIA-GETZ Architecture Prize. L'objectif est de réaliser la compatibilité de la beauté et de la science concernant l'écosystème et d'unifier les architectures et la nature en abolissant les frontières entre elles.
Guidés par ses visions originales, ils conçoivent des « Architectures vacillantes » qui stimulent l'esprit humain et invitent à la communication entre l'homme et la nature. En utilisant une géométrie simple incluant des cercles, des carrés et des grilles uniformes comme méthodologie, et basée sur cinq principes (Nature vacillante, Vides organiques, Agora urbaine, Promenade coulant, Forêts de symbiose), la pratique poursuit l'intégration des architectures et de la nature, Est et Ouest, passé et présent.

YDS Architects es un grupo de arquitectos que se esfuerza por innovar en el diseño con la visión de que «los arquitectos deben ser visionarios del arte y la ciencia». El estudio tiene como objetivo crear espacios hermosos con la naturaleza donde la gente sienta las transiciones de luz y sombras. El estudio ha sido galardonado con numerosos premios, entre los que se incluyen los LEAF Awards, los German Design Awards y el SIA-GETZ Architecture Prize. El objetivo es lograr la compatibilidad de la belleza y la ciencia en relación con el ecosistema y unificar las arquitecturas y la naturaleza rompiendo las fronteras entre ellas. Impulsados por sus visiones originales, diseñan «Arquitecturas vacilantes» que estimulan la mente humana e invocan las comunicaciones entre el hombre y la naturaleza. Empleando una geometría simple que incluye círculos, cuadrados y cuadrículas uniformes como metodología, y basada en cinco principios (Naturaleza vacilante, Vacíos orgánicos, Ágora urbana, Paseo fluído, Bosques de simbiosis), el estudio persigue la integración de arquitecturas y naturaleza, Oriente y Occidente, pasado y presente.

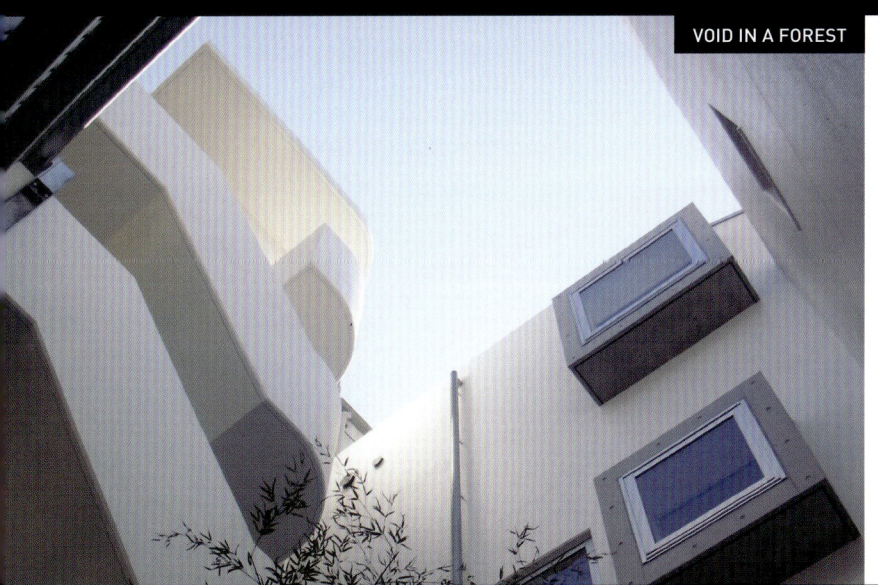

VOID IN A FOREST

Location: Tokyo, Japan

Building area:
1,420 m² / 15,285 sq ft

Architecture team:
Yoshitaka Uchino, Mana Muraki /
YDS Architects

Collaborators:
Toshi Kozo Structural Design

Photo credits: © YDS Architects

FORESTS OF GRIDS

Location: Tokyo, Japan

Building area:
1,530 m² / 16,469 sq ft

Architecture team:
Yoshitaka Uchino, Mana Muraki /
YDS Architects

Collaborators:
Toshi Kozo Structural Design

Photo credits: © YDS Architects

Located in the site next to a very large park, the concept is to take in abundant nature around the site and to create spaces people live feeling light and wind.

A court named 'Urban Garden' is put into the building to insert nature to daily life. The court functions as a square and is softly articulated by louvers from the forest around the site, it would mingle with nature. Stairs over the court functions as vibrant promenades which invoke fondness for nature. The stair and each corridor face the court and provide light and wind when one would come and go to their units, making it pleasant experiences. Through bay windows, one would see trees in the court as well as in the park and feel transitional changes by time and seasons.

At night, the court becomes shining garden with bamboo, providing extraordinary experiences for people with dark sky and wavering forests.

Das Konzept, das sich auf dem Gelände neben einem sehr großen Park befindet, besteht darin, die reiche Natur rund um das Gelände zu genießen und Räume zu schaffen, in denen die Menschen leben und Licht und Wind spüren.

Ein Hof namens „Urban Garden" wird in das Gebäude eingebracht, um die Natur in das tägliche Leben zu integrieren. Der Platz fungiert als Platz und ist durch Lamellen aus dem Wald um das Gelände herum leise gelenkig gelagert, er würde sich mit der Natur vermischen. Die Treppe über dem Hof fungiert als lebhafte Passagen, die die Liebe zur Natur hervorrufen. Die Treppe und jeder Gang zeigen zum Hof und sorgen für Licht und Wind, wenn man zu seinen Einheiten kommt und geht, was es zu angenehmen Erlebnissen macht. Durch Erker würde man Bäume sowohl auf dem Hof als auch im Park sehen und Übergangsveränderungen durch Zeit und Jahreszeiten spüren. Nachts wird der Hof zu einem leuchtenden Garten aus Bambus und bietet Menschen mit dunklem Himmel und schwankendem Wald außergewöhnliche Erlebnisse.

VOID IN A FOREST
TOKYO, JAPAN

Situé sur le site à côté d'un très grand parc, le concept est de profiter de la nature en abondance autour du site et de créer des espaces où les gens vivent dans la légèreté et le vent.

Une cour appelée « Jardin urbain » est aménagée dans le bâtiment pour insérer la nature dans la vie quotidienne. La cour fonctionne comme un carré et est doucement articulée par des persiennes de la forêt autour du site, elle se mêlerait à la nature. Les escaliers au-dessus de la cour fonctionnent comme des passages vibrants qui évoquent l'amour de la nature. L'escalier et chaque couloir font face à la cour et procurent de la lumière et du vent lorsque l'on va et vient à leurs unités, ce qui rend l'expérience agréable. À travers les baies vitrées, on pouvait voir des arbres dans la cour ainsi que dans le parc et ressentir des changements de transition avec le temps et les saisons.

La nuit, la cour devient un jardin brillant de bambous, offrant des expériences extraordinaires aux personnes au ciel sombre et à la forêt vacillante.

Situado en un terreno junto a un parque enorme, el concepto trata de acoger la abundante naturaleza que rodea el sitio y crear espacios donde la gente viva sintiendo la luz solar y el aire.

Un patio llamado «Jardín Urbano» se instala en el edificio para insertar la naturaleza en la vida cotidiana. Este patio funciona como una plaza y está suavemente articulado por medio de elementos del terreno, mezclándose con la naturaleza. Las escaleras del patio funcionan como pasajes vibrantes que invocan el cariño por la naturaleza. La escalera principal y cada uno de los pasillos proporcionan luz y aire, lo que convierte las experiencias en sensaciones agradables. A través de los ventanales se pueden ver los árboles tanto del porche como del parque y sentir los cambios del tiempo y las estaciones.

Por la noche, el espacio se convierte en un brillante jardín de bambú, proporcionando experiencias extraordinarias.

Concept diagrams

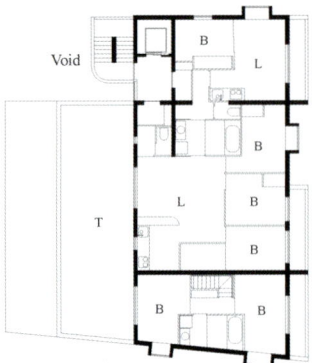

Fifth floor plan

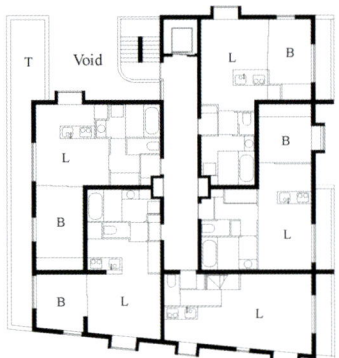

Fourth floor plan

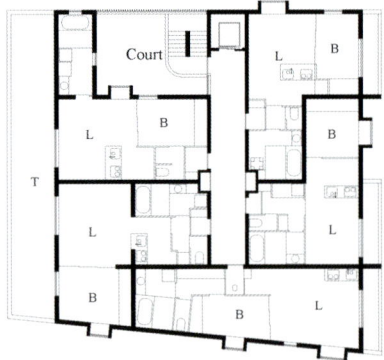

Third floor plan

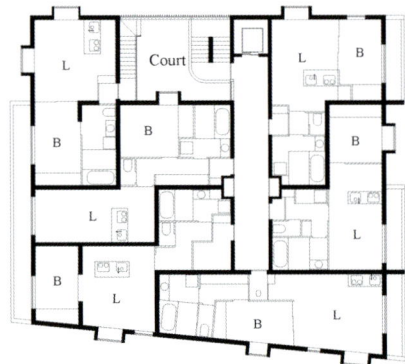

Second floor plan

First floor plan

0 1 2   5M

The vision of creating a forest in cities and buildings demonstrates 'symbiosis with nature'. This building consists of uniform grids of square columns and beams which bring about an order to the daily life and two walls. The forest is placed between the two walls, and stairs are put around the forest to connect it, the square, and every floor, creating three dimensional public spaces. Through the hole dug in the curved wall, the forest is open to the city and is embraced by the people of the city as well as residents. The column inserted into the forest would integrate architecture and nature, signifying the unity of human and nature. Walls freed from the grids fold it like clouds and provide abundant light and wind to the spaces.

Although the forest is small, it is like a minimum universe where everyone would find something important which are lost in our daily life.

Die Vision der Walderschaffung in Städten und Gebäuden zeigt die «Symbiose mit der Natur». Dieses Gebäude besteht aus einheitlichen Gittern aus quadratischen Säulen und Balken, die eine Ordnung im täglichen Leben schaffen, und zwei Wänden. Der Wald befindet sich zwischen den beiden Wänden, und die Treppe wird um den Wald herum gelegt, um ihn, den Platz und jedes Stockwerk zu verbinden, die dreidimensionale öffentliche Räume schaffen.

Durch das Loch in der geschwungenen Wand ist der Wald offen für die Stadt und wird von den Menschen der Stadt sowie den Bewohnern umarmt. Die in den Wald eingesetzte Säule würde Architektur und Natur integrieren und die Einheit von Mensch und Natur symbolisieren. Von den Gittern befreite Wände falten sie wie Wolken und sorgen für reichlich Licht und Wind in den Räumen. Obwohl der Wald klein ist, ist er wie ein Minimaluniversum, in dem jeder etwas Wichtiges finden würde, das in unserem täglichen Leben verloren geht.

FORESTS OF GRIDS
TOKYO, JAPAN

La vision de la création d'une forêt dans les villes et les bâtiments démontre une'symbiose avec la nature'. Ce bâtiment se compose de grilles uniformes de colonnes carrées et de poutres qui donnent un ordre à la vie quotidienne et à deux murs. La forêt est placée entre les deux murs, et des escaliers sont placés autour de la forêt pour la relier, la place et chaque étage qui créent des espaces publics en trois dimensions.

Par le trou creusé dans le mur courbe, la forêt est ouverte sur la ville et est embrassée par les habitants de la ville ainsi que par les habitants. La colonne insérée dans la forêt intégrerait l'architecture et la nature, signifiant l'unité de l'homme et de la nature. Les murs libérés des grilles le plient comme des nuages et apportent aux espaces lumière et vent en abondance.

Bien que la forêt soit petite, c'est comme un univers minimal où chacun trouverait quelque chose d'important qui se perd dans notre vie quotidienne.

La visión de crear bosques en ciudades y edificios demuestra simbiosis con la naturaleza. Este edificio consta de líneas uniformes de columnas cuadradas, vigas y dos muros que dan orden a la vida cotidiana. El bosque está situado entre dos paredes. Se colocan escaleras alrededor de él para conectarlo con la plaza, creando espacios públicos tridimensionales.

A través del agujero excavado en la pared curva, el bosque se abre a la ciudad y es abrazado tanto por la gente de la ciudad como por los habitantes de los apartamentos. La columna insertada en el bosque integraría la arquitectura y la naturaleza, significando la unidad de lo humano y lo natural. Los muros proporcionan abundante luz y aire al resto de espacios.

Aunque el bosque es de dimensiones pequeñas, aparece como un universo mínimo donde encontrar algo importante que hemos perdido en nuestra vida diaria.

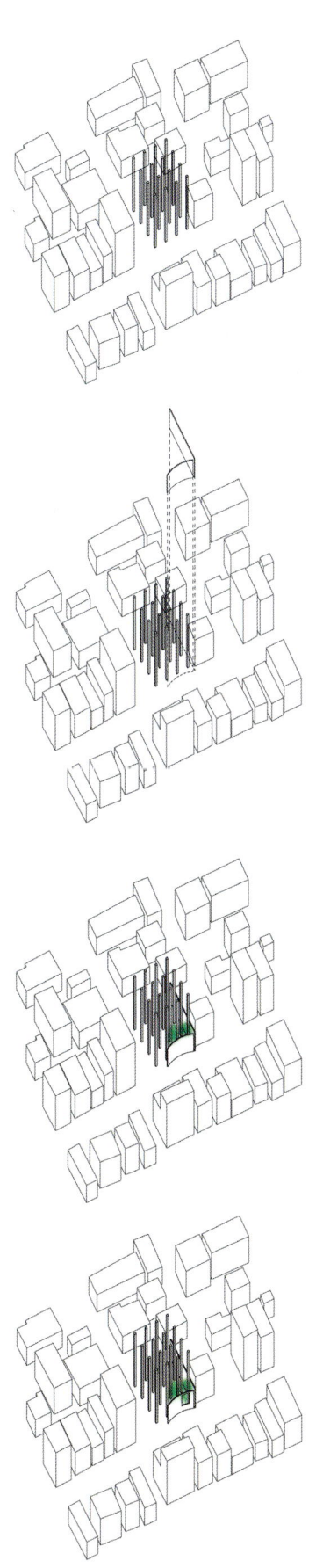

Concept diagram

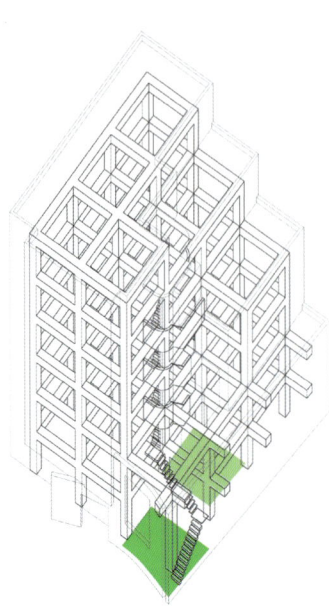

Axonometric view

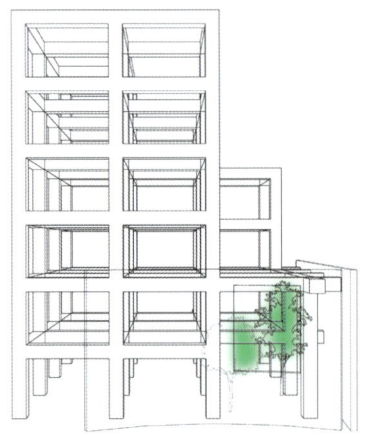

Axonometric view

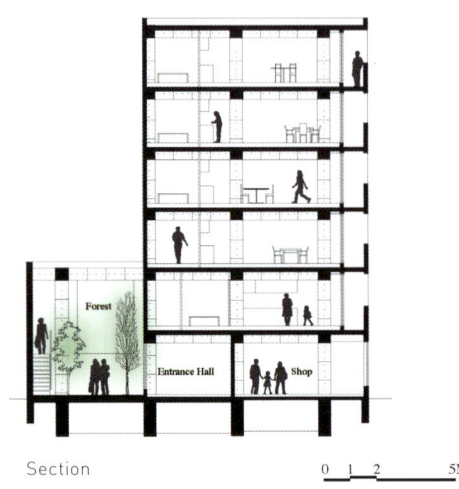

Section   0 1 2   5M

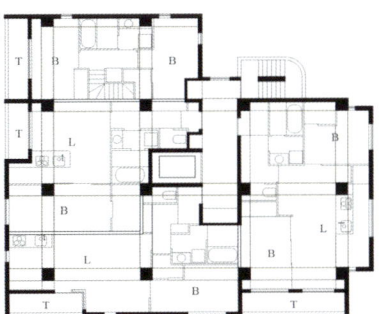

Fourth floor plan

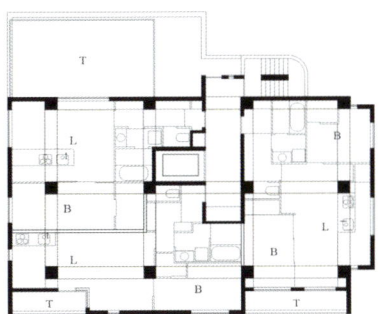

Fifth floor plan

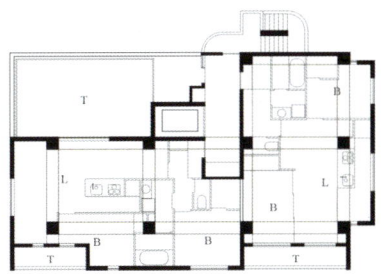

Sixth floor plan

Third floor plan

Second floor plan

First floor plan

YUKIO ASARI

www.lovearchitecture.co.jp

1969 Born in Tokyo
1994 Graduated from Musashino Art University Architecture Department
1996 Completed Master of Architecture Degree at Shibaura Institute of Technology
1996-2001 Worked for Sowa Giken Co.,Ltd.
2001 Established Love Architecture Inc.

Design Philosophy

We believe the best architecture exists in concert with the landscape, nature, culture, and climate of the place where it is built. No matter what genre we are working in, we emphasize livability and particularity.
For us that means not only working out comfortable floor plans or taking an artistic approach to the elements such as light and shadow, materials, and style that sway the moods of those who inhabit a space. Creating livable and unique spaces also requires that we approach design from a logical perspective.

1969 Geboren in Tokio
1994 Abschluss an der Musashino Art University Architecture Department der Musashino Art University.
1996 Abschluss des Masterstudiengangs Architektur am Shibaura Institute of Technology
1996-2001 Arbeitete für Sowa Giken Co.,Ltd.
2001 Gründung der Love Architecture Inc.

Design-Philosophie

Wir glauben, dass die beste Architektur in Verbindung mit der Landschaft, der Natur, der Kultur und dem Klima des Ortes, an dem sie gebaut wird, existiert. Unabhängig davon, in welchem Genre wir arbeiten, legen wir Wert auf Lebensfähigkeit und Besonderheit. Für uns bedeutet das nicht nur, komfortable Grundrisse zu erarbeiten oder sich künstlerisch mit den Elementen wie Licht und Schatten, Materialien und Stil auseinanderzusetzen, die die Stimmung der Bewohner eines Raumes beeinflussen. Die Schaffung von lebenswerten und einzigartigen Räumen erfordert auch, dass wir das Design aus einer logischen Perspektive betrachten.

1969 Né à Tokyo
1994 Diplômé du Département d'Architecture de l'Université d'Art de Musashino
1996 Maîtrise en architecture de l'Institut de technologie de Shibaura.
1996-2001 A travaillé pour Sowa Giken Co. ltée.
2001 Création de Love Architecture Inc.

Philosophie de conception

Nous croyons que la meilleure architecture existe de concert avec le paysage, la nature, la culture et le climat de l'endroit où elle est construite. Quel que soit le genre dans lequel nous travaillons, nous mettons l'accent sur la qualité de vie et la particularité.
Pour nous, cela ne signifie pas seulement élaborer des plans d'étage confortables ou adopter une approche artistique des éléments tels que la lumière et l'ombre, les matériaux et le style qui influencent l'humeur de ceux qui habitent un espace. La création d'espaces habitables et uniques exige également que nous abordions le design dans une perspective logique.

1969 Nacido en Tokio
1994 Graduado por el Departamento de Arquitectura de la Universidad de Arte Musashino
1996 Master en Arquitectura en el Instituto de Tecnología de Shibaura.
1996-2001 Trabajó para Sowa Giken Co.
2001 Se funda Love Architecture Inc.

Filosofía del diseño

Creemos que la mejor arquitectura existe en concierto con el paisaje, la naturaleza, la cultura y el clima del lugar donde se construye. No importa en qué género estemos trabajando, hacemos hincapié en la habitabilidad y la particularidad.
Para nosotros esto significa no sólo elaborar cómodos planos o adoptar un enfoque artístico de los elementos como la luz y la sombra, los materiales y el estilo que influencian los estados de ánimo de quienes habitan un espacio. La creación de espacios habitables y únicos también requiere que enfoquemos el diseño desde una perspectiva lógica.

Architecture: Yukio Asari

Photo credits: © Katsuhisa Kida

Location: Tokyo, Japan

Date of Completion: December 2013

Principal Use: Apartment house / Store

Structure: RC

Site Area: 182.64m²

Total Floor Area: 514.56m² (135.74m² / B1F, 127.73m² / 1F, 135.68m² / 2F, 115.41m² / 3F)

Client: Yoshitou Miyajima, SunTake Hong

Architect:
LOVE ARCHITECTURE Inc.
Yukio Asari, Shigeyuki Suga

Structural Engineer:
NAWAKENJIMU
Kenji Nawa, Nobuyuki Morinaga

Facility: Naoki Matsumoto

Construction:
SHIRAISHIKENSETSU
Kazuhiro Kurita, Takeshi Kikuchi

Bricks:
KUNISHIROTAIKAKOUGYOUSHO
Motoyuki Kamimura
TOKYO BRICKS INC.
Tatsuhiro Ono

SHUGOIN

The project is based on the adjustment of the relationship between the public and the private. The building exhausts the maximum roof allowed, but destines the rest of the plot to a public passage that connects the south and north sides of the city. The programme is structured into four blocks of flats connected by only two staircases which, like the small interior balconies, open towards the passage, encouraging interaction between residents, pedestrians and visitors from the ground-floor premises. The compact brick enclosures of the north and south façades isolate the dwellings from the chaotic urban landscape and full the entry of sunlight. On these façades, huge holes indicate the position of the public passage. On the contrary, the interior façades open up to the passage through openings that reveal the interior of the dwellings.

Das Projekt basiert auf der Anpassung der Beziehung zwischen dem Öffentlichen und dem Privaten. Das Gebäude erschöpft das maximal zulässige Dach, widmet den Rest des Grundstücks jedoch einer öffentlichen Passage, die die Süd- und Nordseite der Stadt verbindet. Das Programm gliedert sich in vier Mehrfamilienhäuser, die durch nur zwei Treppenhäuser miteinander verbunden sind, die sich wie die kleinen Innenbalkone räumlich zur Passage hin öffnen und die Interaktion zwischen Bewohnern, Passanten und Besuchern des Erdgeschosses fördern. Die kompakten Ziegelgehege der Nord- und Südfassade isolieren die Wohnungen von der chaotischen Stadtlandschaft und gewähren den Eintritt von Sonnenlicht. An diesen Fassaden zeigen nur riesige Löcher die Position der öffentlichen Passage an. Im Gegenteil, die Innenfassaden werden durch Öffnungen, die das Innere der Wohnungen freigeben, zum Durchgang geöffnet.

SHUGOIN
TOKYO, JAPAN

Le projet est basé sur l'ajustement de la relation entre le public et le privé. Le bâtiment épuise le toit maximum autorisé, mais consacre le reste du terrain à un passage public qui relie les côtés sud et nord de la ville. Le programme est structuré en quatre blocs d'appartements reliés par seulement deux escaliers qui, comme les petits balcons intérieurs, s'ouvrent dans l'espace vers le passage, favorisant l'interaction entre les résidents, les passants et les visiteurs des locaux au rez-de-chaussée. Les murs de briques compacts des façades nord et sud isolent les habitations du paysage urbain chaotique et tamisent l'entrée de la lumière du soleil. Sur ces façades, seuls d'énormes trous indiquent la position du passage public. Au contraire, les façades intérieures sont ouvertes au passage par des ouvertures qui révèlent l'intérieur des habitations.

El proyecto se basa en el ajuste de la relación entre lo público y lo privado. El edificio agota el techo máximo permitido, pero destina el resto de la parcela a un pasaje público que conecta los lados sur y norte de la ciudad. El programa se estructura en cuatro bloques de viviendas conectados con sólo dos escaleras que, al igual que los pequeños balcones interiores, se abren espacialmente hacia el pasaje, fomentando la interacción entre residentes, traunseuntes y visitantes de los locales de planta baja. Los compactos cerramientos de ladrillo de las fachadas norte y sur aislan las viviendas del caótico paisaje urbano y tamizan la entrada de la luz solar. En estas fachadas, sólo unos enormes agujeros indican la posición del pasaje público. Por el contario, las fachadas interiores se abren al pasaje mediante aberturas que revelan el interior de las viviendas.

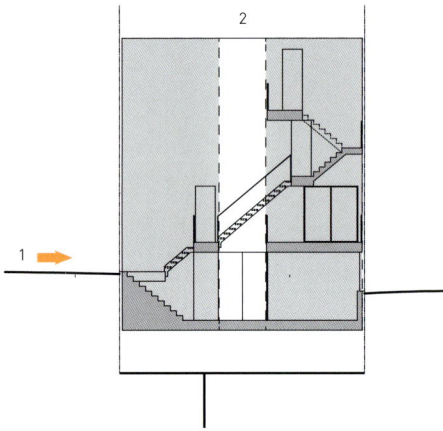

Concept diagram
B-B' section

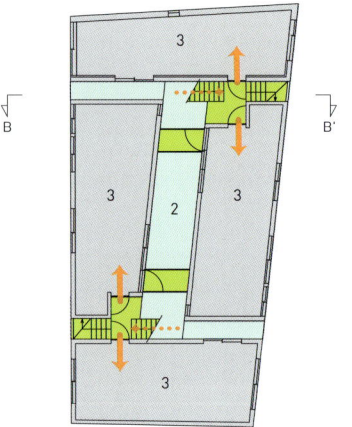

Concept diagram
Floor plan

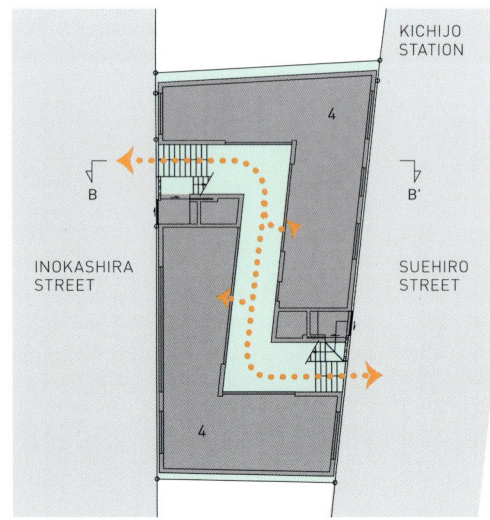

Concept diagram
Shop floor plan

1. Entrance
2. Void
3. Room
4. Shop

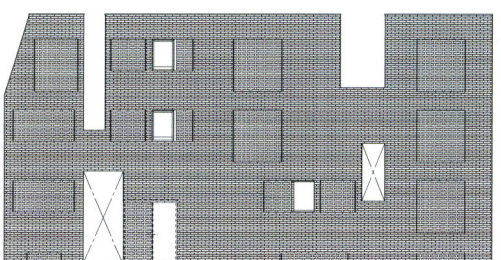

South elevation

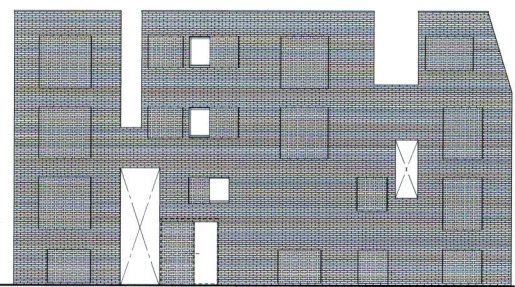

North elevation

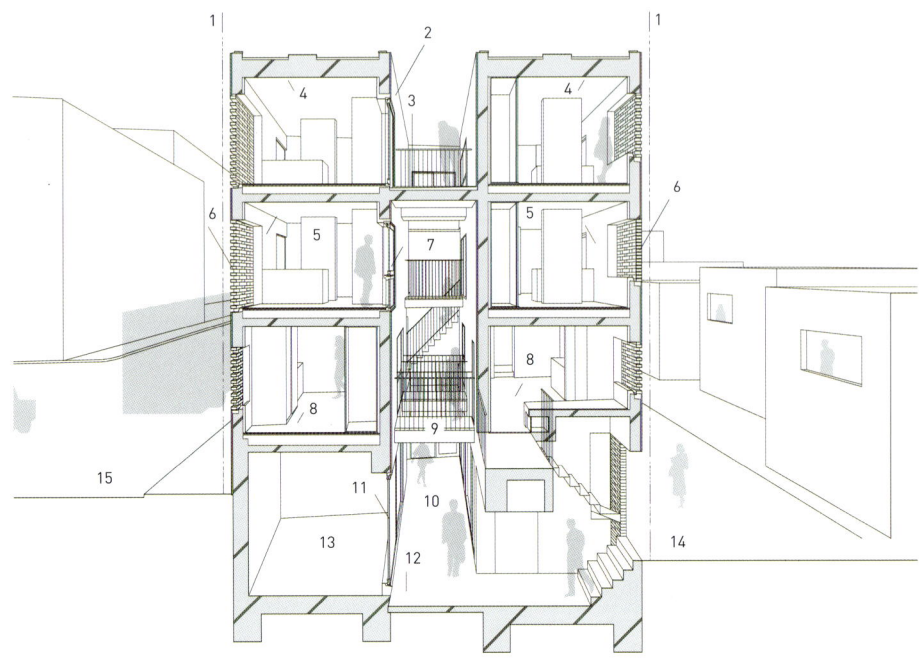

Section

1. Boundary line of street
2. Outer wall: stick brick tile
3. Floor of balcony: natural stone
4. Ceiling: plaster finish
5. Wall: plaster finish
6. Lay brick at intervals + aluminum sash
7. Wodden sash
8. Floor: oak flooring oil finish
9. Balcony
10. Passage
11. Aluminum sash
12. Floor: natural stone
13. Shop 2
14. Level of side walk of Suehiro st.
15. Level of side walk of Inokashira st.

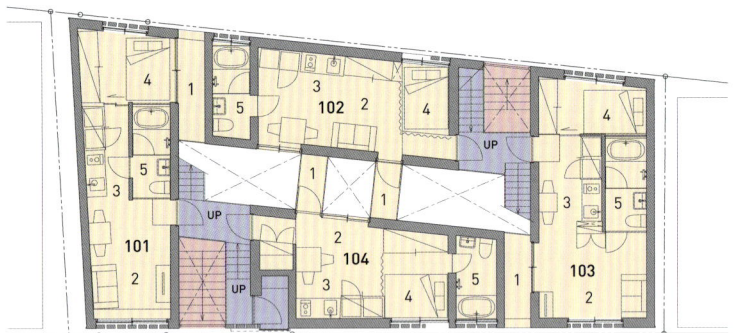

First floor plan

Third floor plan

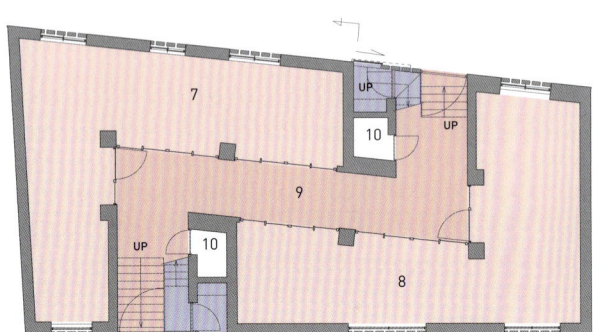

Basement plan

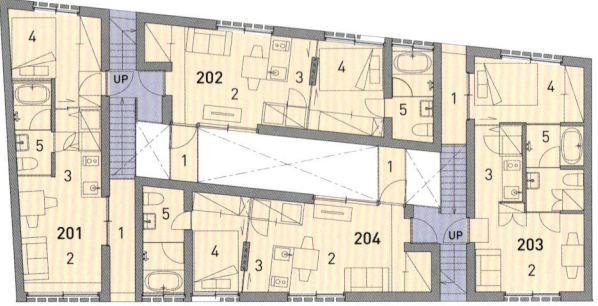

Second floor plan

1. Balcony
2. Living / dining room
3. Kitchen
4. Bedroom
5. Bathroom
6. Inclined ceiling
7. Shop 1
8. Shop 2
9. Passage
10. Machine room